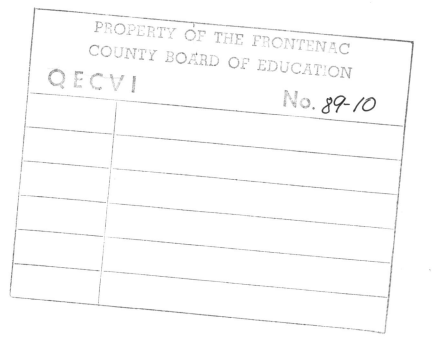

LAND OF

Second Edition

CANADA:

LAND OF DIVERSITY

Second Edition

Bruce W. Clark
John K. Wallace

Prentice-Hall Canada Inc. Scarborough, Ontario

Dedication
To all young Canadians,
especially Graham, Kenyon, David, and Ian.

Canadian Cataloguing in Publication Data

Clark, Bruce, date
  Canada, land of diversity

2nd ed.
For use in secondary schools.
Includes index.
ISBN 0-13-115023-5

1. Canada – Description and travel – 1981 –
I. Wallace, John K., date   . II. Title.

FC57.C52 1989   917.1   C88-095130-3
F1008.C52 1989

Prentice-Hall, Inc., Englewood Cliffs, New Jersey
Prentice-Hall International, Inc., London
Prentice-Hall of Australia, Pty., Ltd., Sydney
Prentice-Hall of India Pvt., Ltd., New Delhi
Prentice-Hall of Japan, Inc., Tokyo
Prentice-Hall of Southeast Asia (PTE) Ltd., Singapore
Editoria Prentice-Hall do Brasil Ltda., Rio de Janeiro
Prentice-Hall Hispanoamericana, S.A., Mexico

ISBN 0-13-115023-5

Production Editors: Eric S. Grace and Jane A. Clark
Designer: Lorraine Hulme
Illustrators: James Loates and Julian Cleva
Manufacturing: Lois Enns
Composition: Colborne, Cox and Burns

Cover photograph: Banff National Park, by Mark Tomalty/Masterfile

Printed and bound in Canada by
Bryant Press Limited
  2 3 4 5   BP   93 92 91 90 89

Note From The Publisher

Prentice-Hall Canada Inc., Secondary School Division, and the authors of *CANADA: LAND OF DIVERSITY Second Edition* are committed to the publication of instructional materials that are as bias-free as possible. This text was evaluated for bias prior to publication.

The authors and publisher also recognize the importance of appropriate reading levels and have therefore made every effort to ensure the highest possible degree of readability in the text. The content has been selected, organized, and written at a level suitable to the intended audience. Standard readability tests have been applied at several stages in the text preparation to ensure an appropriate reading level.

Readability tests, however, can only provide a rough indication of a book's reading level. Research indicates that readability is affected by much more than word or sentence length; factors such as presentation, format and design, none of which are considered in the usual readability tests, also greatly influence the ease with which students read a book. These and many additional features, such as marginal notes and a glossary, have been carefully prepared to ensure maximum student comprehension.

Table of Contents

■ ACKNOWLEDGEMENTS

The development of this Second Edition of *Canada: Land of Diversity* required the talents and dedication of many more people than the two whose names appear on the cover. We would like to extend our sincere appreciation to the staff at Prentice-Hall, especially MaryLynne Meschino, Eric Grace, Judy Dawson, Kateri Lanthier, and Judie Ellis. We would also like to thank our wives, Laurie Wallace and Rosemary Clark, for their editorial suggestions, patience, and tolerance with their often-absent husbands.

Finally, we would like to express our gratitude to our students for field testing the material, and to the many companies, government departments, and individuals who provided materials for this book. Their generosity and cooperation were invaluable.

Bruce Clark/John Wallace

■ TO THE STUDENT

Canada has been described as a country that exists in spite of its geography. It remains united and prosperous despite problems created by vast distances, harsh climates, different physical regions, and a variety of cultures. Canada's diversity of geographical features has, in fact, helped Canadians become one of the most fortunate people in the world. Canadians enjoy a high standard of living, a variety of lifestyles, peace, and freedom.

Canada, nevertheless, faces many challenges to its existence and growth. *Canada: Land of Diversity* examines some of these challenges and will help you understand their origins, nature, and scope.

■ HOW TO USE THIS BOOK

Before beginning your study of Canada's geography, you should know how this book is organized and how to use its many parts. Knowing this will improve your study skills.

- Seven major themes are presented in this book. Each theme is examined in a *Unit* composed of several *Chapters*. An additional unit (Unit Eight) contains exercises that will help you develop some of the skills necessary to study the geography of Canada.

- Several chapters in the book contain *Complementary Studies*. These studies examine in detail a specific geographic situation related to the material in the chapter.

- The names of all the units, chapters, and complementary studies are listed in the *Table of Contents*.

- When you wish to discover where a particular topic or place is discussed, you should look in the *Index* at the back of the book.

- As you read through the text, you will notice that some words are printed in **bold type**. These words have special geographical meaning. If you do not know their meaning, you will find them defined in the *Glossary*.

- At the beginning of most chapters is a section called *Key Terms*. Major geographical ideas discussed in the chapter are listed here. Remember, if you do not know the meanings of the key terms, you can look them up in the glossary.

- You will see two types of *margin notes* in this book:
  - i. some non-geographical words are explained in the margin because they may be difficult to understand.
  - ii. geographical information and hints are also found in the margin, and help explain something discussed in the text.

- The text, maps, photos, and diagrams in each chapter provide the starting point for your study. They are followed by *Questions*. The questions are divided into four groups according to the kind of answers required:

  - i. *Checkback* questions ensure that you have learned the most important ideas in the chapter. The answers are found right in the chapter.

  - ii. *Analyze* questions can also be answered from information in the text. You may be asked to use this information to express ideas in new ways, combine ideas, or draw maps, graphs, or diagrams.

  - iii. *Investigate* questions are similar to Analyze questions except that you will have to find some information from other sources. These sources might include government documents, encyclopedias, newspapers, magazines, library vertical files, computerized data bases, audio-visual materials, and personal interviews.

iv. *What Do You Think?* includes questions that encourage you to study the information given, evaluate various points of view, and give your own opinion. Many of the issues facing Canada have a geographical basis. You should be well informed about these issues because some day you may have to deal with some of them yourself.

Now that you understand the structure of this book, you are ready to begin your study of Canada's geography. In the following units you will

- learn about Canada's physical geography;
- investigate the origins of Canada's people;
- study where Canadians live and why they live there;
- examine how and where Canadians earn a living;
- discover where Canada's natural resources are found and how they are used;
- consider Canada's relationships to other countries;
- develop the skills required for your geographic study of Canada.

UNIT ONE

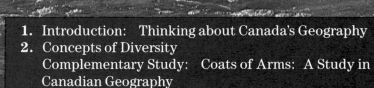

CANADA
LAND OF DIVERSITY

1 Introduction: Thinking about Canada's Geography

As you work with *Canada: Land of Diversity* you will have a chance to learn much about the country, and in particular how geographers study Canada. Try the questions below. They will introduce you to some different topics in the study of Canadian geography.

Your teacher may keep these maps so that if you do another "mental map" at the end of the course, you will be able to see how your image of Canada has changed.

1. On a blank sheet of paper, draw a map of Canada from memory. On this "mental map" label as many features as you can, such as provinces, lakes and rivers, mountains, towns and cities, and oceans.

2. The 1976 Summer Olympics were held in Montréal and the 1988 Winter Olympics in Calgary. Toronto applied to stage the Summer Olympics in 1996.
   a) In a small group, discuss and make a list of the characteristics that cities like Montréal, Calgary, and Toronto need in order to hold
      i) Summer and ii) Winter Olympic Games.
      Characteristics you might consider are size, economic and physical characteristics, and the surrounding regions.
   b) Use an atlas and your list from part a) to select another Canadian city that you think would make an ideal site for either the Summer or Winter Olympic Games.
   c) Imagine you are the mayor of the city that you selected in part b). Write a letter to the Olympic Committee proposing that your city be chosen for the next Games. Read the letters in class. Based on the proposals, have the class choose the winning city.

3. How well do you know the names of Canadian cities? Below are clues to the names of seven cities. Use the clues to determine the name of each city.
   a) Named after a queen.
   b) Begins like the name of its province.
   c) A colourful cutting tool.
   d) A knight in shining armour rides a . . .
   e) A goose's mate.
   f) Three rivers, en Français.
   g) Napoleon met his . . .

4. Below is a list of the ten largest cities in Canada and their populations. Are most of these cities located in the northern or southern parts of the country? Why do you think this pattern exists?

a)	Toronto	3 427 000	f)	Calgary	671 000
b)	Montréal	2 921 000	g)	Winnipeg	625 000
c)	Vancouver	1 381 000	h)	Québec City	603 000
d)	Ottawa-Hull	819 000	i)	Hamilton	557 000
e)	Edmonton	785 000	j)	St. Catharines-Niagara	343 000

5. a) Name the cities in Canada that have National Hockey League teams (Fig. 1–1).
   b) Give two reasons why these cities have teams while other major Canadian cities do not.
   c) Which major cities are not represented?
   d) Does this surprise you? Explain.

6. List as many of the communication and transportation links as you can that join your community with other communities in Canada. Why are these links especially important in a country like Canada?

7. a) Name any three items you use that were not made in Canada. Why do Canadians import these products from other countries?
   b) List three products that Canada exports to other countries. Why do people in other countries buy Canadian products?

8. Which four provinces produce the most agricultural products? Why do these provinces lead in agriculture?

Fig. 1–1 Which Canadian cities have NHL teams?

Fig. 1–2 When people think of Canada, they do not usually imagine scenes like this.

As part of this course you and your fellow students may decide to produce this magazine for distribution to other students in the school.

9. In which part of Canada do you think the photo in Fig. 1–2 was taken?

10. You have been made chief editor of a newsmagazine in another country (you pick the country). Your magazine is doing a feature issue called "Canada Today."
    a) What would you put on the cover? You may wish to draw the cover.
    b) List the subjects for six stories you would include.
    c) Why would you make these choices?

If you were able to do a good job on most of these questions, congratulations! You must already have some knowledge of the geography of Canada. If you were not sure of the answers to some of the questions, do not worry because you are just starting your study of Canada's geography.

In trying to answer these questions you began to deal with some of the most important ideas in Canadian geography:

interact: having contacts and exchanges such as telephone calls, business deals, television programs, transportation links, etc.

- regions and their differences
- who the people of Canada are, where they live, and how they support themselves
- how we interact with each other across a huge land
- how we use our natural resources
- what ties we have with other countries

You will have the opportunity to explore these ideas in detail in this book. At the end of your study you will better understand Canada and the world in which you live. Learn and enjoy!

Key Terms

equator	prime meridian	temperate zone
hemisphere	tropical zone	population density
meridian	polar zone	per capita GNP

CANADA'S LOCATION IN THE WORLD

If you were asked to describe where Canada is found in the world, how would you do it? One way is by dividing the world into different sections. Then you could describe Canada's position in relation to these divisions. Three ways of dividing the world are described below.

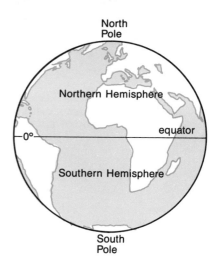

Fig. 1–3 The earth's hemispheres (north-south division)

NORTHERN AND SOUTHERN HEMISPHERES

Fig. 1–3 shows a line that divides the world into north and south.

1. a) What is the name of this line?
   b) From what word does the name of this line come? What does this suggest about the line?

2. What is a **hemisphere**?

3. Is Canada in the northern or southern hemisphere?

EASTERN AND WESTERN HEMISPHERES

The world can be divided into eastern and western hemispheres, sometimes called the Old World and the New World. The line that divides the world in this way follows the 0° and the 180° lines of longitude (see Fig. 1–4).

The 0° line is called the **prime meridian** and extends from the North Pole to the South Pole through Greenwich, England. The 180° **meridian** is halfway around the world from Greenwich. It runs from the North Pole to the South Pole across the Pacific Ocean. Look at a globe to check this.

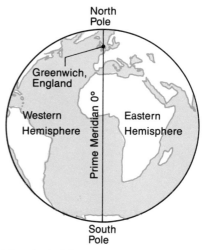

Fig. 1–4 The earth's hemispheres (east-west division)

1. Is Canada located in the eastern or western hemisphere?

2. Why is the eastern hemisphere called the Old World and the western hemisphere called the New World?

3. a) In which direction does the sun seem to travel across the sky?
   b) Which province of Canada has i) sunrise first? ii) sunset last?

CLIMATE ZONES

The world can be divided into climate zones (see Fig. 1–5). Each of these zones has a different pattern of temperatures during the year. The **tropical zone** has warm to hot temperatures all year long, ranging from 23°C in winter to 26°C in summer. The **polar zones** have cool to cold temperatures throughout the year, ranging from -25°C to 10°C. Between the polar and tropical zones are the **temperate zones**, where both warm and cold seasons occur. Temperatures generally range from 0°C to 20°C.

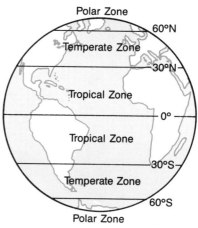

Fig. 1–5 Climate zones. Which climate zone is not found in Canada?

1. a) In which climate zones is Canada found?
   b) How do you know this?

2. What annual temperature ranges are typical for Canada?

■ CANADA COMPARED WITH OTHER COUNTRIES

One way of learning about Canada is to compare its area, population, and wealth with those of other countries. These comparisons will show us how Canada is similar to, or different from, other nations of the world.

AREA

Examine Fig. 1–6. It gives information about the areas of the ten largest countries in the world.

1. How many times larger than Canada is the U.S.S.R.?

2. How much larger, in square kilometres, is Canada than China?

3. Add the areas of Canada and the U.S.A. together. Compare this total to the area of the U.S.S.R. Which is larger?

4. How many times larger than India is Canada?

5. a) Find the location of the ten countries using a globe or atlas.
   b) Which continent (Asia, Australia, Africa, Europe, North and South America, or Antarctica) has most of the world's ten largest countries?

Fig. 1–6 Areas of the ten largest countries (in km²)

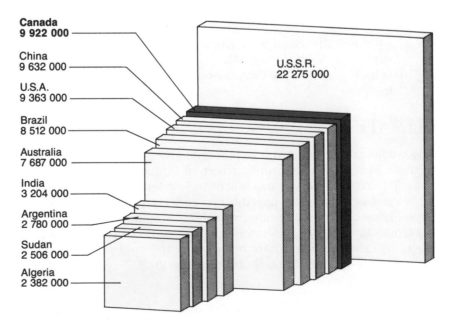

Canada
9 922 000

China
9 632 000

U.S.A.
9 363 000

Brazil
8 512 000

Australia
7 687 000

India
3 204 000

Argentina
2 780 000

Sudan
2 506 000

Algeria
2 382 000

U.S.S.R.
22 275 000

POPULATION

Compare the list of largest countries (Fig. 1–6) to the list of the largest populations (Fig. 1–7). You will see many of the same countries on both lists. The U.S.S.R., U.S.A., China, India, and Brazil appear on both lists, but does Canada?

Canada ranks 31st in population among the nations of the world, with a population of 25 950 000 in 1988. While this is a large number of people, it is not a large population in comparison to other countries when you consider Canada's enormous area.

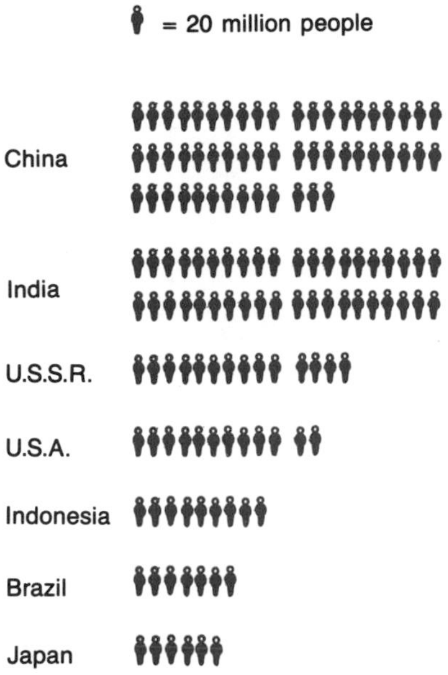

POPULATION DENSITY

We have just discovered that Canada has a very large area but a small population. The relationship between the area and the population of a country is called the **population density**. To calculate the population density of a place, divide the population by the area.

$$\text{population density} = \frac{\text{population}}{\text{area}}$$

The result is expressed in units of "people per square kilometre." For example, the population density of Canada is

$$\frac{25\ 950\ 000}{9\ 922\ 000\ \text{km}^2} = \text{approximately 3 people/km}^2$$

This does not mean that there are three people living in each square kilometre of Canada. It means that for every square kilometre, there is an average of three people living somewhere in the country.

When we compare population densities, we can tell how sparsely Canada is populated. Hong Kong is one of the most densely populated regions in the world, with 5 529 people/km². At the other extreme is Greenland, with 0.02 people/km². Other countries, including Canada, fit somewhere in between. Fig. 1–8 shows Canada in relation to some other countries.

Country	Population Density (people/km²)
United Kingdom	247
China	111
U.S.A.	26
U.S.S.R.	13
Canada	3

= 20 million people

China

India

U.S.S.R.

U.S.A.

Indonesia

Brazil

Japan

Fig. 1–7 The world's most populated countries. How many symbols would Canada have?

Fig. 1–8 Population densities in selected countries (numbers have been rounded off)

1. Define the term "population density."

2. a) Draw five boxes, 2 cm x 2 cm each, in your notebook. Each box represents 1 km².
   b) Label each box with the name of a country from Fig. 1–7.
   c) Within each box, draw the number of dots needed to show the population density of that country. For example, in the box labelled Canada, draw 3 dots to represent 3 people/km².

3. What surprises you most in what you see? Explain.

Although the population density for all of Canada is very low, some places (e.g. large cities) have very high population densities.

This exercise demonstrates that places with a high population density are more crowded than places with a low population density. As you can see, Canada's population density suggests that it is not a crowded country. Imagine drawing the box for Hong Kong!

WEALTH

Canadians have higher incomes than people in most other parts of the world. Even those Canadians in lower income brackets would be considered well-off by the standards of many who live in Asia, Africa, and South America. Our standard of living is matched only by that of a few countries in the world.

standard of living: how well-off people are in terms of the necessities and luxuries of life

per capita: per person

It is difficult to measure wealth. One of the measurements used most often is **per capita Gross National Product (GNP)**. This is the yearly value of everything produced in a country divided by the number of people in the country. It is often used to compare the wealth of one country to that of another. A country with a high per capita GNP should have citizens who are well-off. They should be able to afford the basics of living—food, shelter, and clothing. They may also afford luxuries, such as automobiles, stereos, and computers.

Canada is compared to other countries in several ways in Chapters 26 and 29

Only six countries in the world have per capita GNPs higher than that of Canada, while more than 150 have lower ones.

1. a) Define the term "Gross National Product per capita" and explain how it is often used.
   b) Suggest three countries with higher and three countries with lower GNPs than Canada.
   c) What would the lifestyle be like for citizens in each group of countries?

Now that you have learned some basic facts about Canada compared with other countries, review this section by answering the following questions.

QUESTIONS

CHECKBACK

1. Complete the crossword puzzle in Fig. 1–9 in your notebook.

Fig. 1–9

Across
- 3 weather patterns over a long period
- 4 population/area
- 5 a product brought to Canada
- 6 opposite of 5 across
- 7 number of people
- 10 most northerly settlement in Canada
- 11 0° longitude is the ■ ■ ■ ■ Meridian
- 14 coldest climate zone
- 16 our nearest neighbour
- 17 the size of a country is its ■ ■ ■ ■
- 18 gross national product (abbrev.)
- 19 climate zone that is hot all year
- 20 line of longitude
- 21 country with the world's biggest population
- 22 city named after a bird
- 23 Canada: Land of ■ ■ ■ ■ ■ ■ ■ ■

Down
- 1 climate zone where most Canadians live
- 2 world's largest country
- 3 movement of information
- 8 Europe is part of the ■ ■ ■ World.
- 9 half of the world
- 12 place with very high population density
- 13 high standard of living
- 15 Winter Olympic site in '88

ANALYZE

2. **a)** On a globe, use a piece of string to measure the distance from St. John's, Nfld. to Victoria, B.C. Where would you be if you travelled this same distance:
   i. east from St. John's?
   ii. northwest from Victoria?

   b) Use your string to measure the distance from Windsor, Ont. to Alert, N.W.T. (northern tip of Canada). Where would you be if you travelled this same distance:
   i. south from Windsor?
   ii. north from Alert?

   c) From your comparisons above, what conclusion(s) can you draw regarding distances within Canada?

3. There is one country in the world which has a pattern of area, population, population density, and wealth similar to Canada's. Use what you learned about Canada in this chapter and your atlas to name this country by following these instructions.

Hint: The country's name was mentioned in this chapter.

   a) Construct a chart using the headings shown in Fig. 1–10. Make a list of countries that you think might be similar to Canada in these categories.
   b) Obtain statistics for each country under the four categories. An atlas will help you with this task.
   c) Compare the data. Which country seems to be the most similar to Canada?

Fig. 1–10

Organizers like this one will be found throughout the book to help you answer some questions. Copy them into your notes or use the copies given to you by your teacher. Please do not write in your textbook.

Country	Area	Population	Population Density	Wealth

4. Canada is one of the world's four largest countries. How does its size and position compare with those of the three other largest countries? Copy the following table (Fig. 1–11) into your notebook and complete it using your atlas.

Fig. 1–11

	Latitude			Longitude		
	Farthest North	Farthest South	North-South Extent (in degrees)	Farthest East	Farthest West	East-West Extent (in degrees)
Canada U.S.S.R China U.S.A.						

5. You wish to send a telegram to a friend in another country describing what makes Canada different from other countries in the world. You can only afford to send 50 words. What would you say?

Concepts of Diversity 2

People have described Canada in many ways. The quotations below are a sample of what has been said about Canada.

1. "Canada has never been a **melting pot**; it is more like a **tossed salad**."

2. "In the eyes of Canadian men and women I have seen a new hopefulness. Perhaps it is bred by the wider spaces of our plains, the greater height of our mountains or the vast extent of our indented shorelines. Or perhaps it arises from the fact that here they stand on soil they can own."

3. "The land was black and rich...the water clear and abundant ...the forests huge and green and I knew I was in the greatest country in the world."

4. "O Canada! Where pines and maples grow,
   Great prairies spread and lordly rivers flow,
   How dear to us thy broad domain,
   From east to western sea,
   Thou land of hope, for all who toil!
   The True North, strong and free."

5. "In Canada there is too much of everything. Too much rock, too much prairie, too much tundra, too much mountain, too much forest."

What do these quotations tell us about the Canadian land and people? Answer the questions below to find out.

1. The U.S. often refers to itself as a "melting pot" because immigrants to that country seem to give up the culture of their country of birth and adopt the American way of life. In quotation 1, Canada is called a "tossed salad". What do you think this means? Is this distinction between the two countries a valid one?

2. Why do you suppose the author of quotation 2 thought the people looked hopeful?

3. a) What is the source of quotation 4?
   b) What mental images of Canada are created in quotations 3 and 4?
   c) How do the images presented in quotation 5 compare to those presented in quotations 3 and 4?

4. What might have caused a traveller to write quotation 5?

Key Terms

melting pot   physical diversity   cultural diversity
diversity   culture   economic diversity
cultural fabric

■ INTRODUCTION

Many people would say that **diversity** is the single most important characteristic of Canada's geography. But what is diversity and how does it apply to the geography of our country? Let's check the dictionary first.

di ver si ty (di vur se tee): noun. "The condition of having differences or a great variety."

The two key words are *differences* and *variety*. Let's examine them in more detail.

Your life is filled with your individual likes and dislikes, responsibilities, and goals. You go to school and you may have a part-time job. You may be interested in sports and you may love music. You may speak French and study biology in school. You may be an excellent cook. Your life is filled with diversity and you are different from your friends.

Now consider the diversity which exists among television shows that you might watch. Choose five popular television shows and answer the following questions about each one:

1. What type of show is it (music, police, soap, sports, etc.)?

2. Are the stars male or female? young or old?

3. For what type of audience is the show designed?

4. Where is the show made?

5. When is the show broadcast (daytime, evening, late night)?

You probably found out that significant differences exist among the shows that you examined. This is another way of saying that there is diversity in television programs.

■ DIVERSITY IN CANADA

You have examined some of the diversity that exists within your own life. Now expand your vision to include all of Canada. Canada has a great variety of physical environments. There are rocky harbours by the sea, areas of rugged lake country, flat plains, mountain ranges, and deserts. As well, Canada has a great diversity of environments created by people. These range from a single cabin in the woods to a very large city. There is enough choice to please just about everyone. These different types of physical and human environments provide people with many different ways of earning a living, such as lumbering, farming, working in an office, or driving a truck. This results in a diversified Canadian economy.

Canadians have a wide variety of cultural backgrounds. People have come to Canada from all over the world. They have brought with them different customs, languages, attitudes, and skills. The result is a rich **cultural fabric**.

Canada's great diversity can also have negative effects. As Canadians we have the difficult task of trying to understand the needs and thoughts of other Canadians who may:

- live far from where we live
- speak a different language
- have different religious beliefs
- be either richer or poorer

Not only does diversity make being a Canadian difficult, it makes the job of governing the country tricky. The federal government must try to pass laws and spend money to meet the needs of people all over the country. But these needs are not all the same: what might help people in one area might harm people in another. Trying to find solutions that are acceptable to everyone is sometimes an impossible task.

federal: national

You may ask, "If diversity causes such problems, why should we make it the basis of our study of Canada's geography?" The answer is that many people feel that diversity makes Canada a more interesting and exciting place in which to live. This book will help you to discover Canada's diversity, why this diversity exists, and how it contributes to Canadian life.

PHYSICAL DIVERSITY

If you flew from Victoria, B.C. across Canada to St. John's, Nfld., you would see a variety of landforms. Some are shown in Fig. 2-1. But landforms like these are not the only aspect of Canada's **physical diversity**. There are also differences in climate, soil, and vegetation all across the country.

Fig. 2-1 The photographs here and over the page show some of the physical diversity found in Canada.

ECONOMIC DIVERSITY

1. Name the jobs shown in Fig. 2–3.

2. Where in Canada would you find people doing these jobs? (In some cases there may be more than one location.)

3. Construct a chart similar to Fig. 2–2. For each of the job categories, provide a specific job. The first one is done for you.

Fig. 2–2

Category	What Is Done	Sample Job
Forestry	Using forest resources	tree planter
Mining	Using mineral resources	
Manufacturing	Making products from raw materials	
Construction	Building things	
Transportation	Moving people and things	
Communications	Moving information	
Retailing	Selling to the public	
Finance	Handling money	

The answers to these questions demonstrate that Canadians earn their livings in many different ways. The products that Canadians make, buy, and sell, together with the services they provide and use, make up the Canadian economy.

In some parts of the country, the jobs of many people are concentrated in one industry and the economy of an entire area is based on this industry. For example, many jobs in the Atlantic provinces depend on the fishing industry, and we think of the economy of this area as fisheries-based. In contrast, the economy of the Prairies is largely dependent on farming, while the economy of Niagara Falls is dependent on tourism. These examples illustrate Canada's **economic diversity**.

Fig. 2–3 Canada's economic wealth is based on a wide diversity of activities. These are just a few examples. What other types of activity can you think of?

CULTURAL DIVERSITY

Culture includes a person's skills, interests, and way of life. Let's compare two typical Canadians who illustrate Canada's cultural diversity (Fig. 2–4). Steve and Hélène have different cultural backgrounds: for example, they speak different languages and have different religions. In addition, they have different kinds of jobs and choose different leisure-time activities. The fact that these and many other types of cultural differences exist within our country makes Canada a land with enormous **cultural diversity**.

Fig. 2–4 The cultural backgrounds of two Canadians

Steve Hyrich		Hélène Marchand
Belmont, Manitoba	**Born**	Saint-Rémi-de-Tingwick, Québec
School principal	**Job**	Editor
Ukrainian	**Ethnic origin**	French
English, Ukrainian	**Language(s) understood**	French, English, some Greek
Eastern Orthodox	**Religion**	Roman Catholic
Photography, curling, baseball, cooking	**Interests**	Theatre, dancing, calligraphy, swimming

■ IN CLOSING...

When we talk about Canada's diversity we are referring to the differences and variety that exist within all aspects of Canadian life. Diversity is one of the most important characteristics of Canada's geography and accounts for many of our country's strengths and problems. In *Canada: Land of Diversity* we will investigate the nature of Canada's diversity and how it makes us different from people in other parts of the world.

QUESTIONS

CHECKBACK

1. In your own words, define the following terms:
   a) diversity
   b) culture
   c) economy
2. Give three examples of:
   a) physical diversity
   b) cultural diversity
   c) economic diversity

3. a) Describe, in one or two sentences, the type of landforms shown in each photo in Fig. 2–1.
   b) Where in Canada might each photo have been taken?
4. a) Using the examples of Steve Hyrich and Hélène Marchand as guides, write a cultural summary for yourself, or one of your parents, or another person.
   b) Compare your summary to the summaries produced by at least two of your classmates. What evidence of cultural diversity do you see?

INVESTIGATE

5. Study the amount of cultural diversity in the area where you live by doing the following exercise.
   a) Select one of the cultural groups in your community. Using the phone directory, find the telephone numbers and the addresses of restaurants, stores, places of worship, and clubs or associations frequented by members of the cultural group you selected.
   b) Locate these places on a map of your community.
   c) Are they grouped together or are they spread throughout the community? Explain why this pattern exists.
6. What evidence of economic diversity is there in your community? List ten economic activities you have observed. Choose as wide a variety as possible.

WHAT DO YOU THINK?

7. At the beginning of this chapter, you read what some people have said about Canada. Now it is your turn. Describe either Canada's people or Canada's land using one of the following:

   • written description
   • drawing or painting
   • collage
   • audio tape
   • video tape

Coats of Arms: A Study in Canadian Geography

Canada's coat of arms is found on all our paper money

You have likely seen the **coats of arms** of at least some of the provinces of Canada (Fig. 2–5). But have you ever thought about what the symbols on the "coat" represent? Before you can understand the coats of arms you have to understand how they came into being.

Key Terms

coats of arms   heraldry   ethnic

Coats of arms are drawn according to the rules of the science of **heraldry**. In heraldry, every symbol has a meaning that tells something about the person or place represented by the coat of arms. Provincial coats of arms use the following kinds of symbols:

- **ethnic** and royal symbols
- plants and animals that are found in the province
- important natural features of the province's geography
- natural resources of the province
- symbols related to the province's history

Let's look at some provincial coats of arms to see what they can tell us. Newfoundland's coat of arms (Fig. 2–5) includes an interesting mistake. The white cross, lions, and unicorns are of British origin. The two Indians are Beothuks, who were the original inhabitants of Newfoundland. The mistake is the elk at the top. There never were elk in Newfoundland. When the coat of arms was drawn, the designer in England confused the elk with the caribou which is native to Newfoundland.

unicorn: a fictional horse with one large horn

The coat of arms of the Northwest Territories has many interesting features. The star represents the magnetic north pole, which is in the Northwest Territories. The narwhals inhabit the seas of this territory, and the double wavy lines represent the Northwest Passage through the Arctic islands. The red area with a fox head represents the **tundra** and the fur trapping industry. The single wavy line is the **tree line**. The green area and rectangles represent the **boreal forest** and mining industry.

narwhal: a small arctic whale

Fig. 2–5 The Provincial and Territorial coats of arms.

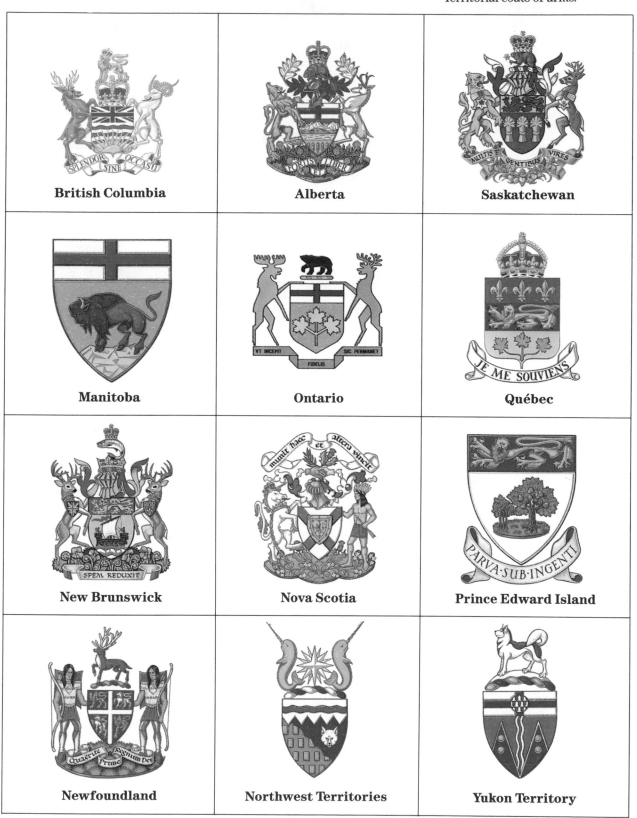

British Columbia

Alberta

Saskatchewan

Manitoba

Ontario

Québec

New Brunswick

Nova Scotia

Prince Edward Island

Newfoundland

Northwest Territories

Yukon Territory

The coat of arms of Nova Scotia reflects the origins of this province's Scottish settlers. The blue cross, thistles, unicorn and standing lion are all symbols of Scotland. The hands and the thistle and laurel refer to the friendship between Scotland and Nova Scotia.

QUESTIONS

INVESTIGATE

1. Choose at least four of the other provincial or territorial coats of arms. For each, list in a table like the one below (Fig. 2–6), the symbols used and the reason(s) why each was chosen.

Fig. 2–6

Province	Symbol	Reason(s) for Use

WHAT DO YOU THINK?

2. a) Design a coat of arms for your town, city, or district. Be sure to think carefully about the symbols you choose.
   b) List the symbols you used and give the reason why you chose each.

Concept of Regions

3

We can study and remember information much more easily if it is organized into categories. This is something that all of us do even if we may not be aware of it. For example, knowledge is organized at school into subjects like mathematics, languages, geography, history, music, and physical education. This organization allows for easier study.

Canada is such a large and diverse country that organization of information is needed here as well. Geographers have many ways of organizing knowledge. In this chapter we will examine one very important way that this is done — by the creation of **regions**.

Key Terms

region   transition zone   multi-factor region
single-factor region

DEFINING REGIONS

The following exercise will give you an idea of what a region is and how it is created.

1. Draw a sketch map of your school property.

2. Divide the school property into different parts (or regions) based on their use. For example, the part of the property with the school building is a different "region" from the part with the playing field.

3. How many regions did you find? What differences exist between your regions?

An area of almost any size can be divided into regions: a classroom, a country, or the whole world. Regions are created by geographers to allow them to study the great diversity of physical and cultural features on the earth. But how are regional boundaries determined? Consider the fictional island of Adanac (Fig. 3-1).

On Adanac, it was easy to create regions based upon the occupations of the people living on the island. This illustrates how regions are determined. A region is an area which has similar characteristics throughout. This similarity might include climate, landforms, vegetation, or human activity. One or more characteristics of a region make it different from other regions. Is it as easy to create regions in the real world?

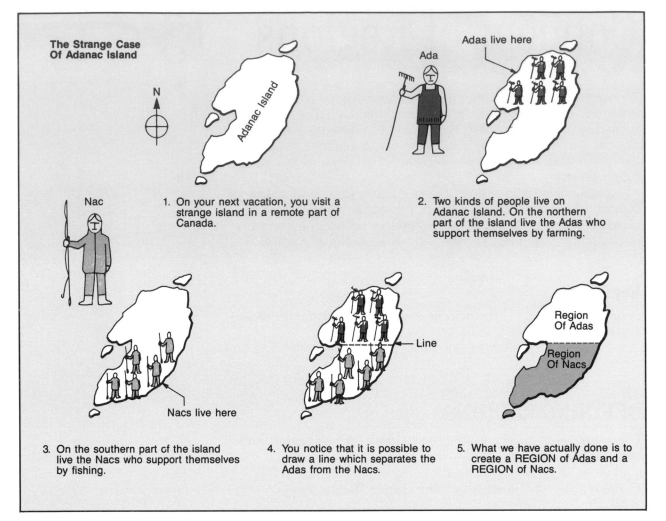

The Strange Case Of Adanac Island

N

1. On your next vacation, you visit a strange island in a remote part of Canada.

2. Two kinds of people live on Adanac Island. On the northern part of the island live the Adas who support themselves by farming.

Ada

Adas live here

Nac

Nacs live here

3. On the southern part of the island live the Nacs who support themselves by fishing.

4. You notice that it is possible to draw a line which separates the Adas from the Nacs.

Line

5. What we have actually done is to create a REGION of Adas and a REGION of Nacs.

Region Of Adas

Region Of Nacs

Fig. 3-1 The strange case of Adanac island

Fig. 3-2 What two regions can be seen in this photograph? Where is the boundary between these regions?

In many real-world situations, it is not very easy to see regional boundaries, but Fig. 3-2 shows an exception to this rule. It is a photograph taken in southern Alberta where the Interior Plains region meets the Rocky Mountains region. As you can see, the two areas have very different landforms and therefore can be considered as different regions.

In each of the two examples above, the regions have been determined on the basis of only one factor. On Adanac, the single factor that distinguished the two regions was the occupation of the people. In southern Alberta, the factor was the type of landform. Regions like these, which are determined by only one factor, are called **single-factor regions**.

Not all boundaries between regions can be determined as easily as that on Adanac Island. On the island next to Adanac, the pattern of the Adas and Nacs is a bit different (Fig. 3-3). On this island it is obvious that there is not a sharp division between the region of the Adas and the region of the Nacs. Instead there is an area, or

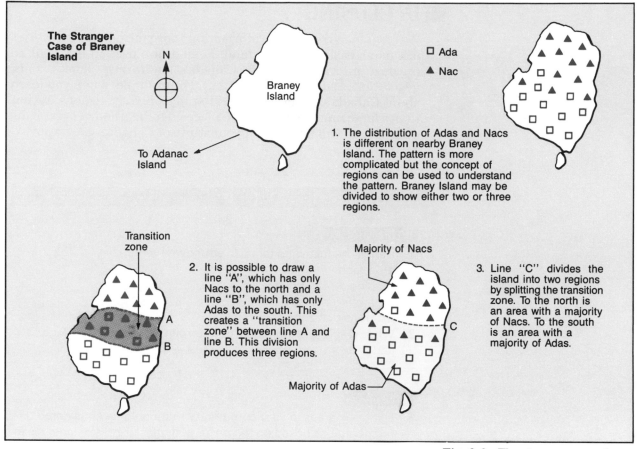

The Stranger
Case of Braney
Island

N

Braney
Island

To Adanac
Island

☐ Ada
▲ Nac

1. The distribution of Adas and Nacs is different on nearby Braney Island. The pattern is more complicated but the concept of regions can be used to understand the pattern. Braney Island may be divided to show either two or three regions.

Transition zone

A
B

2. It is possible to draw a line "A", which has only Nacs to the north and a line "B", which has only Adas to the south. This creates a "transition zone" between line A and line B. This division produces three regions.

Majority of Nacs

C

Majority of Adas

3. Line "C" divides the island into two regions by splitting the transition zone. To the north is an area with a majority of Nacs. To the south is an area with a majority of Adas.

Fig. 3-3 The stranger case of Braney Island

region, where both types of inhabitants live. This region, situated between the other two, is called a **transition zone**.

In the real world there is often a transition zone between regions. If it is large enough, the transition zone is considered to be a separate region. For example, between the grassland region and forest region of western Canada is a large area containing both grasses and trees. Because of its size, this transition zone is treated as a separate region called parkland (see Fig. 7-1).

Not all regions are based on a single factor. Many are determined by several factors and are called **multi-factor regions**. For example, if similar geologic structure, landforms, climate, vegetation, and soils are found throughout an area, then the area can be treated as a multi-factor region. In Canada, the Prairies are a multi-factor region (Fig. 3-4).

Fig. 3-4 The Prairies: a multi-factor region

Factor	Similar Conditions Throughout the Prairies
geology	sedimentary rock
landforms	generally flat with rolling portions
climate	semi-arid (dry) in most places
vegetation	short and long grasses in most places
soils	dry climate soil types

■ IN CLOSING . . .

We have seen that when information is organized into categories it is much easier to understand. Regions are used in this book to organize information about Canada's landforms, climate, soils, vegetation, and human settlement. For example, when you learn about Canada's climate, you will study only six regions, rather than a large number of separate places. This method of organizing information will help you in your study of Canada's geography.

QUESTIONS

CHECKBACK

1. Define the following terms in your own words:
   a) region
   b) single-factor region
   c) multi-factor region
   d) transition zone
2. What was the factor used to determine the regions in Figs. 3-1 and 3-3?

ANALYZE

3. List three areas in your community that could be considered different regions based on the major activities or type of land use in each area.
4. How do urban regions and rural regions differ? Consider the following: population density, number of buildings, and major economic activities.
5. a) Examine the climatic regions map (Fig. 6–12). Are these single-factor or multi-factor regions? How did you determine this?
   b) Examine the vegetation regions map (Fig. 7-1). Identify a vegetation region, other than parkland, which is a transition zone between other regions.

INVESTIGATE

6. Check your atlas and determine:
   a) two examples of single-factor regions
   b) two examples of multi-factor regions.
      For each of these regions give the determining factor(s).

PHYSICAL DIVERSITY

4 Geologic History

Canada is a land of great physical diversity (Fig. 4–1). This physical diversity is largely the result of the country's geologic development.

Just as your physical appearance has changed as you have grown older, so has the earth's. Ancient seas have disappeared and left behind dry land. Mountains that were once very high are now worn flat. Volcanic eruptions built up new land, and rivers wore down the continents. Today, the earth's physical appearance continues to change, and will do so into the future. A hundred million years from now Canada's physical landscape will look very different from how it looks today.

Fig. 4–1 Locations of major landform types.

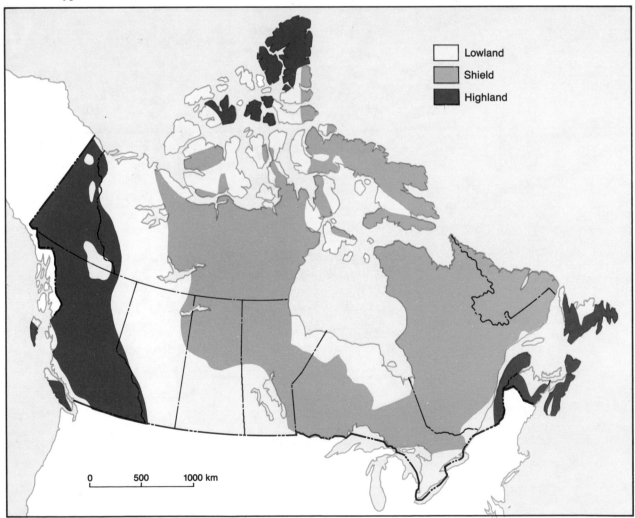

Lowland
Shield
Highland

0 500 1000 km

Canada's physical landscape is the result of conflict between forces that build the land higher and those that wear it down. Land that is pushed upward by great forces within the earth may form mountains. Mountains, in turn, are worn down by wind, rain, running water, and ice. At different times and in different places, one force has been stronger than the other. As a result, the land has either been built up or been worn down. This conflict has taken place over hundreds of millions of years, and forms the story of the earth's geologic history.

Current theories hold that the land masses that today form separate continents were once a single supercontinent. This land mass broke up. Separate continents drifted apart and sometimes collided again. These movements affected the shapes of the oceans and land surfaces.

Key Terms

geologic time	sediments	folding
eras	sedimentary rock	faulting
Precambrian era	bedrock	glaciers
erosion	fossils	mammals
Canadian Shield	Mesozoic era	
Paleozoic era	Cenozoic era	

■INTRODUCTION

How can we find out about the earth's early physical history? One approach is to make a careful analysis of the evidence provided by rocks, landforms, and fossils. While different people reach different conclusions after examining the evidence, the following account gives the analysis that is most widely accepted at present by scientists and geographers.

fossil: the remains of plants or animals that have been preserved in rock

The earth is very old. Some scientists estimate that the world was formed about 4 600 000 000 years ago. How long is this? Most of us cannot even imagine how long a million years is! Here are two tricks to help you understand how long **geologic time** really is.

Thousand million is the preferred term, now used instead of the term "billion"

- How many times does your age divide into a million years? The answer will tell you how many of your lifetimes equal one million years. For example, if you are 15, you would have to live your life approximately 66 667 (1 000 000/15) times before you would live a million years.
- In this chapter, another comparison is used. The age of the earth is compared to just 12 hours. As you study the chapter, you will be able to see how much of the 12 hours is taken up by each part of the earth's geologic history. The times are shown on watch faces in the margin.

To make geologic time easier to understand, geologists have divided the earth's history into four periods called **eras**. Each era represents a time of major sediment deposition and earth movement. These eras are shown in Fig. 4–2. We will refer to these eras

Eras	Time Period (millions of years ago)		Major Events	
	Began	Ended	Geological	Biological
Cenozoic (recent life)	70	–	• ice sheets cover much of North America • continents take on their present shape • formation of the Rocky Mountains completed	• human beings • modern forms of life evolve • fossils present
Mesozoic (middle life)	225	70	• formation of Rocky Mountains begins • shallow seas in the interior of North America at various times	• age of reptiles, such as dinosaurs • first birds and mammals evolve • fossils present
Paleozoic (ancient life)	600	225	• periods of mountain building • Appalachians formed • periods when large parts of North America are covered by shallow seas	• age of fishes • first plants and animals appear on land • fossils present
Precambrian (earliest life)	4600	600	• Precambrian shields, such as the Canadian Shield, are formed	• primitive life forms appear in the oceans • no fossils present

Fig. 4–2 Geologic history is broken down into four major time periods called *eras*. The eras are separated by major periods of mounting building.

Fig. 4–3 Precambrian era begins (4 600 000 000 years ago)

12:00 noon

when describing the major events in the formation of Canada's landforms. Landform regions named in the following section are shown in Fig. 4–1. As you read, relate each geological event to the location and time the event occurred.

■ PRECAMBRIAN ERA

Scientists believe that the earth was formed from a mass of gas floating in space. This occurred at the beginning of the **Precambrian era** (Fig. 4–3). The Precambrian lasted for about 4 000 000 000 years—long enough for many cycles of mountain building and **erosion** to take place (Fig. 4–4). This means that entire mountain ranges thousands of metres high formed and then were worn down. As millions of years passed, areas of land and ocean developed and then disappeared. The surface of our continent was formed by a series of such changes. These changes continue today.

Canada has many features that have survived since the Precambrian era. The **Canadian Shield** was created during this time (Fig. 4–5). The Canadian Shield is the most important region in Canada, around which the other regions have formed. The rest of Canada as we know it did not even start to exist until hundreds of millions of years later. Near the end of the Precambrian era, the first living organisms appeared in the oceans.

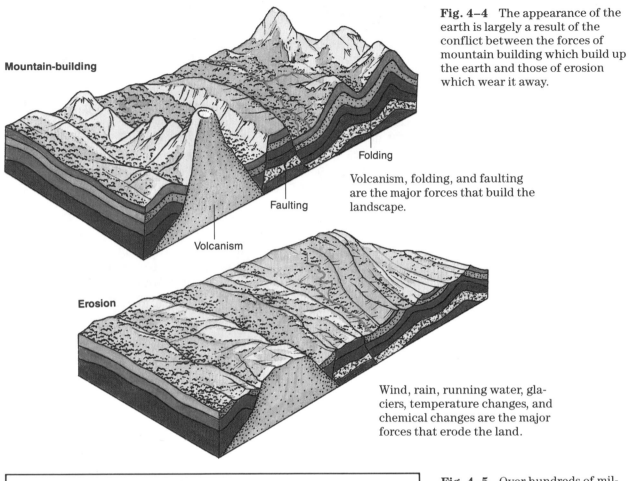

Mountain-building

Folding

Faulting

Volcanism

Fig. 4–4 The appearance of the earth is largely a result of the conflict between the forces of mountain building which build up the earth and those of erosion which wear it away.

Volcanism, folding, and faulting are the major forces that build the landscape.

Erosion

Wind, rain, running water, glaciers, temperature changes, and chemical changes are the major forces that erode the land.

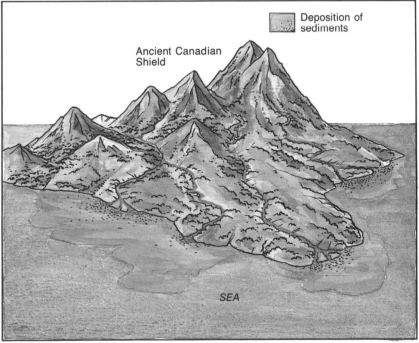

Deposition of sediments

Ancient Canadian Shield

SEA

Fig. 4–5 Over hundreds of millions of years, starting in the Precambrian, the mountains of the ancient Canadian Shield were eroded. The sediments produced were carried by rivers to nearby seas.

■ PALEOZOIC ERA

When the **Paleozoic era** began, 87% of the earth's history to date was already over (Fig. 4–6). This era lasted approximately 375 000 000 years, and during this time Canada continued to form. The Canadian Shield was as high as 12 000 m above sea level. These enormous mountains were taller than any that exist today. They were gradually worn away by the forces of erosion. (Now most parts of the Shield are less than 500 m high.) The eroded rock particles, called **sediments**, were moved by rivers and deposited in the shallow seas which surrounded the Shield. Very gradually over millions of years, these sediments were compressed into **sedimentary rock**. Today these rocks form the **bedrock** of parts of every province. At the end of the Paleozoic era, the sedimentary rock to the east of the Shield was forced upward to form the Appalachian Mountains (Fig. 4–7).

At the beginning of the Paleozoic era, the only living organisms were probably single-celled plants and animals in the seas. As time passed, more complex organisms began to evolve. These included fish, shellfish, and amphibians. The amphibians were the first animals to live on land. Some of the remains of these organisms are found in Canada's sedimentary rocks as **fossils**. Fossils help scientists estimate the age of the rock in which they are found.

The tallest mountain today, Mount Everest, is almost 9000 m in height.

10:24 p.m.

Fig. 4–6 Precambrian ends and Paleozoic begins (600 000 000 years ago)

Fig. 4–7 The Appalachian Mountains were formed during the Paleozoic from the eroded deposits from the Canadian Shield. Deposition continued in the Western Sea.

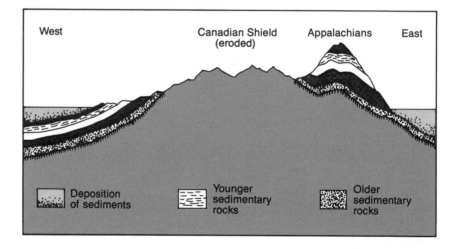

■ MESOZOIC ERA

The **Mesozoic era** lasted for approximately 155 000 000 years (Fig. 4–8). At the beginning of the era, the rocks of the eastern Arctic were folded to form the Innuitian Mountains. During the middle of the era, seas covered much of central and western Canada. While this area was under water, new layers of sedimentary rock were formed on top of those formed in the Paleozoic era. At the end of the Mesozoic era, the Rocky Mountains started to form.

The climate in the Mesozoic era was warm, and huge swamps and forests developed. Dinosaurs and other reptiles lived in this humid environment. The vegetation that grew in or fell into swamps became covered with water, sand, and silt. The pressure created by these many layers of sediments gradually, over millions of years, compressed the layers of vegetation into the coal deposits now found in Alberta and Saskatchewan. In a similar way, in the shallow seas that periodically covered this area, the remains of tiny creatures and plants fell to the sea floor and were covered by sediments. Over millions of years they were compressed and altered, eventually forming oil and gas.

■ CENOZOIC ERA

During the **Cenozoic era**, the final changes occurred which gave Canada's landforms their present shape (Fig. 4-9).

The uplifting of the mountains of western Canada (which began in the Mesozoic era) continued. The process of uplifting was accomplished by **folding, faulting**, and by the action of volcanoes which released huge amounts of lava to form plateaus. The seas that had occupied the area that is now the Prairies disappeared as the land slowly rose.

Beginning approximately 1 000 000 years ago, Canada and much of the world experienced four periods of glacial activity. Because of a slight cooling of the earth's climate, huge masses of ice, called **glaciers**, developed. As the glaciers moved, they acted like giant bulldozers, scraping and gouging the land they covered. The Appalachians and the Canadian Shield were rounded by moving ice that was often more than a kilometre thick. As the glaciers formed and then melted away, large amounts of clay, silt, sand, and gravel were dumped on the lowlands surrounding the Shield. Because it happened very recently (at least in geologic terms!), glaciation had an enormous impact on Canada's geography. The current patterns of lakes and rivers were created, along with areas of hills, plains, and swamps. While other geologic forces may have been more powerful than glaciation, none has been as important in shaping the land that we see today in Canada.

The last ice age ended for most of Canada about 10 000 years ago, but glaciers are still found in some mountain and Arctic areas. Some scientists think it is possible that the glaciers will advance a fifth time as part of a future ice age.

The Cenozoic era is the age of **mammals**. Probably because of a change in climate, the dinosaurs died out and mammals, which include human beings, became dominant. Humans have only been on the earth for a very short period of geologic time (see Figs. 4-10 and 4-11). The impact that people have had on the earth is enormous considering the short time we have been here. For example, we have created huge lakes by building dams, and have increased rates of erosion by cutting forests. In geologic terms, however, these impacts are of little lasting importance.

11:24 p.m.

Fig. 4-8 Paleozoic ends and Mesozoic begins (225 000 000 years ago).

11:49 p.m.

Fig. 4-9 Mesozoic ends and Cenozoic begins (70 000 000 years ago).

See the complementary study at the end of Chapter 5 for more information on glaciers.

Some scientists believe that the effects of a large comet hitting the earth caused the dinosaurs to die out.

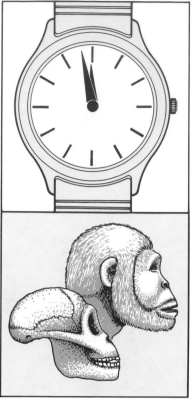

11:58:45 p.m.

Fig. 4–10 Prehuman ancestors evolve (8 000 000 years ago).

■ IN CLOSING . . .

Many geologic events have occurred since the Precambrian era to create Canada's diverse landforms. These events took place over hundreds of millions of years. Most people live less than a hundred years, and as a result, do not live long enough to see many geologic changes taking place. Because of this we tend to forget that geologic changes are still occurring today.

QUESTIONS

CHECKBACK

1. "Canada's physical landscape is the result of conflict between two forces." Describe the forces involved in this conflict and how they combine to produce the landscape we live in.

2. Define the **bold** words:
   a) **Geologic time** can be divided into four **eras**.
   b) The rocks of the Canadian Shield were **eroded**. The **sediments** were moved to nearby seas and **deposited** there.

3. a) What part of Canada was created during the Precambrian era?
   b) How did it differ in appearance from today? Make a sketch of how it looked in your notebook.

4. a) What happened to the Canadian Shield during the Paleozoic era?
   b) Where was the eroded material from the Shield deposited and what did this material become?
   c) At the end of the Paleozoic Era, what mountains were formed to the east of the Shield?
   d) What life forms existed during this era?

5. a) Describe the physical features that were created in Canada at the beginning, middle, and end of the Mesozoic era.
   b) Describe the climate and the life forms during the Mesozoic era.
   c) How were (i) coal deposits and (ii) oil and gas formed at this time?

6. a) How many glacial periods have there been during the last million years?
   b) Describe the impact of the glaciers on the Appalachians, the Canadian Shield and the surrounding lowlands.

7. Construct a geologic time chart using the headings in Fig. 4–12. List the eras from the most recent at the top to the oldest at the bottom. Fill in the chart using information from this chapter.
   a) How old is the earth?
   b) What percentage of the earth's age does each era represent?
   c) Why is the Precambrian put at the bottom of the chart?
   d) What is the name of the era that we live in?

Fig. 4–12

Name of era	When era began	How long era lasted	Major geological events in Canada

8. a) Draw a line 25 cm long on a piece of paper. Divide it into eras based on the percentages calculated in 7 b).
   b) Along the line, label the main geological events which occurred in each era.
9. Most geologic events happen very slowly. List two geologic events that happen fast enough for people to see.
10. What were the main geologic events that occurred in the area of Canada where you live? In which era did they occur? What evidence of these events can you see?

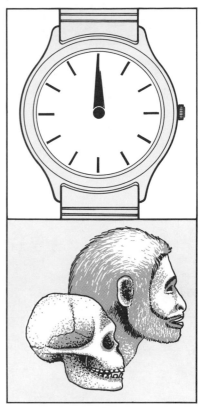

11:59:58 p.m.

Fig. 4–11 Modern human beings evolve (300 000 years ago).

INVESTIGATE

11. It is widely believed that the earth was formed about 4 600 000 000 years ago from a mass of gas and dust floating in space. Investigate other theories of when and how the earth was formed.

5 Landform Regions

If you remember these three words—**shield**, **lowlands**, and **highlands**—you will find the physical diversity of Canada easier to understand. Fig. 5–1 shows the location of these types of landforms. With a classmate, examine Fig. 5–1.

1. What is a landform region?

2. How many landform regions are there?

3. Which landform region is the largest? Which is the smallest?

4. a) In which landform region do you live?
   b) What does the landform region in which you live look like?
   c) How does it differ from other parts of Canada that you have visited or seen pictures of?

Fig. 5–1 Landform regions of Canada

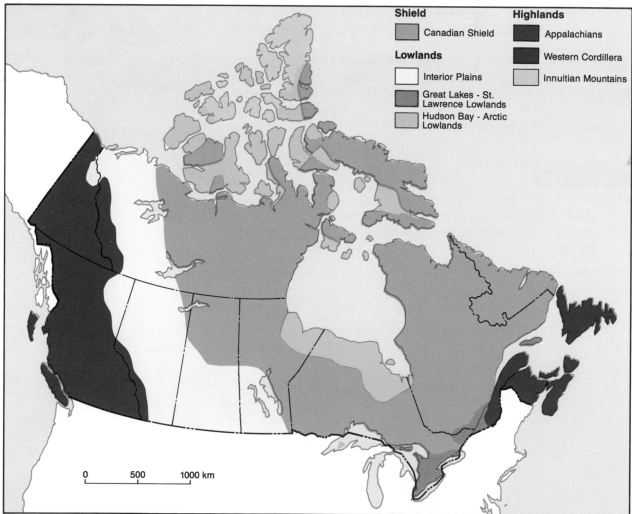

Shield
- Canadian Shield

Lowlands
- Interior Plains
- Great Lakes - St. Lawrence Lowlands
- Hudson Bay - Arctic Lowlands

Highlands
- Appalachians
- Western Cordillera
- Innuitian Mountains

0   500   1000 km

In this chapter the **topography** of each of Canada's landform regions, including the one in which you live, will be examined. As well, you will have a chance to learn how landform features affect Canada's people.

Key Terms

Canadian Shield	metallic minerals	rift valley
lowlands	sedimentary rocks	faulting
highlands	escarpment	drainage
topography	metamorphic rock	plateaus
igneous rock	non-metallic minerals	fiords
bedrock		

■ THE CANADIAN SHIELD

The Canadian Shield is the geographic foundation of Canada. More than half of Canada's area is covered by it (Fig. 5–1). Some of the world's oldest rock—over 3 500 000 000 years old—is found here. Two rock types, **igneous** and **metamorphic**, make up most of the Shield. These rocks form the platform on which the rest of Canada is built (Fig. 5–2). Because lead, gold, nickel, copper, zinc, and other valuable minerals are found in great quantities in these two types of rock, the Canadian Shield is often called the storehouse of Canada's **metallic minerals**.

How did these mineral deposits form in the Shield? Originally the minerals were mixed in the molten rock (magma) beneath the earth's crust. This molten rock then forced, or intruded, its way into cracks and cavities in the Shield rock. As the magma cooled to form igneous rock, water and other substances containing the minerals escaped. Sometimes these hot, mineral-bearing solutions made their way through cracks in the rock and chemically

Metamorphic rock is the more common

Fig. 5–2 Cross-section of Canada's landforms

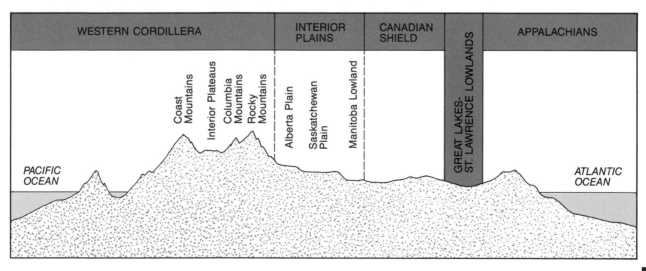

Fig. 5–3 Minerals are deposited when molten rock intrudes into existing rock formations.

Before

After

Older rock

Older rock

crack

molten rock

Mineralization occurs here. Older rock here has been "metamorphosed"

Older rock

Older rock

Intrusion of molten rock into crack in older rocks

A simple experiment will show you how liquids separate into layers:
1. Put 20 ml of vinegar and 60 ml of vegetable oil into a jar with a lid.
2. Shake well and let stand. What happens? Why?
3. Do not throw away the result of your experiment. Shake again and pour it on a salad!

See the complementary study on glaciation at the end of this chapter for more information on the effects of glaciation on the Canadian Shield.

habitat: natural living conditions

changed the surrounding rock to form metamorphic rock. The minerals were deposited in this contact zone (Fig. 5–3). In other cases, the minerals combined with sulfur, separated from the magma, and formed deposits. As the minerals slowly cooled, they separated into layers according to their density. The lighter ones floated on top of the heavier ones. Minerals that had similar density floated to the same level. For example, because nickel and copper have similar density, they are often found together.

The presence of metallic minerals attracts mining companies to the Shield. Many cities and towns (such as Sudbury, Thompson, and Yellowknife) rely on the mining industry for jobs. Factories in Canada and in other parts of the world use the raw materials mined in the Shield to create products we use every day.

During the ice ages of the Cenozoic era, glaciers removed enormous amounts of soil, clay, rock, and gravel from the Shield. Today, most of the Shield is covered by only a thin layer of soil, and the **bedrock** is visible in many places. Coniferous (needle-leaved) trees, which are better suited to thin, sandy soil than most other plants, cover most of the area. Canada's most extensive forest grows on the Shield, and provides lumber and pulp and paper for Canada and other parts of the world. The forest is also a habitat for a great number of animals.

The action of the glaciers affected the **drainage** of the Shield. Rivers were dammed up or forced to flow in different directions by sand, gravel, and clay deposited by the glaciers. The result is a very disorganized pattern of winding rivers, lakes, and swamps (Fig. 5–4). These swamps provide breeding grounds for the mosquitoes and blackflies for which the Shield is famous.

Since the Shield has thin soils, it is not very good for farming. However, its scenic rivers, waterfalls, lakes, rock outcrops, and vast forests make it ideal for recreation. People visit the Shield to

Fig. 5-4 Canadian Shield. Notice the many lakes.

camp, fish, hike, and "get back to nature". The tourist industry is very important in the southern parts of the Shield near centres with large populations.

The centre of the Shield is much lower than its outer portion. This gives the Shield the appearance of a saucer, with Hudson Bay occupying the low-lying centre. As a result, most of the rivers of the Shield flow toward the centre of the Shield and into Hudson Bay.

Many of these rivers provide sites for hydro-electric generating stations. The energy produced by these stations is transmitted by power lines to cities and towns both on and off the Shield.

QUESTIONS

CHECKBACK

1. **a)** What types of rock make up the platform on which the rest of Canada is built?
   b) Describe the ways in which these rocks are similar and the ways in which they differ.
2. Why is the Shield called Canada's storehouse of metallic minerals?
3. **a)** Using your own words, describe how mineral deposits form.
   b) Why are nickel and copper often found together?
4. Describe the effects of glaciers on:
   a) the surface material, and
   b) the drainage of the Shield.

ANALYZE

5. The natural beauty, the minerals, the rivers, and the forests are the economic backbone of the Shield. How have these resources aided in the economic development of this region?

6. Many products that you regularly use are made from different kinds of raw materials that originate in the Canadian Shield. Make a chart to show at least five products and the raw materials from which they are made.

WHAT DO YOU THINK?

7. a) On an outline map of Canada, draw the Canadian Shield.
   b) On this map locate the major cities (population over 100,000) found on the Shield. See your atlas for this information.
   c) How many such cities are there?
   d) Discuss the following questions with a small group of your classmates:
      i. What does this map and your knowledge of the Shield's landforms and natural resources tell you about the ability of the Shield to support a large population?
      ii. Why would this be so?
      iii. Could this change in the future? How?

THE LOWLANDS

There are three lowlands regions surrounding the Shield: the Interior Plains, the Great Lakes-St. Lawrence Lowlands, and the Hudson Bay-Arctic Lowlands (see Fig. 5–1). The bedrock under these lowlands is formed of sediments eroded from the Shield. The sediments were laid down under the seas that existed at various times and locations millions of years ago. The **sedimentary rocks** found in the different regions are of different ages.

INTERIOR PLAINS

The Interior Plains of Canada are part of the Great Plains of North America that extend from the Arctic Ocean to the Gulf of Mexico.

The main sedimentary rock layers underlying the Interior Plains were formed by the compression of sediments deposited in warm, shallow seas. The rock layers are several thousand metres thick, and took millions of years to form. Part of this sedimentary rock consists of coral reefs that once formed close to the surface of the seas but are now thousands of metres below the surface of the land. Much of the oil and gas of Alberta and Saskatchewan is found in these ancient coral reefs.

When some of the shallow seas covering the region that is now Saskatchewan evaporated, thick layers of mineral deposits were left in the dried-out sea bed. These layers are now deep in the earth, covered by newer rocks and glacial deposits. Today, potash is mined from these layers and used as a fertilizer in Canada and overseas.

See the complementary study on potash in chapter 24 for more information.

Fig. 5–5 Interior Plains

Some of the sedimentary rocks are very hard and resistant, and some are quite soft. The softer rock usually erodes more quickly than the harder rock. This difference in rates of erosion has caused three different levels of elevation to develop on the prairies. Each level is separated by a sharp rise called an **escarpment**. The escarpments are found where a rock layer resists erosion and therefore stands out above the others.

resistant: able to withstand the forces of erosion

The Interior Plains, like the rest of Canada, were subjected to glaciation. The glaciers left deposits that produced a rounded, gently rolling landscape in many areas. When the glaciers melted, they formed a large lake over much of what is now southern Manitoba and Saskatchewan. Later, the land rose, causing most of the water to drain into the ocean. Small portions of the lake remain today as Lake Winnipeg, Lake Manitoba, Lake Winnipegosis and Cedar Lake. The lake bottom was covered with sediments, making it remarkably flat. Consequently, the surface of the land in southern Manitoba is very flat today. The soil that developed on these sediments is deep and fertile.

This lake, called Lake Agassiz, was larger than all of the Great Lakes combined.

Locate these lakes by referring to your atlas.

Grain is grown in many southern locations of the Interior Plains. In locations where the climate is too dry for crops, cattle are raised. Agricultural products from this region are used both in Canada and in many other parts of the world.

Although many people think of the Interior Plains as flat, there are relatively few areas where this is true (Fig. 5–5). In most places the landscape is composed of rolling hills and deep, wide river valleys. Overall, the land slopes gently downward from west to east.

GREAT LAKES-ST. LAWRENCE LOWLANDS

South of the Canadian Shield is a smaller landform region, the Great Lakes-St. Lawrence Lowlands (Fig. 5–1). As you might suspect from the name, the region consists of two parts. The two parts are separated by a thin wedge of the Canadian Shield that cuts across the St. Lawrence River and extends into the U.S. near Kingston, Ontario. Like the bedrock of the Interior Plains, the bedrock of these lowlands is made of sedimentary rock formed during the Paleozoic era. (The presence of sedimentary rock should give you a hint as to how these lowlands were formed.

This part of the Canadian Shield is called the Frontenac Axis.

Fig. 5–6 Great Lakes Lowlands

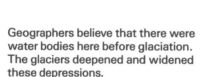

Geographers believe that there were water bodies here before glaciation. The glaciers deepened and widened these depressions.

Fig. 5–7 The cross-section in B shows how the St. Lawrence Lowlands were created as a result of faulting.

Refer to the previous chapter if you cannot remember.) The Paleozoic bedrock is seen in several escarpments, the best known being the Niagara Escarpment that extends from Niagara Falls to Manitoulin Island.

The Great Lakes section of the lowlands has a rolling landscape created mainly by glaciation (Fig. 5–6). Flat plains are broken by glacial hills and deep river valleys. The basins where the Great Lakes are today were gouged out by glaciers. When the glaciers melted, the enormous volume of water made these lakes even larger than they are today. The lakes eventually shrank to their present size as the water drained into the ocean. Flat plains of sediment were left on what used to be lake bottoms. In many parts of the Great Lakes Lowlands these sediments formed soil that is excellent for farming.

The St. Lawrence Lowlands were formed in a different way from the Great Lakes Lowlands. **Faulting** took place and a **rift valley** was formed (Fig. 5–7). Toward the end of the last ice age, this rift valley was flooded by a part of the Atlantic Ocean called the Champlain Sea. The deposits laid down under this sea have made this flat lowland very good for farming. The flat land is also ideal for transportation routes and the development of cities.

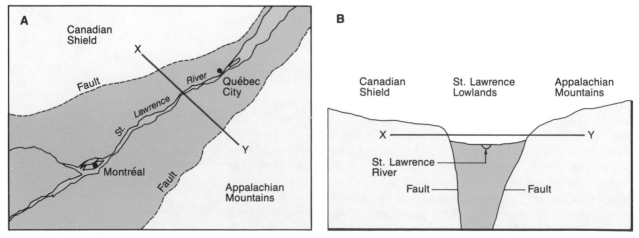

Rising above the floor of the St. Lawrence Valley is a series of hills, extending to the east of Montreal. Mont Royal, Mont St. Hilaire, and others are known as the Monteregian Hills. Geologists believe they are the result of igneous intrusions into the sedimentary rocks of the lowland. After millions of years of erosion the softer sedimentary rocks were worn away, leaving the igneous rocks as hills.

HUDSON BAY-ARCTIC LOWLANDS

You learned previously that the Canadian Shield is shaped like a saucer, with Hudson Bay occupying the low-lying centre (Fig. 5–1). Around the southwestern shore of Hudson Bay is a very flat lowland covered by swampy forest. Sedimentary rock underlies this region as it does in the other lowland areas you have learned about.

The Arctic Lowlands are made up of a series of islands located north of Hudson Bay. They are also formed of sedimentary rock and have a gently rolling surface. The harsh climate does not permit farming, but the animals and minerals of the region are important resources.

Q U E S T I O N S

CHECKBACK

1. a) How was the bedrock of the lowlands formed?
   b) Why are the sediments of different lowlands regions of different age?
2. a) How thick is the bedrock in the Interior Plains and why is it this thick?
   b) Of what modern significance are the ancient coral reefs?
   c) Describe how the three prairie levels were formed.
   d) How did glaciation affect the Interior Plains?
3. Describe the topography of the Interior Plains as you would see it if you were to drive across the region from west to east on the Trans-Canada Highway.
4. What separates the Great Lakes Lowlands from the St. Lawrence Lowlands? Where does this occur?
5. Copy the paragraph below into your notebook. Wherever there is an asterisk (*) insert the correct word from this list:

sedimentary	escarpment	lowlands
rift	soft	south
faults	erosion	glaciation

   To the * of the Canadian Shield is the Great Lakes-St. Lawrence *. Like the Interior Plains, these lowlands are made of * rock. The St. Lawrence Lowlands were created when land between two * collapsed creating a * valley. The landscape of the Great Lakes Lowlands is largely the result of *. The Niagara * is the biggest single feature of the lowlands.

6. Describe the characteristics of the Hudson Bay and Arctic lowlands.

Save your map for a further activity later in this chapter.

ANALYZE

7. a) Draw the three different lowlands regions on an outline map of Canada. (Use the same map that you used to draw the Shield.)
  b) Name the different lowlands regions.
  c) Locate the major cities (populations of 100 000 and over) in each region.
  d) How many of Canada's major cities are found in the lowlands?
  e) Compare the number of major cities in the lowlands with the number found in the Canadian Shield earlier in this chapter. Which region has more? Why?
8. Parts of the southern portion of the Interior Plains are often called Canada's breadbasket. Why?

■ THE HIGHLANDS

Canada's three highland areas lie to the east, north and west of the Shield and lowlands areas. Each has a different geological history and as a result each has a different appearance.

APPALACHIAN MOUNTAINS

The Appalachian Mountains stretch from the state of Georgia in the southern U.S. through the Maritimes to Newfoundland in the north (see Fig. 5–1). The Appalachians were formed about 300 000 000 years ago, near the end of the Paleozoic era, when sedimentary rock layers were uplifted and folded. They are the oldest highland region in Canada. Later, igneous and metamorphic rocks were created in parts of this region from the stresses and strains of folding and faulting. The Appalachians were once jagged peaks, but erosion over hundreds of millions of years has reduced their height. They are now rolling mountains and hills separated by wide valleys (Fig. 5–8).

Non-metallic minerals, such as coal and salt, are found within the sedimentary rock layers of the Appalachians. Between the ridges of the mountains are **plateaus** of igneous rock. Metallic minerals, such as iron and zinc, are mined from these plateaus.

During the ice ages the Appalachians were pressed down as well as eroded by the mass of ice. As the land sank, small inlets along the east coast became long bays. Today, many of these bays provide excellent harbours for ocean freighters and fishing boats. A coastline that has been depressed below the seas is called a "drowned coastline". The jagged coastline of the Atlantic provinces is the result of this sinking process.

Fig. 5–8 Appalachians

INNUITIAN MOUNTAINS

In Canada's far north, the Innuitian Mountains stand like icy watchtowers, measuring over 3000 m in height in some parts (see Fig. 5–1). These mountains were formed in the middle of the Mesozoic era. They are composed mainly of sedimentary rock but have some metamorphic and igneous rocks as well.

They are younger than the Appalachians, and erosion has not had time to reduce them to rounded hills. These mountains are barren because trees cannot survive the very cold winter temperatures or grow much in the short summer. Ice and permanent snow cover vast areas of the northern mountains. The Innuitian Mountains resemble the Appalachians in composition and contain similar types of minerals, but the mineral resources have not been exploited because the region's remote location makes development too costly.

remote: far away from where most Canadians live

WESTERN CORDILLERA

The Western Cordillera (see Fig. 5–1) stands along the western edge of Canada like a great wall: range after range of mountains separated by plateaus and valleys (Fig. 5–9). What does the great height and rugged appearance of these mountains tell us about their age?

Apart from those in the Arctic, the mountains of the Western Cordillera contain the only remaining glaciers in Canada. These glaciers add to the beauty for which the Canadian West is famous.

Many people tend to use the name "Rocky Mountains" and "Western Cordillera" interchangeably. This is a mistake. There are three major divisions in the Western Cordillera. The Rocky Mountains form a narrow mountain range along the eastern edge of the Cordillera and are only one of many mountain ranges found in the region. Further west are two other divisions, both of which are much wider than the Rockies: the Interior Plateaus and Mountain Ranges, and the Coast Mountains. Refer to Fig. 5–10 as you read about each division.

interchangeable: can be used in place of another

Fig. 5-9 Western Cordillera

Fig. 5-10 Cross-section of the Western Cordillera

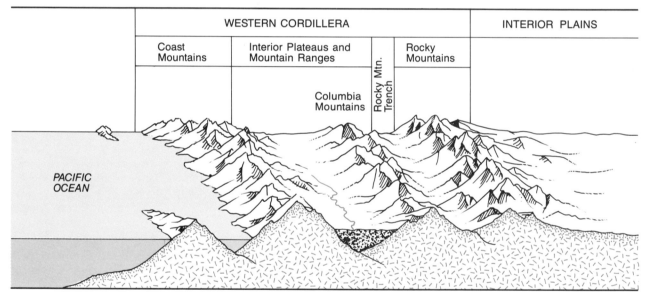

WESTERN CORDILLERA				INTERIOR PLAINS
Coast Mountains	Interior Plateaus and Mountain Ranges	Rocky Mtn. Trench	Rocky Mountains	
	Columbia Mountains			

PACIFIC OCEAN

Rocky Mountains

The Rocky Mountains on the eastern side of the Cordillera are formed of folded and faulted sedimentary rock. This rock contains many fossils of ancient life, proving that it was formed of sediments deposited in ancient seas. Millions of years later great forces inside the earth forced this rock up, causing it to bend, crack, and be heaved upward to form Canada's youngest and most scenic mountains.

Today, as in the past, the Rockies present an obstacle to transportation across the Cordillera. The mountain ranges and valleys run northwest-southeast and the transportation routes run east-west. Only in a few spots are the gaps or passes low enough to allow highways and railways to be built.

The Rocky Mountain Trench separates the Rockies from the next series of mountain ranges. This valley was created by erosion along a zone of faults.

Interior Plateaus and Mountain Ranges

In the centre of the Cordillera is a series of mountain ranges and plateaus. The mountain ranges are composed of metamorphic and igneous rocks. In southern British Columbia there are three mountain ranges known collectively as the Columbia Mountains.

Although not as high as the Rockies, the Columbia Mountains are still difficult to cross. Many of the interior plateaus are formed from lava flows, indicating that there was volcanic activity here in the past. The lava flows have been deeply cut by the major rivers of the region.

Coast Mountains

The Coast Mountains, a mountain range of igneous rock, extend along the west coast of Canada. The islands off the coast of British Columbia are part of this range. The igneous rock of the Coast Mountains formed below the earth's surface and was then uplifted to create a wall of granite along the Pacific Coast. Mount Logan in the Yukon Territory is part of this range. It is Canada's highest peak (6050 m).

The western slopes of the Coast Mountains receive a great deal of rainfall. This, coupled with the warm climate, encourages the growth of the tall coastal Douglas fir, Sitka spruce, cedar, and hemlock. Further inland, dry conditions exist and the tree species are different. Nevertheless, the Cordillera is one of Canada's major regions for forest products.

During the last ice age many coastal valleys were occupied by glaciers. These glaciers eroded the valleys below sea level. When the ice melted, these valleys became long narrow inlets of the sea, called **fiords**. The steep sides of these fiords and the towering mountains create spectacular scenery that attracts thousands of tourists every year (Fig. 5-11). These tourists, however, must travel by boat or seaplane. There are few roads along the coast of British Columbia because of the rugged landscape and the many fiords.

Fig. 5-11   British Columbia fiord

■ IN CLOSING...

"A core of ancient rock, surrounded by lowlands and then highlands on three sides." This may be a simple description, but it does summarize the diversity of Canada's physical landforms.

QUESTIONS

1. Why does the Appalachian region have many excellent harbours?

2. a) Describe the composition and appearance of the Innuitian Mountains.
   b) Which other mountain system do they resemble?
   c) Why has this region not been developed as much as other regions?

3. Compare the three major divisions of the Western Cordillera under the following headings: formation, rock type, and appearance.

4. Why are the mountain ranges of the Western Cordillera viewed as a barrier to transportation?

5. a) How were the fiords of British Columbia created?
   b) What effect do the fiords have on transportation along the coast?

ANALYZE

6. a) Draw the highland regions on your outline map of Canada.
   b) Name each region.
   c) Locate the major cities (population 100 000 and over) in each region.
   d) Compare the number of major cities in these highland regions with the number in the lowlands and the Shield. Why does this pattern exist?

7. Examine the photo of the Appalachians on page 43 and the photo of the Western Cordillera on page 44. Which mountains are older? How can you tell?

8. Cut out a piece of cardboard or paper 14 cm by 9 cm to make a postcard. Select one of the landform regions and draw a picture typical of the region. On the other side of the postcard write a short letter to a friend describing this region.

9. Draw a profile of the Western Cordillera according to the following instructions.
   a) On a piece of graph paper draw a horizontal line 15 cm long. Label the left end of the line Vancouver and the right end Calgary.
   b) Draw a vertical scale on the left showing elevations from 0 to 3600 m. The vertical scale should be 1 cm = 700 m.
   c) Put dots at the elevations and distances provided in Fig. 5–12. Now join the dots.
   d) Label the following features on your profile:
      Rocky Mountains   Rocky Mountain Trench
      Columbia Mountains   Interior Plateaus
      Coast Mountains
   e) Look at your profile and suggest what problems for farming and transportation might exist in this region.

Distance from Vancouver on profile (cm)	Elevation at this point (m)	Distance from Vancouver on profile (cm)	Elevation at this point (m)
0.5	350	9.0	2200
1.0	1500	10.5	3200
1.5	2700	11.5	3300
2.5	1800	12.0	1000
3.5	2500	12.5	2800
4.0	1400	13.0	3500
6.0	1200	14.0	1800
7.5	1400	15.0	1050
8.0	1600		

Fig. 5–12

10. **a)** Name four lakes in Manitoba and five lakes in southern Ontario which are remnants of glacial lakes. (Use an atlas).

b) Why are these lakes smaller than they were in the glacial period? Why did the lakes not disappear completely?

INVESTIGATE

11. Many advertisements in magazines use photos of different geographical locations and landforms in Canada to help sell their products. Let us call these advertisements "geo-ads". Obtain at least five "geo-ads" from Canadian magazines and answer the following questions for each advertisement.

a) What landform region is shown in the "geo-ad?"

b) Explain how you were able to identify the region.

c) Why is the landform being used to sell this product?

d) Is the advertisement successful in selling this product by using the landform? Explain your answer.

12. Find postage stamps, or copies of stamps that show how Canada differs from place to place. Attach the stamps in the correct locations on a map of Canada's landform regions.

If your parents have a stamp collection, DO NOT use their most valuable stamp!

WHAT DO YOU THINK?

13. **a)** Using an atlas, draw the major physical regions (Shield, Lowlands and Highlands) on a blank map of Canada.

b) Draw the Trans-Canada Highway and the major CN and CP railway lines on the map.

c) Indicate the largest city in each province on the map.

d) With the help of this map, discuss the following quotation: "Canada is an east-west country trying to live in a north-south continent."

Glaciation

Whenever winter is particularly long or cold, newspapers and magazines publish stories about the possibility of a future **ice age** (Fig. 5–13). People seem fascinated by the possibility of a mass of ice advancing over the landscape, sweeping away everything in front of it. But this is more than science fiction. Ice sheets have covered most of Canada several times during the past few million years, causing enormous changes in our geography. How did this glaciation happen? What were its effects? Could it happen again soon? This study will provide some answers to these questions.

Fig. 5–13 While some scientists think that glaciers may cover Canada in the future, others think that the glaciers that are left may melt away. Which do you think would be a more serious problem?

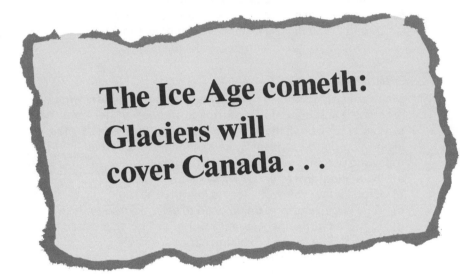

The Ice Age cometh: Glaciers will cover Canada . . .

Key Terms

ice age	zone of accumulation	till
glacier	advance of glacier	till plains
alpine glacier	retreat of glacier	moraines
continental glacier	U-shaped valley	

■ INTRODUCTION

Did you know that ice is one of the hardest substances on earth? This seems strange when we see fragile ice crystals on window-panes or ice cubes floating in cool drinks. Yet ice has the power to crush the hulls of steel ships and to transform the shape of the land.

The earth has experienced many **ice ages**. For reasons not yet fully understood, the earth's climate cooled and the snow that fell in the winter did not completely melt in the summer. Over thousands of years the snow got deeper and became hundreds of metres thick. The tremendous weight of the snow on top caused the bottom layers to turn to ice. Over many years this mass of ice, or **glacier**, could grow to several thousand metres in thickness.

Almost as remarkable as the size of the glacier is the fact that it can move. Solid ice acts like a very thick liquid and flows very slowly.

Glaciers move in different ways, depending on their location and on the climate. In mountainous regions, **alpine glaciers** move down valleys from high elevations to low elevations under the force of gravity. A **continental glacier** is found on level, low-lying land. The enormous weight of snow and ice causes the glacier to spread outward from its centre or **zone of accumulation** (Fig. 5–14). Although the ice of a continental glacier is constantly moving outward, the outer edge or margin of the ice sheet may advance, retreat, or stay in one place. Fig. 5–15 explains the conditions under which each of these movements might occur.

For comparison, the CN Tower in Toronto stands only 553 m high

You can demonstrate the movement of a continental glacier with a ball of bread dough. Place the dough on a flat surface and press down on it slowly with your palm. Notice how it spreads outward in all directions.

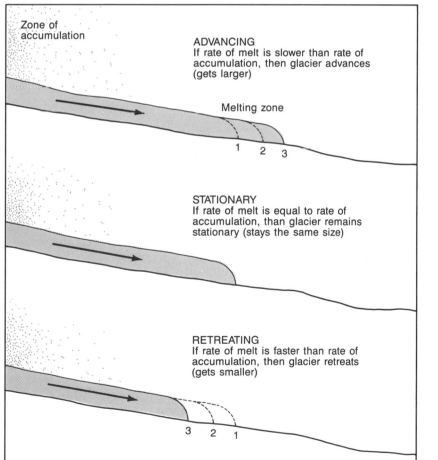

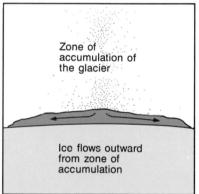

Fig. 5–14 Glaciers move like very thick liquid.

Fig. 5–15 The advance or retreat of a glacier is determined by the balance between ice accumulation and ice melt. In all cases the ice continues to move outward from the zone of accumulation.

During the past two to three million years, great glaciers have **advanced** and **retreated** at least four times. Each of these advances and retreats is called an ice age. The last ice age began about 100 000 years ago and ended in most parts of Canada about 10 000 years ago. During each ice age almost all of Canada and parts of the U.S., Europe, and South America were covered by huge glaciers. A large amount of the world's water was frozen in glaciers. This caused the level of the oceans to fall well below current levels. Continental glaciers give the landscape a smoother appearance by eroding higher points on the land and filling in lower areas with the eroded material. Today, continental glaciers exist only in Greenland and Antarctica.

These ice ages occurred during a part of the Cenozoic era called the Pleistocene.

Alpine glaciers leave the high-altitude landscape scoured and rugged, and sharpen the upper portions of the mountains. When they moved down river valleys, they scraped away the valley walls to produce broad **U-shaped valleys**. The result is beautiful scenery that attracts many tourists. Alpine glaciers exist today in parts of the Western Cordillera and the Arctic islands, as well as in very high mountains around the world.

■ GLACIATION OF CANADA

Glaciation is the process most responsible for the topography that we see in Canada today. There are two reasons for this:

- glaciation is an extremely powerful force;
- glaciation happened very recently in geologic terms, and there has not been enough time for the glacial features to be worn away.

To understand what happened to shape the land, we will examine a series of maps which portray the last stages of the ice age in Canada (Fig. 5–16):

1. Fig. 5–16a shows the maximum extent of glaciation during the last ice age. This occurred about 18-20 000 years ago. As the glacier moved, it eroded huge amounts of soil, sand, gravel, and rocks and carried them along with it. This eroded material is called **till**. In some places, the glacier deposited the till underneath the ice, forming a gently rolling landscape called **till plains**. In other places, the till was deposited at the edges of a glacier when the ice began to melt. This till formed **moraines**, which tend to be hillier than till plains.

2. Fig. 5–16b shows that the ice melted back from its farthest limit over a period of 7-10 000 years. The enormous amounts of meltwater flowing from the glaciers during this time caused the creation of temporary lakes along the margins of the ice. Some of these lakes, known as glacial ponds, were very small. Others, like Lake Agassiz in Manitoba, were much larger than any lake in the world today.

Imagine the amount of water released by the melting of a glacier 2 km thick!

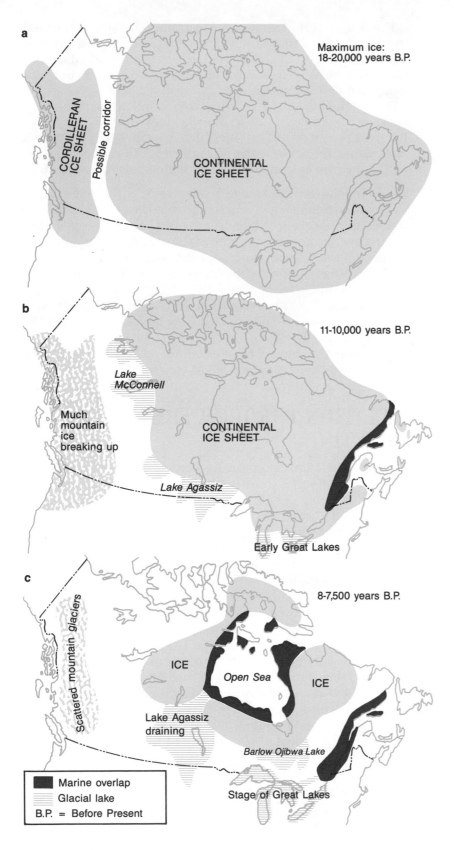

Fig. 5–16 Retreat of the glaciers.

a

CORDILLERAN ICE SHEET

Possible corridor

CONTINENTAL ICE SHEET

Maximum ice:
18-20,000 years B.P.

b

Much mountain ice breaking up

Lake McConnell

CONTINENTAL ICE SHEET

Lake Agassiz

Early Great Lakes

11-10,000 years B.P.

c

Scattered mountain glaciers

ICE

Open Sea

ICE

Lake Agassiz draining

Barlow Ojibwa Lake

Stage of Great Lakes

8-7,500 years B.P.

◼	Marine overlap
▦	Glacial lake
B.P.	= Before Present

The land is rebounding at a rate of approximately 1 to 2 cm per century.

The ancient sea that occupied parts of the St. Lawrence and Ottawa Valleys is called the Champlain Sea

The weight of the ice sheet had a dramatic effect on the land. Over a period of thousands of years, it compressed the land downward. When the ice melted, the land rebounded upward but at a relatively slow rate. In fact, this rebound continues today in much of Canada.

During this period, the sea was able to roll in and cover large areas of depressed land in the St. Lawrence River Valley. Today, these areas are dry land, but we can see beaches and sand dunes far above current sea levels. These beaches and sand dunes are evidence of what is called "marine overlap".

3. Fig. 5–16c shows a later stage in the retreat of the glaciers. The ice sheets are almost gone. In some areas the glacial lakes have almost disappeared, while in others they have expanded. Marine overlap continues in the St. Lawrence River Valley and has become very significant along the edges of Hudson Bay. By 7500 years ago, most of the landforms had appeared that we can see in Canada today.

The action of the glaciers produced features which are very important to our economy today. Clay is the raw material for making bricks. The flat bottoms of glacial lakes, as well as gently rolling till plains, have excellent soil for farming. Sand and gravel deposits may be used as construction materials.

■ GLACIATION THROUGH THE EYE OF THE ARTIST

Canadian artists have dramatically portrayed the effects of glaciers on the landscape in different parts of Canada. Fig. 5–17 portrays what many people regard as typical of Canada. On the Canadian Shield, much of the soil was eroded by moving ice, leaving bare, rocky hills. The eroded materials were deposited in valleys, blocking the natural drainage system of streams and rivers. This created many swampy areas and scenic lakes. In time, new soil and new drainage patterns will develop.

Fig. 5–18 shows a common scene in many parts of Canada south of the Shield. By the time the ice sheets reached this far they had lost much of their ability to erode and were mainly depositing material. This painting shows till that has been deposited by the glacier. If you were on a field-trip to this area, you could easily identify till because it contains the angular-shaped stones and boulders typical of material deposited by ice.

Examine the third painting (Fig. 5–19). Many people think that this extreme flatness is what all of the Canadian Prairies look like. In fact, it is only typical of those parts of the Prairies that were covered by glacial lakes. These lakes were formed when a glacier melted. Parts of the region that were not covered by glacial lakes have the more hilly landscape typical of deposition by ice. Similar flat glacial lake areas are also found in parts of Ontario, Québec and the Northwest Territories.

Fig. 5–17   **White Pine** by A.J. Casson, is an artist's view of how glaciation affected much of the Canadian Shield.

Fig. 5–18   **Hillside, Lake Alphonse** by William Goodridge Roberts, shows the rolling landscape that was created by deposition of soil materials by ice in many parts of southern Canada.

Fig. 5–19   William Kurelek's **No Grass Grows on the Beaten Pathway** vividly shows the flat land produced in parts of Canada that were covered by glacial meltwater lakes. (Taken from *FIELDS*, by Wm. Kurulek, published by Tundra Books, 1976).

Fig. 5–20   **Mount Jacobsen #2** by James Spencer illustrates the results of alpine glaciation.

Materials carried by meltwater from the glaciers were smoothed and sorted by the action of the moving water. In consequence, materials deposited in a glacial lake have a smooth rounded appearance, and there are usually particles of only one size in a given location. Where a fast moving glacial stream existed, you might find a deposit of gravel. Where once there was a quiet lake, you may find only fine clay.

The spectacular scenery of Canada's mountainous regions shown in Fig. 5–20 is largely due to the action of alpine glaciation. Glaciers flowing in the valleys between mountain peaks have eroded and "sharpened" the landscape.

■ IN CLOSING . . .

There is no reason why another ice age could not happen. In fact, some scientists think that there may be another ice age soon! Average yearly temperatures would only need to drop about 4C° for this to happen. Many questions about ice ages and the reasons why climates change remain to be answered.

QUESTIONS

CHECKBACK

1. a) What causes snow to turn to glacial ice?
   b) What causes alpine and continental glaciers to flow?
2. During the ice ages:
   a) which parts of the earth were covered by glaciers?
   b) what happened to the oceans? Why?
3. Construct a chart to compare the effects on the landscape of alpine and continental glaciers. Before you begin, decide under what headings you will make the comparison.
4. By observing the deposited materials, how can you tell those that were deposited directly by a glacier from those deposited by glacial meltwater?

ANALYZE

5. Many important activities today are directly related to the effects of glaciation on Canada. For each of the areas portrayed by the paintings (Figs. 5–17 to 20) describe an economic activity related to glacial effects. Be sure to state the relationship that exists.
6. Which glacial process was most important where you live? What evidence is there of this?

7. Determine what each of the following continental glacial features looks like and how it was formed:
   a) drumlin
   b) striations
   c) spillway
   d) esker
   e) kettle lake
   f) kame

8. a) Some scientists think it is possible that a new ice age may develop and that glaciers will advance a fifth time. What effects would this have on i) the land, and ii) the people of Canada?
   b) Other scientists think that the remaining glaciers in the world may be melting. If this happens, sea levels might rise by 100 metres. Using an atlas as a reference, draw these new ocean levels on a map of North America.
   c) Explain why scientists cannot agree on whether another ice age will happen.

9. a) Is the use of paintings an effective way to study geography? Why?
   b) What are the advantages and disadvantages of this approach compared to more conventional methods of presenting geographic information?

   conventional: ordinary

   c) Use art galleries, picture stores or books to find some paintings which portray other aspects of Canada's physical or human geography. Record the name of the painting and the artist and the geographical features shown.

6 Climate

"And now for the weather forecast (Fig. 6–1). Good evening. Typically we have had quite a diversity of early March weather across the country today. . .

"A storm moving through the southeastern part of Canada left 25 cm of snow in its wake. This low pressure system is expected to cross the Maritimes early tomorrow and move eastward over the Atlantic by tomorrow evening. Temperatures will remain from -5°C to -10°C throughout the eastern part of the country.

"In the Prairies today the cold snap continued under sunny skies. Temperatures of -25°C were recorded in Winnipeg and -20°C in Calgary. Arctic air flowing southward is the cause of this current cold weather.

"On the coast, Vancouver had cloudy skies and rain today with a high temperature of 6 degrees above zero. Tomorrow the city will have a touch of spring with sunny skies and a high of 14°C.

"Finally, the coldest spot in the nation today was Resolute in the Northwest Territories at -40°C under clear skies.

"That's the weather across the country for today. Until tomorrow, goodnight."

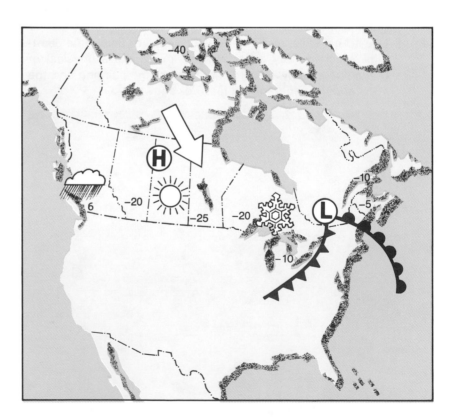

Fig. 6–1 A typical TV weather map.

Key Terms

weather

climate

air pressure

winds

air mass

prevailing winds

front

warm front

cold front

maritime climate

continental climate

relief precipitation

cyclonic precipitation

convectional precipitation

■ INTRODUCTION

Weather is a result of the day-to-day condition of the atmosphere. Descriptions of the weather include details about temperature, precipitation, humidity, wind speed and direction, cloud cover, and air pressure. This is the type of information normally given in a weather forecast. The weather is important to us all and affects us personally in many ways. For example, a rainstorm may wash out a baseball game you were planning to attend. A snowstorm may mean you have to leave home a half hour earlier to reach school on time. A dry summer often means smaller crop yields for farmers. This will affect your family's food bills as the prices of some goods at the supermarket are forced up. In what ways has the weather affected your activities over the past two weeks?

Over the years, records have been kept of the weather in different parts of Canada. These records show the patterns of weather which have occurred over a long period of time. A long-term pattern of weather is called a **climate**. Different parts of Canada have different climates.

In this chapter you will learn about:

- the factors that affect climate
- the three types of precipitation
- the climate regions of Canada.

In summer the air temperature can be estimated by listening to a cricket. Try this:
i. count the number of chirps in 8 seconds
ii. add 8 to the count to get the air temperature in degrees Celsius

The year 1816 is known as the "summerless summer." Snow was on the ground in many parts of southern Canada by August and few crops could be harvested.

■ FACTORS THAT AFFECT CLIMATE

Climate is affected by the following factors:

- *L*atitude
- *O*cean currents
- *W*inds and air masses
- *E*levation (altitude)
- *R*elief (mountain barriers)
- *Near*ness to *water*

The first letters of the first five factors and the italic portion of the last factor can be used to make a simple phrase. This phrase will help you remember the six climate factors. Write this phrase in your notebook.

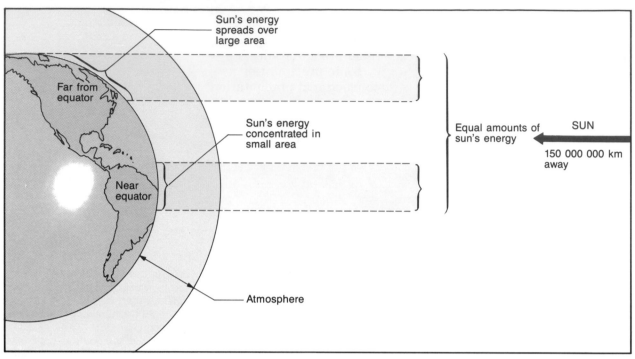

Fig. 6–2 Effect of latitude on climate

LATITUDE

Usually the further a region is from the equator, the cooler its climate will be (Fig. 6–2). The following questions will help you examine the effect of latitude on climate.

1. Which is closer to the equator, Regina or Yellowknife?

2. Examine the climate graphs for these two locations (Figs. 6–15 and 6–16). What is the January temperature and the July temperature at each location?

3. Based on these observations, describe the effect that latitude has on climate.

OCEAN CURRENTS

Canada is affected by three ocean currents. To learn about the effect of ocean currents on climate, answer the following questions.

1. The coast of British Columbia has a yearly average temperature of 9°C. The eastern coast of Newfoundland has a yearly average temperature of 5°C. Explain how this temperature difference can be partially accounted for by looking at the differences in ocean currents along these coasts (Fig. 6–4).

2. a) The east coast of Canada has a special situation—a warm current meeting a cold current. Examine Fig. 6-4 and describe the characteristic weather conditions of this area.

   b) What navigational problems do these weather conditions create for ships and how might these problems be overcome?

3. The Labrador current brings icebergs southward from arctic regions. This area of the ocean is referred to as "iceberg alley". What effects does this have on shipping and oil exploration off the east coast of Canada?

In 1912, an iceberg that drifted down "iceberg alley" was struck by a passenger ship. The ship sank, killing 1500 people. What was the ship's name?

WINDS AND AIR MASSES

Air, like everything else on earth, has weight. Its weight is created by the force of gravity and is called **air pressure**. If you climbed to the top of a mountain there would be less air above you than there was when you were at sea level. Since there is less air at high altitudes, there is less air pressure.

The average pressure of air at sea level is 101.3 kilopascals (kPa).

Winds are created by differences in air pressure. These differences are caused not only by altitude but also by temperature differences. Convection currents are created by the rising air (Fig. 6-3).

Around the world, there is a system of high and low pressure belts. The movement of air between these global high and low pressure belts has created a well-established pattern of winds which blow from west to east over most of Canada. We say, therefore, that the **prevailing winds** are westerly. Within this prevailing westerly wind belt, high pressure areas or cells, alternating with low pressure cells, create our changing weather conditions.

Fig. 6-3 Differences in air pressure produce convection currents and winds.

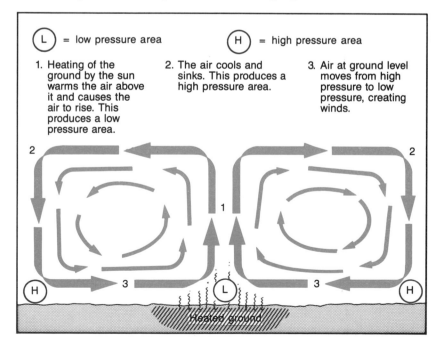

L = low pressure area   H = high pressure area

1. Heating of the ground by the sun warms the air above it and causes the air to rise. This produces a low pressure area.

2. The air cools and sinks. This produces a high pressure area.

3. Air at ground level moves from high pressure to low pressure, creating winds.

Heated ground

Moisture content is usually measured in terms of relative humidity (RH).
RH = (Amount of moisture in air/ Moisture holding capacity) x 100%

As an air mass moves southward, it becomes warmer and picks up moisture. Nevertheless, it remains colder and drier than the air in the region that it moves into.

An **air mass** is a large volume of air with almost the same temperature and moisture content throughout. As it moves, an air mass takes with it the climatic conditions of the area where it was formed (Fig. 6–4). For example, an air mass that forms in Canada's Arctic is cold and dry. As it moves southward, its cold, dry conditions are carried across Canada by the prevailing westerly winds. To test your understanding of winds and air masses, try these questions.

1. Why is the air pressure lower at the top of a mountain than it is at sea level?

Fig. 6–4 Canada's climate is affected by air masses and ocean currents.

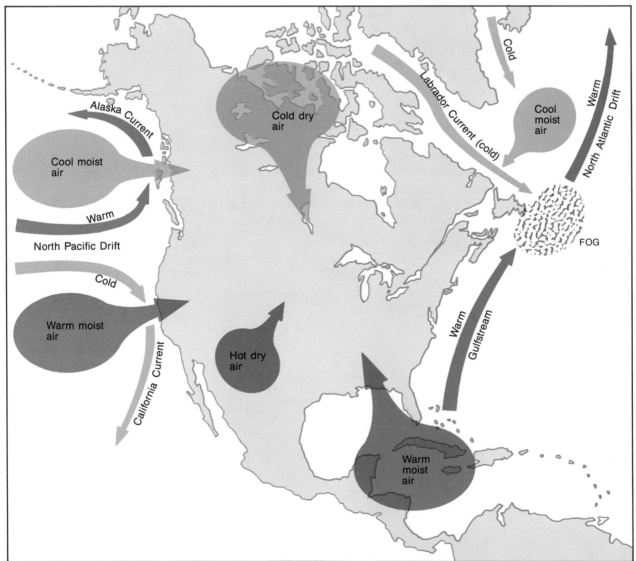

2. a) What causes a low pressure cell to develop?
   b) What causes a high pressure cell to develop?

3. Define the terms: i) wind and ii) prevailing winds.

4. What is an air mass?

5. Explain what happens to the weather in southeastern Canada when warm, moist air comes up from the Gulf of Mexico.

6. Why doesn't the cold, dry air mass from the Arctic affect the Pacific Coast near Vancouver?

ELEVATION

If you were to hike from sea level to the top of a high mountain, you would notice that the temperature dropped steadily as you went up. As you approached the top, you might even find ice and snow all around you. Why does it get colder even though you are getting closer to the sun? Consider what happens as a mass of air moves up a mountain. As the air rises it expands because there is less air pressure. As the air expands, it loses heat.

The rate of cooling varies according to the moisture content of the air. When the air has a relative humidity of 100%, **condensation** begins, and this affects the cooling rate:

- When condensation is *not* occurring, an air mass loses 1.0C° for every 100 m it rises.
- When condensation *is* occurring, an air mass loses heat at a rate of only 0.6C° for every 100 m.

   Let's explore why this difference occurs. When water vapour condenses into liquid water, heat is given off. Thus, when air is rising and condensation is occurring, two opposing changes are taking place. The rising air is cooled by expansion while it is heated by condensation of its water vapour. The result is a lower rate of cooling.

   Fig. 6–5 illustrates how you can calculate the temperature of an air mass as it rises up a mountainside. Now, try these questions.

1. Mount Garibaldi is a 2700 m high mountain just outside Vancouver. The temperature at the waterfront in Vancouver is 24°C. What will the temperature of this air mass be at the mountain top if condensation starts at 1200 m?

2. The temperature of an air mass at sea level is 10°C. What will its temperature be at the top of a mountain 1800 m high, if condensation begins at 900 m?

When discussing an actual temperature, use "degrees Celsius". For example, "the temperature today is 20°C." When discussing a temperature change or a range of temperatures, use the term "Celsius degrees". For example, "the temperature fell by 10C°."

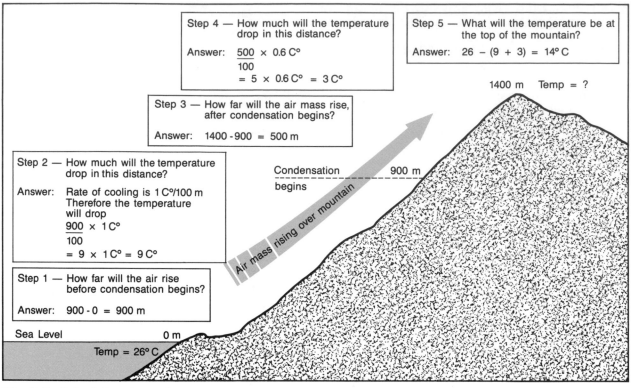

Step 4 — How much will the temperature drop in this distance?

Answer: $\dfrac{500}{100} \times 0.6\,C°$
$= 5 \times 0.6\,C° = 3\,C°$

Step 5 — What will the temperature be at the top of the mountain?

Answer: $26 - (9 + 3) = 14°\,C$

1400 m   Temp = ?

Step 3 — How far will the air mass rise, after condensation begins?

Answer: $1400 - 900 = 500$ m

Condensation begins   900 m

Air mass rising over mountain

Step 2 — How much will the temperature drop in this distance?

Answer: Rate of cooling is $1\,C°/100$ m
Therefore the temperature will drop
$\dfrac{900}{100} \times 1\,C°$
$= 9 \times 1\,C° = 9\,C°$

Step 1 — How far will the air rise before condensation begins?

Answer: $900 - 0 = 900$ m

Sea Level   0 m

Temp = 26° C

Fig. 6–5 Calculating change in temperature of a rising air mass

RELIEF

Relief refers to the differences in elevation of the earth's surface. Mountain ranges affect climate because they act as barriers to the movement of air masses. For example, Vancouver often has warm, rainy weather in winter while Calgary, on the other side of the Western Cordillera, has cold, dry weather. Mountain barriers also tend to cause precipitation to occur. We will examine the effect of relief on precipitation later in this chapter.

NEARNESS TO WATER

As an air mass passes over a large body of water, such as an ocean or a big lake, it absorbs moisture. Then, as the air passes over land, the moisture may be released in some form of precipitation. As a result, areas closer to bodies of water usually receive more precipitation than areas farther away from water.

When the water body is a lake, this moderation of the nearby land temperatures is called the "lake effect."

Water bodies can also affect climate by moderating land temperatures. Water gains and loses heat more slowly than land. In summer, this means that wind blowing off the water will keep the surrounding countryside cooler than it would be if no water were present. In winter, the opposite occurs—at least until the water body freezes over. Therefore, in a region near a body of water, the winters are not as cold and the summers are not as hot as similar areas in the middle of a land mass. The temperatures have been "moderated" by the water body.

Areas that are close to an ocean have a **maritime climate**. Areas that are located far from an ocean have a **continental climate**. The following table (Fig. 6–6) shows the differences that exist between the two climates.

Fig. 6–6 Characteristics of Continental and Maritime Climates

Climate	Typical Weather	Annual Temperature Range	Annual Precipitation
continental	warm to hot summers; cold winters	25–50 C° (large range)	200–1000 mm (low to moderate)
maritime	cool to warm summers; cool winters	10–30 C° (small range)	1000–2500 mm (moderate to high)

1. Examine the climate graphs for Prince Rupert (Fig. 6–13) and Regina (Fig. 6–15).
   a) Calculate the temperature range for both locations. Which one has the larger range? Why?
   b) Which location has the lower annual precipitation? Why?
2. On the basis of your answers to Question 1, what types of climate do Prince Rupert and Regina have?

Temperature range = average temperature of warmest month minus average temperature of coolest month.

▪ TYPES OF PRECIPITATION

Precipitation is one of the most important elements of weather and climate. It is easy to understand why precipitation occurs if two key ideas are understood:

- **Precipitation occurs when air containing water vapour cools to the point where condensation of the vapour takes place.**
- **Air cools when it is forced to rise.**

An air mass may rise for any of the following reasons:

1. It may be forced to rise to cross an area of higher elevation. This causes **relief precipitation** (sometimes called **orographic precipitation**).

2. It may rise because it absorbs heat from the earth's surface. This causes **convectional precipitation**.

3. It may be forced to rise by a cooler, denser air mass flowing beneath it. This causes **cyclonic precipitation**.

A region's location and physical features determine the type and amount of precipitation that occurs.

RELIEF PRECIPITATION

Mountain barriers create relief precipitation (Fig. 6–7). As moist air is forced to rise up the **windward** slope of a mountain range, it cools. As it cools it is unable to hold as much water vapour. At a certain temperature (called the dewpoint) the air becomes saturated with water vapour and condensation occurs. This produces clouds. As more and more moisture condenses, the water droplets get larger until rain is produced. In colder conditions, water vapour can change directly into snow.

As the cool air descends on the **leeward** slope of the mountain range, it gets warmer. Because warm air is able to hold more water vapour than cooler air , the clouds evaporate and the relative humidity drops. The result is a very dry climate area called a **rain shadow**. The following questions will help you understand the effect of relief on precipitation.

dewpoint: temperature at which condensation occurs

saturated: the air is so full of water vapour that it is not able to hold any more at that temperature.

Fig. 6–7   Effect of relief on precipitation

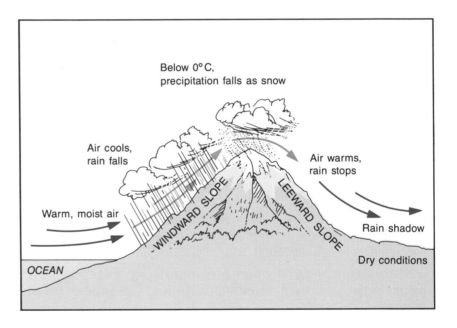

Features other than high mountains may also cause relief precipitation. Southern Ontario's snowbelt is a result of wind blowing from Lake Huron and Georgian Bay over hilly areas.

1. Describe, in your own words, what happens to the temperature and moisture content of the air as it passes over the mountain in Fig. 6–7.

2. Examine the climate graphs for Prince Rupert (Fig. 6–13) and Prince George (Fig. 6–14). Which one is on the windward side and which one is on the leeward side of the mountain barrier? How could you tell from the climate graphs? Check their locations on a map to confirm your answer.

CONVECTIONAL PRECIPITATION

Convectional precipitation develops as a result of the uneven heating of the earth's surface by the sun. For example, the south side of a hill receives more of the sun's rays than the north side of the hill. The air above such a hot spot becomes warmer than the surrounding air and starts to rise, creating convection currents or updrafts (see Fig. 6–3).

Convection currents may be seen in Fig. 6–3

If you are in an area where this process is occuring, you can see evidence of it over the course of a day. The rising air expands and cools, and the water vapour within it condenses to form puffy white clouds. During the course of a day more and more moisture is carried up by the rising warm air. By mid-afternoon the sky may be covered with very large clouds.

Within these towering clouds, the water droplets get larger and larger. They may even freeze at very high altitudes. The weight of the water droplets and ice pellets (or hail stones) causes them to fall, often in violent downpours (Fig. 6–8). As they fall to the ground the raindrops cool the air and drag some of it downward, creating downdrafts. Eventually, the cooling effect of the rain on the ground stops more updrafts from forming. At this point the precipitation-forming process stops and the storm is over.

Convectional precipitation is very common during the summer in the Prairies, Ontario, and Québec, where the land is subject to intense heating during hot summer days. Summer thunderstorms, although very short-lived, may cause considerable damage to crops and property because of violent winds, lightning, heavy rainfall, or hail. In extreme cases, strong convectional heating may even cause tornadoes. These violent storms can lift trees and cars into the air.

Fig. 6–8 Summer thunderstorms like this are a familiar sight to many Canadians. Where would the strongest currents of rising air be in this storm?

1. Without looking at the textbook, draw a series of diagrams to demonstrate how convectional precipitation occurs.

2. Describe three characteristics of summer thunderstorms that can cause damage to property and crops.

3. Examine the climate graphs for Prince George (Fig. 6–14) and Regina (Fig. 6–15). Which one represents an area of mainly convectional precipitation? How did you know?

CYCLONIC PRECIPITATION

Air masses that are different in temperature and moisture content do not mix. Instead a boundary or **front** is established between them. Cyclonic precipitation occurs along these fronts.

A cyclonic storm is a large low pressure cell that forms when a warm air mass and a cold air mass collide. The warm air mass forms a wave-like wedge with the cold air mass. The air rotates inward in a counter-clockwise direction about a cyclonic storm (Fig. 6–9).

The warm air is forced to rise above the colder air at two locations: the leading edge of the warm air (**warm front**) and the leading edge of the cold air (**cold front**). A variety of weather occurs as a cyclonic storm passes over an area (Fig. 6–10).

In North America these low pressure storm systems move from west to east at all times of the year and spread precipitation over a large area. Most of the precipitation in Ontario, Québec, and the Maritimes is of the cyclonic type. Much of the relief precipitation of the West Coast develops out of cyclonic storms that blow in from the Pacific Ocean and rise over the western mountains.

Cyclonic precipitation is also known as frontal precipitation.

Fig. 6–9 Satellite images of cyclonic storms help the weather office to predict our weather. The names of the parts of the storm have been added to help you. In what direction is the storm likely to be moving?

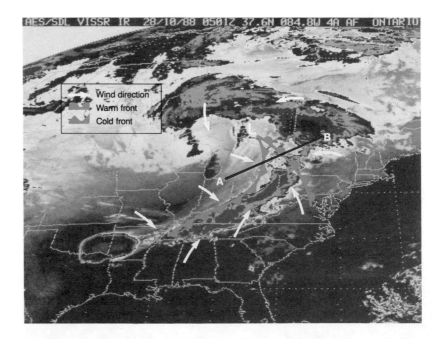

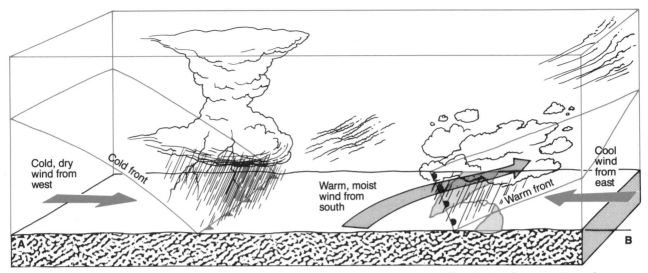

Cold, dry wind from west

Cold front

Warm, moist wind from south

Warm front

Cool wind from east

A

B

1. A cyclonic storm is approaching the area where you live. Using the headings in Fig. 6–11, construct a chart to compare the weather conditions you will experience as the storm passes over you.

Fig. 6–10   Cross section of cyclonic storm. Compare to Fig. 6–9

Fig. 6–11

	Temperature	**Sky Cover**	**Precipitation**	**Wind Direction**
Before Warm Front	Cool	Increasing Cloudiness	Likely	Easterly
At Warm Front				
Between Fronts				
At Cold Front				
After Cold Front				

2. Some people say that the weather that Winnipeg has today, Calgary had yesterday, and Toronto will have tomorrow. Explain why this is often true.

■ CANADA'S CLIMATIC REGIONS

Areas with similar climates may be grouped together to form a climatic region. A climatic region is a single-factor region since it is established on the basis of one factor, that is, climate. Canada has seven climatic regions (Fig. 6–12). They are:

- West Coast (maritime climate)
- Mountain (much variation)
- Prairie (continental climate)
- Boreal (continental climate)
- Arctic (mainly continental)
- Southeastern (elements of continental and maritime climates)
- East Coast (maritime climate)

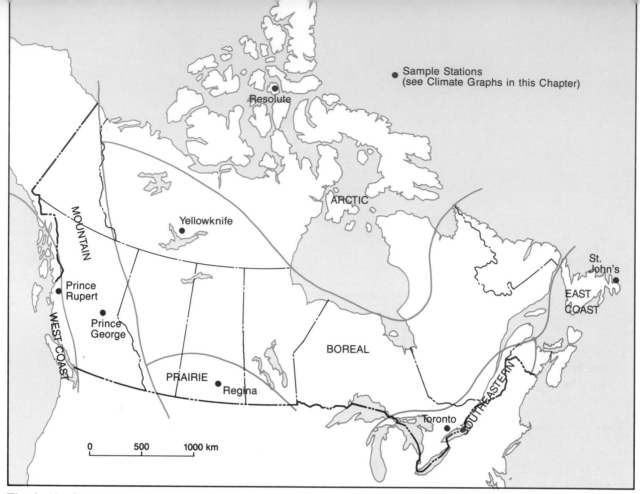

Fig. 6–12 Canada's climatic regions

WEST COAST (see Fig. 6–13, Prince Rupert, B.C.)

In February, while the rest of Canada may shiver in the cold, the West Coast usually remains quite mild. Most coastal locations remain above freezing during winter. In the summer, however, when hot air covers much of the country, residents of the West Coast may be reaching for a sweater. The reason for this is the Pacific Ocean, which gives the region a typical maritime climate. Many people find this moderate climate very attractive. They move to the West Coast to escape the harsh winters of the Canadian interior.

MOUNTAIN (see Fig. 6–14, Prince George, B.C.)

There are many different climates in the Mountain climatic region. Places only a few kilometres apart may have very different temperature and precipitation patterns. This is caused by differences in elevation and aspect. Windward slopes (those facing west) often receive a great deal of relief precipitation. On the other hand, leeward slopes and interior valleys are often very dry because of rain shadow conditions. The Okanagan Valley in British Columbia is an example of such a dry area.

aspect: the direction a place faces, (e.g. the window has a western aspect)

PRAIRIE (see Fig. 6–15, Regina, Sask.)

Because the Prairie region is in the heart of the country far from any ocean, it is an excellent example of a continental climate. In winter, cold polar air blankets the land. In summer, warm dry air covers the region. As a result, there is a great annual temperature range. The Prairie climate region is quite dry. It is in the rain shadow of the Western Cordillera. Few cyclonic storms bring precipitation, and air masses coming from the north are dry. Most of the small amount of moisture that the region receives usually occurs in the summer in the form of convectional precipitation.

The highest temperature ever recorded in Canada was 45°C at Midale and Yellow Grass, Saskatchewan on July 5, 1937.

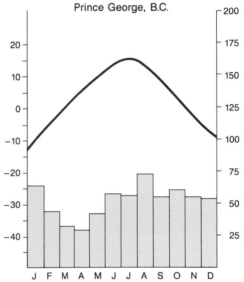

Fig. 6–14 Mountain Climate

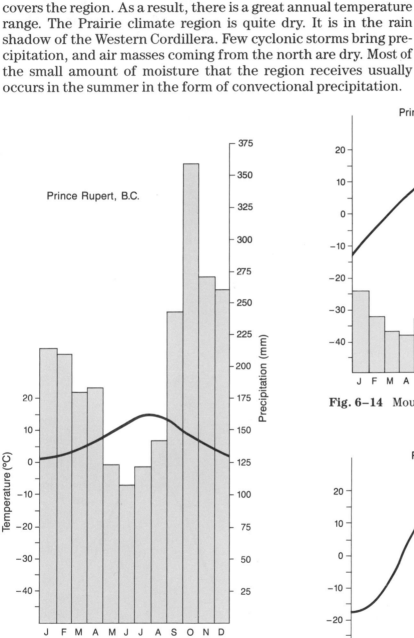

Fig. 6–13 West Coast Climate

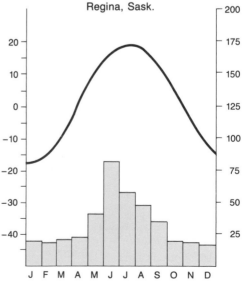

Fig. 6–15 Prairie Climate

BOREAL (see Fig. 6–16, Yellowknife, N.W.T.)

Although the Boreal climate region extends to Hudson Bay and the Atlantic Ocean, it is not influenced very much by these water bodies. Give two reasons why this is so.

The Boreal climatic region is vast and stretches in a wide band across most of Canada. Because of its northern location and interior position, the climate is a continental one. The winters are cold and may last six months or more. The summers are short and relatively cool. Precipitation occurs mainly in the summer when the land heats up, causing convectional precipitation. A small amount of winter precipitation is the result of cyclonic storms.

ARCTIC (see Fig. 6–17, Resolute, N.W.T.)

The lowest temperature ever recorded in Canada was -63°C in Snag, Yukon on Feb. 3, 1947.

The Arctic has a very harsh climate. In the most northerly locations winter lasts as long as ten months. Summer is very short and not very warm. It is too cold for trees to grow.

One surprising feature of the Arctic climate is its small amount of precipitation. You could say that the Arctic is really a cold desert. Less than 350 mm of precipitation fall each year. Precipitation is scarce because there are few open bodies of water from which the air can pick up moisture. For most of the year the Arctic Ocean and other water bodies are frozen. In addition, cold air can hold very little moisture.

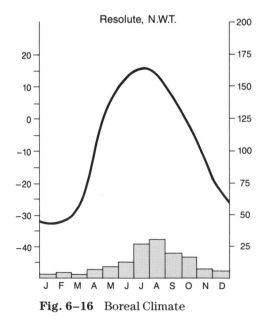

Fig. 6–16 Boreal Climate

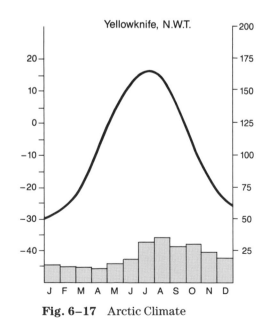

Fig. 6–17 Arctic Climate

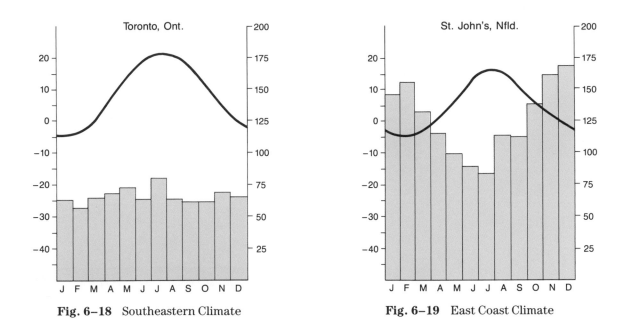

Fig. 6–18 Southeastern Climate

Fig. 6–19 East Coast Climate

SOUTHEASTERN (see Fig. 6–18, Toronto, Ont.)

The Southeastern climatic region has characteristics of both a continental and a maritime climate. While it has mainly a continental climate, the Atlantic Ocean and the Great Lakes produce maritime conditions in some areas. For the entire region, winter temperatures vary from cool to cold and the summers from warm to hot.

Cyclonic precipitation is brought to the Southeastern climatic region by storms that come from two directions — west and south. The cyclonic storms from the west are brought by westerly winds. Storms from the south begin in the Gulf of Mexico and move up the Mississippi River Valley. They usually cross the Great Lakes and move down the St. Lawrence Valley toward the Maritime provinces.

EAST COAST (see Fig. 6–19, St. John's, Nfld.)

The East Coast climatic region has a maritime climate. The nearness of the ocean moderates the temperatures so the winters are not very cold nor the summers very hot. The prevailing westerlies bring cyclonic storms throughout the year. The region receives more than 1000 mm of precipitation.

■ IN CLOSING . . .

drought: an unusually long period of dry weather

The weather and climate of the region we live in has a direct impact on us. For example, it determines the type of clothing we must wear each season. But weather in other parts of Canada also affects our lives. A drought in the Prairies can raise the price of bread in the Maritimes. The harsh climate of the Arctic makes exploration for oil and gas very costly, and these costs are passed on to customers. In these ways and many more, the weather and climates of Canada are very much a part of our lives.

QUESTIONS

CHECKBACK

1. **a)** In which climatic region do you live?
   b) Describe the climate of this region.
   c) Which factors affect the climate in your region the most?
2. Correctly spell the word that means
   a) rain and snow
   b) day-to-day changes in the atmosphere
   c) the climatic region of the Far North
   d) a long period of time with much less precipitation than normal
   e) the climatic region that covers most of the Canadian Shield.

ANALYZE

3. List five ways in which the weather affects your life.
4. Study the sample climate graphs for each climatic region (Figs. 6-13 to 6-19). Make a chart like Fig. 6-20 to compare the climates in each region. One region is done for you.
   a) Which location has
      i. the coldest winter temperature?
      ii. the warmest winter temperature?
      iii. the coldest summer temperature?
      iv. the warmest summer temperature?
   b) Which location has the largest temperature range? Why?
   c) Which location has the smallest temperature range? Why?
   d) Which station receives the most precipitation? Why?
   e) Which station receives the least precipitation? Why?
   f) Check back in the chapter to find what type of precipitation is most common in each region. How is this related to the season of maximum precipitation?

Region and Location	Average Temp. of Coldest Month	Average Temp. of Warmest Month	Annual Temp. Range	Average Annual Temp.	Annual Precipitation	Season of Maximum Precipitation
West Coast — Prince Rupert, B.C.	5°C	17°C	12°C	10.8°C	2415 mm	winter

Fig. 6–20

5. a) Using the climate statistics in Fig. 6–21, construct climate graphs for these two mystery climate stations.
   b) Using the same headings as in Fig. 6–20, determine the values for each climate station.
   c) Determine whether each station is in a continental or maritime location. Explain how you arrived at your answer.
   d) In which climatic region is each climate station located?

	J	F	M	A	M	J	J	A	S	O	N	D	Annual
Climate Station A													
Temperature (°C)	−14	−12	−6	4	11	14	17	16	11	5	−4	−10	2.7
Precipitation (mm)	24	20	21	28	46	80	85	65	34	23	22	25	473
Climate Station B													
Temperature (°C)	−9	−9	−3	4	11	16	19	18	14	8	2	−6	5.4
Precipitation (mm)	91	86	73	81	88	86	90	86	87	91	120	105	1084

Fig. 6–21 In what regions would these climate stations be found?

6. Toronto averages about 24 thunderstorms per year whereas Vancouver only has about 4. Why does Toronto experience so many more thunderstorms than Vancouver?

WHAT DO YOU THINK?

7. Which season do you like best? Why?
8. If you could live in any one of Canada's climatic regions, which one would you choose? After discussing this question with a group of your classmates, write a short paragraph explaining your choice.

The Effect of Weather and Climate on the Lives of Canadians

"Everyone talks about the weather, but no one ever does anything about it."

What can be done about the weather? There are two possibilities. First, we can try to change the weather itself by modifying its causes. Second, we can try to change the impact that weather has on people. So far in our history we have done little to deliberately change the weather, but we have done a lot to change its effects. In fact, ever since prehistoric people first clothed themselves in skins or huddled around a fire for warmth, attempts to modify the effects of the weather have been an important part of human life. In this study you will be introduced to some ways in which weather and climate affect human activity.

Key Terms

wind-chill factor   frost-free period   greenhouse effect

■ WEATHER AND FARMING

People have been farming for about 10 000 years. For most of this time they learned about the effects of climate through trial and error. They learned from experience that one area was too cold to grow cotton, or another was too dry for wheat. Today, we apply more scientific methods to study the effect of climate on farming.

Two important climatic conditions for farming are the length and warmth of the growing season. We cannot grow oranges in southern Ontario or peaches in the Prairies because of limitations in the growing season in these areas. How can we measure the quality of the growing season? One way is by measuring the length

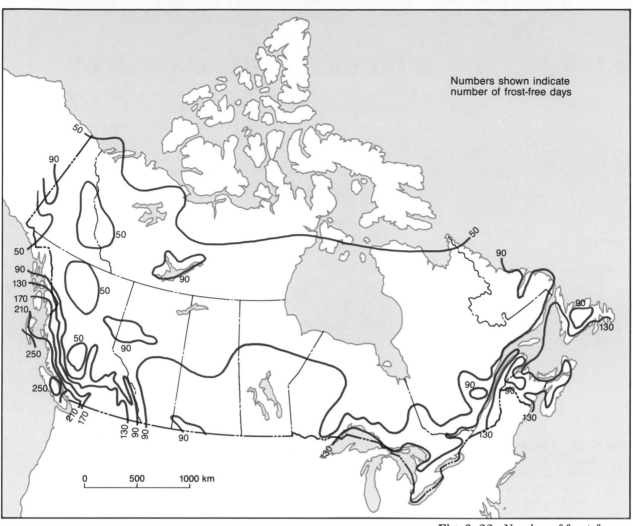

Fig. 6–22 Number of frost-free days

of the **frost-free period** (Fig. 6–22). The frost-free period is the length of time between the last expected frost in the spring and the first expected frost in the fall. This measurement recognizes that a late spring or early fall frost can destroy a farmer's crops.

▪ WEATHER AND WINTER COMFORT

Winter can be one of Canada's most pleasant experiences — or one of its least. It all depends on what activity you are involved in and on the particular weather conditions.

One thing that can make any winter day unpleasant, and even dangerous, is a strong wind. Meteorologists measure the effect of wind by determining the **wind-chill factor**. The wind chill combines the effect of temperature and wind to give an "effective" temperature (Fig. 6–23). The wind-chill reading tells you how cold it feels; that is, what the equivalent temperature would be if it felt that cold but there was no wind.

Fig. 6–23 Wind chill values reflect the effect of both temperature and wind.

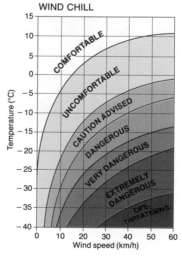

WIND CHILL

■ ARE WE CHANGING OUR CLIMATE?

Earlier in this study we quoted a famous saying which said that, although everyone talks about the weather, no one changes it. In fact, many scientists think people *are* changing the weather — at least by accident. Some believe that we may cause average world temperatures to rise by as much as 4.5C° over the next 50 years. While this amount of temperature change may not seem like much, it is a larger change than has ever occurred in human history, and it is happening very quickly. The effects of this change could be enormous for people all over the world. Because Canada is a northern country, with large extremes in climate, we would be affected more than most people.

At first glance the idea of a warmer climate might seem very appealing to the many Canadians who do not like our long, cold winters. Some advantages of a warmer climate would be:

- longer growing seasons, allowing more northerly areas to be used for commercial farming (Fig. 6–24) and forestry
- lower costs to heat homes and other buildings
- longer shipping seasons in the North and on the Great Lakes
- warmer and less snowy winters in most areas.

Many people, however, fear that the negative effects of this warming would be worse than the positive ones. A warmer climate could mean:

- severe droughts would be more common in southern Canada
- water levels in lakes and rivers in the south would be lower
- increased flooding could occur in northern Canada

Fig. 6–24 A warmer climate would allow Canadians to expand commercial agriculture northward. What current agricultural lands might become too dry to be farmed?

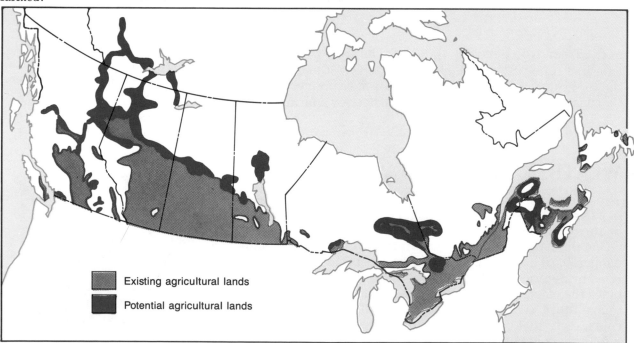

Existing agricultural lands

Potential agricultural lands

- coastal flooding could occur as sea levels increased as a result of ice cap melting
- winter recreation such as skiing and snowmobiling would be harmed by shorter, less snowy winters.

How are people causing this global warming? The warming is the result of what is called the greenhouse effect. This is caused by an increase in the amount of certain gases in the atmosphere (Fig. 6–25). The sun's rays pass through the atmosphere and heat the earth's surface. This heat energy is then radiated back into the atmosphere. The so-called greenhouse gases in the atmosphere absorb this heat, and trap it near the earth. As you see in Fig. 6–25, most of the gases are produced as by-products of our everyday activities.

Fig. 6–25 These gases are causing the greenhouse effect. What can be done to reduce this problem?

Type of Gas	Reason(s) for Increase
carbon dioxide (CO_2)	• burning of huge amounts of oil, coal, wood, and natural gas • removal of forest in many areas (plants change carbon dioxide to oxygen)
freons (chlorofluorocarbons)	• use in foam insulation, spray can propellant, coolant in refrigerators and air conditioners, and as a solvent
methane (CH_4)	• produced by rice paddies, grazing cattle, burning of wood, mining of coal and natural gas
nitrous oxide (N_2O)	• from production of chemical fertilizers, burning of wood and fossil fuels
ozone (O_3)	• formed in air from pollutants coming mainly from auto exhausts and coal burning

■ IN CLOSING . . .

If we could learn more about weather and climate, we might be able to improve our lives. Perhaps we could grow more food in areas where it cannot now grow. We might be able to reduce the hazards of droughts, floods, hurricanes, blizzards, and frost spells. Only time will tell how much control we can develop over the weather.

1. **a)** Define "frost-free period."
   b) Examine Fig. 6–22. In what parts of Canada could you successfully grow the following vegetables:
      i. Cabbage (growing period of 88 days)?
      ii. Sweet corn (77 days)?
      iii. Pumpkin (110 days)?
      iv. Tomato (72 days)?
2. On the basis of information given in Fig. 6–22:
   a) name Canada's best areas for farming.
   b) name four other parts of Canada that are good for farming.
   c) check the map of agricultural regions in an atlas — were your answers to a) and b) correct? Did you miss any important farming areas? If you did miss any, why did this happen?
3. In your notebook, draw a fully labelled diagram to explain the greenhouse effect.

INVESTIGATE

4. The concept of "degree-days" can be very useful in measuring the heat or cold of a region. Investigate the meaning of degree-days and how the concept is used in farming, for heating, and for air-conditioning.
5. Investigate the effect of weather and climate on each of the following aspects of our lives. Your school or public library should have information to help you. Your teacher will tell you whether you are to do a written report or an oral report and whether you are to work independently or in a group.

a) climate and transportation
b) climate and the problems of supplying energy
c) climate and shelter: comfort without wasting energy
d) climate and problems of water supply in Canada
e) climate and clothing design
f) weather hazards (e.g. hail, drought, excessive rain, blizzards, lightning)
g) summer comfort
h) climate and recreation (e.g. characteristics needed for ski resorts, cottaging, camping, boating)
i) effect of climate on cities and cities on climate
j) weather and air pollution
k) potential for climate modification

6. **a)** Describe the wind-chill effect.

    b) Try to remember the coldest conditions you have ever experienced. What do you estimate the temperature and wind chill were? What particular weather conditions made that occasion so cold?

    c) What role did clothing play in making the experience in b) pleasant or unpleasant? What effect did the activity that you were involved in have on the experience?

7. **a)** Name the gases responsible for the greenhouse effect.

    b) State the major sources of each gas.

    c) How could people cut back on the production of each of these gases?

    d) What effect(s) might these cutbacks have on society?

8. **a)** Name at least four positive effects and four negative effects of the greenhouse effect.

    b) Which do you think will be more significant? Why?

7 Vegetation

It is not difficult to understand that a region's vegetation is determined mainly by its climate. Plants must have moisture, heat, and light for their survival. The relative amounts of these three things influence the types of plants that grow. For example, a hot, wet climate may support a forest of large trees; a drier climate may support only short grasses. Areas with different types of natural vegetation are classified as different vegetation regions (Fig. 7–1).

Fig. 7–1 Natural vegetation regions of Canada

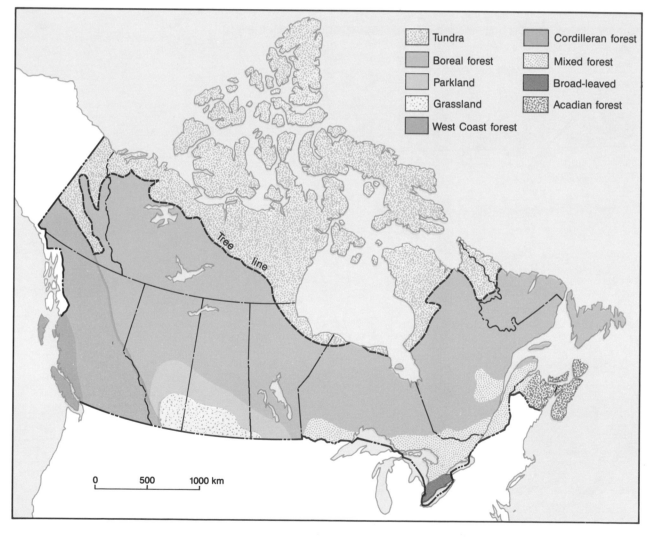

Legend:
- Tundra
- Boreal forest
- Parkland
- Grassland
- West Coast forest
- Cordilleran forest
- Mixed forest
- Broad-leaved
- Acadian forest

Tree line

0   500   1000 km

Key Terms

natural vegetation
Cordilleran vegetation
permafrost
boreal forest
tree line

needle-leaved trees
broad-leaved trees
mixed forest
Acadian forest
broad-leaved forest

grassland
parkland
tundra

■ VEGETATION REGIONS

Natural vegetation refers to those plants which grow without any human interference. Natural vegetation is usually quite different from plants which people cultivate for food and for use in industry. Different types of natural vegetation grow in response to different climatic and soil conditions. Figs. 7–2 and 7–3 show the types of natural vegetation that grow as precipitation and temperature vary from place to place. Because Canada's climate differs across the country, natural vegetation differs as well. Geographers have identified large areas which have distinctive natural vegetation. We will study nine natural vegetation regions across Canada.

Fig. 7–2 Vegetation changes as precipitation levels change

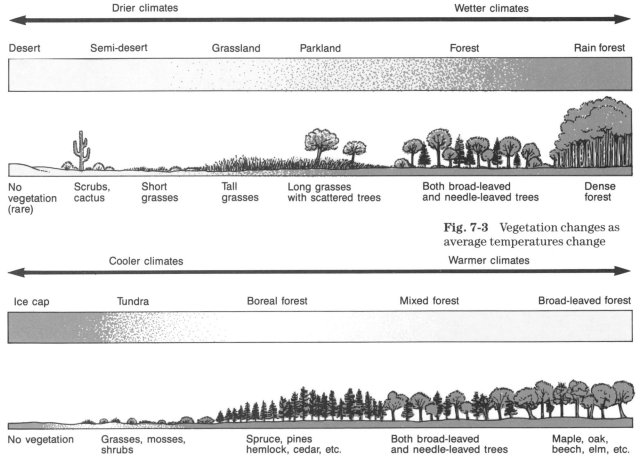

Drier climates → Wetter climates

Desert | Semi-desert | Grassland | Parkland | Forest | Rain forest

No vegetation (rare) | Scrubs, cactus | Short grasses | Tall grasses | Long grasses with scattered trees | Both broad-leaved and needle-leaved trees | Dense forest

Fig. 7-3 Vegetation changes as average temperatures change

Cooler climates → Warmer climates

Ice cap | Tundra | Boreal forest | Mixed forest | Broad-leaved forest

No vegetation | Grasses, mosses, shrubs | Spruce, pines hemlock, cedar, etc. | Both broad-leaved and needle-leaved trees | Maple, oak, beech, elm, etc.

TUNDRA (see Fig. 7–4)

The most northerly vegetation region of Canada is the **tundra**. Most of this region has **permafrost** or permanently frozen ground. No trees grow here because the climate is too cold and dry, and only a thin layer of soil on the surface thaws in the short summer. Small shrubs, mosses, and lichens grow close to the ground where they soak up as much heat as possible from the earth. Tundra plants bloom with colourful flowers and mature very quickly to produce their seeds before the cold weather returns.

Lichens are slow-growing plants that cling to rocks. At first glance, they look like dead mosses, but are actually a combination of an alga and fungus.

BOREAL FOREST (see Fig. 7–5)

To the south of the tundra is the **boreal forest**. It is separated from the tundra by a zone known as the **tree line**, which marks the northern boundary of tree growth. Trees grow south of the tree line because there is a longer growing season and more precipitation than in the tundra. **Needle-leaved trees** grow sparsely along the northern edge of the boreal forest but further south they grow much more thickly. They are harvested for use by pulp and paper and lumbering companies. Spruce, pine, and fir are dominant, but **broad-leaved trees** such as poplar and white birch are also present.

MIXED FOREST (see Fig. 7–6)

South of the boreal forest in eastern Canada is a **mixed forest** of needle-leaved and broad-leaved trees. Spruce, fir, pine, cedar, and hemlock are found in the same forest with maple, beech, ash, oak, and birch. The mixed forest is a transition zone between the boreal forest to the north and the broad-leaved forest to the south. In the autumn, tourists visit these forests to admire the magnificent colours of the changing leaves.

ACADIAN FOREST (see Fig. 7–7)

The **Acadian forest** of Prince Edward Island, Nova Scotia, and southern New Brunswick is very similar to the mixed forest. It is a transition zone between the boreal forest and the broad-leaved forest. Red and white spruce, balsam fir, birch, beech and maple are the most common trees. Along exposed coastlines where the cold winds create a harsher climate, the forest may give way to small shrubs, such as junipers, that grow close to the ground for protection.

Fig. 7–4 Tundra vegetation

Fig. 7–5 Boreal forest

Fig. 7–6 Mixed forest

Fig. 7–7 Acadian forest

Fig. 7–8   Broad-leaved forest

Fig. 7–9   Grassland vegetation

Fig. 7–10   Parkland vegetation

Fig. 7–11   Cordilleran vegetation

Fig. 7–12   West Coast forest

BROAD-LEAVED FOREST (see Fig. 7–8)

The only **broad-leaved forest** in Canada is found in the south-western part of Ontario. Here the summers are long and hot, the winters mild, and the precipitation plentiful. Only small woodlots of maple, beech, hickory, and black walnut are left because most of the region has been taken over for farmland.

GRASSLAND (see Fig. 7–9)

In the driest areas of Saskatchewan and Alberta, short grasses, sagebrush, and cactus are the only types of vegetation which can survive. Taller grasses grow in areas with slightly more precipitation. These are known as **grassland** areas. Trees, such as trembling aspen, willow, and spruce, grow only in river valleys where more moisture is available.

Sagebrush and cactus are plants that have adapted to growing in dry conditions

PARKLAND (see Fig. 7–10)

Between the drier grassland and the cooler and wetter boreal forest is a vegetation region called **parkland**. This is a transition zone of grassland dotted with clumps of trees. Needle-leaved trees grow in the northern part and broad-leaved trees grow in the southern part.

CORDILLERAN VEGETATION (see Fig. 7–11)

Within the Cordillera, the climate changes rapidly from valley to mountain, and from one side of a mountain to the other. As a result, the **Cordilleran vegetation** varies greatly. Grasses and cactuses grow in dry valleys. Ponderosa pine and other needle-leaved trees grow on the slopes where precipitation is heavier. These forests are important to the logging industry of British Columbia.

On the higher slopes of the Cordilleran mountain ranges, the vegetation is similar to that of the tundra. There are no trees, only meadows of flowers and shrubs. On the highest slopes, vegetation cannot survive. Here, there is only bare rock, snow, and ice.

WEST COAST FOREST (see Fig. 7–12)

Along the west coast of Canada grow lush forests of Douglas fir, Sitka spruce, red cedar, and western hemlock. The large amounts of rainfall and the mild climate provide excellent growing conditions for the trees of this forest. Trees more than 1 m in diameter and over 50 m high are common. These splendid trees have played a crucial role in British Columbia's forest industry.

Douglas fir reach heights of 100 m and diameters of almost 5 m

crucial: of great importance

■ IN CLOSING . . .

Natural vegetation refers to the types of grasses, trees, and other plants that grow without human interference. In southern Canada, there is little natural vegetation left because most of the land has been taken over for farming or the building of cities. In many forested areas, forestry companies have cut down the original trees and have not replanted seedlings.

The different vegetation regions in Canada provide us with many products. The needle-leaved trees of the boreal forest are the raw materials for pulp, paper, and lumber. Broad-leaved trees provide wood for eastern Canada's furniture industry. The huge trees of the West Coast forest provide lumber for use in Canada and for export. The beef in your barbecued hamburger may come from cattle raised on the short grasses of the western plains. You may even have cooked your hamburger using charcoal from the hardwood trees of eastern Canada.

QUESTIONS

CHECKBACK

1. In your own words, explain the meaning of the term "natural vegetation".
2. There are two classes of trees. Which one can survive a harsher climate? Why?
3. Select the best answer for each of the following multiple-choice questions.
   a) The broad-leaved forest is found in
      i. southern British Columbia
      ii. northern Québec
      iii. southern Ontario
      iv. none of these places
   b) The vegetation region located between the boreal forest and the grassland is
      i. parkland
      ii. mixed forest
      iii. broad-leaved forest
      iv. tundra
   c) Tundra vegetation consists of
      i. cactuses, sagebrush, and short grasses
      ii. needle-leaved trees such as spruce, pine, and fir
      iii. small bushes, flowers, mosses, and lichens
      iv. clumps of trees surrounded by grassland
   d) The trees of the boreal forest are mainly used
      i. to make furniture
      ii. to make pulp and paper and lumber
      iii. as Christmas trees
      iv. as tourist attractions when the leaves change colour

e) Which one of the following statements is incorrect?

    i. There is tundra vegetation in the Cordilleran forest region.

    ii. Parkland and grassland vegetation regions are in approximately the same location as the Prairie climate region.

    iii. The largest trees in Canada are found in the broad-leaved forest.

    iv. In the parkland region, needle-leaved trees grow in the north and broad-leaved trees grow in the south.

ANALYZE

4. Prepare a poster with drawings or photographs of at least six trees which grow in Canada. Indicate whether each tree is needle-leaved or broad-leaved, and describe its main commercial use.

5. Are vegetation regions single-factor or multi-factor regions? Explain.

6. Examine Figs. 7–2 and 7–3 and answer the following questions.

    a) What climatic characteristic causes tall grasses to grow instead of short grasses?

    b) Which type of trees, broad-leaved or needle-leaved, require warmer climates to grow? (Check with a biology teacher to discover why this is so.)

7. "Trees grow wherever there is enough precipitation to support them."

    a) About how much precipitation do trees need to grow? Try to find this out by comparing the annual precipitation map from your atlas and the vegetation map in this chapter.

    b) Where do trees seem to stop growing? Describe the climate of this region.

8. a) Using Figs. 7–1 and 6–12, match each vegetation region to the corresponding climatic region.

    b) The mixed forest and the broad-leaved forest regions are found in the same climatic region. Explain how two vegetation regions can both occur in the same climatic region.

INVESTIGATE

9. a) From which Canadian tree can a type of candy be made?

    b) Is this tree needle-leaved or broad-leaved?

    c) In which vegetation regions do we find this tree?

10. a) What types of trees are used for Christmas trees in Canada?

    b) Describe the process used by commercial growers to produce Christmas trees.

    c) Where are the markets for Canadian Christmas trees?

    d) What is the impact of artificial trees on the Christmas tree market?

8 Soil

The words were spoken by Neil Armstrong, the first person to set foot on the moon, on July 20, 1969

You may have heard the famous words, "One small step for a man, one giant leap for mankind." The person who spoke these words was about to walk on the moon, a landscape totally lacking in true **soil**. Why is there soil on the earth but none on the moon?

Mud, sand, dirt, clay, loam, silt — these are some of the terms we use to describe the substances that cover much of the earth. Together they can be considered as soil. Just as vegetation, climate, and landforms differ from place to place, so does soil. A large area with a type of soil that is different from that found in surrounding areas can be referred to as a soil region.

In this chapter you will learn what a soil is, and where different soils are found in Canada. You will also begin to see how soil influences the pattern of vegetation, agriculture, and settlement.

Key Terms

soil	soil profile	leaching
nutrients	weathering	calcification
humus	parent material	permafrost

■ WHAT SOIL IS MADE OF

A true soil is a very complex substance. It is made of four main parts. If one of these parts is missing, the material cannot be considered a true soil.

- Mineral Materials.

    The mineral materials of soil came originally from rock. They become part of the soil when the rock is broken down by weathering into smaller particles called sand, silt, or clay. Many of these minerals, such as calcium, phosphorous, and potassium, are **nutrients** needed by plants for growth.
- Organic Materials.

    When plants die, they decay and form **humus**. Perhaps you have noticed this happening to old piles of leaves or grass clippings. Humus is important because it is a source of nutrients for plant growth. The nutrients are released when bacteria in the soil break down organic matter so that it can be recycled. Humus gives the soil its dark colour.

bacteria: microscopic organisms

- Air.

   We must not forget the importance of air in soil. Plants need air around their roots. This means that the soil must have many air spaces in it. A high humus level helps to produce these air spaces. They are also created by worms and other small animals which tunnel through the soil.

- Moisture.

   Moisture is an important part of soil. Plants need it to grow, and water is necessary in the chemical and physical processes that weather rock and decay organic materials.

■ SOIL FORMATION

A basic **soil profile** is shown in Fig. 8–1. New mineral materials are added at the bottom of the profile by the **weathering** of the **parent material**. At the same time, organic materials are added at the top of the profile as plants drop their leaves or die off in winter.

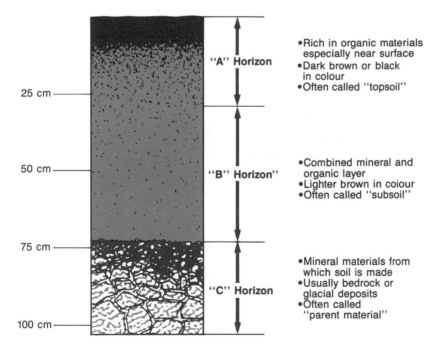

Fig. 8–1   A typical soil profile

25 cm

"A" Horizon
- Rich in organic materials especially near surface
- Dark brown or black in colour
- Often called "topsoil"

50 cm

"B" Horizon"
- Combined mineral and organic layer
- Lighter brown in coiour
- Often called "subsoil"

75 cm

"C" Horizon
- Mineral materials from which soil is made
- Usually bedrock or glacial deposits
- Often called "parent material"

100 cm

Two other processes, which are related to climate, contribute to soil formation. The first is called **leaching**. In areas where there is a great deal of precipitation, there is a continual downward movement of water through the soil (Fig. 8–2). As the water moves down, it dissolves the chemical nutrients out of the soil and carries them away. This downward movement of water removes nutrients that plants need. Leaching creates a soil that lacks most of its water-soluble minerals. You can identify a leached soil by its poor, often thin, topsoil layer.

soluble: able to be dissolved

Fig. 8–2 A leached soil profile

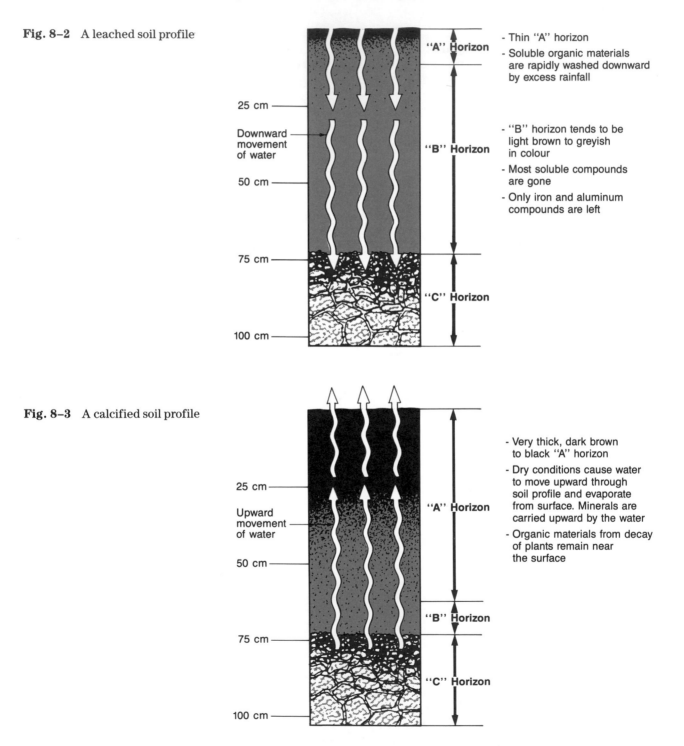

25 cm

Downward movement of water

50 cm

75 cm

100 cm

"A" Horizon
- Thin "A" horizon
- Soluble organic materials are rapidly washed downward by excess rainfall

"B" Horizon
- "B" horizon tends to be light brown to greyish in colour
- Most soluble compounds are gone
- Only iron and aluminum compounds are left

"C" Horizon

Fig. 8–3 A calcified soil profile

25 cm

Upward movement of water

50 cm

75 cm

100 cm

"A" Horizon
- Very thick, dark brown to black "A" horizon
- Dry conditions cause water to move upward through soil profile and evaporate from surface. Minerals are carried upward by the water
- Organic materials from decay of plants remain near the surface

"B" Horizon

"C" Horizon

The second process, known as **calcification**, occurs in areas with drier climates (Fig. 8–3). Where there is little precipitation, water is not available to move downward through the soil. Instead, there is an upward movement of water because of the evaporation that occurs on the surface of the soil. When water reaches the surface and evaporates, it leaves behind the minerals that were dissolved in it. The result is the creation of a thick topsoil layer which is rich in minerals. This process is called calcification because calcium is the main mineral deposited near the surface. In very dry climates, the amount of mineral deposition can be so great that a poisonous salt layer can be created.

As the water on the surface evaporates, water from below is drawn up to replace it.

■ SOIL TYPES

Fig. 8–4 Soil Regions of Canada

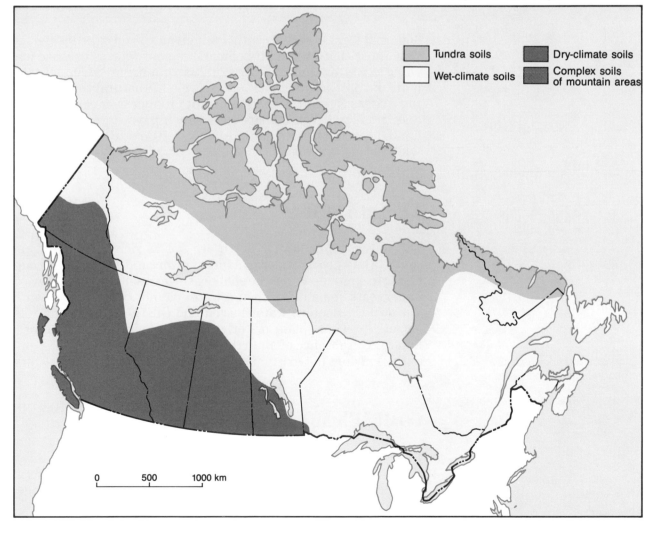

SOILS FOUND IN AREAS WITH A DRY CLIMATE

Canada's dry-climate soils are found mainly in the southern prairies (Fig. 8–4). You will remember from Chapter 6 that there is relatively little precipitation (less than 450 mm per year) in this region. The natural vegetation here is grass because the region is too dry for trees to grow. Because of the lack of rain, soils are calcified. In the drier parts of the prairies, only shorter grasses can grow. As a result, very little humus is formed and the topsoil layer is thin and brown in colour. Soils here are limited in terms of which crops can be grown. In wetter areas of the prairies, by contrast, taller grasses grow. When they decompose to humus, the rich vegetation produces a thick, black topsoil. The black soils of the prairies are among the richest soils in Canada and are excellent for growing crops.

SOILS FOUND IN AREAS WITH A WET CLIMATE

Soils that form in regions with a wet climate tend to be less fertile than those that form in dry climatic regions. This is because leaching in wetter climates carries valuable nutrients deep into the earth out of reach of plant roots. As well, the natural vegetation in these areas is forest, and trees do not produce as much humus as does grassland. Wet climate soils which have experienced only limited leaching, however, are quite fertile and can produce a wide variety of crops.

TUNDRA SOIL

The soils of Canada's far north are not as rich as soils farther south. The subsoil is permanently frozen and is called **permafrost**. In summer, when the shallow surface soil thaws, the layers underneath remain frozen and water cannot escape downward. The surface remains water-logged and this, along with the cold climate, prevents plant material from decaying quickly to form humus. The absence of air in the water-logged ground means that a true soil does not exist, and agriculture is impractical.

Climatic conditions also severely affect agriculture in this area.

COMPLEX MOUNTAIN SOILS

Dry climate, wet climate, and tundra soils are all found on the mountains of the Western Cordillera. The distribution of each soil type depends on the particular elevation, slope, rainfall and vegetation cover of each area within the mountain range.

■ IN CLOSING...

Knowledge of the soil patterns shown in Fig. 8–4, along with the landform, climate, and vegetation patterns presented earlier in this unit, will help you understand the cultural and economic patterns of Canada. These will be discussed in later chapters.

QUESTIONS

CHECKBACK

1. Choose the correct definition in Column 2 to match the word in Column 1. Write the answers in your notebook.

Column 1	Column 2
a) weathering	i. removal of nutrients from soil by water
b) humus	ii. all air spaces in the soil are filled with water
c) waterlogged	iii. decaying plant material
d) soil profile	iv. permanently frozen soil
e) leaching	v. rocks are broken down into smaller pieces
f) permafrost	vi. deposition of soluble minerals near surface
g) calcification	vii. layers within a soil section

2. List the things that make up soil. Briefly describe the importance of each.
3. Why are some prairie soils brown while others are black?
4. With the help of Fig. 8–1, describe the steps involved in making soil.

ANALYZE

5. Examine Figs. 8–2 and 8–3. Why is the topsoil layer shallow in leached soils and deep in calcified soils?
6. Fig. 8–5 shows the relationship between precipitation and soil fertility. Copy the graph in your notebook, and on it mark the following:
   a) a brown prairie soil
   b) a lightly leached soil
   c) a black prairie soil
   d) a heavily leached soil
   e) the boundary between wet-climate and dry-climate soils
7. Why are there soils on the earth but not on the moon?

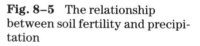
Fig. 8–5 The relationship between soil fertility and precipitation

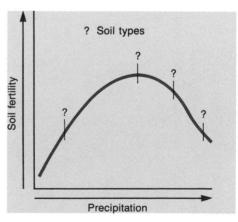

modify: change

8. **a)** Farmers can sometimes modify the natural soil conditions of their region. What can be done to overcome each of the following problems:
   i.   too much moisture
   ii. too little moisture
   iii. infertile soils
   iv. soils that have too much clay
   v.   soils that have too much sand
   vi. highly acidic soils
   vii. highly alkaline soils

   b) What improvements to the soil are most needed in each of the following regions:
   i.   Atlantic Canada
   ii. southern Ontario and Québec
   iii. the Prairies

UNIT THREE

CULTURAL DIVERSITY

9 Native Peoples

The **Native peoples** are the original inhabitants of the land that is now Canada. They came to this continent in two separate groups many thousands of years ago. Six major cultural groups developed in Canada (Fig. 9–1).

What happened when the Native peoples first came into contact with European culture? What opportunities does the future hold for Canada's Native peoples? These and other questions will be examined in this chapter.

Key Terms

Native peoples   reserve   economic base
land bridge   aboriginal rights   cultural groups
Inuit   Métis   assimilation
Indian

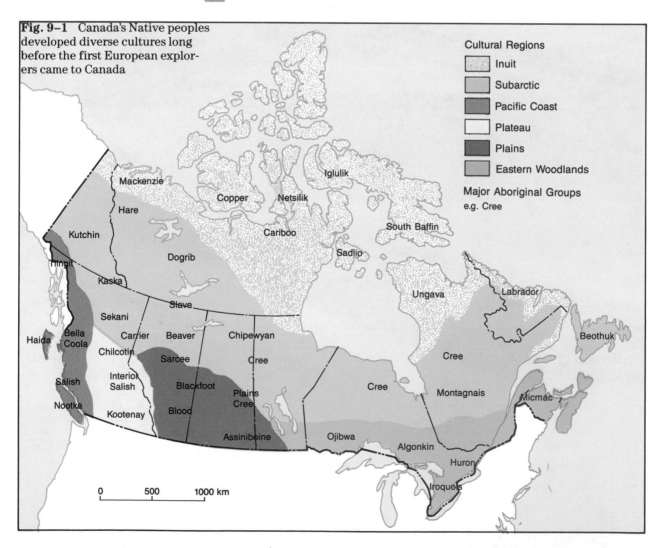

Fig. 9–1 Canada's Native peoples developed diverse cultures long before the first European explorers came to Canada

Cultural Regions
- Inuit
- Subarctic
- Pacific Coast
- Plateau
- Plains
- Eastern Woodlands

Major Aboriginal Groups
e.g. Cree

Mackenzie
Hare
Kutchin
Tlingit
Kaska
Sekani
Haida
Bella Coola
Carrier
Chilcotin
Salish
Interior Salish
Nootka
Kootenay

Copper
Netsilik
Cariboo
Dogrib
Slave
Beaver
Chipewyan
Sarcee
Blackfoot
Plains Cree
Blood
Assiniboine

Iglulik
South Baffin
Sadlio
Ungava
Labrador
Cree
Cree
Cree
Montagnais
Beothuk
Micmac

Ojibwa
Algonkin
Huron
Iroquois

0   500   1000 km

■ NORTH AMERICA'S FIRST PEOPLE

How long ago did the Native peoples come to Canada? Where did they come from? How did they get here? There are a number of theories that try to answer these questions, but one in particular is now widely accepted. To understand this theory we must review Canada's recent geological history.

The last ice age began approximately 100 000 years ago and ended about 10 000 years ago. During this time most of Canada was covered with ice, which in some parts was more than 2 km thick. Where did all this ice come from?

Water that evaporated from the oceans during the ice age fell as snow on the land and did not melt. Over thousands of years, the piled up layers of snow were compressed by their own weight into ice. These masses of ice are called glaciers. Because so much of the oceans' water was now in the form of ice, the level of the seas dropped. In some places the ocean bottom became dry land. The Bering Strait between Asia and North America was one place where this happened. The land that was exposed became a "bridge" between the two continents.

See the complementary study in Chapter 5 for more details about glaciers.

Most anthropologists believe that nomadic hunters followed wild animals across the Bering **land bridge** (Fig. 9–2) and became

anthropologist: a person who studies the development, customs, and beliefs of human groups

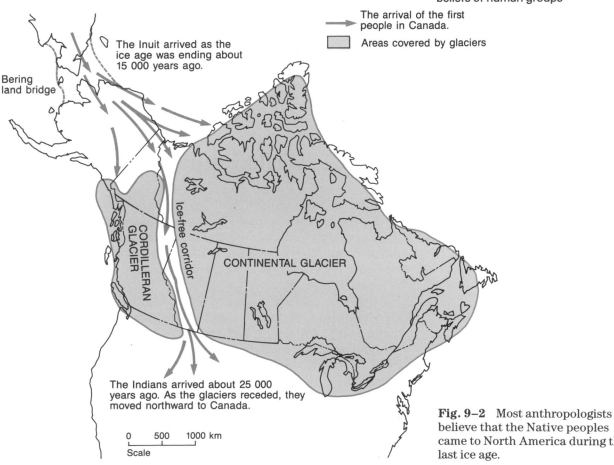

The arrival of the first people in Canada.

Areas covered by glaciers

The Inuit arrived as the ice age was ending about 15 000 years ago.

Bering land bridge

CORDILLERAN GLACIER

Ice-free corridor

CONTINENTAL GLACIER

The Indians arrived about 25 000 years ago. As the glaciers receded, they moved northward to Canada.

0   500   1000 km
Scale

Fig. 9–2 Most anthropologists believe that the Native peoples came to North America during the last ice age.

the first humans to live in what is now the Americas. It appears that they crossed the bridge from Asia about 25 000 years ago. Later generations of hunters travelled further south through an ice-free corridor between two ice sheets. During the thousands of years that the land bridge was exposed, many waves of peoples came to North America. Eventually some of these people **migrated** as far south as South America. Their descendants are the **Indians** who live in North, Central and South America today.

As the hunting bands migrated into different areas they developed into several major **cultural groups**. These included the Indians of North America, the Mayans of Central America, and the Incas of South America. Each of these cultural groups developed communities with different religions and methods of hunting and farming. Anthropologists think that some groups moved into parts of Canada from warmer areas to the south as the ice age was ending about 10 000 to 13 000 years ago.

The last groups to cross the land bridge as the ice age ended had probably lived in the Arctic environment of northeastern Asia. When they came to North America they stayed in the Arctic regions. Later generations migrated eastward through the islands and mainland areas of northern Canada and into Greenland. These people were the ancestors of today's **Inuit**.

Canada had great cultural diversity long before the arrival of Europeans. Different groups of Native peoples in Canada developed different cultures. There are six major cultural areas in Canada (see Fig. 9–1). Groups within each area have similar languages and lifestyles, but there is still much cultural diversity. The differences among each of the major cultural groups are summarized in Fig. 9–4.

It is commonly accepted that the Vikings were the first Europeans to visit North America in about the year 1000, but some people think that earlier visitors came from Ireland or even China.

■ CONTACT WITH EUROPEANS

technology: scientific knowledge applied to practical uses

To understand the impact that the arrival of Europeans had on Native peoples, try to put yourself in the place of a Native person living in eastern Canada. One day unfamiliar people appear. They look different from you, speak in a language that is different from yours, and have a technology totally foreign to you. How would you react? (Fig. 9–3).

By the late 1500s Europeans were trading for furs with the Native peoples of eastern Canada. During the 1600s the fur trade expanded into the heart of the continent, and European settlers occupied more and more land in eastern Canada. The arrival and spread of the Europeans had some unforeseen and disastrous effects on the Native peoples. European diseases such as measles and smallpox, for which the Native peoples had no immunity, killed thousands.

Settlement of the land by Europeans had an enormous influence on the lifestyle of the Native peoples, especially the Indian peoples in southern and central Canada. The new settlers used resources in a different way from the Native peoples. They created a demand for large quantities of fur-bearing animals, cut large areas of forest to obtain lumber and to make room for farming, plowed the Prairies, and developed mines. The European immigrants changed the natural environment so much that the Native peoples found it difficult to carry on their traditional ways of life and were constantly in conflict with the society set up by the new settlers. The Indians were often forced off their land and resettled on reserves. Other things that have happened over the years include the following:

Fig. 9-3 Early contacts between Native peoples and Europeans are portrayed in paintings such as this.

- It has been estimated that about 300 000 Indians and Inuit lived in Canada in 1500. The population of Native peoples today is between 700 000 and 1 000 000, within a total Canadian population of about 26 000 000. The larger population now in Canada makes it practically impossible for Native peoples to live in a traditional nomadic and hunting way of life.

- Many Indian peoples in Canada now live on **reserves**. These are parcels of land set aside by the federal government for the exclusive use of Indian peoples. There are more than 2200 reserves, with a total area of less than 26 000 km^2. Many of the reserves, however, are small and poor in resources. It is difficult, if not impossible, to make a good living under such conditions. The creation of the reserves under treaties speeded up the end of nomadic life.

- The new settlers from Europe often changed the natural environment. Southwestern Ontario, for example, was once covered by dense forests, but is now almost clear of trees. The Eastern Woodlands Indians depended on this forest for their livelihood. Their food, clothing, houses, and canoes came from the plants and animals of the forest. Without the forests, they could not live in their traditional way. The reduction in number of game and fur-bearing animals and the decline of the fur trade also reduced the Indian peoples' traditional livelihood. They were forced to look for new ways to live. Native peoples who lived on reserves with fertile soil could develop farms. Those on reserves that lacked resources, however, did not have an **economic base** to support themselves. Many were forced to move to cities to find employment.

- With the introduction of welfare, family allowance, and other forms of government assistance, most Native peoples were able to avoid the worst problems of poverty. The effect of this, however, was often to replace self-reliance with dependance on government help. Many young Native people are trapped between two worlds. They find it difficult to earn their living either in the traditional ways of the Native peoples or as wage earners in the larger society.

- Native peoples traditionally hunted and fished anywhere that game was plentiful. But laws have now been made by the provincial and federal governments to protect populations of fish,

Fig. 9-4

	PACIFIC COAST INDIANS	PLATEAU INDIANS	PLAINS INDIANS	EASTERN WOODLANDS INDIANS	SUB-ARCTIC INDIANS	INUIT
Environment	Along the rugged Pacific coastline the mild climate and abundant rainfall created forests of huge trees.	The mountains, plateaus, and valleys of the Western Cordillera form a rugged environment. The variety of climate types created dense forest in some areas, while others remained barren and desert-like.	In this region of rolling prairies with its climate of cold winters and hot summers, the small amount of precipitation allowed the development of grasslands but not forests. Trees were found in river valleys near water.	The landscape varies from flat lowland to rugged uplands. The moderate climate created very large forests of broadleaf and coniferous trees.	Rugged mountains, rocky lake country and flat muskeg lowlands are some of the many landscapes of this area. The cold winters and short summers combined to create the vast boreal forest covering much of this region.	Months of darkness and months of sunlight cover this region of barren rock, tundra and ice. The short summers and long cold winters make this Canada's most difficult environment to live in.
Population	75 000 - 100 000	18 000 - 23 000	30 000 - 40 000	50 000 - 70 000	60 000 - 80 000	10 000 - 20 000
Housing	Wooden house	Wooden or bark house near the coast Tipi near the plains	Tipi made of skins	Birch-bark-covered dome lodge Long house	Wigwam (dome- or cone-shaped) covered with hide or bark	Snow house Stone and turf dens Skin tents
	Permanent villages were composed of wooden homes (lodges) built along the Pacific shoreline. Totems at the entrance denoted family ancestry.	The homes of the Plateau Indians in the western part of the Interior or Mountains resembled the lodges of the Pacific Coast Indians. The tipis used in the eastern part of this mountain region were similar to those of the neighbouring Plains Indians.	Tipis were made by tying three or four wooden poles together and covering them with skin. Tipis could be set up easily and taken down quickly. The opening at the top allowed smoke from the cooking fire to escape.	These two types of lodges were constructed of poles and bark. A wall made out of logs surrounded each village.	This type of housing could be quickly put up or taken down. In the southern parts of the sub-arctic, birch-bark covered the lodge. In northern parts caribou hides were used.	The stone and turf houses were the most permanent type of housing. Skin tents and snow houses were built on hunting expeditions.
Food	Salmon	Fish Bear Deer Bison	Bison	Corn Deer	Caribou Moose Fish	Seal Walrus

Major Source	Minor Source	Transportation
	Whale Musk ox Bear Fish 	Kayak (single hunter) Umiak (6-9 m in length) Dog sledge Transport was essential to a people who were often on the move.
	Duck Beaver Bear 	Birch-bark canoe Canoe made from hides Snowshoes Toboggans
	Bear Beaver Berries 	Birch-bark canoe Snowshoes Toboggans Lightweight canoes were suitable for transporting goods and people through rough terrain. Snowshoes and toboggans were essential for use in the winter.
	Deer Antelope 	Horse dragging a travois Dogs were used to drag or carry household goods until the Plains Indians obtained horses from the Europeans. A travois was made from two poles to which a platform or net was attached.
	Berries Roots 	Dugout canoe Bark canoe Horse Near the coast, canoes of bark or dugouts of pine were used. On the eastern side of the region the horse was used to hunt bison on the plains near the mountains.
	Seal Whale Fish Berries 	Dugout canoe Large cedar canoes were used for fishing and travel from village to village.
Major Source	**Minor Source**	**Transportation**

mammals, and birds. These laws restrict traditional practices. Fishing regulations, for instance, control when, and how many, fish may be caught. Native leaders maintain that hunting and fishing are **aboriginal rights** and that hunting and fishing laws should not apply to Native peoples. They say that such laws destroy the economic base of Native peoples in many parts of Canada.

- Native peoples are often harmed by developments over which they have no control. The Bennett Dam in B.C., for example, is one of Canada's largest hydro-electric projects. It produces many benefits for the people and industries of the province. At the same time, however, it reduces stream flow downstream in the Peace River delta at Fort Chipewyan, Alberta. The Indian peoples in this area traditionally earned their living by trapping the muskrats that lived in the river. The reduced stream flow harmed both the size and quality of the muskrat habitat. Consequently, the muskrat population declined and the quality of the pelts decreased. Many of the trappers of Fort Chipewyan are no longer able to make an adequate living. In another example, the Inuit of Broughton Island in the eastern Arctic used to support themselves by seal hunting. Protests over the wearing of furs brought about a big decline in the demand for seal fur in Europe and destroyed this local industry.

One-third of the young people of Broughton Island attempted suicide during the first two years after the seal hunt was stopped.

■ CHALLENGES TODAY

In the previous section we examined the results of contact with Europeans on the Native peoples. What is the situation today?

Native peoples face many problems that are similar to those faced by other Canadians. These problems, however, are often more widespread within the Native communities. We can divide these problems into three major groups.

NO COMMON VOICE

Canada's Native peoples are divided into three groups: Indians, Inuit and **Métis**. The Indian group can be further divided into two categories — status and non-status Indians. Status Indians are registered as Indians under the Indian Act and have guaranteed rights. Most live on reserves. Non-status Indians do not have rights or obligations under the Indian Act even though they are Indian by birth, culture and heritage. This may be a result of having never signed treaties with the government.

Under the Indian Act, Indian women lost their status if they married a non-Indian. This discriminatory rule was amended in 1985, allowing many Indian women and their children to regain their status.

Each group faces different challenges. Each group, therefore, seeks something different from provincial and federal governments. The lack of one strong voice to speak for Native rights has reduced the Native peoples' political power in the past. Recent co-operation among many Native groups is changing this situation.

LACK OF AN ECONOMIC BASE

As described earlier, most Native peoples have lost their traditional ways of earning a living. Many have not found alternatives. Often, the reserves do not have enough natural resources to support the people who live on them. The Six Nations Reserve in southern Ontario is in an area that has fertile soils on which fine farms have been developed. In contrast, the Parry Island Reserve on the east side of Georgian Bay has land that is unsuitable for agriculture. The impact of this lack of an economic base is shown in Fig. 9–5.

Fig. 9–5 Without a sound economic base, Native peoples face serious social and health problems.

Unemployment	About 30% nationally. On some reserves 90% are unemployed.
Income	Substantially below the national average.
Working Population	The percentage of adult Indians who work is about two-thirds of the national average.
Housing Conditions	In addition to the severe lack of housing on reserves, over half of the reserve homes have no central heating and three of every ten have no bathrooms.
Health	Indian children (ages 5–14) are 27 times more likely to contract tuberculosis than other Canadian children of the same age.
Life Expectancy	Indian men and women live on average between 8–11 years less than other Canadians.

SOCIAL CONDITIONS

The social conditions of the various Native peoples are different from those of the majority of Canadians. Some of these social conditions are shared by other minority groups; others are unique and result from the Native peoples' particular culture and history. The following social conditions apply to those living on reserves.

Note that the description does not include non-status Indians, Métis, or Inuit.

Population

Canada's population of Native peoples has been growing at a faster rate than the national average since the 1950s. The reinstatement of thousands of people who had lost their Native status has also contributed to the growth of the Native population. As a result, Native communities have a greater demand for education, jobs, and services.

Housing

Over the past ten years the federal government has spent over $600 000 000 on housing for Native peoples. Spending, however, is not keeping up with the demand. There are more people returning to the reserves and the birthrate is increasing. Overcrowding is ten times more common on reserves than elsewhere. About 24% of houses on reserves need major repair work, compared to about 7% of housing elsewhere. More housing with proper sanitation and heating facilities is still required.

Education

Native culture and knowledge have traditionally been pased on by the elders outside of a formal school setting.

The proportion of Native children attending elementary school is similar to the national proportion. There is a large drop, however, in secondary school attendance. Only 20% of Native children who begin in elementary school complete grade 12. This compares with 60% for other children. One reason for the high drop-out rate is that Native children often have to travel long distances to school or even have to board away from home during the school term.

Health

Although their health care has been improving over the past 20 years, the death rate for Native peoples is about three times the national average. Many of the deaths are related to the poor housing conditions, poverty and lack of medical facilities often found on reserves.

Another important factor is violence and accidents. The number of violent deaths on reserves is three times the national average — similar to that of people living in rural areas. There are several reasons for this:

- unsafe housing and poor fire-fighting facilities
- family breakdown and demoralization
- alcoholism and frustration

Conditions are made worse by the lack of an independent economic base in Native communities. One Native leader has said that these are "conditions of poverty and not of race."

■ MEETING THE CHALLENGES

Although Canada's Native peoples face many difficult problems, there are several reasons to be optimistic about the future. There is economic, political, and cultural potential for resolving many of the issues.

ECONOMIC POTENTIAL

Many reserves have the potential for considerable economic development. Thirty percent (600 000 ha) of all reserve lands have a high potential for farming. In addition, more than 1 000 000 ha can be harvested for forest products and over 100 000 ha have a high potential for recreational development. Such areas could be developed for commercial camping, hunting and fishing, skiing, and other activities. The full development of these resources will take time and large amounts of money, but many jobs would be developed.

Some Native peoples have gone beyond the development of natural resources. They own and operate more than 800 businesses across Canada. These include such activities as welding operations, recreational resorts, lumber mills, weaving and craft industries, airlines, farming and ranching, shoe manufacturing, canoe construction, and a variety of retailing and service industries (Fig. 9–6).

When the James Bay hydro-electric project was built in Québec, the Crees of the area reached an agreement with the Québec government that gave them full control over 5500 km² of land and hunting and fishing rights over another 65 000 km². They also received $135 000 000. This money was invested and the interest, about $10 000 000 per year, has allowed them to make improvements to homes and schools throughout the area, form a construction company, create a boat building company with the Yamaha company of Japan, and to set up an airline – Air Creebec (Fig. 9–7).

Most people of working age still hunt and trap full-time. But the economic base of natural resources, capital investment, and business development is allowing the Cree of the James Bay region to control their own future.

POLITICAL POTENTIAL

Many Native peoples have stated that the federal government has had too much control over their affairs. Today, many groups of Native peoples have self-government, which gives them more power to determine their own future. Native councils now make many decisions that used to be made by the Department of Indian

Fig. 9–6 A worker at Yukon Native Products in Whitehorse.

Fig. 9–7 The formation of Air Creebec.

Crees move to expand their northern airline

By Rudy Platiel
The Globe and Mail

The Northern Québec Crees, who muscled their way into an airline service in Québec several years ago, are making a bid to move into Northern Ontario by taking over "certain assets" of Air Ontario Inc., a regional carrier.

Affairs. They have more responsibility for administration. This includes passing by-laws, administering schools, and controlling reserve police forces. In recent years, a number of Native associations have given Native peoples greater access to all levels of the Canadian political structure.

CULTURAL POTENTIAL

assimilation: to lose your culture and adopt the culture of the larger cultural group.

Should Native peoples be assimilated into the mainstream of Canadian society? Some people view **assimilation** as a solution to the problems that Native peoples face. Most Native peoples oppose assimilation. They do not want to lose their cultures and believe that an improved self image is the best defence against this.

Several changes in recent years may lead to schooling that is more useful to Native students. Many Native groups now run their own school boards, and help decide what will be taught. There are more Native peoples teaching Native languages and values along with courses better suited to Native students. Nine universities across Canada currently offer Native studies programs and the University of Regina has established an Indian Cultural College.

There has been a growth of interest in Native cultures in recent years. In 1964 there were only six Native-oriented newspapers and magazines. Now there are more than 35. There are also regular radio and television broadcasts for and by Native peoples.

Many Canadians have become more aware of Native cultures through Native Studies courses in secondary schools and universities. Modern Native art is now highly prized and is included in the collections of major art galleries and museums. For example, the National Museum of Civilization in Ottawa has collected hundreds of pieces of Native art since 1967.

■ IN CLOSING...

Canada's Native peoples are in a unique position. They are Canada's first inhabitants but their relationship with the rest of Canadian society is still developing. Native organizations are creating economic, political, and cultural resources to ensure that the future of their people is brighter.

QUESTIONS

CHECKBACK

1. Describe the stages by which it is thought that Native peoples arrived in North America. Be sure to indicate how the arrival of the Indians and the Inuit differed.
2. Was conflict between the Native peoples and early European settlers inevitable in southern and central Canada? Explain.

3. Explain how each of the following affected the traditional life-style of Canada's Native peoples.
   a) Canada's greatly increased population
   b) changes in the natural environment
   c) fish and game laws
   d) resource development projects
4. Briefly describe the conditions faced by Native peoples on reserves under the following headings:
   a) population
   b) education
   c) health
   d) housing
5. What types of activities are some reserves engaged in to improve their economic base?

ANALYZE

6. a) Define "cultural groups."
   b) List Canada's Native cultural groups.
   c) Which cultural group lived in your area?
   d) Is this group still living in your area? If not, explain why.
7. a) List at least two social problems faced by many Native peoples today.
   b) How might these problems be related to each other and to economic problems?

INVESTIGATE

8. a) How did the Native peoples help the early European explorers and settlers?
   b) What benefits did Native peoples gain from the Europeans?
   c) What problems were created for Native peoples by early contacts with Europeans?
9. Why were the Inuit less affected by Europeans than were the Indians?

WHAT DO YOU THINK?

10. a) Some Native peoples today lead lifestyles much like those of their ancestors. Others have adopted a way of life completely different from that of their ancestors. Most Native peoples are somewhere in between. What factors help determine the particular lifestyle chosen by a Native person?
    b) Will the traditional lifestyle become easier or more difficult to follow in the years to come? Give evidence to support both viewpoints.
11. "There is a tendency to see Native peoples only when problems exist. Successful Native peoples blend in." Comment on this statement.

Resource Development in the Far North

To the Inuit, the Far North is home. To most Canadians, the Far North is a largely unknown region (Fig. 9–8). We all have some idea about what the region is like: vast, treeless spaces; bitter cold; polar bears; and snow houses (igloos). Are these impressions accurate?

The lifestyle of the Inuit has changed under the influence of people who came from outside the Far North. This lifestyle will likely change even more in the future as the Far North is increas-

Fig. 9–8 The Far North as an Inuit might see it.

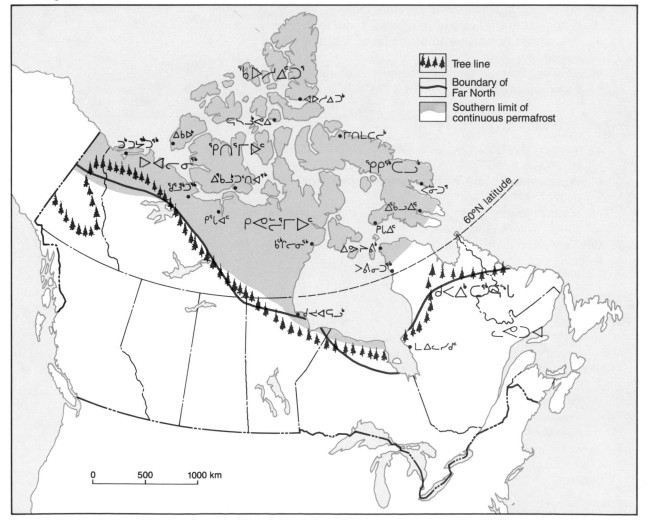

ingly seen as a new source of raw material and energy for the industries of southern Canada.

This complementary study will examine the events that are now taking place in the Far North, and what effect they may have on its future.

Key Terms

ecosystem	environmental impact	sovereignty
land claims	resource development	food web
permafrost		

THE LAND OF THE FAR NORTH

If you were to tune your television to a broadcast of one of the many hearings dealing with the possible future development of the Far North, it could sound like this...

Announcer: "From Iqaluit the CBC brings you live coverage of hearings to discuss the future of the Far North. Before the hearings begin, we would like to give a brief description of the Far North for those of you who are not familiar with this region.

"It is difficult to put an exact boundary on the Far North. Most of the area is situated north of 60° latitude. The greater part is north of the tree line, and is roughly bounded on the south by the southern limit of continuous permafrost. Although these two physical features do not always occur in the same place, they tend to follow the same pattern. The region north of these lines makes up almost one-third of Canada's land area.

"To understand the economic geography of the Far North, we must understand its physical geography, which is very different from that of southern Canada where most Canadians live.

"The eastern part of the Far North is mainly mountainous. The western part is composed of flat lowlands. In the most northerly parts, the snow and ice do not melt from year to year and there is no vegetation at all (Fig. 9–9). In some of these areas, glaciers exist.

This is a fictional account, based on what has happened at similar hearings in the Far North.

Iqaluit: formerly known as Frobisher Bay

The CBC has a special Northern Service designed to meet the needs of Native peoples and others living in the north

continuous permafrost: permafrost that is found everywhere without any interruption

Canada's Far North covers more than 3 000 000 km². It stretches 4000 km from the Yukon to Labrador and nearly 3500 km from Cape Columbia in northern Ellesmere Island to James Bay.

Fig. 9–9 The mountains of the eastern Arctic.

"The waters in and around Hudson Bay aren't free of ice until June, and they freeze over again by November. Most of the Far North gets less than 250 mm of precipitation per year, and we can say that it is a cold desert. Yet in the summer the ground may be wet and swampy (Fig. 9–10). That is because the **permafrost** under the surface does not allow water to drain into the earth, and there is little evaporation.

"The Far North is often referred to as the 'Land of the Midnight Sun.' In summer, the northernmost areas have sunlight 24 hours a day for days or weeks. In the winter, the sun is not seen for days or weeks.

"Largely because of these physical features, the economic geography of the north is less developed than in other parts of Canada. Its isolated settlements have small populations, and are located beside stretches of water. Since there are few roads, boats are used for transport in summer and snowmobiles in winter. Airplanes are used all year to bring in supplies of food and equipment. Boats also bring supplies in the summer. During the short shipping season, when Hudson Bay and the Arctic Ocean are mostly free of ice, larger vessels bring in goods and take out products from the mines. Icebreakers must be used in the most northerly parts, where ice may never leave the channels.

"The earliest inhabitants of the Far North were the Inuit and Indians, who led semi-nomadic lives. Their economy was based on hunting, fishing, and trapping. It is likely that the Vikings were the first Europeans to make contact with these peoples. More frequent contact between Native peoples and Europeans started during the 1600s, when other Europeans arrived in search of a Northwest Passage to India. They did not find one, but they did find animals valuable for their fur – muskrat, beaver, mink, seals and fox. They established trading posts and began to trade with the Native peoples. The assistance of Native peoples was important to the Europeans. It helped them survive in the northern environment.

Canada is building the world's most powerful icebreaker to make travel between the islands easier.

The Northwest Passage was not travelled through until the beginning of the 20th century.

Fig. 9–10 The Mackenzie Delta in the western part of the Far North.

DISCOVERY AND DEVELOPMENT

"Gold was found in the Yukon in 1898 and thousands of Canadians and Americans moved north to seek their fortunes. In the 1930s, gold was found at Yellowknife, and silver and radium at Radium City. After World War II, companies became even more interested in the resources of the Far North as resources in southern Canada began to run out. Today, we know that in the Far North there are deposits of lead, zinc, uranium, silver, copper, gold, oil, and gas.

"At present, there are about 60 000 to 70 000 people living in isolated settlements in this vast area. Many Native peoples still hunt, fish, and trap for a living. Most other people work for the government, mining companies, or the military. Some live in temporary settlements made up of trailers. These are used, for example, by exploration teams that move from place to place in search of oil and gas deposits.

"The oil, gas, and mineral deposits of the Far North are currently the subject of much controversy. Should these resources be developed? Residents, governments, businesses and conservation groups all have different opinions on the matter. One point of view suggests that modern society needs the resources. Another states that resource development will cause Native ways of life to disappear and could seriously damage a fragile environment. People from all walks of life – trappers, gas company executives, shopkeepers, parents, and children – have been invited to present their views at these hearings."

■ LOOKING AT THE ENVIRONMENT

Commission Chair: "We will now call on Dr. Cynthia Brown, a geography professor, to acquaint us with the environmental aspects of this region."

Dr. Cynthia Brown: "The **ecosystems** of the Far North, both on land and in the water, are fragile. By fragile I mean that any damage to the physical environment can easily upset the delicate balance of animals and their food supply. You see, the harsh climate here not only prevents animal and plant life from growing quickly: it also limits the variety of living things. Consequently, there is a relatively small number of species in the North (Fig. 9–11). If any one of these species is wiped out, then the **food web** will be affected, and other species may also die out as a result. The ecosystems of the Far North are simple ones compared to those further south. Normally, if a food web is interrupted, most animals can find something else to eat. Here in the north when a species is wiped out, there is little else for its predators to eat. This interruption works its way right through the food web until it reaches the top.

Ecosystems exist everywhere. In this study we are interested in the ecosystems of the Far North.

Fig. 9–11 Few species of mammals live in the Far North compared with ecosystems closer to the equator.

Area	Number of Species
Tropical rain forest (10°N)	163
Temperate desert (35°N)	100
Boreal forest (50°N)	45
Low tundra (60°N)	30
High tundra (75°N)	8

Fig. 9–12 Vehicle tracks may remain on the tundra for many years.

The caribou move from one area to another depending on the season. They always follow the same route.

calving grounds: the area where the calves are born in the spring.

"The cold climate and slow growth mean that the land of the Far North takes a long time to recover from damage. For instance, a bulldozer passing over the tundra will kill vegetation, which will take years to grow back. The scars remain on the land for a long time because biological action is slow in such a cold climate (Fig. 9–12). When garbage is dumped, it takes years to decay. Building projects sometimes cause the permafrost to thaw, allowing the soil to shift and erosion to occur. These are just a few of the problems affecting the land.

"The caribou and musk oxen rely on the sparse tundra vegetation for their survival. If this vegetation were destroyed on a large scale, these animals would not have enough to eat and their numbers would decrease. If they are disturbed during their breeding periods, they will not reproduce in sufficient numbers to survive. The caribou are migratory, and if their paths are cut by pipelines or blocked by construction, they will not follow their normal routes. This change affects the size of herds by preventing them from reaching their normal feeding and calving grounds.

THREATS TO THE OCEAN

"As we all know, resource exploration has now moved offshore. The environmental problems that can arise in the oceans are perhaps even more serious than those on land. The ice of the Beaufort Sea and Arctic Ocean is an unpredictable force. In the summer, the ice floes are a hazard to drilling rigs and oil tankers. In the winter, the ocean currents force huge heaps of ice together to form pressure ridges. These are so big they reach right down to the sea floor. What would happen if an oil pipeline under the sea were broken by a pressure ridge?

"There is an abundance of life in the oceans despite the cold. The results of an oil spill would be terrible. The thousands of migratory birds that make their summer homes in the Arctic would be killed by oil on the water. Whales, seals, and walrus, which come to the surface to breathe, would be killed by oil blocking their nostrils or breathing holes. The fur and pores of many arctic animals would be coated with oil, making it impossible for them to stay warm. They would most certainly die.

"The waters of the North are not like waters in other parts of the world. They are always at the freezing point or just above it. Oil trapped in ice could be moved long distances before being released by warmer water. It could be trapped under the ice or freeze into the polar ice cap where it could remain for years.

"Any damage that is done to the environment would have very serious consequences for the residents of the Far North. The Native peoples' survival in the north depends to a large extent on hunting, fishing, and trapping. Any disruption of the natural environment threatens their well-being.

"In conclusion, the question we must ask ourselves is this: how much damage can the land and sea tolerate? Unfortunately, the answer to this question is not known. Much more research is needed before we can decide. Development should not go ahead until we know what the dangers are."

■ THE NEED FOR DEVELOPMENT

Commission Chair: "Thank you for your presentation Dr. Brown. We will now hear from Stewart Hansen, a business manager from Inuvik."

Stewart Hansen: "I believe the development of the Far North's mineral, oil, and gas resources should begin on a larger scale immediately. The business community believes that this development will benefit all northerners. When I say development, I mean the mining of lead, silver, zinc, iron ore, oil, and gas. The industries in southern Canada need these raw materials, and if we do not supply them someone else will. When the resources in the south run out, Canada will have to import them. This will cost Canadians, including ourselves here in the north, more money. We must promote the country's economy as well as our own, and keep this money in Canada. We should not let this opportunity go by.

"I agree that the environment is fragile. Development, however, is planned for only a small portion of the Far North. With our current knowledge and technology we can prevent significant damage to the environment.

"Mining will bring us jobs and prosperity. Workers who come here will have to live somewhere. New towns will have to be built. Among other things, people will need stores, hotels, banks, and movie houses. Our business community will grow to meet these needs. All residents will benefit from the new schools, better health care, and improved living conditions. Roads and airfields will be built. Transportation systems, including pipelines, will be constructed to ship the raw materials. All these developments will produce a thriving northern economy with jobs for everyone. The business community has waited a long time for this opportunity. We cannot throw it away."

prosperity: wealth

■ NATIVE PEOPLES AND THE LAND

Commission Chair: "Thank you Mr. Hansen. We will now hear a report from George Nadeau, a trapper from Baker Lake."

George Nadeau: "Although I cannot speak for all Native people, I can speak for most of those in my community. Those of us who live on the land see it as our security. Our occupations and our lifestyle go hand in hand. We hunt and fish (Fig. 9–13). The new jobs that Mr. Hansen talks about are not important to us. We are more concerned about the effect of development on our land and on the lives of our people.

"We are in the majority in the north now, but if thousands of people come into our land, we will be in the minority. We will have little say in how we are governed. The needs of others will be treated as more important than ours.

"The development of oil, gas and mineral resources on a large scale will require many huge construction projects. It will take 15 to 20 years to build pipelines, roads, and mining towns. Our children will go to work on these projects. We will be less able to pass on our knowledge and heritage to them and they will lose our cultural values. Television will teach them different cultural values. Some will be attracted to the lifestyle that they see southern workers enjoying. Alcoholism will likely become a bigger problem (Fig. 9–14).

"Besides all this, our lifestyle does not depend on the oil, gas, or mineral industries. Native people will not benefit from their development. They will only suffer. Our lifestyle relies on wildlife for food, clothing, and shelter. But the animals do not breed

heritage: the values, customs, and history of a people that are passed on from parents to children

Fig. 9–13 Many of the Native peoples of the Far North still live by hunting and fishing.

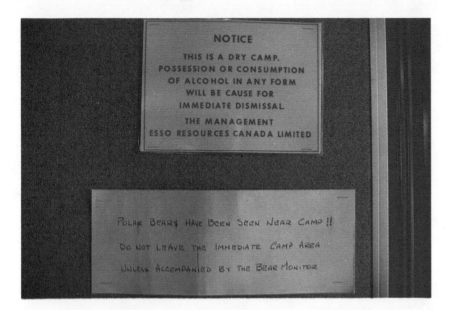

Fig. 9–14 Alcohol abuse is a common problem in many areas of the Far North.

successfully when they are disturbed. Helicopters used for construction and transportation stampede the caribou. Ships in the Arctic Ocean and Hudson Bay disturb the seals. This causes their numbers to decrease. Visitors to the north kill for sport the animals that we depend on. How will we survive if our sources of food and clothing disappear?

"There is one very important part of our way of life that others find hard to understand: our special relationship with the land. Our feeling for the land is a spiritual one, and it is part of everything we do. If the land is altered and the environment changed, our very existence is threatened."

spiritual: sacred or religious

■ A THREATENED COMMUNITY

Commission Chair: "Thank you Mr. Nadeau. We will now hear from Marie Whitefish, a Dene Indian social worker from Fort Simpson."

Marie Whitefish: "In the past, hunting and trapping were respected activities that were necessary to our survival. Whenever we hunted and trapped, we shared among the people in the village. But now that we have money, things are different. Holding down a job is becoming more important than hunting and trapping. But nobody shares money or the things it can buy. Money creates an individual lifestyle rather than the shared one by which our people have always lived.

"Today, some of our people feel that hunting is less important. They do not feel worthwhile without a paid job. Some turn to alcohol and drugs for escape. Large-scale development of resources will not help. Our people will not get the skilled jobs anyway, just the lowest-paid ones.

"Many people in the north foresee more family break-up when **resource development** comes. Our children will be torn between the traditional values of our people and the values that they pick up from their contact with southerners and from television. Even now we do not have as much influence on our children as in the past. The strong ties that used to bind families together are breaking as younger members leave home to work on construction projects. This leads to the break-up of families. The support and sense of belonging that give people their self-worth are lost.

"When thousands of southern workers come to the north, the housing shortage will get worse. We will suffer because we have less money to buy housing. The presence of so many people will add to our social problems, not reduce them as Mr. Hansen suggested. There will be drugs and alcohol for anyone who goes looking for them. Who will pay for the services to deal with these problems?"

■ MEETING THE CHALLENGES

Commission Chair: "Thank you for your presentation Ms. Whitefish. We will now hear from Pierre Tremblay, President of the All Canadian Oil and Gas Corporation."

Pierre Tremblay: "The development of resources on a large scale is the issue being examined at this meeting. Although I can only speak for my company, I am sure other resource-based companies share my feelings.

"Oil and gas are but two of the resources of the Far North. It is our purpose to develop these potentially vast reserves to serve all Canadians. Canada's easily recoverable reserves of oil and gas in other areas will not get us much beyond the year 2000. If society is to survive as we know it, we must begin exploration and development here in the north now. We have already found some oil and gas. It is likely that much more will be found. Canada will need these resources in the near future. Fifteen to twenty years for development is not a long time in an area of such great distances and harsh climates.

"I would now like to give our side of the argument to some items raised by earlier speakers.

"Dr. Brown raised several points about the **environmental impact** of large-scale development. We too have done studies and offer solutions to the issues raised. Consider these examples.

• Drilling operations in Arctic waters are controlled by very strict regulations set by the federal government. There has never been a major blowout from any of the drilling rigs operating in these waters (Fig. 9–15).

Fig. 9-15 Artificial islands have been built to allow drilling for oil in the Beaufort Sea. These islands offer the maximum protection possible from damage by moving ice.

- The oil that is presently found in Arctic waters comes from ships pumping out their tanks. We must have stricter control over their activities.
- Roads can be built in a way that reduces damage to the land. Bulldozers can be modified to prevent their treads from digging up the ground.
- Pipelines can be insulated so that the permafrost will not be melted by the heated oil flowing through the pipes.
- During biologically important times for wildlife – mating and birth periods – we do not have to work in sensitive areas. We will not travel through breeding grounds at critical times of the year. In the past, developers in the north were not aware of these cycles. Now that we know such cycles exist, we can organize construction programs to prevent further damage.

  "Mr. Nadeau said that aircraft frighten the animals on which the Native peoples depend for their livelihood. In the oil industry we can solve the problem by restricting air travel to the special areas that are away from important animal habitats. In other areas, where mining research is conducted, planes will fly higher to avoid disturbing the animals.

  "The two previous speakers have raised the question of social problems created by large-scale resource development. I would like to make some points in this regard.

- After leaving school, young Native people are often well qualified for good jobs. In the past, these jobs were not readily available in the Far North. With large-scale development, there will be jobs available for Native youth in their own region.
- Without permanent employment there will always be a need for welfare. Development will provide jobs so people will not need as much economic assistance.
- The development of resources in the Far North, even on a large scale, would not use more than one or two percent of the total land area. There is still a great deal of land available for traditional hunting, fishing, and trapping.

- In order to prevent social problems caused by the flow of large numbers of workers into the region, the construction camps can be built away from Native settlements. When permanent settlements are created, they can also be located where contact with Native peoples will be minimal.

"Ms. Whitefish was worried that Native peoples would get only the lowest-paid jobs available. We would put special hiring practices into effect so that those who wished to work in our industry would have first choice at jobs for which they are qualified.

"Let me leave you with one last question: Should 0.3% of Canada's population decide the future for the remaining 99.7%?"

■ MAKING THE CHOICES

Commission Chair: "Thank you Mr. Tremblay. Now I would like to call upon Anne Kataoyak, a journalist from Inuvik."

Anne Kataoyak: "Native peoples are often pictured as being against all development in the Far North. While some feel this way, there are others who feel differently. I wish to speak for those who realize that large-scale resource development in the Far North will come. What we are concerned about is when and how it occurs. We say that before any large-scale development takes place, our **land claims** must be settled. Most Native groups agree on this issue.

"As the first people to inhabit this land, many of us see it as our own. We want to govern ourselves, and determine on our own what is to be done to the land. The settlement of our land claims involves the following issues.

- We want to be recognized by the government as owners of the land. This will allow us to negotiate with governments and industries on any proposed development (Fig. 9–16).
- Ownership and control of the land mean that we can safeguard our traditional economy and way of life.
- Recognition of our ownership of the land means that we will be paid when development occurs. The money we receive will help us to solve our own problems.
- If we own the land, we can influence the rate of development and decide our future.
- We must have guarantees against the future loss of any of our land.

"I am not saying that resource development should never take place. I am saying that we want our claims recognized so that we can prepare for development and control it as we see fit. This will allow us to preserve our culture for future generations.

"Many of us in the Northwest Territories would like to see two provinces created so that we would have more control. Discussions have been taking place for several years between

Under government laws, owning the land does not necessarily mean ownership of the oil and minerals under the land. Most Native peoples want mineral rights as well as land ownership.

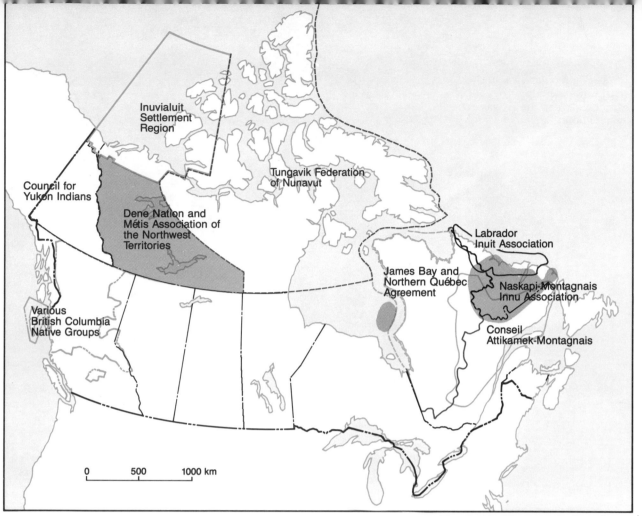

Fig. 9–16 The negotiation of
Native land claims is critical in
determining the future direction
of development in the North.
This map shows areas where
land claim negotiations are
underway.

Indian and Inuit organizations over the division of the Northwest Territories into two territories. The Inuit organization
would like to establish an Inuit homeland, possibly called
Nunavut ('our land' in Inuktitut), in the eastern portion of
the Northwest Territories. The western portion could be
called Denendeh ('our land' in Dene) and would be a Dene
and Métis homeland. I feel the federal government should
look at this possibility very seriously."

■ CANADIAN SOVEREIGNTY IN THE FAR NORTH

Commission Chair: Thank you Ms. Kataoyak. Now I would like
to call on Dr. David Kenyon of the Canada North Foundation in
Montreal."

Dr. David Kenyon: "While I in no way wish to downplay what
has been said at this hearing, I feel that we may be ignoring the
most important challenge that faces us in the north today. The
very **sovereignty** of our north is threatened by our neighbours
both to the north and to the south.

Fig. 9–17 A polar view of the earth shows Canada's strategic position between the U.S. and the Soviet Union.

New Fighter Bases

cruise missiles: missiles that fly very close to the ground to avoid radar.

The Canadian forces are planning to build a permanent military base in the Far North during the early 1990s. This base would be a training centre and, more importantly, would assert Canadian sovereignty in this region. The community of Nanisivik is being considered as a possible location. It is located on northern Baffin Island near the eastern entrance to the Northwest Passage.

"A glance at a globe of the world shows that Canada is sandwiched between two superpowers. If the U.S. and the Soviet Union ever fight a nuclear war, Canada's Far North will be a major battleground. The Soviets have a large fleet of cruise missiles. In time of war these would be released from bombers flying over our Far North. The new "North" radar system and the fighter plane bases at Yellowknife, Inuvik, Rankin Inlet, Kuujjuaq, and here at Iqaluit are designed to counter this threat (Fig. 9–17).

"Both the Soviet and U.S. navies have nuclear submarines that are capable of operating under the ice of the Arctic. These submarines can carry small but deadly missiles. The Canadian Armed Forces do not have the ships and planes needed to patrol the ice-choked passages between the islands.

"We have three choices:

- One—continue to expand defence co-operation between the U.S. and Canada. The U.S. is already paying for most of the Arctic air defence system. Perhaps we should get the Americans to use their nuclear submarines to patrol our part of the Arctic Ocean. Many Canadians, however, would view the resulting loss of national pride as unacceptable. Many Northerners would say that this choice might increase the basic threat of war.

- Two—pursue a defence policy that is more separate from that of the U.S. We could build our own air defence and submarine defence systems. Many Canadians would have difficulty

Fig. 9-18 The construction of a super ice breaker like this will allow Canada to patrol the waters of the Far North year round.

accepting the enormous cost that would come with this choice. For example, the cost of a fleet of small nuclear-powered submarines to patrol the Arctic islands would be more than $8 000 000 000.

Canada's total defence budget is about $10 000 000 000.

- Three—declare the Far North a nuclear weapons-free zone. Those who support this idea say that it is the only way to secure a future that would be safe from fear for the people of the region. Opponents of the scheme feel that it would be a dangerous idea and would actually increase the chance of war.

"The Soviets are not the only threat to our sovereignty in the north. Although the Americans are certainly not a military threat to us, they believe that the waters of the Northwest Passage are international and that they can use them any time without asking permission from Canada. In the past, they have sent icebreakers through the Passage to emphasize their point. In the future, they might decide to use this route to move oil and natural gas from Alaska to the U.S. east coast. The environmental impact of a serious oil spill here would be catastrophic. Furthermore, the Northwest Passage may be used some day as the shortest sea route between Asia and Europe.

"Until recently Canada has not had the ability to "show the flag" in the Arctic during heavy ice conditions. The new Polar-8 icebreaker (Fig. 9-18) will allow us to do this more easily. The presence of the Polar-8, along with increased economic and military activity, should make it more obvious that this land and water is indeed part of Canada. At the same time, by negotiation or in international court, we must get the U.S. and all other countries to acknowledge our sovereignty."

Commission Chair: "Thank you for your presentation Dr. Kenyon. That is all the time we have for today. We will continue with more presentations tomorrow."

■ IN CLOSING...

This hearing provides only an outline of some of the issues surrounding resource development in the Far North. Building pipelines, drilling for oil and gas, developing mines, and all the changes these activities will bring, will certainly affect the land and the people who live on it. But will the results be harmful or helpful?

CHECKBACK

1. Write the following definitions in your notebook. Beside each, write the word that matches the definition.
   a) ground that does not completely thaw during the summer
   b) a community of organisms interacting with one another and with the environment
   c) an accident on a drilling rig that allows oil to escape
   d) the values, customs, and history of a people
   e) the area where caribou calves are born in the spring
2. Briefly describe four physical characteristics of the Far North.
3. Why is the Far North referred to as the "Land of the Midnight Sun?"
4. a) What is meant by the "fragile" ecosystem of the Far North?
   b) How is this fragility shown by
      i the effect of development on life in the tundra?
      ii an oil spill in arctic waters?
5. What methods have been suggested by resource companies that would deal with the environmental and social issues raised at the hearing?
6. a) Examine Fig. 9–16. How much of the Far North has been claimed by Native groups?
   b) Where have land claims been settled? How much of the land in these areas has been selected by Native peoples?
   c) Which Native groups have claimed land in the Far North?
   d) What do Native peoples want in any land claims settlement? Why?

ANALYZE

7. Compare the views of the northern business community and northern Native peoples regarding large-scale resource development.
8. a) Examine the equatorial view of Canada and its neighbours in Fig. 26–10. Select Canada's three closest neighbours.
   b) Examine the polar view of Canada and its neighbours in Fig. 9–17. Select Canada's three closest neighbours.
   c) Which view, polar or equatorial, are Canadians most familiar with?
   d) Generally speaking, countries have a large number of contacts with their nearest neighbours. Is this true for Canada? Why or why not?
9. On a blank map of Canada, draw the location of the five new fighter plane bases. What reasons can you suggest for the choice of these locations? Refer to Fig. 9–17 for help.

10. Choose the side of the development issue with which you most agree. Research information to back up the side you have chosen. Find your information and materials in the library, in newspapers, and in magazines. You might also contact resource-based companies in your area or speak to representatives from Native organizations. Work in groups, and present your findings in a report, debate, or other form. You should investigate such aspects of the situation as:
    a) the status of Native land claims
    b) specific plans for oil and gas developments and mines
    c) the routes of proposed pipelines and tankers
    d) environmental impact studies
    e) how (and by whom) political decisions will be made.

11. In 1982, a vote was held in the Northwest Territories on whether the territory should be divided into two. This vote was not binding on the federal government (the federal government would still make the final decision). It did, however, indicate that the people of the area are interested in the way that important government decisions about their region will be made.
    a) What was the result of this vote?
    b) What did this result indicate about the feelings of the residents of the Far North?
    c) What progress has been made over this issue since April 1982 when the vote was held?

12. a) Surface ships have traversed the Northwest Passage only a handful of times. Research the different routes used by:
        i. Gjoa (1904-1906)
        ii. St. Roch (two trips in the early 1940s)
        iii. Manhattan (1969)
    b) Trace these routes on a map of the Far North.
    c) Trace the limit of permanent polar ice on your map.
    d) Why has the apparently obvious route through McClure Strait never been used?

The S.S. Manhattan was a specially designed oil tanker. When it was built it was the most powerful non-military ship in the world. The purpose of its voyage was to prove the feasibility of oil shipments through the Northwest Passage and to demonstrate to Canada that the U.S. considers the Northwest Passage as international waters.

13. a) Describe two threats to Canada's sovereignty in the Far North.
    b) How do these threats differ?
    c) What do you think we should do to counter each?

14. Are there reasonable grounds for Native peoples to:
    a) claim independent status from Canada?
    b) claim provincial status within Canada?

10 Cultural Diversity

In Chapter 2, Canada's population was described as a "tossed salad." This image suggests that our population is made up of people whose ancestors came from many other countries. These people have maintained much of their original **culture**, even though they have become Canadian citizens. This has created a **multicultural society** in Canada.

What makes people want to leave one country and move to another? Why do they decide to come to Canada? What do they face when they arrive? You will find some of the answers to these questions in this chapter.

Key Terms

culture	push factor	emigrant
multicultural society	immigrant	pull factor

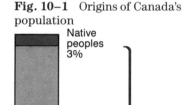
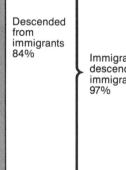

Fig. 10–1 Origins of Canada's population

Native peoples 3%

Descended from immigrants 84%

Immigrants or descended from immigrants 97%

Foreign born 13%

■ CANADA: A LAND OF IMMIGRANTS

Most Canadians are **immigrants** or are the descendants of immigrants. In fact, about 97% of Canada's citizens fit into this category. (Fig. 10–1). They or their ancestors were born in another country. The remaining 3% are the original Canadians – the Native peoples who have inhabited this land for thousands of years.

More than 3 000 000 of today's Canadians were born in other countries. In an average year, more than 100 000 new immigrants come to Canada. Why has Canada become the new home of millions of people from all over the world?

■ CANADA'S IMMIGRATION HISTORY

Examine Fig. 10–2. It shows the numbers of people who came to Canada at different times in the past century. As you can see, the numbers of immigrants changed greatly from year to year. Immigration to Canada is related to events happening elsewhere in the world. For example, hundreds of thousands of people came to Canada from Europe between 1946 and 1958 because much of Europe lay in ruins as a result of World War II. Try to think of other world events that have produced periods of high and low immigration to Canada.

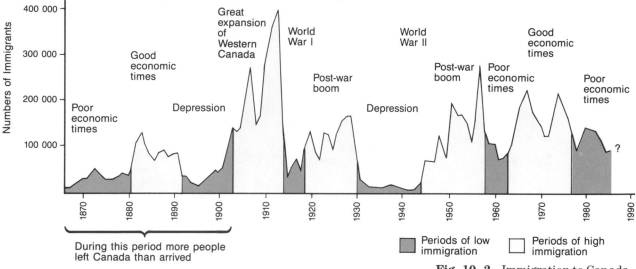

Fig. 10-2 Immigration to Canada, 1867 - 1985

Not only do the numbers of immigrants change from year to year, but the places of origin of immigrants change as well. France supplied most of the country's immigrants until the British conquest of New France in 1759. Until the 1960s, Great Britain was the source of the largest number of new Canadians. The second largest number of immigrants over the past two centuries has come from the U.S. Between 1900 and 1920, great numbers of immigrants came to Canada from the Ukraine and Scandinavian countries. In the years following World War II many people came from Italy. More recently, many citizens of Portugal, Hong Kong, India, African countries and the West Indies have immigrated to Canada.

Where will future immigrants come from? Only time will tell. It is safe to speculate that our traditional immigrant sources—Great Britain, Europe and the U.S.—will continue to send us more people. But Canada will probably continue to accept increasing numbers of immigrants from **Third World** countries.

Where do immigrants go when they arrive here? Examine Fig. 10-3. The large cities of Toronto, Montreal, and Vancouver have traditionally been the first destination of most immigrants. Why is this not surprising?

speculate: predict what may happen

■ WHY PEOPLE BECOME IMMIGRANTS

Imagine that you are thinking of leaving Canada and moving to another country. What might make you want to leave your home for a new country? Perhaps you have lost your job and cannot find a new one. Perhaps you disagree with the decisions made by Canadian politicians. In some countries people fear for their safety because of war, revolution or poverty. Reasons that cause people to leave their country are called **push factors**. People who leave their country to live in another one are called **emigrants**.

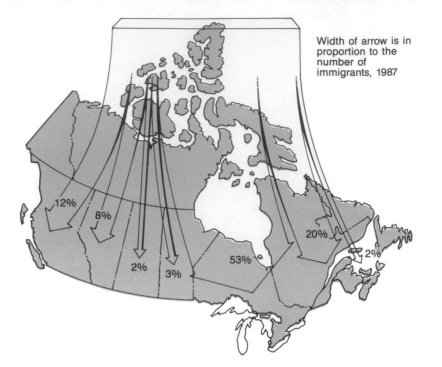

Width of arrow is in proportion to the number of immigrants, 1987

12%
8%
2%
3%
53%
20%
2%

Fig. 10–3 When immigrants come to Canada, where do they go?

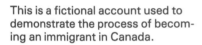

This is a fictional account used to demonstrate the process of becoming an immigrant in Canada.

Canadian unemployment rates in recent years have averaged less than 10%

What might make you choose a particular country as your new home? Perhaps you are engaged to marry someone there. Jobs may be plentiful. Reasons which attract people to another country are called **pull factors**.

To understand how push and pull factors work, consider the case of Emerson and Barbara Robinson. The Robinsons used to live in Kingston, Jamaica. They moved to a suburb of Toronto in 1984. Why did they decide to move to Canada?

Mr. Robinson worked as a diesel mechanic in Jamaica. He earned about $85 (Canadian) per week. His wife sometimes worked as a dressmaker. They had two young children and lived in an apartment in a middle-class section of Kingston. All, however, was not well. The unemployment rate was about 25% and Mr. Robinson was worried about losing his job. Three of his workmates had already been laid off. Furthermore, Kingston had experienced street violence between rival political groups. Mr. and Mrs. Robinson were increasingly concerned about the future for themselves and their children.

Canada offered what Mr. Robinson felt were certain advantages. Both he and his wife had friends and relatives who had moved to Canada, many of them to the Toronto area. He learned from his cousin in Toronto that he could get a steady job in Canada that would pay more than $350 per week. His family would not have to learn a new language. A final advantage was that so many people from the West Indies had recently moved to Canada that Jamaican-style food, stores, music, and social clubs were quite common in some large urban areas. This would make it easier for the Robinsons to adjust to their new home.

The decision was made. The Robinsons would try to move to Canada. Mr. and Mrs. Robinson decided to visit the Canadian government office in Kingston to find out how to go about it.

HOW PEOPLE BECOME IMMIGRANTS TO CANADA

The Robinsons found out that moving to Canada was harder than they had anticipated. The Canadian government uses a point system to evaluate potential immigrants. This system ensures fairness and makes certain that immigrants possess skills that will enable them to earn their living in Canada. Each person must obtain at least 70 points to qualify for entry into Canada. How did the Robinsons fare? (See Fig. 10–4)

Fig. 10–4 The spouse with the higher number of points is considered to be head of the household when determining eligibility for immigration. The passing mark is 70 points.

Points Can Be Obtained For	Maximum Points Possible	Points Received by Mr. Robinson
1. Education One point per year of formal education (up to twelve). Points are based on equivalents to Canadian school system. Mr. Robinson had eight years of schooling.	12	8
2. Vocational training Points are given for specific training for a trade or a profession, e.g., 1–3 months training — 3 points; 1–2 years — 9 points; 10+ years — 15 points. Mr. Robinson had 18 months of training as a mechanic.	15	9
3. Experience Points are given for experience in the occupation mentioned in (2). Mr. Robinson had two years' experience as a mechanic.	8	4
4. Demand for occupation Points are given if there is a shortage of people in Canada with the immigrant's job skills. A zero here will bar a potential immigrant from entering Canada. Diesel mechanics are in moderate demand.	10	6
5. Arranged job Points are given if the immigrant has a job offer in Canada. The employer must state that he is unable to find a Canadian to fill the job. Mr. Robinson had a written offer for a job in Toronto.	10	10
6. Age Ten points if 21 to 44 years old. Two points subtracted per year if older or younger.	10	10
7. Knowledge of English/French A person fluent in English and French receives 15 points. Mr. Robinson knows only English.	15	10
8. Personal suitability Up to 10 points given as the result of an interview with a Canadian immigration official.	10	6
9. Levels control This value changes from time to time to reflect demand for immigration. All immigrants coming at the same time receive the same number of points.	10	5
TOTAL	100	68
KINSHIP BONUS An immigrant with relatives in Canada willing to guarantee financial assistance receives 10 points. Mr. Robinson's cousin agreed to this condition.	10	10

Immigration officials keep these point totals confidential and they are unavailable to the public. Entry to Canada can also be obtained in other ways:
1. Sponsorship: by relatives in Canada who guarantee that the immigrant will be supported until he or she is established.
2. Refugee status: those who have been forced to leave their country because of war, revolution, or threat of jail or death because of their political beliefs.
3. Investor: a wealthy individual who can create jobs in Canada.

The Robinsons' score of 78 points was enough to qualify them to move to Canada. Not everyone qualifies. Immigrants allowed into Canada have certain characteristics. They may be well educated, have vocational training, and useful job experience. They are usually young. Finally, immigrants to Canada are likely to be highly ambitious. They want to improve life for themselves and their families and are prepared to work hard for what they want.

■ WHAT IS IT LIKE BEING AN IMMIGRANT?

Unless you have experienced it, it is very hard to understand what it is like to be an immigrant. Try to imagine what it would be like to get off an airplane in Toronto, Montreal, or Vancouver, and know no one, have little money, and perhaps not speak English or French well. What would your first day of school or work be like? Here are the reactions of some Canadian high school students who are recent immigrants to Canada (Fig. 10-5).

Tony *(from Italy—age 17)*
"Not being able to speak English was the biggest problem. I learned to speak English at school and with my friends. It didn't take too long — about two years — but my mother still doesn't speak much English. She goes to Italian stores and has Italian friends. Most of the members of our church speak Italian, including the priests."

Andrea *(from Hong Kong—age 15)*
"I couldn't believe how big and how quiet Canada is. Hong Kong was so crowded and noisy. It took me a long time to get used to the space and privacy we have here."

Diana *(from South Africa—age 16)*
"There were two big things I noticed. Canada has few of the racial problems of South Africa. The second thing I noticed was that people here do not have servants."

John *(from Trinidad—age 14)*
"The biggest change was the weather. Before I came to Canada, the coldest weather I had experienced was about 7°C. I couldn't believe how cold I was during my first winter here. It made me want to go home."

Mohammed *(from Pakistan—age 16)*
"Most Canadians are friendly but there are some who don't want to accept you because you are different."

Ruth *(from Israel—age 15)*
"The biggest problem for me when I came to Canada was not knowing what to expect. In Israel we learned nothing about Canada at school. Everything here came as a surprise."

All these students are adapting well to their new country. Most plan to become citizens as soon as they can. But other

immigrants may find that Canada is not what they had expected. Because of this they may decide to return to their native countries. Why might this happen?

IN CLOSING...

Canada has benefited a great deal from immigration. Immigration has meant an inflow of millions of people. The impact of immigration on the Canadian landscape may be seen in many ways: many different languages are taught in schools across the country; restaurants specialize in the foods of different nationalities; supermarkets and specialty shops supply food and clothes from around the world; and **ethnic** communities have a great cultural impact in some large cities. But perhaps the most important things brought to Canada by immigrants are their skills and enthusiasm.

QUESTIONS

CHECKBACK

1. a) Name two countries that have been major sources of immigrants for more than 100 years.
   b) Name two other countries from which many people have recently immigrated to Canada.

ANALYZE

2. a) What percentage of Canadian residents fit into each of these categories:
   i. Native peoples?
   ii. people born in other countries?
   iii. people born in Canada but descended from immigrants?

    b) Which category are you in? Which category are your parents in? Which category are your grandparents in?

3. a) Examine Fig. 10–2. Name two periods when immigration to Canada was high.

    b) What factor(s) caused these periods of high immigration?

4. a) Examine Fig. 10-2. Name two periods when immigration to Canada was low.

    b) What factor(s) caused these periods of low immigration?

5. a) Examine Fig. 10–3. Which areas of Canada attract the most immigrants?

    b) Why do you think immigrants go to these areas? List three reasons.

    c) Could the pattern change in years to come? Why?

6. a) Define "push factors" and "pull factors".

    b) Give at least two push and two pull factors for the Robinsons' decision to come to Canada.

7. a) Examine Fig. 10–4. What are the characteristics of the people favoured by the system?

    b) Is this system fair to Canada? Explain.

    c) Is this system fair to the countries that the immigrants come from? Explain.

8. It is interesting to note that many Canadian-born citizens might not obtain entry into Canada if they had not been born here.

    a) Calculate the points your family would receive if it were applying for entry into Canada.

    b) Would your family gain entry into Canada? Why was it successful or unsuccessful?

9. a) Examine the reactions to Canada by recent immigrants to Canada on p. 128. State two reactions that you found surprising. Why did they surprise you?

    b) From your own experience, or that of a friend, describe at least two other reactions a recent immigrant might have to life in Canada.

INVESTIGATE

10. a) Using resources in your school or public library, prepare a series of graphs to show the percentages of people from major ethnic groups in each province.

    b) Compare the provincial patterns. What differences do you see?

WHAT DO YOU THINK?

11. a) What role did family assistance play in qualifying the Robinsons as immigrants to Canada?

    b) Why is family assistance considered important?

    c) Do you think this is fair? Why?

12. Over the past 10 years an average of about 50 000 people per year have emigrated from Canada.
    a) Give three reasons why you think people might leave Canada.
    b) Where do you think they move to? Why?
    c) This number is lower than during previous decades. Why might this be so?
13. a) The U.S. has been called a "melting pot" of immigrants. What does this mean?
    b) How is this different from the Canadian idea of a "tossed salad" (or "cultural mosaic")?
    c) Construct a chart to compare the positive and negative features of each approach.
    d) Based on your analysis, which do you think is a better idea for a country that receives many immigrants?
14. a) Examine Fig. 10–2. In which year was immigrant flow to Canada highest? How many immigrants arrived that year? The population of Canada at that time was 7 200 000. What percentage of the population did the new immigrants represent?
    b) If immigrants came to Canada at this rate today, how many would come in a year? (The population of Canada is now about 26 000 000).
    c) What problems might be created if this many immigrants came to Canada today?
    d) What advantages would result to Canada if this many immigrants came today?
15. How would Canada be different
    a) if it had no limits on immigration?
    b) if it stopped all immigration?
16. A new immigration policy allows people with few points into Canada if they are **entrepreneurs**. It has been suggested that this allows wealthy business people to "buy" their way into the country. What do you think?

    entrepreneur: a person who takes the risk of starting a business

17. Political refugees are often allowed into Canada without meeting the 70 point level and without waiting in line for their turn to be considered for immigration. With a group of classmates, discuss the following questions:
    a) What is a political refugee?
    b) Why are political refugees permitted to immigrate into Canada more easily than other people?
    c) Is this policy fair to the refugees? Why?
    d) Is the policy fair to the people who are waiting in line for their chance to enter Canada? Explain.

    refugee: someone who leaves their country because of war, revolution, or threat of jail or death because of their political beliefs

Portrait of a Family

When we study the geography of Canada we usually concentrate on rivers and mountains, cities, mines, and transportation routes. We tend to forget that the study of Canada and its geography is also the study of people and their achievements. In this study we will look at Canada from the perspective of one family.

The picture opposite (Fig. 10–6) is from the family album of Mr. Anton Horvath. In 1988 Mr. Horvath celebrated his 100th birthday at a huge family reunion held on the family farm near Swift Current, Sask. This occasion gave him the opportunity to share some of the family history with younger members of the family.

Key Terms

migration   section   mechanization
Depression

■ LIFE IN THE OLD WORLD

Mr. Horvath's great-grandchildren wanted to know how he came to Canada. He explained that he was born in 1888 in a remote part of the Austro-Hungarian Empire. He was the fourth of five children born to Josef and Maria Horvath (Fig. 10–7).

The Horvaths were a farm family. They had a hard but rewarding life. Only occasionally did their crops fail because of insect damage or early frosts. There were, however, problems. Their government gradually increased taxes during the latter half of the 19th century in order to pay the costs of running the Empire. In time of war or national emergency, Josef (or his sons when they became old enough) could be forced to serve in the Imperial Army. Josef would then be unable to work the farm, and the rest of his family might starve. On top of this, if the Horvaths criticized their government, they could be thrown into jail.

Josef accepted the restrictions placed on his life as his father and grandfather had. Maria, however, would not accept that her sons might one day be slaughtered in a distant war. She also could not understand why so much of her family's income was taken in taxes to pay for things which she felt did not benefit them at all.

For several years Maria worried about these problems, but she could not see a way out. One day a stranger came to their village and put up a poster on a wall (Fig. 10–8). Neither Maria nor Josef could read, so they asked the local priest to read the poster to them. The poster told of the opportunities in western Canada. The Horvaths had no idea where this place was, but they were very interested in what the poster announced.

Fig. 10–6 The Horvath family.

Fig. 10–7 Horvath family tree

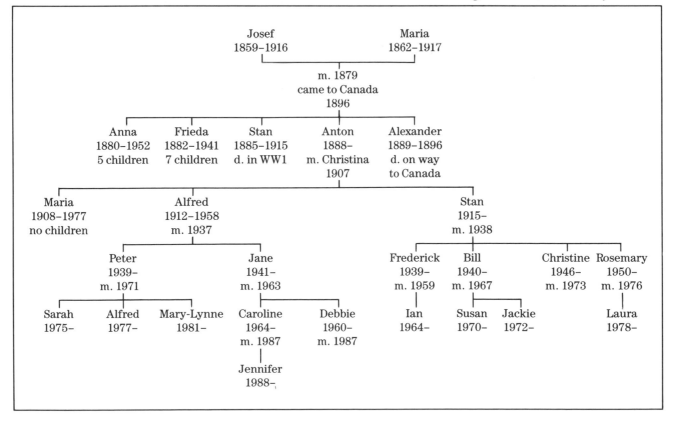

Fig. 10–8 Posters like this were distributed in many languages to encourage settlers to come to Canada.

diphtheria: an infectious disease that used to kill many children. Now children receive a vaccine to prevent this dangerous disease.

The settlement pattern of the Prairies will be discussed in more detail in Chapter 11.

The government of Canada wanted a large-scale **migration** of settlers to the Canadian West in order to farm an almost empty region of grasslands. The immigrants had to be prepared to work hard, but the Canadian government would help them. It would pay part of the cost of moving to Canada, and would also give the settlers a farm of about 64 ha. This was an enormous amount of land—almost 10 times the size of the Horvath's present farm. And they would get the land free! They could keep this land as long as they kept it cleared and under cultivation.

On Maria's prompting, Josef travelled to the nearest large city to talk to the Canadian immigration agent. This city was 80 km away and Josef had never travelled so far before. Although the agent had never been to Canada, he answered all Josef's questions. Josef thought that this Canada must indeed be a wonderful place—free land, no compulsory military service, and the right to vote. He went home to Maria to discuss the matter. After a few sleepless nights spent thinking about their future, the Horvaths decided to move to Canada. They left their village for Canada on March 1, 1896.

■ COMING TO CANADA

The trip to Canada was a long and unhappy one. The Horvaths travelled by oxcart, train, and ship. They were able to take only a few of their most prized possessions. Their life savings were very small and they had to be sure not to waste any money. The most tragic event occurred when their ship was only three days from Québec City. Alexander, Anton's younger brother, died. The ship's doctor said that he died of diphtheria but everyone knew that Alexander had never been strong and that the trip had just been too hard for him.

When the Horvaths reached Québec City on April 7, 1896, they were shocked to learn that they were still thousands of kilometres from their goal. This last part of the trip was completed more easily, however, because special railway trains had been provided to move settlers to the West. The early days in Canada passed in a haze of unfamiliar faces, languages, and customs. Finally, after several days on the train, the Horvaths reached the Prairies where the free land was being given out.

It was here, in the new village of Swift Current in what is now Saskatchewan, that the Horvaths learned how the survey system worked. With the aid of a translator, Josef was told that all of the land of the Prairies had been divided into blocks called townships. Each of the townships was subdivided into **sections** and each section into quarter-sections. Josef found that his family was entitled to one quarter-section of land. To obtain ownership of the quarter-section he would have to pay $10 and farm the land for three years.

Little was left of the family's savings, and they still had to buy a team of mules or oxen, a plow, seed, and other essentials. Having

Fig. 10–9 Most settler families lived in sod houses like this until they could afford to build a better home.

made these purchases, the family set out in early May to find their land. The search was made more difficult by the fact that the land had few identifying features such as large hills, rivers, or forests.

The task facing the Horvaths seemed almost impossible. They had to plow the prairie, plant and harvest crops, and build a shelter before winter came. They found the plowing harder than any they had done before. The tangled turf had never been broken and resisted the plow. The work was very slow. Luckily, the family had arrived in spring and had the whole summer to prepare for winter.

For the first few months the family lived in a rough tent. Insects, dust, and heavy thunderstorms bothered them all summer. They needed a house but there were few trees to cut for lumber. Lumber bought in town had been shipped from northern Ontario or British Columbia and was far too costly. The alternative was a sod house (Fig. 10–9). The house had only two small rooms, but for the Horvaths it would be home for the next five years. Later on, when they had more money, they would build a better home.

Almost before they realized it, fall came. The Horvaths harvested their crops and made ready for winter. The winter weather was more severe than the Horvaths could have imagined. For weeks on end the temperature stayed far below 0°C. On several days in January and February the temperature dropped below -30°C. Maria wondered if they had made a mistake in leaving their homeland.

At last spring arrived and the new year's plowing and planting began. Josef, with the help of his family, was able to plant more land the second year. At harvest time, the farm showed a small profit. At the end of the third year, Josef was given the title deed for his land. He was also given the opportunity of "pre-emption." This meant that he could buy an additional quarter-section of land from the government quite cheaply.

Some settlers hired trained guides to lead them to their land.

An old saying about the Prairies: "Anyone who foretells Prairie weather is either a newcomer or a fool."

Life in Canada seemed almost unbelievably good to Maria and Josef. They had worked tremendously hard, but after three years they owned a farm larger than any back home. They also had the freedom that they had lacked in their homeland.

Anton Horvath was now old enough to help out more around the farm and in the new house that the family built in 1902. In this same year he left school after finishing grade nine, and he met Christina Kostic who lived on a farm several kilometres away.

QUESTIONS

CHECKBACK

1. **a)** Define "migration".
   b) Describe how migration can occur because of both "push" and "pull" factors. List at least two push and two pull factors in the Horvath's decision to come to Canada.

Push and pull factors are discussed earlier in this chapter on Canada's Cultural Diversity.

2. Earlier in this chapter you learned about Canada's immigration history. To which major immigration period did the Horvaths belong?

ANALYZE

3. Why did settlement of the Prairies come so late?
4. List at least three characteristics of the kind of person who would be likely to move to a new country.
5. Three farmers moved to the Prairies in 1900. One came from the Ukraine, one from southern Ontario, and one from Scotland. Which would probably have had the most useful experience? Explain your answer. How might this experience contribute to the farmer's success?

Check your atlas's world agricultural map for help.

INVESTIGATE

6. **a)** Trace the route followed by the Horvaths on a map of the world. Their starting point was Bratislava, Czechoslovakia.
   b) How far did they travel?
   c) Describe how the Horvath family and other settlers might have felt about taking such a long trip.

WHAT DO YOU THINK?

7. Put yourself in the position of Josef and Maria Horvath. You have arrived in Canada and are going to become a homesteader. There will be no stores near your farm. In a group, make a detailed list of all the things your family will need for the first season. Do some research to find out if the items you chose were available at the end of the last century.

■ BOOM AND BUST

In 1907 Anton married Christina and they built a small house on the farm. The following year their first child, Maria, was born. In the years that followed, the Horvaths prospered. Not every year was good, but there were more good years than bad. In 1910 Anton's father, Josef, was seriously injured in an accident on the farm. After this, the day-to-day operation of the farm fell more and more to Anton and Christina. In 1912, their son Alfred was born.

World War I lasted from 1914 to 1918. During that time, tens of millions of people were killed, including 60 000 Canadian troops. Stan Horvath, Anton's older brother, was killed fighting for his new country. Josef died in his sleep in 1916, happy in the belief that he had provided a good future for his family. Maria died a few months later.

The war made Europe more dependent on imported food. As a result, food prices increased and farm incomes boomed. The boom continued even after the war ended because Europe continued to need food imports as it slowly rebuilt itself.

The farm boom helped the Horvath family. The higher farm income allowed Anton and Christina to improve and modernize the farm. The major change was the purchase of a steam tractor (Fig. 10–10). It was the beginning of **mechanization.**

As the Roaring Twenties ended, the Horvaths and other Prairie farmers looked forward to a future of continued prosperity. The first news they heard of "Black Tuesday," which occurred in October of 1929, did not alarm them. That day marked the beginning of the collapse in stock market prices. Anton and Christina did not think Black Tuesday affected them since they did not own any stock. But they were mistaken.

Roaring Twenties: time of great prosperity during the 1920s

Fig. 10–10 Powerful steam tractors meant that one person could do the work of many and allowed prairie farmers to expand their farms.

Depression is the name used to describe the economic conditions of the 1930s. Sometimes this decade is called the "Dirty Thirties". After Black Tuesday, a great many companies went bankrupt. As a result, the number of unemployed people rose dramatically. The many unemployed had little money to spend. Therefore the demand for products was low. This, in turn, caused even more layoffs and more unemployment. Canada's economy slowed almost to a halt and thousands of people crossed the country looking for work.

The economic slowdown caused serious problems for the Horvaths. Lower demand for food in Canada and abroad caused lower prices and thus lower farm incomes. The reduction in income came at a very bad time for most Prairie farmers. Many of them, including the Horvaths, had long-term debts to pay.

Natural hazards increased the trials facing Prairie farmers. Many years were drier than normal. The effect of these dry conditions was devastating. Many farmers lost their farms because they could not pay their debts. The Horvaths were able to survive this period only because they were lucky enough to have a very good farm and because they made great sacrifices and lived very simply.

By the end of the 1930s, Anton, Christina, and their son Alfred, who now helped run the farm, were wondering if they were going to see good times again. In Europe, events were taking place that would end the Depression—but at great cost.

■ PROSPERITY RETURNS

World War II and the end of drought conditions both occurred at the end of the 1930s. The war put an end to unemployment because every able-bodied worker was required for military service, factory work, or farm labour. The demand for agricultural products shot up. At the same time that economic conditions changed, the pattern of rainfall and snowfall returned to normal. Crop yields again reached normal levels. With the higher prices and higher yields, farm income soared. In just a few years, Prairie farmers went from bust to boom.

In the 1930s, almost every day would bring a drifter to the Horvaths' farmhouse asking for work or for a handout. During the war, however, hired workers were not available. Often the whole family had to work full days in the fields as well as look after the three farmhouses and many barns that dotted the farm.

After the war, the great demand for food continued. Large areas in Europe and Asia had been damaged and were no longer in a condition to produce food crops. People needed food imports and there were only a few countries, including Canada, the U.S. and Australia, with the resources to produce the required extra food. The Horvaths prospered. They continued to add new machinery and new land to their farm. This expansion was made possible by the high farm income of these years.

It was during this period that the world's largest wheat field was laid out. This field, near Lethbridge, Alberta, was twice as big as the island of Bermuda!

As the years passed, the family changed. In 1968, Christina died at the age of 83. Maria, Anton's first child, had been a travelling nurse in northern Saskatchewan for more than 30 years. She had often been the only person who could provide medical care in the remotest regions of the province. She died in 1977. Anton's son Stan was the first Horvath to move to the city. A diesel mechanic, he settled in Winnipeg after serving in the airforce in World War II. Many of Anton's grandchildren and great-grandchildren have also done well. Alfred's son Peter decided that he wanted to become a farmer and eventually took over the family farm. Christine is a stockbroker in Toronto. Bill became a Member of Parliament in Ottawa. Debbie works in the Canadian High Commission Office in Hong Kong and is fluent in Chinese. Ian, who works on offshore drilling rigs, has been stationed in the Beaufort Sea.

■ IN CLOSING...

That night, after the crowd of relatives had left his birthday celebration, Anton thought about what had happened to his family since its arrival in Canada more than 90 years before. Someone in the family calculated that Anton's parents, Josef and Maria Horvath, had 152 Canadian descendants. These descendants of immigrants have helped enrich the economic and cultural life of Canada.

QUESTIONS

CHECKBACK

1. **a)** Why did World War I have positive effects for the Horvaths?
   b) How did they respond?
2. What are the characteristics of an economic depression?
3. How were the Horvaths affected by the Depression and the weather of the 1930s?
4. How did World War II affect the Horvaths?
5. Why did prosperity continue after the war?

INVESTIGATE

6. Prepare *your* family tree. If possible, try to trace it (on both parents' sides) back to its arrival in Canada. If you are a recent immigrant, trace your family tree back as far as possible. Try to determine how many members of your family are in Canada, where they live, and what sorts of jobs they have.
7. When the Horvaths arrived in Canada, the government was encouraging people to immigrate to Canada. Investigate current government policy on immigration.
8. Investigate how a person becomes a citizen today.

Metro International Caravan

Canada's population is made up of people from all over the world. How can we understand and appreciate Canadians whose culture, food, and religion may be different from our own? An ideal way would be to visit the countries from which people have emigrated. But this would be very expensive and time-consuming. There is an easier way to get to know our fellow Canadians. Many communities hold special events to recognize their cultural heritage. Those who live in the Toronto area, for example, can become world travellers without ever having to leave the city! This is done through an annual event called Caravan.

Key Terms

heritage

■ WHAT IS CARAVAN?

Is there a similar cultural festival where you live?

Caravan was started in 1969 as a non-profit event to highlight the artistic talents, culture, and food of the many ethnic groups in Metropolitan Toronto. The event encourages different ethnic communities to share their **heritage** with others. It gives people a chance to experience for themselves the uniqueness of each culture.

The name "Caravan" was chosen because it means a group of travellers going from place to place. Caravan is organized with this idea in mind. Each cultural organization (there are over 40) sets up a pavilion in a community centre, school, or church basement during the last nine days of June. Over 20 000 volunteers prepare the food and drink, decorate the halls, and provide the entertainment. Each pavilion is given the name of a city, such as Athens, Hong Kong, Kiev, St. John's, Waikiki, Port of Spain, or New Delhi. The pavilions are spread out across Metropolitan Toronto and are connected by special Caravan buses.

To attend Caravan you must first purchase a passport that gives you access to any of the pavilions. Caravan is financed by the sale of these passports. When you enter a pavilion, your passport is stamped, just as it is when you enter a country. Once inside, you

Fig. 10–11 In what Caravan pavilion would these dancers be found?

can hear traditional music, view arts, crafts and stage productions, sample the food and drink of the country, and maybe try one of the dances (Fig. 10–11).

It takes a great deal of work throughout the year to prepare for Caravan. Community members, however, find that the planning and practising together help them appreciate their own culture. Young people in particular become more familiar with their own heritage, which may be vastly different from what they are used to in their daily lives. Through the sale of handicrafts, food, and beverages, the pavilions raise money to maintain the cultural activities of their members.

Do people think Caravan is worthwhile? One way to judge is to remember that over two million passports are stamped during Metro Toronto International Caravan Week. What a great way to learn about other cultures!

QUESTIONS

CHECKBACK

1. Why was Caravan started?
2. a) Why was the name "Caravan" chosen?
   b) How is a visit to a pavilion like visiting a real country?
3. How does a community's participation in Caravan help its members?

4. **a)** Is there an ethnic festival where you live?
    b) What ethnic group or groups are involved?
    c) What activities are held?
    d) How does this festival reflect the cultural makeup of your community?
5. Organize a "mini-Caravan" in your class or school. You might be surprised at the number of cultural groups represented.

WHAT DO YOU THINK?

6. Do you think an event like Caravan is worthwhile? Why?

RURAL AND URBAN LANDSCAPES

UNIT FOUR

Settlement Patterns

Colleen Ryan is a fictional character but her account of flying over Canada is based on the experiences of an actual person.

Colleen Ryan is a Grade 10 student who lives in Calgary. During a discussion in her geography class, she told her friends about what she had seen on a recent trip.

"Last summer I flew to Halifax to visit my relatives. I had a window seat and as we flew eastward I noticed some interesting things about the land and the number of people who lived on it. There were large areas in which only a few people lived. For example, the Prairies had huge farms, and there were small isolated villages on the Shield. Occasionally we flew over a large town or city, and I was amazed to see how many people were packed into such a small area. And yet most of the time we were flying over huge areas of Canada that were almost empty."

The class raised two key questions after hearing about Colleen's trip. Where do people live in Canada? How many people live in a particular area? The teacher told the class that what they were discussing is referred to in geographic terms as population distribution and population density.

In Chapter 10 you learned how, when, and why people came to live in Canada. In this chapter you will learn about population distribution and density, and the patterns of population which exist outside Canada's towns and cities. Population patterns within towns and cities will be examined in Chapter 12.

Key Terms

population distribution	urbanization	concession system
population density	survey system	section system
urban	long lot system	settlement pattern
rural		

■ POPULATION DISTRIBUTION

In 1954, the Quaker Oats Company had a sales promotion in which 21 000 000 building lots in the Yukon were given away with cereal purchases. However, this promotion did not change Canada's population distribution very much because each of the lots was only 6.3cm² (1 in²) in area!

Population distribution refers to where people live. Distributions can be classified into one of two patterns. The first exists when the population is **dispersed** over an area (Fig. 11–1). The second pattern occurs when the population is **concentrated** in a few small areas, leaving other, larger areas almost empty of people (Fig. 11–2).

Canada's population is not evenly dispersed throughout the country. More than 90% of Canadians live in southern Canada within 600 km of the border with the U.S. This area represents only 10% of Canada's land area, but most of the major cities, farmland, and manufacturing industries are located here. The majority of Canadians today live in towns or cities.

POPULATION DENSITY

Population density refers to the number of people who live in a given area. Density is usually measured in terms of people per square kilometre. To calculate density, divide population by area. Population density, therefore, is an average of all the people in a given area, not a measure of where people live in that area. The average population density for Canada is 3 people/km². By comparison, the population density in the U.S. is 26 people/km² and in the United Kingdom it is 231 people/km². Canada's density is low because it is a large country (the second largest in the world) with a relatively small population (about 26 million).

Canada's population density varies from province to province and from area to area. For example, in the Northwest Territories there is an average of less than 1 person/km². Prince Edward Island has about 22 people/km². In large cities the density is naturally very high. Some areas with many apartments have densities of close to 10 000 people/km².

Sometimes two different areas have the same density but different distributions (Fig. 11–3). Each area has the same number of people per square kilometre, but the people in one area are spread out, and the people in the other are grouped together. Therefore, both density and distribution must be considered when describing an area's population pattern.

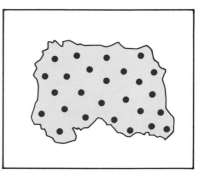

Fig. 11–1 Population on this island is evenly distributed

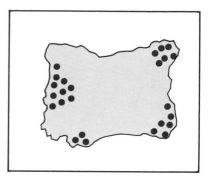

Fig. 11–2 Population on this island is unevenly distributed. It is concentrated in several places.

RURAL SETTLEMENT

When an area of Canada was settled, the population distribution which developed there depended on several factors.

The natural environment played an important role. The physical features of the land determined where people built their new homes. For example, pioneers settling in a mountainous area were restricted to the river valleys where flatter land and a good water supply could be found.

Another factor that affected the pioneer's choices was the period of settlement. An area settled in the 1700s was usually located near water because the most efficient transportation available at that time was by boat. Areas settled after 1850, on the other hand, were usually located along rail lines or roads.

A final but very important factor that determined where newcomers settled was government policy. The government created regulations that established one or more of the following:

- which land was to be settled
- where roads would be located
- the size of farms
- the location of townsites, schools, and churches
- the cost of land

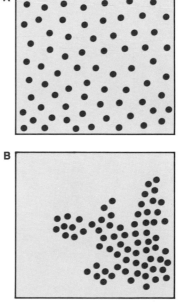

Fig. 11–3 These two areas have the same population density but different population distributions.

A set of regulations that determines the location of roads and the distances between them, the size and layout of farms, and the locations of towns, schools and churches, is called a **survey system**. Different survey systems were used by the governments in different parts of the country.

What exactly did all these different factors, and the choices made by the pioneers, do to the landscape of Canada? They created different **settlement patterns**. This means that the newcomers built their farms, roads, and towns, and used the land in different ways in different regions of the country. If you fly across the country today (or study topographic maps and aerial photographs), you can see how Canada's diversity results in part from differences in the way people settled the land. In the rest of this chapter you will learn about the major settlement patterns found in Canada, and why they developed where they did.

SOUTHERN QUÉBEC SETTLEMENT PATTERN (LONG LOTS)

The French settlers who first came to the St. Lawrence River Valley found a land and a climate entirely different from those of France. Settlers were faced with dense forests, long, cold winters, a few villages scattered along the river, and no roads. They developed a unique settlement pattern that enabled them to overcome the problems of the land.

In the earliest years of French settlement, the settlers used the rivers, particularly the St. Lawrence, for transportation. In winter they sledded across the frozen surfaces; in summer they sailed or paddled from place to place. Since each settler had to have access to the river, farmhouses were built side-by-side on narrow lots along the shore. The farms stretched back from the river in long, narrow strips called **long lots**. Taxes were based on the width of the long lot. The narrower the lot, the lower the farmer's taxes.

Eventually all the river lots were settled. By this time, however, there were enough people with sufficient time to build roads. These roads were built parallel to the rivers (Fig. 11–4). As each new family moved to the area, it was granted a narrow lot with frontage on a road. Just as the lots along the rivers were long and narrow, so too were those stretching away from the roads. The result of this settlement was the creation of **linear villages** that grew up along rivers and roads.

When French-Canadian settlers moved to other parts of Canada, they often took the linear settlement pattern with them. The long lot pattern is found today not only in Québec but also in parts of southwestern Ontario near Windsor, in southern Manitoba, in Saskatchewan, and in the Peace River district of Alberta.

What is it like to live in an area with the long lot settlement pattern? Anne-Marie is 16 and lives on a farm situated on the highway between Trois Rivières and Québec City.

Fig. 11–4 The long lot system is visible in southern Québec. Because neighbours lived close together, they helped each other build houses, barns and fences. In times of sickness and trouble neighbours aided a family in need.

"I really like living here because I can live on a farm and yet be close to my friends. Our nearest neighbours, the Tremblays and the Doucettes, are less than 100 m away. The nearest town is less than 1 km away. The only problem is that when we have some work to do on the property at the back of our farm, we have to walk more than 1 km to get there. It would be easier if we did not have to go so far."

This is a fictional account based on the experiences of many people living on farms.

SOUTHERN ONTARIO SETTLEMENT PATTERN (CONCESSION SYSTEM)

A survey system known as the **concession system** enabled immigrants to settle southern Ontario in an orderly and efficient manner. A main road called the **base line** was built either parallel or perpendicular to the shoreline of a Great Lake. This was the first concession road. More concession roads were built parallel to the first one at equal distances from one another. Side roads were constructed perpendicular to the concession roads and they too were the same distance apart (Fig. 11–5).

The intersection of concession roads (lines) and sideroads created blocks of land known as concessions. Within concessions, land was divided into farm lots of equal size. Farmhouses were built near the roads and square or rectangular farm fields stretched back into the interior of each block. **Townships** were formed by grouping concession blocks together. Counties, the largest political groups in Ontario, were formed by grouping several townships together (Fig. 11–6). Townships and counties differ in size and shape throughout the province.

The distances between concession roads and sideroads, and the size of individual farm lots, varied from county to county and from township to township in southern Ontario. As a result, the roads between townships often did not connect, unless a noticeable jog made the connection possible.

As you will see later in this chapter, townships in the Prairies are different from those in southern Ontario.

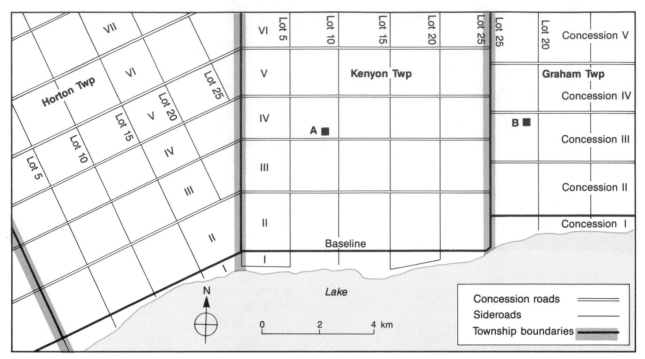

Fig. 11–5 The concession system of southern Ontario. Roads running parallel to the base line are concession roads and those running perpendicular to the base line are side roads. The strips of land between the concession roads are called *concessions* and are numbered with Roman numerals. The strips of land between sideroads are divided into *lots* and are numbered with Arabic numbers.

Early settlers needed waterpowered mills nearby to cut lumber and to grind wheat into flour.

Why did this block pattern, rather than the linear pattern, develop in southern Ontario? Southern Ontario was settled at a much later date than Québec. By this time road building techniques had improved so much that it was easier to build roads. Towns and villages grew up at the intersection of major roads or at mill sites on rivers, not in long straight lines as in Québec.

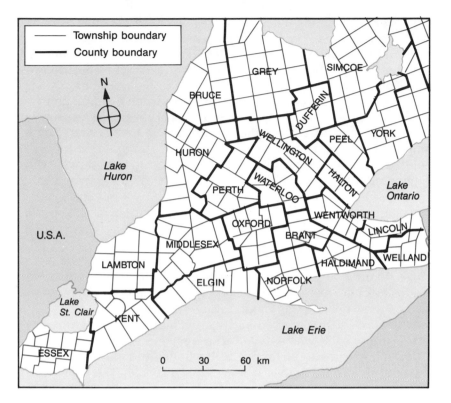

Fig. 11–6 Townships are grouped together to form counties.

What effect does such a settlement pattern have on peoples' lives today? Laura lives on a farm near Lake Huron, and will tell us how she feels about living there.

"I like living on our farm. My family works hard, and this land has provided my family with a living for more than 120 years. In the summer we swim in our pond and in the winter we can skate and go cross-country skiing. In the morning and evening I help my father milk our few dairy cows. Most of our cattle are raised for beef. I also raise some chickens for eggs, and sell vegetables from our garden to tourists who drive by on the highway. The main problem with living here is that it takes a long time to go anywhere. It's a three hour drive to go to Toronto for a concert or for shopping. The school bus trip is 45 minutes, and in the winter we often get snowed in. And sometimes, living on a farm can be a bit boring."

This is a fictional account based on the experiences of many people living on farms.

PRAIRIE SETTLEMENT PATTERN (SECTION SYSTEM)

In western Canada the government decided to survey the land before many settlers arrived. There were three major reasons for this. First, Canada was afraid that the U.S. might take over the Prairies. Second, the increase of the population in Ontario was creating a demand for new land. Third, the government wished to avoid the kinds of disputes that had arisen in parts of the western

The survey system sometimes caused problems in areas where the land was already settled by the Métis and others.

U.S. over land claims. These disputes occurred because the area had not been surveyed before settlement. A survey system that was fast and efficient was needed. The government therefore decided to copy the American system known as the **section system** (Fig. 11–7).

The 49th parallel (49°N), the border between Canada and the U.S. in the west, was used as a base line. Survey lines were drawn 6 miles (9.7 km) apart, parallel to the base lines, to create townships. Lines were then drawn 6 miles (9.7 km) apart in a north-south direction to create **ranges**. Both townships and ranges were numbered for easy identification (Fig. 11–8). The squares formed by the intersection of ranges and townships were also called townships. Each township was 36 miles² (94 km²) in area. A township was then subdivided into 36 one-square-mile blocks called sections.

The result was a pattern that looked like a chessboard. Some of these sections were granted to settlers for farming, some were set aside for schools, some for the railways, and some for the previous owner, the Hudson's Bay Company.

When the settlers arrived in the area, many of them from eastern Europe, each was entitled to a quarter-section plot of land called a homestead. If a family built a house and plowed a certain amount of land each year, it was allowed to keep the property it had been granted.

The farms on the Prairies are larger than those in other parts of Canada. Farmers need larger farms because climate and soil conditions make profits per hectare lower than in other farming regions.

Most towns and villages on the Prairies were located along rail lines so that farmers could store grain in elevators and load their products on the trains for shipment to the east and west. "Elevator towns" developed to serve farmers living in the surrounding countryside. When transportation was by horse and wagon, these towns grew up close together. As automobiles became common,

Fig. 11–7 The Prairie section system is visible in this aerial photograph. Originally each settler was given one section to farm. Many farmers expanded their farms by purchasing neighbouring farms. Is there evidence of this in the photograph? Why did some farmers expand their farms while others sold out?

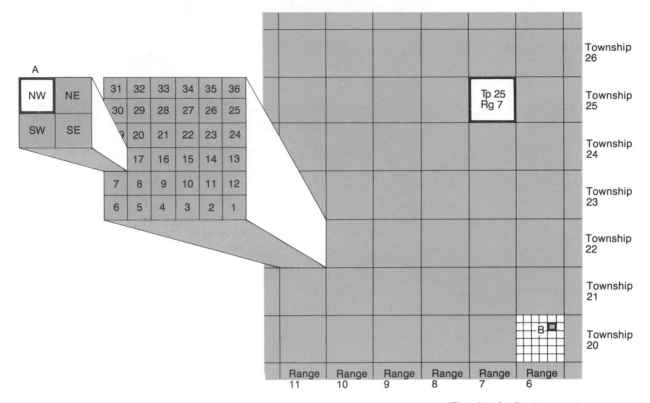

Fig. 11–8 Prairie section system. The intersection of Township rows and Range columns create *Prairie Townships*. The Townships are easily identified (for example, Tp 25 Rg 7).
Each *Township* is subdivided into 36 blocks called *sections*. Each section is given a number from 1 to 36. Each section is then subdivided into four quarter-sections. These can also be labelled.
The location of farm A is: subdivision NW, section 18, township 22, range 11.

farmers could travel further in the same amount of time. This meant that "elevator towns" could serve more farmers over a larger area, and thus be farther apart. As a result, some towns grew larger while those in between no longer provided elevator services.

Would you like to live on the Prairies? Dave is 15 and lives on a farm in southwestern Manitoba. What are his thoughts on living there?

"This must be the best place in Canada to live. I really like the wide-open spaces. I hope to take over the farm from my father later on. The main problem out here is that things are so spread out. I don't have my driver's licence yet and it can be difficult getting to my best friend's house. He lives on the next farm 3 km away. I also have to go 20 km each way to school every day."

■ ISOLATED SETTLEMENTS

In southern Ontario and Québec, and on the Prairies, survey systems were imposed by the government. The physical features of the land were carefully noted in the Dominion Land Survey. Survey lines did not need to follow physical boundaries because the land in these regions is relatively flat.

In other areas of Canada, however, the land is more rugged and is not suitable for farming. Most of these regions offer something quite different—a natural resource such as fish, trees, minerals or hydro-electric power sites. People are attracted to certain areas by these resources and live in communities located far from the main populated areas of Canada. Such **resource-based settlements** are frequently isolated, and are settled as the resource is demanded.

The fishing communities on both coasts developed because of the rich offshore fishing grounds. The fact that the interior of the country was almost impassable was not important. The people used the sea as their highway. The result was a pattern of settlement consisting of a scattering of villages along the coast with few, if any, land connections by road (Fig. 11–9). Most road connections have been built in the last 50 years.

Other **isolated settlements** are found in Canada's north. Many of them are resource-based towns that have grown up where minerals such as nickel, silver, lead and zinc are present and can be mined. Others are government centres for the district in which they are located. They provide such services as medical care, R.C.M.P. stations, schools, and stores.

For many of these isolated settlements, the only year-round contact with the outside is by air. For some, such as those on the Arctic islands, the summer months also bring contact by ship. Some settlements are serviced by convoys of tractors that travel over the frozen muskeg during the winter.

What is it like to live in an isolated town? Grant is 15 and lives in a small community in the Yukon where lead, zinc, and silver are mined.

"I like living in our small town because I know everyone. Most of us were born in southern Canada and moved to the north when our parents got jobs with the mining company. I would rather live here than in a big city because there's no air pollution or traffic noise. Also, I enjoy exploring the wilderness that surrounds us. I like to go hunting and fishing with my family. At the same time I am glad that we get Canadian and American television programs and many radio stations now that our community has a satellite dish. My biggest complaint about living in the north is the high cost of things like clothes, records, and magazines. My parents sometimes complain about the cost of such things as milk, eggs, and vegetables. Much of our food has to be brought in from the south. Some day I will probably have to leave my town to go to college in a city in southern Canada. But I hope to return and get a job in the north."

■ URBANIZATION

In 1867, when Canada first became a country, 82% of its people lived on farms in the countryside — that is, in **rural** areas. Very few people lived in cities, or **urban** areas. The country's population was dispersed across the land. Since that time, however, cities and towns have grown enormously in both size and number. Today, more than 75% of Canada's population lives in urban areas, and the density of population in these areas is usually very high.

Canada's urban geography is examined in Chapters 12-14.

It is possible to calculate the proportion of the population that lives in towns and cities, and the proportion that lives in the countryside in the following way:

$$\frac{\text{rural population}}{\text{total population}} \times 100\% \quad \text{OR} \quad \frac{\text{urban population}}{\text{total population}} \times 100\%$$

When the percentage of the population that is urban increases over the years, the country is in the process of **urbanization.**

What caused the change in the distribution of population, and why do urban areas now have such high densities? Over the years, as agricultural machinery improved, fewer workers were needed on the farms. These workers came to towns and cities in search of work. As more jobs in manufacturing and service industries were created in the cities, both farm workers and immigrants flocked to the cities to take advantage of these jobs.

Urbanization changed not only the distribution of Canada's population but also affected population density. City dwellers live in houses built on small lots, or in apartments. These housing patterns create a high population density.

■ IN CLOSING . . .

In this chapter we have seen that settlement patterns are determined by the physical landscape, the decisions of government, the date of settlement, and the needs of people. Because these factors were never the same, the rural settlement patterns are different all across Canada. As new areas in Canada's north are opened up in the future there will, perhaps, be new settlement patterns to add to the list.

1. **a)** Define the terms "distribution" and "density" in your own words.

   b) Draw two squares of the same size. Add dots to show the same population density but different population distributions.

   c) Is Canada's population dispersed or concentrated? Explain.

2. Briefly describe three factors that helped to determine the settlement pattern which developed in different regions of Canada.

3. **a)** Identify the survey systems shown in Figs. 11–4, 11–5, and 11–7.

   b) Describe in words how the land has been divided in each system. Each description should be two or three sentences in length.

4. **a)** Why do Prairie farms tend to be larger that those in other parts of Canada?

   b) The relatively great distances between farms on the Prairies often caused problems for settlers. What might these have been? Do such problems exist today? Why or why not?

5. **a)** State two reasons why isolated settlements exist.

   b) How can modern transportation and telecommunications help to overcome isolation?

6. Define the terms "rural" and "urban."

Fig. 11–10 The increasing urbanization of Canada between 1881 and 1981.

Year	Rural Population	Urban Population	Total Population
1881	3 215 000	1 110 000	4 325 000
1901	3 357 000	2 014 000	5 371 000
1921	4 436 000	4 352 000	8 788 000
1941	5 254 000	6 252 000	11 506 000
1961	5 538 000	12 700 000	18 238 000
1981	5 907 000	18 436 000	24 343 000

7. **a)** Fig. 11–10 shows Canada's rural and urban populations since 1881. Draw a graph to illustrate the rural and urban population changes. Fig. 11–11 shows you how to get started.

   b) What has happened to the rural population between 1881 and 1981?

   c) What has happened to the urban population during the same time period?

   d) What do you think will happen by the year 2001? Show this on your graph.

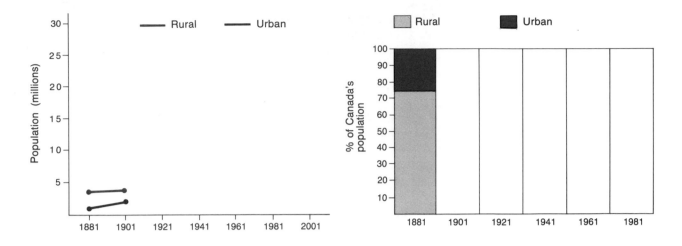

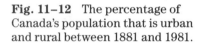

Fig. 11–11 Urban and rural population changes between 1881 and 2001.

Fig. 11–12 The percentage of Canada's population that is urban and rural between 1881 and 1981.

8. **a)** Calculate the percentage of the population that was rural and the percentage that was urban in each of the years shown in Fig. 11–10. Use these percentages to complete Fig. 11–12 in your notes.
   b) What happened to the rural/urban balance?
   c) Why did this occur?

9. **a)** Draw a sketch map of a farm in Québec based on the following description:
   Because taxes were based on the amount of river frontage owned, most farms were long and narrow (150 m by 1.5 km for example). The farmhouse was built close to the river to make travel easier. Behind the house, a garden provided fruits and vegetables. Beyond the garden would be fields of wheat, oats, and barley. Farther still from the farmhouse were pastures where horses, cows and oxen would graze. At the very back of the farm was the woodlot that provided lumber for construction and firewood.
   b) Why is this organization of land not surprising?

   Hint: consider the daily chores to be done on the farm.

   c) In Québec, as in many places, when sons reached adulthood, the farmer would divide the land and give each son a strip of the farm.
   i. Draw a rectangle 2 cm by 10 cm to represent a Québec farm. Divide this farm so each of four sons receives an equal share.
   ii. What problems can you see developing after two or three generations?
   iii. How might these problems be solved?

10. Examine Fig. 11–5. Give a full description of the location of farm B.

11. Examine Fig. 11–8. Locate Township B in the southeastern corner of the map. One of the sections is shaded in. Give a full description of the location of the farm in the northeast quarter section of the shaded township.

INVESTIGATE

12. What type of settlement pattern exists in the rural area near you? From the aerial photograph or map of your area provided by your teacher, draw an overlay map on acetate or tracing paper to show the location of farms and communities.
13. If you live in a large city, can you find any evidence of the rural settlement pattern that existed before the city grew to its present size? Draw a sketch map to illustrate this evidence.
14. Will Canada become even more urbanized in the future? What countries of the world are most urbanized today? Could Canada reach this level?

WHAT DO YOU THINK?

15. a) What are the advantages and disadvantages of living in an isolated community?
    b) If you live in an isolated community:
       Would you like to live in a large city? What adjustments in your life would be necessary?
    c) If you live in an urban community:
       Would you like to live in an isolated community? What adjustments in your life would be necessary?
16. There are increasing numbers of people who are moving to rural areas but who do not farm the land. This group is known as the rural non-farm population.
    a) Why would people want to live in a rural setting but not want to farm the land?
    b) How might these people earn a living?

Urban Patterns and Growth

Do you live in a city, a small town, or in the country? Most likely you live in a town or city. This is a safe guess since more than 75% of Canadians live in urban areas. This concentration of people is shown well by an isodemographic map (Fig. 12–1). Most maps are drawn in proportion to their land areas. On an isodemographic map, however, areas are drawn in proportion to their population. The concentration of population in the urban centres in southern Canada is clearly shown on this map.

Why do towns and cities develop in certain places and not in others? What roles do towns and cities play? What is it like to live in urban places of different sizes? In this chapter you will find out.

Fig. 12–1 On this isodemographic map, the areas of provinces, territories, and cities are in proportion to their populations.

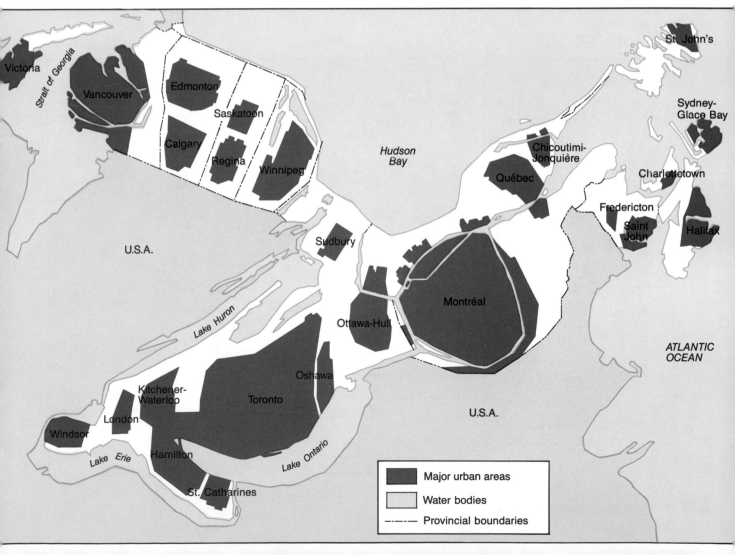

Key Terms

hamlet	city	census metropolitan area (CMA)
services	urban functions	diversified urban centre
village	multiplier effect	service centre
town	economic base	resource-based community

■ THE STORY OF LITTLETON

To help you understand how and why towns and cities develop, we will look at a geographical model of an imaginary city. A model is a simplified description of real life. It makes real life situations easier to understand. In our model we will concentrate on the characteristics of urban growth that are common to most cities. Once you understand why our model city grows, you can more easily understand the particular growth pattern of any other city.

When a certain fertile area in Canada was settled over a century ago, almost all the pioneers were farmers. The one exception was a miller. He opened a gristmill (building #1 in Fig. 12–2) by a

gristmill: a mill where grain is ground into flour

Fig. 12–2 Hamlet of Littleton

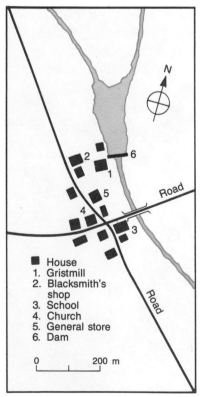

House
1. Gristmill
2. Blacksmith's shop
3. School
4. Church
5. General store
6. Dam

0   200 m

Fig. 12–3 Village of Littleton

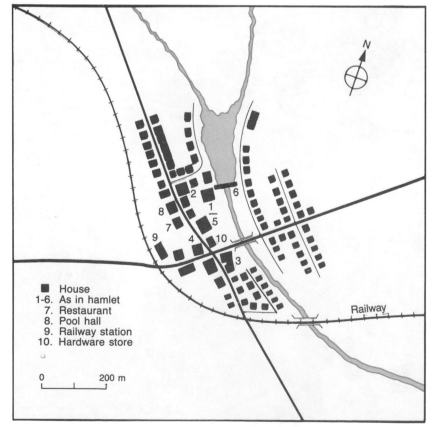

House
1-6. As in hamlet
7. Restaurant
8. Pool hall
9. Railway station
10. Hardware store

0   200 m

waterfall. This waterfall was situated near a crossroads. Two years later, a blacksmith arrived and set up a shop in the area (building #2). The following year a merchant opened a general store (building #5) next to the blacksmith's shop. Within ten years, a small community with a church and a one-room schoolhouse had grown up. Such a small community is called a **hamlet**. This hamlet became known as Littleton.

With the passage of time, some hamlets grow larger than others. Littleton was one that grew. Why? Littleton was located at a crossroads where a great deal of traffic passed by. When farmers drove through, they found it convenient to stop and do some shopping. Therefore, in addition to its basic **services**, Littleton soon had a hardware store, a restaurant, and a pool hall (Fig. 12-3).

As services increased, more people moved into Littleton to take jobs. When the one-room schoolhouse became too small to hold all the children, a three-room elementary school took its place. When a railway was built in the region, it passed through Littleton and brought more newcomers with it. The population increased to 800. Littleton was now a **village**.

As the years passed, Littleton continued to grow. The expanding population needed more services. A weekly newspaper was published; many new stores and a regional high school were built. The local carpenter began constructing new homes on the outskirts of the village. Soon the population numbered 2000. Littleton had become a **town** (Fig. 12–4).

Thirty years later the population of Littleton had grown to more than 10 000. The town could now be called a **city**. The city council changed the name of the community to Bigton (Fig. 12–5). Other things changed as well. The area near the waterfall was made into a park, and the old gristmill was converted into a museum. The weekly newspaper became a daily publication. Factories were built on the outskirts of Bigton on what had been farmers' fields. Bigton soon became the district capital, and more people moved into the city to help run the local government. Large housing developments were built to accommodate the influx of people. The population of Bigton and its surrounding region was now large enough to support services such as a college, a hospital, and a large department store. These are all **urban functions** not found in smaller urban communities.

Bigton grew because of the **multiplier effect**. For example, when a new factory was built, 100 workers moved to Bigton to work in it. These workers and their families (about 300 people in all) needed housing, schools, shops, banks, restaurants, and medical facilities. In order to supply all these goods and services, more workers and their families—an additional 600 people—moved to Bigton. The total addition to the city's population was approximately 900—all as a result of the original 100 jobs in the new factory.

influx: the coming in, or arrival of people

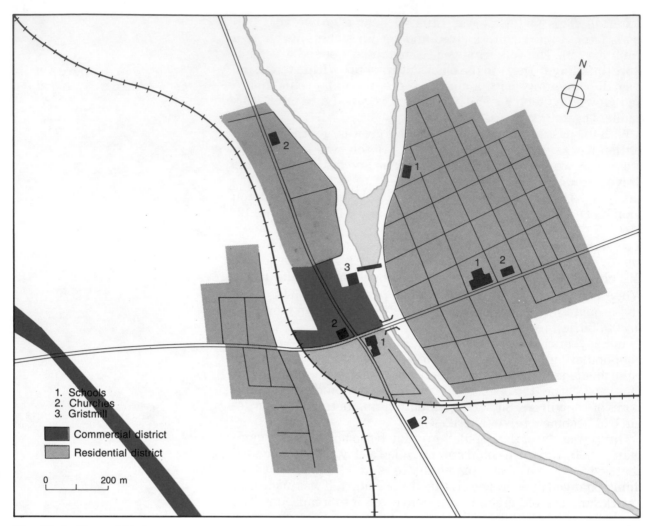

Fig. 12–4   Town of Littleton

1. Schools
2. Churches
3. Gristmill

■ Commercial district

▨ Residential district

0   200 m

Canada's census metropolitan areas (CMAs) are listed in Fig. 18–1 on page 235.

Only a few cities across Canada have grown to more than 100 000 people, and Bigton is one of them. Because of its size and importance, the city of Bigton is now referred to as a **census metropolitan area (CMA)** (see Fig. 12–6). It now contains many manufacturing industries, retail businesses, and services such as insurance, banking, and government. Bigton's downtown area has many large office buildings, and it is here that most of the major business and government decisions are made.

Fig. 12–6   Populations in different types of urban centres.

hamlet:	less than 100
village:	100 - 1000
town:	1 000 - 10 000
city:	10 000 or more
census metropolitan area:	a city with more than 100 000

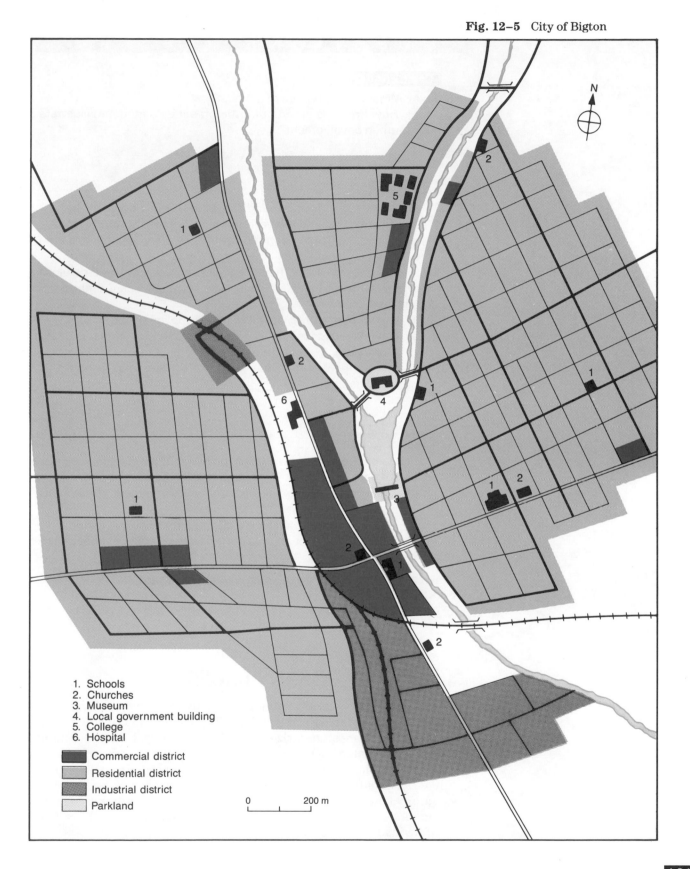

Fig. 12–5 City of Bigton

1. Schools
2. Churches
3. Museum
4. Local government building
5. College
6. Hospital

▮ Commercial district
▮ Residential district
▮ Industrial district
▮ Parkland

0   200 m

1. **a)** What is the purpose of a model?
   b) How does the growth of Littleton act as a model to illustrate urban development?

ANALYZE

2. **a)** Where did i) the miller and ii) the blacksmith locate? Why?
   b) How did their location affect the future of Littleton/Bigton?
3. How does the size of a community influence the number and type of activities found in it?
4. Make a chart to show the differences in population and services offered among a hamlet, village, town, city, and census metropolitan area.
5. **a)** In your own words, describe the multiplier effect.
   b) How would the multiplier effect work in a town that has a new factory employing 500 people?
   c) The multiplier effect can work in reverse. Explain how this could happen.

INVESTIGATE

6. Research the historical roots of the community in which you live, or one near your home. Examine the following:
   a) The original location of the community and the reasons for its location at that spot.
   b) The factors that caused the community to grow or shrink.
   c) When and why change occurred from one size of community to another.

TYPES OF URBAN PLACES

In the previous section you learned why and how the hamlet of Littleton grew into the major city of Bigton. The major steps in the city's growth are summarized in Fig. 12–7. Today, Bigton has many functions, including providing services, acting as a transportation centre, and manufacturing. A city that has many urban functions like this is called a **diversified urban centre**.

Many communities have a variety of urban functions. In some communities, however, one function dominates the others. The following four cities are examples of this.

Event	Role of the Urban Place
1. Littleton formed as a hamlet	provided services to nearby farmers (mill, blacksmith)
2. Littleton grew	more services (general store, church, school)
3. Littleton became a village	transportation centre (railway) more services (retail stores, restaurant, pool hall, larger school)
4. Littleton became a town	more services (weekly newspaper, high school, more retail stores) some manufacturing industries
5. Littleton became a city	more services (daily newspaper, government, hospital, large department store, college) more manufacturing industries

Fig. 12–7 Stages in the growth of Littleton

THUNDER BAY: A TRANSPORTATION HUB

Thunder Bay is located on a flat area between Lake Superior and the highlands of the Canadian Shield (Fig. 12–8). The city was created in 1970 when the cities of Fort William and Port Arthur were combined. The importance of Thunder Bay's location on the western shore of Lake Superior was recognized as long ago as the early 1800s. At that time, the community of Fort William was the most important inland fur-trading centre for the North-West Company. The Canadian Pacific Railway was built through the area in 1885, and the Canadian Northern Railway (now part of the Canadian National Railway) in 1902. This link meant that grain could be shipped by rail from western Canada to Thunder Bay, where it was loaded onto ships for transport through the Great Lakes. This was done because ships can carry bulk cargoes, like grain, more cheaply than can trains. With the opening of the St. Lawrence Seaway in 1959, ocean-going ships could travel directly from abroad to Thunder Bay to load grain. Thunder Bay now has the world's largest facility for handling grain. There are 15 grain elevators in the port that are capable of storing over two million tonnes of grain. Railway lines and the Trans-Canada Highway pass through the city.

Grain is not the only commodity handled by this transportation centre. Forest products from the Shield, as well as coal and potash from the west, are funnelled through the port.

FREDERICTON: A SERVICE CENTRE

Fredericton was founded by Loyalists in 1783. At that time, large amounts of land were set aside for various services. Government buildings, a military headquarters, churches, and schools were later built on this land. Fredericton became the centre of provincial government as well as the military, religious, and cultural focus of the British colony of New Brunswick.

The Loyalists are people who came to Canada from the U.S. after the American Revolution. They preferred to continue to live in a British colony.

Fig. 12–8 Notice how the land use of Thunder Bay is dominated by transportation facilities.

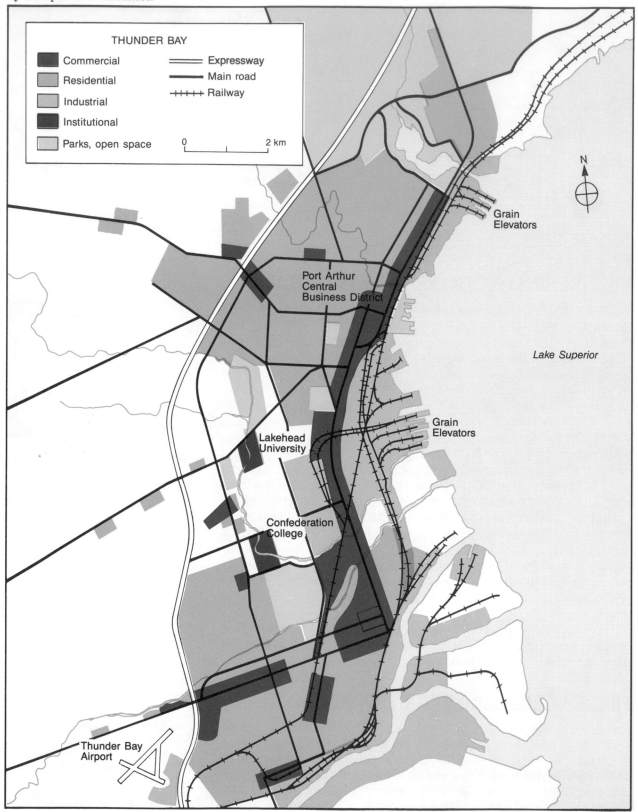

THUNDER BAY

- Commercial
- Residential
- Industrial
- Institutional
- Parks, open space

=== Expressway
━━━ Main road
++++ Railway

0   2 km

Grain Elevators

Port Arthur Central Business District

Lake Superior

Lakehead University

Grain Elevators

Confederation College

Thunder Bay Airport

Fig. 12–9 Fredericton provides services for a large area.

Today, Fredericton is the capital city of New Brunswick (Fig. 12-9). As the centre of government for the province, it offers employment to many people. These people need services such as stores, banks, medical facilities, and schools. The presence of government contributes to Fredericton's function as a **service centre**.

Fredericton is a centre of higher education. It is the home of the University of New Brunswick and attracts students from across the province and other parts of the country. The city must provide these students with services such as food stores and lodging facilities. The presence of the university further contributes to Fredericton's function as a service centre.

PORT ALBERNI: A RESOURCE-BASED COMMUNITY

Many cities and towns in Canada are **resource-based communities**. They exist because of the presence of a natural resource such as timber, minerals, or water that can be harnessed for hydro-electric power. Port Alberni is located about 200 km north of Victoria on Vancouver Island at the head of Alberni Inlet (Fig. 12-10). It was founded at this location because the timber resources of the region could be easily shipped out of the Inlet. Today, the lumber industry is still Port Alberni's major industry. Equipment for the lumber industry is manufactured and serviced in the city. It is British Columbia's third largest port by volume of shipments.

Fig. 12-10 Port Alberni exists because of the combination of forest resources and easy transportation.

Not all resource-based communities are as close to major urban centres as Port Alberni. Some are located in remote areas and lack road access to the rest of the country. In the past, people worked only for short periods in these isolated places because they became lonely away from friends, relations, and the activity of populated areas. To counteract this isolation, companies built communities nearby for workers and their families. Many of these resource-based communities are well-planned and pleasant places in which to live. They have shopping plazas, recreation centres, and modern schools. Thompson, Manitoba, built by the International Nickel Company, is an example of such a community.

PETERBOROUGH: A MANUFACTURING COMMUNITY

Peterborough began as a resource-based community. During the 1870s it was Ontario's major timber producer. As the local timber resources ran out, the community needed a different **economic base**.

For a long time, lumber and grist mills had used the rivers of the Peterborough region as a source of power to drive the water wheels on the mills. These rivers were later used for the development of hydro-electric power. This resource was very attractive to manufacturing industries needing cheap power.

Hydro-electricity was developed along the Trent River system even before the development of power at Niagara Falls in 1881.

Peterborough was well-connected by rail and roads to Toronto and other major urban markets of southern Ontario and Québec. The city further increased its attractiveness to manufacturing companies by offering cheap land and tax benefits. As a result, large corporations such as Canadian General Electric and Quaker Oats, as well as many smaller manufacturing companies, settled in Peterborough.

1. Make a list of five services that a town or city can offer to its surrounding region.
2. **a)** What are resource-based communities?
   b) Describe the characteristics of this type of community.

ANALYZE

3. A large, skilled labour force and transportation facilities are two things that make manufacturing possible. Name three additional factors that make manufacturing possible in an urban area and explain how each helps manufacturing industries to develop.
4. Most of Canada's manufacturing occurs in the cities of southern Ontario and southern Quebec. Explain how the concentration of manufacturing here makes it difficult for cities in other regions to develop manufacturing industries.

INVESTIGATE

5. Name five port cities in Canada. What types of products are shipped through each?
6. The following Canadian cities and towns have one main function. In your notebook, match the city with the function.

   1. Hamilton, Ont.   a) service centre (government)
   2. Banff, Alta.   b) service centre (university)
   3. Ottawa, Ont.   c) mining centre
   4. Iqaluit (Frobisher Bay),
      N.W.T.   d) manufacturing centre
   5. Labrador City,
      (Labrador) Nfld.   e) service centre (tourism)
   6. Thunder Bay, Ont.   f) service centre (region)
   7. Waterloo, Ont.   g) port city

■ WHAT IS IT LIKE TO LIVE IN. . .?

What is it like to live where you live? If you were asked to write about where you live, what would you say?

Let's make a brief comparison between two communities that are quite close together in distance and yet quite far apart in lifestyle. Let's see what it is like to live in the small town of Picton, Ontario and in Canada's largest city, Toronto.

PICTON

What would one expect a small town to be like?

To the casual visitor, Picton is very much what one would expect a small southern Ontario town to be. Picton is a quiet, historic town, situated about 185 km east of Toronto on the Bay of Quinte.

Picton was founded in 1837 by descendants of United Empire Loyalists. These were people who had left the U.S. because they were loyal to the British king. Even today, more than 80 percent of Picton's inhabitants have British ancestry.

county seat: the location of the county government

Picton developed as a main service centre for Prince Edward County because it was the county seat and a trading centre. Today it has another function as a centre for tourism. People who spend their holiday in the southern part of the Bay of Quinte or at the nearby resorts and campgrounds (such as Sandbanks Provincial Park) use the services that Picton offers.

In 1921, Picton's population was 3356. Today it is 4235. As you can see, it has grown quite slowly. Consequently, few of Picton's buildings are new and many are historic. The town has attractive streetscapes with many mature trees (Fig. 12–11).

Because Picton has few job opportunities, many of the town's young people leave to find employment elsewhere. On the other hand, it is an attractive place to live for retired people. This has contributed to an older population.

Picton's Amenities

amenities: anything that increases comfort or convenience.

Picton has most of the services that a family might want. These include:

- elementary and high schools
- hardware, clothing, and other stores
- restaurants
- fair grounds
- bowling alley
- golf course
- drive-in cinema (summer only)
- hospital
- supermarkets
- library
- arena
- hotel and motels
- cable television
- yacht club

Fig. 12–11 Picton is typical of many small towns in Canada.

Advantages and Disadvantages of Living in Picton

In a survey of attitudes toward living in Picton, the following opinions were given:

Advantages

- "In Picton, you get to know everyone. Community spirit and community activities are important. In a pinch you know you can depend on the people in town."
- "Picton's just the right size. No traffic, no pollution, no noise. If you can't buy things here, it's a short trip to Belleville or even Kingston."
- "I don't have to spend my life in the car here. It's five minutes to work and five minutes to shop."
- "Everything is here for recreation. I can walk to the yacht club in ten minutes. In winter we can go ice fishing or skating on the harbour."

Disadvantages

- "It's a great spot for kids and old people, but there just aren't enough jobs. Some local factories have closed down. Kids graduating from school have to go to Belleville, Trenton, Kingston, or even Toronto for a job."
- "It's pretty boring here for teenagers. The movie theatre is closed, there are no big record stores, no drive-in restaurants, and the nightlife is really limited. If you don't have a car to take you to Belleville, you're stuck."

TORONTO

To some, Toronto is "the city that works" — a world-class city that has grown enormously and yet has avoided the problems that plague many other cities. To others, it is still "Hogtown". In either case, Toronto is a city about which people have strong opinions.

Before we can discuss Toronto, it is necessary to decide exactly what (and where) we are talking about. The built-up area centred around Toronto extends from Oshawa in the east to Hamilton in the west, and north to Richmond Hill. Within this area it is difficult to decide where one city begins and another ends. At least three "Torontos" can be identified (Fig. 12–12).

The City of Toronto is only one of the six municipalities that make up Metropolitan Toronto. It currently has a population of 612 000. When most people refer to Toronto, they are talking about Metropolitan Toronto (population 2 193 000). But Toronto has grown far beyond the Metropolitan Toronto boundaries. The Toronto census metropolitan area (CMA) is the continuously built-up area which extends beyond the other two Torontos. It has a population of 3 427 000. In this chapter, when we talk of Toronto we will be referring to the CMA definition.

Hogtown: Toronto was given this nickname during the early part of the 20th century. It referred to the fact that Toronto dominated the economic life of Ontario, had an excessive share of the province's wealth, and was an unexciting place without a big-city outlook.

Fig. 12–12 "Three Torontos"

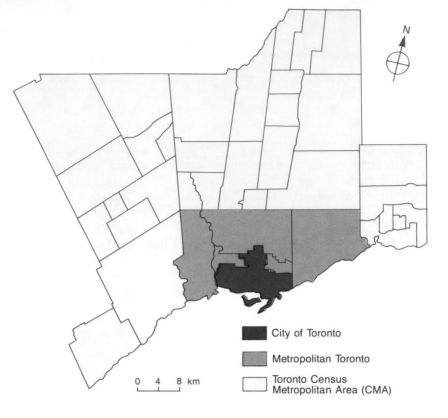

City of Toronto

Metropolitan Toronto

Toronto Census
Metropolitan Area (CMA)

0   4   8 km

Toronto (originally known as York) was founded by John Graves Simcoe in 1793. It became the new capital of Upper Canada (now Ontario) in 1794. When new roads were built to link the capital with the rest of the province, Toronto became the focus of road and rail routes. Manufacturing and business services developed and Toronto became the most important commercial city in the province. The result is that Toronto, like most large cities, has a diversified economy.

Fig. 12–13 Ethnic composition of Toronto (1986)

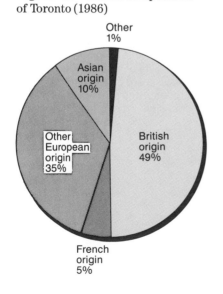

Other
1%

Asian
origin
10%

Other
European
origin
35%

British
origin
49%

French
origin
5%

Toronto's Population

Before World War II, Toronto's population was much like Picton's — predominantly British. In 1921 the population was 522 000, of which 85% were of British origin. After World War II this changed completely. Hundreds of thousands of immigrants moved to Toronto from all over the world. Today, only 49% of Toronto's population has British ancestry (Fig. 12–13).

The first major influx of new immigrants came from Italy in the 1950s and 1960s. Then came Portuguese in the 1960s and 1970s. More recently, there have been major influxes of Chinese, West Indians, and South Americans. Today, Toronto is one of the most multicultural cities in the world (Fig. 12–14).

Toronto's Amenities

In a city as large as Toronto, it is impossible to list all of the services available. In fact, there are relatively few things that are not available. Some of the major features of the city are:

- more than 25 hospitals
- two major universities
- thousands of restaurants of all types
- more than 175 movie theatres
- several major museums and art galleries
- professional hockey, baseball, football, and soccer teams
- the third largest number of live theatres in any North American city
- appearances by the world's leading performers

Advantages and Disadvantages of Living in Toronto

A survey of attitudes about living in Toronto yielded the following.

Advantages

- "Everything is here. Toronto has almost all the advantages of New York or Los Angeles with few of the problems."
- "The city's many cultures produce an exciting, stimulating place in which to live."
- "The growth of Toronto means that there are many jobs available. The unemployment rate is the lowest in the country."

Disadvantages

- "Toronto's great if you have the money to take advantage of what's here. If you're poor it's a tough place to live."
- "Toronto is too large and too busy. The traffic is awful. I have a one-hour trip each way on a crowded bus and subway to and from work."
- "Toronto's not as perfect as people say. Some people sleep in the street and search garbage cans for food. Too many people care too much about earning a buck and not enough about people."

Fig. 12–14 Toronto has a greater multicultural mix than other Canadian cities.

The cultural diversity of Canada is discussed in Chapter 10. Toronto's multicultural festival, Caravan, is described in a complementary study in that chapter.

■ IN CLOSING...

There are both positive and negative aspects to living in a large city like Toronto or in a small town like Picton. What one person considers an advantage, another might view as a disadvantage. Regardless of the size of your community, it probably suits your interests and meets your needs. If not, Canada has a wide variety of urban and rural places from which you could choose a new home in the future!

ANALYZE

1. **a)** Construct a chart to summarize the positive and negative features of living in Picton and Toronto.
   b) Prepare a similar summary chart for the place where you live.

WHAT DO YOU THINK?

2. **a)** Discuss with a group of your classmates the characteristics of an ideal community in which to live.
   b) Write a short report describing the characteristics of the community you would like to live in after you leave school. Be sure to describe both the advantages and disadvantages of your choice.

Urban Dominance

When we think about France, we usually think first of the city of Paris. When we think about England and the Soviet Union, London and Moscow come quickly to mind. These are the dominant cities of their countries. A country's dominant city is referred to as its **metropolis**. It is a city that is very important in the life of a country. A metropolis has a large population. It also has great political, economic, and cultural influence over the country in which it is found. This is referred to as **metropolitan dominance**. Most countries have only one metropolis. A few have more than one.

Key Terms

metropolis   metropolitan dominance

■ DETERMINING CANADA'S METROPOLIS

How can we determine which city is Canada's metropolis? In this study we will compare Vancouver, Edmonton, Calgary, Winnipeg, Toronto, Montréal and Halifax. Each of these cities is very influential in its own region, but which is most important in Canada? Fig. 12–15 lists the information that we will use to determine which city is Canada's metropolis.

1. For each item in Fig. 12–15, score each city according to the following system:

15	10	6	4	2	1	0
for 1st	for 2nd	for 3rd	for 4th	for 5th	for 6th	for 7th

   In the case of ties, average the points of the tied cities (round to the nearest whole point). Example: Toronto and Montréal are tied for 4th and 5th place for item 3. Points earned are $(4+2)/2 = 3$. Give each city 3 points.

2. Draw a chart similar to Fig. 12–16 in your notebook, and place the number of points earned in the correct spaces on it. (See examples calculated for population.)

If you have access to a microcomputer and a spreadsheet program you may wish to use them for this exercise.

	Vancouver	Edmonton	Calgary	Winnipeg	Toronto	Montréal	Halifax
1. Population in thousands	1381	785	671	625	3427	2921	296
2. City's population as percentage of province's population	48	33	28	58	38	45	34
3. Distance to nearest other city on list (Km)	700	300	300	1150	500	500	850
4. Number of House of Commons seats	13	8	7	7	31	29	3
5. Attractiveness to migrants from other provinces	moderate	moderate	moderate	low	high	moderate	low
6. Stock market sales ($millions)	4485	0	476	0.6	63 684	15 982	0
7. Bank head offices	4	1	0	0	52	8	0
8. Number of years with NHL team	21	10	9	10	58	58	0
9. Number of major professional sports teams	2	2	2	2	3	2	0
10. Number of magazines published	130	39	48	60	695	244	14
11. Number of professional theatres	9	5	1	3	26	12	2
12. Percentage of Canada's manufacturing	3.7	3	1.2	1.6	16	12	0.8

Fig. 12–15 Some measures of a city's metropolitan importance

QUESTIONS

CHECKBACK

1. Define metropolis and metropolitan dominance.

ANALYZE

2. Indicate how each of the following items in Fig. 12–15 helps show the importance of a city.
   a) items 1 and 2   e) items 6 and 7
   b) item 3   f) items 8 and 9
   c) item 4   g) items 10 and 11
   d) item 5   h) item 12
3. a) Using total scores, rank the cities in the study.
   b) Which city(ies) would qualify as Canada's metropolis(es)?

	Vancouver	Edmonton	Calgary	Winnipeg	Toronto	Montréal	Halifax
1. Population	6	4	2	1	15	10	0
2. Percentage of provincial population							
3. Distance to nearest large city							
4. House of Commons seats							
5. Attractiveness to migrants							
6. Stock market sales							
7. Bank head offices							
8. NHL history							
9. Professional sports teams							
10. Magazines							
11. Theatres							
12. Manufacturing							
TOTALS							

Scoring system: first – 15 points; second – 10 points; third – 6 points; fourth – 4 points; fifth – 2 points; sixth – 1 point; seventh – 0 points.

Fig. 12–16 Metropolitan city scoreboard

INVESTIGATE

4. In this question, consider only Brazil, Mexico, U.S.A., Australia, Italy, and Japan.
   a) Choose three countries, each of which has only one metropolis.
   b) Choose three countries, each of which has two metropolises.
   c) To which group would you expect Canada to belong?
   d) Is this in fact the case?

13 Urban Land Use

Fig. 13–1 illustrates several familiar urban scenes. It represents the amount of land used for each major land use category in a typical Canadian city.

Match the photographs with the land-use categories and write a definition for each in your notes.

The purpose of this chapter is to help you become familiar with the principal types of urban land use. In addition, you will see the ways these land uses combine to produce the patterns we see in cities and towns.

Fig. 13–1 The percentage of a city's area occupied by major land uses

Key Terms

land use

central business district (CBD)

residential density

zoning

■ TYPES OF LAND USE

The majority of Canadians work, live, travel, shop, and spend leisure time in a city. Urban activities require buildings and facilities such as factories, offices, houses, apartments, roads, rail lines, stores, parks, golf courses and schools. All of these features of the city can be classified into one of five major **land use** groups: industrial, residential, commercial, transportation, and other.

INDUSTRIAL

You hear that a new factory, employing 200 people, is to open near your home. What does such news mean to different people? To an unemployed worker it means a job prospect. To the town's mayor, it will mean higher tax revenues. To people in your neighbourhood it could mean increased traffic, noise, and pollution.

Industrial land use is an important feature of most towns and cities. On average, about 11% of the developed land in most communities is used for factories, warehouses, and related uses. Industrial land uses can be grouped according to the nature of the business carried on and the transportation method on which each depends.

Large industries are often found in locations next to water bodies. They locate there to take advantage of cheap transportation by water or to use water as part of their processing. These industries include steel factories, oil refineries, and cement plants, which all tend to produce noise, smells, and air and water pollution. They are therefore best located far from residential areas.

Many factories, especially those built before World War II, were located on railway lines so that raw materials and finished goods could be easily transported. They were built before urban planning and concerns for pollution were common. They were located close to residential areas so that workers could walk to work. Today, most people do not want to live close to factories. Many older factories are now obsolete and are eventually torn down or replaced.

Most modern factories and warehouses are built away from residential areas in industrial parks. They may have landscaping to hide them from view, as well as specially designed water, sewage, power, and fire and police protection facilities. They are usually located close to highways to take advantage of modern truck transportation.

RESIDENTIAL

Residential land uses include all places where people live — everything from single-family houses to huge apartment buildings. It is the single largest land use in most cities, often taking up 40% or more of the developed land.

Perhaps the single most important housing characteristic is the density of housing. **Residential density** refers to the number of housing units per hectare. Low residential density consists of detached houses on relatively large lots (Fig. 13–2). Medium density housing ranges from 20 to 80 units/hectare. Typical housing of this type includes townhouses and low-rise apartment buildings (Fig. 13–3a). High density housing has more than 80 units/hectare and consists mainly of high-rise apartment buildings (Fig. 13–3b).

Two factors influence residential density patterns. The first is the cost of land. Where land values are lowest, usually on the outskirts of cities, single family homes are built on large lots. Downtown or along major transportation routes, where land is costly, large apartment buildings are built because they generate enough income to pay for the land.

The second factor that influences density patterns is the age of the neighbourhood. Residential areas built before 1930 tend to have higher densities than those which developed after World War II (Fig. 13–4). Before World War II, most people used streetcars or walked to work, school, or shops. Neighbourhoods did not need driveways or wide streets for cars. Since most people had to walk (at least to the streetcar stop), it made sense to have narrow house lots. This made the neighbourhood very compact. Today, because most families have one or more cars, new residential areas are designed with wide streets and driveways.

Fig 13–2 Low residential density – detached and semi-detached houses on large lots

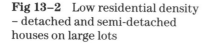

- Non-residential
- Semi-detached houses
- Detached houses

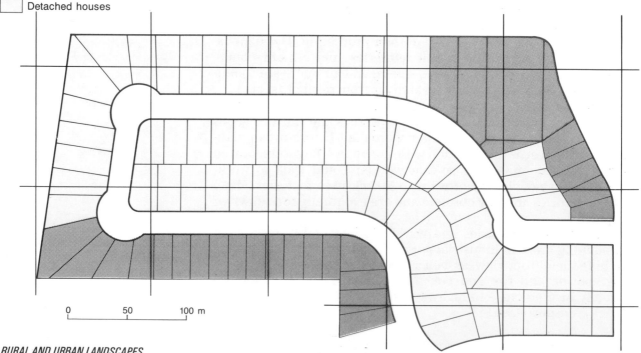

0   50   100 m

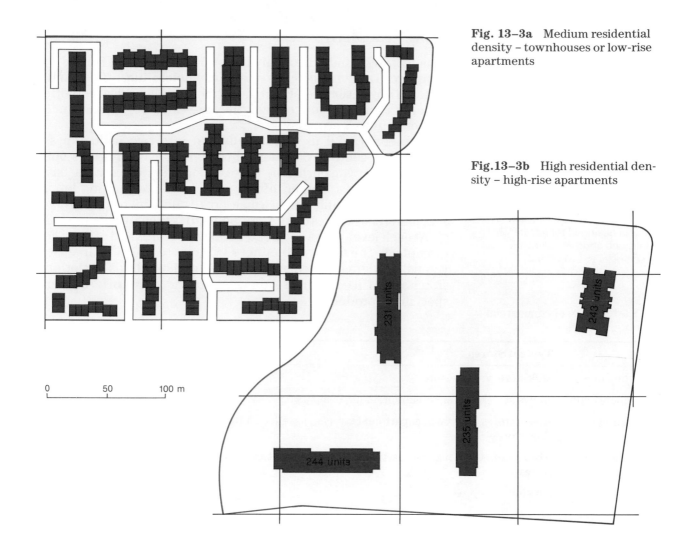

Fig. 13–3a Medium residential density – townhouses or low-rise apartments

Fig. 13–3b High residential density – high-rise apartments

231 units

243 units

235 units

244 units

0   50   100 m

Fig. 13–4 Streetscapes before and after World War II

COMMERCIAL

In most towns and cities, only about 5% of the land is used for commercial activities such as retailing, wholesaling, offices, and a wide variety of services. Even though these commercial activities use only a small amount of land, they are extremely important to the community's economy.

Commercial land use can be divided into two main types—ribbons and centres. Commercial ribbons consist of stores built along major transportation routes. Commercial centres have stores clustered together, often around a large parking lot. A centre is usually built beside a major road and is highly accessible.

Commercial centres can be grouped into five categories (Fig.13–5). At each level, there is a greater choice of stores and offices. For example, in the **Central Business District** (CBD) of a large city, you will find several department stores and hundreds of clothing stores and office buildings. You will also find stores offering very specialized products.

An inspection of the CBD of one large city revealed a store selling products designed for left-handed people, and another selling old comic books to collectors.

Fig. 13–5 Types of commercial centres

Type	Typical Stores	Number of Stores
Convenience	Milk store, variety store	1–5
Neighbourhood	Above stores, and supermarket, bank, beauty salon	5–30
Community	Above stores, and small department store(s), jeweller, clothing stores, shoe stores	20–100
Regional	Above stores, and major department store(s), bookstores, specialty stores	75–300
CBD	All kinds of stores	Depends on population of city and its region

In many Canadian towns and cities, the single most important issue affecting commercial land use is the decline of the CBD. Shopping centres and office buildings in the suburbs draw shoppers and retail tenants from the centre of the city. Why? Some downtown stores and offices are old and in need of major renovation or even replacement. At the same time, the CBD may be increasingly difficult for many people to reach. Most Canadian CBDs were built more than 70 years ago and were never meant to accommodate large numbers of automobiles. As a result, roads are often clogged, and parking is costly and in short supply.

Québec City was founded almost 400 years ago.

Canadians can see examples of urban decay in the CBDs of many U.S. cities.

Downtown businesses and local governments are trying many things to prevent the decline of the CBD in Canadian cities and towns (Fig. 13–6). It is obvious from this list that not all solutions are practical for all communities. Some, like the widening of sidewalks and roads, are in conflict with each other. Each town or city must choose the solutions that make most sense for the local situation.

Problem	Solutions
old buildings	• tear down and replace • modernize and expand existing structures • renovate but maintain "historic" character
congested roads	• widen roads • have one way streets • expand public transport • encourage car pooling • restrict private car access to CBD • eliminate on-street parking
limited parking	• build parking garages • expand on-street parking • subsidize parking
crowded, unattractive pedestrian areas	• widen sidewalks • ban cars on some streets (malls) • "landscape" sidewalks • build mini-parks

Fig. 13–6 Some solutions to problems of a declining CBD

TRANSPORTATION

Many people are surprised to find that almost 25% of the developed land in most Canadian cities is used for roads and highways. This large amount of land is needed to transport people and goods. Transportation land uses include roads, highways, railroad rights-of-way, and electricity transmission corridors.

Roads and highways can be grouped into three major categories according to their size and purpose (Fig. 13–7).

The largest highways are expressways. They are designed to carry huge amounts of traffic quickly over long distances. Access to expressways exists only at a limited number of interchanges.

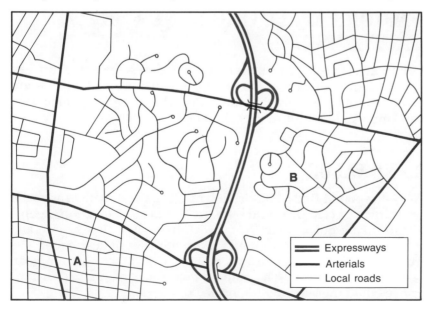

Expressways
Arterials
Local roads

Fig. 13–7 Three major categories of roads. The local roads at A are in a grid pattern. Roads at B are in a garden pattern.

Arterial roads are smaller than expressways and carry moderate amounts of traffic over shorter distances. Arterial roads are the major transportation routes that link local roads to expressways. Commercial ribbons develop along arterial roads.

Local roads are smaller than arterial roads and carry moderate amounts of traffic between arterial roads and peoples' houses.

There are other transportation land uses. Parking lots, particularly in the downtown area, take up large areas. Airports use a great deal of land and can cause serious noise pollution and traffic problems. Rail and hydro lines, as well as highways, tend to divide communities into identifiable districts.

OTHER LAND USES

There are several other land uses that are important to the functioning of our towns and cities.

- Institutional. Included in this category are such buildings as schools, hospitals, government offices, and churches.
- Vacant. This important part of the urban scene includes all unused, empty land in the city. It includes land which has never been developed as well as previously developed land which is awaiting a new use.
- Open Space. It is sometimes easy to confuse vacant land and open space. Just remember that open space has already been developed, while vacant land awaits use. Open space includes such uses as parks, playgrounds, golf courses, and cemeteries.

■ FACTORS AFFECTING LAND USE PATTERNS

Why is an office building built in one location, a sewage treatment plant in another, and a golf course somewhere else? There are many factors affecting this choice but the three most important are land value, zoning, and technology.

LAND VALUE

Why do you not find a golf driving range in the downtown area of your town or city? It would seem to be a perfect location. People could take a quick break from work to get a little exercise and fresh air. There certainly would be no shortage of customers! The reason is land cost. Land in a major city's downtown area can easily cost $3000/m^2$. The land needed for even a small driving range could therefore cost $20 000 000!

In general, land costs are highest in the areas of the city that are most accessible. This means that the highest land values are found in the CBD. High land values are also found along major transportation routes, especially where such routes intersect. Not surprisingly, land uses that produce the highest income per unit area occupy the most expensive land. This is why the CBD has the tallest buildings and high density retailing — but no driving ranges!

Land costs are a factor in other parts of the city as well. In many larger cities (where land costs are higher than in smaller centres) new house lots in many parts of the city are smaller than they were 10 to 15 years ago. And what of our driving range? Land uses that require large amounts of land and produce relatively low income must find cheap land on which to locate. They find this on the edge of the city, and in most cases will locate there only temporarily until the land is needed for other more permanent uses.

ZONING

Governments pass laws stating which land uses are allowed in an area. Fig. 13–8 is a typical **zoning** map. Zoning laws are meant to avoid conflicts between land uses. For example, dirty, smelly factories are zoned well away from residential areas. Conflicts frequently exist in older, non-planned areas. Some cities still lack effective zoning laws, while others have had such laws for decades.

Accessible: most easily reached from all parts of the city

Fig. 13–8 Zoning maps use a standard code to identify land uses.
R is single family residential (schools may also be built in these zones)
RM is multiple family residential (higher numbers represent higher densities)
01 is open space — park
03 is open space — utilities

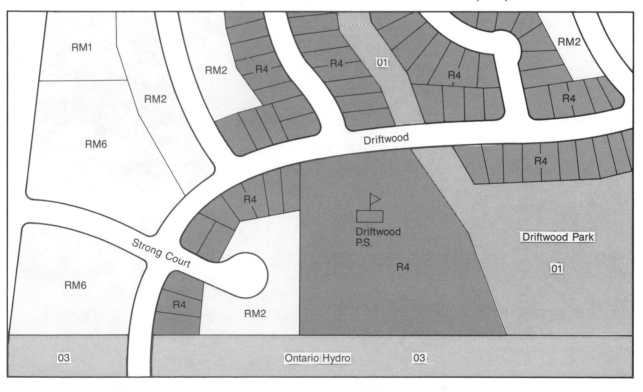

TECHNOLOGY

Land use reflects the technology that exists when the land is developed. When horses were the major method of transportation, horse-watering troughs could be found along roads. Today, automobiles are the major method of transportation and gas stations are found along roads. Other examples tell similar stories. Compare the two aerial photographs (Fig.13–9). One shows a district built about 70 years ago, the other shows a district built in the past 20 years. There are some obvious differences (Fig. 13–10).

Clearly differences exist, but why? The principal reason is the nearly universal ownership and use of automobiles since World War II. Urban areas built since then feature wider arterial roads with local roads designed to make through-traffic difficult. Shopping and working areas include their own parking areas.

The division between older and newer districts is very clear in most Canadian cities because of a unique historical coincidence. During the economic depression of the 1930s and World War II (1939-45) few homes were built. As a result, there exists a clear break between the older pre-1930 districts and the post-1945 suburbs.

Fig. 13–9 These two aerial photographs show two parts of the same city and are at the same scale. Which area is older? How can you tell?

	Road Pattern	Road Width	Housing Density
Older Area	grid	narrower	higher, smaller lots
Newer Area	garden	wider	lower, larger lots

Fig 13–10 Comparing older and newer residential areas. Which kind of area do you live in?

IN CLOSING . . .

Land-use patterns in towns and cities do not develop by chance. They result from decisions made by people about such things as where to work, what type of home to live in, what kind of local government to have, and what to spend money on. The decisions that you make about these things may affect the way your community looks in the future.

QUESTIONS

CHECKBACK

1. **a)** Explain the differences between low, medium, and high density residential land use.
    b) What factors influence these differences?
2. Compare older factories with modern ones in terms of location, landscaping, closeness to residential areas, and pollution control.
3. Describe the main differences that exist between the three major types of roads.
4. Cities contain both open space and vacant land. Give examples of each and state their different purposes.
5. How do land values, technology, and zoning affect land use patterns?

ANALYZE

6. Examine Figs. 13–3a and 13–3b.
    a) Calculate the housing density in each case. To do this, divide the number of housing units by the area covered by housing.
    b) What are the advantages and disadvantages of each type of housing?
    c) What is the housing density in the neighbourhood where you live?
7. Examine Fig. 13–5.
    a) Where would you go to buy a loaf of bread?
    b) Where would you go to buy an expensive piece of clothing?
    c) Are specialized stores more or less likely to be close to where people live? Explain.

8. **a)** What evidence, if any, is there of CBD decline where you live?

   b) If you found that there is a problem in a), what has been done to halt this decline?

9. **a)** When did a 15-year gap occur in the growth of most Canadian towns and cities?

   b) What two events caused this gap and how did each prevent urban growth?

   c) What evidence of this gap is there in i) residential land use, ii) commercial land use, and iii) transportation land use?

INVESTIGATE

10. If possible, give examples of each of the five kinds of commercial centres in the community where you live. How did you determine which category each was in?

11. Describe three industries in your community that are different in terms of size, age, nature of product, landscaping, or pollution controls. How did each come to locate on its present site? Consider such factors as transportation needs, zoning, and land cost.

12. **a)** Name the two road patterns found in most towns and cities.

    b) How does the road pattern in older parts of cities tend to cause traffic problems? What can be done to overcome these problems?

    c) How are roads in newer districts designed to avoid traffic problems?

Can you think of any other road patterns? Hint: look at a street map of Paris or Washington.

13. **a)** What governmental bodies are responsible for zoning where you live?

    b) How long have zoning laws existed? How strict are they? To find out, talk to a builder or someone in a zoning office in your area.

14. Describe an example of a land use conflict in your community. Which land use was there first and how did the conflict come into being?

WHAT DO YOU THINK?

15. **a)** Are older districts of cities or newer suburbs the more interesting place in which to live? Construct a chart to compare the advantages and disadvantages of each. Why do you prefer one over the other?

    b) Where do you live now, and where do you expect to live when you establish your own household? Why might you not be able to live in the choice that you made in a)?

16. Your teacher will organize the class into groups. Each group will construct a town plan showing the locations of various types of land use discussed in this chapter. Your town is to be located in the area shown in Fig. 13–11.
   a) The group should brainstorm ideas to determine what type of community it wants to achieve with its town plan. Use the information contained in this chapter as a guide to the location of various land uses.
   b) On a sheet of blank paper, draw the area shown in Fig. 13–11. Experiment with various designs within this area until you obtain the one that best meets the goals of your group.
   c) Draw this area on a large sheet of paper or bristol board and construct the town plan. You will need a border, title, direction arrow, legend, and names for the features you draw.
   d) Write a short report explaining why you located the land uses where you did. Be prepared to defend your design in front of the other groups.

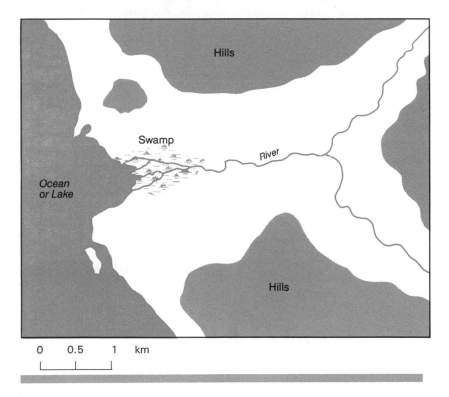

Fig. 13–11 Make copies of this base map to design your new community.

14 Canadian Cities — Coping with Change

What thoughts come to your mind when you see a photograph of an old building (Fig. 14–1)? Do you think about its past? About the many families who lived there since it was new? Do you think about how it came to be old and obsolete? Or do you think about its future? Will it be torn down and replaced by a modern building or will it be restored to its former glory? Buildings which provoke questions such as these can be found in most Canadian cities and towns. They illustrate how urban places are always changing. These changes make our towns and cities exciting and challenging places in which to live.

Key Terms

urban renewal	day care	domestic response teams
economic base	quality of life	community relations police
public transit	mobility	greying of the population
livable winter city	Block Parents	Neighbourhood Watch

Fig. 14–1 Old, worn-out buildings tell us about the past but they also offer us choices for the future.

■ INTRODUCTION

The quality of life in Canadian cities depends on how well we meet the challenge of change. In this chapter, you will be given a brief sketch of a number of current urban problems. You should choose one to study in detail, and prepare a written essay, an oral presentation, or some other kind of report.

■ URBAN CHANGE ISSUES

- *Urban Renewal or Replacement?* — Examine Fig. 14–2. It shows the same street as Fig. 14–1. What has happened here?

  When an existing building or even a whole neighbourhood is run-down, how do we determine whether to tear down the existing building(s) or to fix them up? In different places and in different times both solutions have been used. What is the case where you live?

- *Dealing with Rapid Growth* — The population of the Toronto suburb of Mississauga grew from 250 000 in 1976 to 374 000 in 1986. An increase like this, of almost 50% in only 10 years, puts enormous strain on the resources of a community. Schools, roads, and shopping centres must be built, and social services need to be provided. Growth of this sort is typical of the suburbs that surround our largest cities.

Fig. 14–2 This is the same area as in Fig. 14-1. What changes do you see?

Fig. 14–3 What will happen to Nanisivik in the Northwest Territories when the mineral resource on which it depends is gone?

Canada's climate was once described as ten months of winter and two months of tough sledding.

- *Dealing with Decline* — While some Canadian communities are dealing with frantic growth, others must face the opposite problem. Typical is the case of Schefferville, Qué. Schefferville was built as a model town in the 1950s to house the workers brought to northern Québec to mine a rich iron ore deposit. By the 1980s, the richest ore deposits had been mined and the demand for iron ore was weak. The mine's owners, the Iron Ore Company of Canada, decided to close the mine. The **economic base** for the town was gone, but not the desire of many of the residents to keep their town going. What problems are there in a situation like this?

  Other isolated resource-based communities, such as Nanisivik on Baffin Island (Fig. 14–3), will face similar problems in the future. What other communities have faced similar problems?

- *Traffic Problems Downtown* — Many larger Canadian cities must face the problem of traffic congestion in their downtown areas. The number of roads and parking lots and the width of roads were not designed to handle modern traffic loads. Is the solution to widen roads, install one-way street systems, and build more parking lots? Or does the solution lie in the opposite direction? Should we limit automobile access to the downtown and expand **public transit**? What is being done where you live?

- *Dealing with Climate* — Winnipeggers will tell you that the corner of Portage and Main is the coldest place in the world on a -30° C morning in January. People in other Canadian cities all have their own "coldest place in the world". Because Canada is a northern nation, winter conditions can make even simple acts such as shopping and getting to work or school an ordeal for several months each year.

Most Canadian towns and cities have responded to this problem by building indoor shopping malls in the suburbs or by building underground or covered walkways in downtown areas. Toronto and Montréal each have an underground "city" that stretches for many blocks. The West Edmonton Mall has hundreds of stores and extensive indoor recreation facilities, including an amusement park and water park. These are all part of what is called the **livable winter city**. What can or should be done about this problem varies from city to city.

- *Day Care* — For many families, finding affordable and reliable **day care** for their pre-school children is one of the biggest problems of urban life. It is a problem both for single parents and for families with two wage-earners. Is the lack of day care a serious problem where you live?

- *Teenagers in the City* — What special problems are faced by teenagers in the city? Do existing programs and facilities for young adults meet their needs? If you were put in charge of meeting teenagers' needs, what would you do about such concerns as unemployment, recreation, public health, and education?

- *Greying of the Population* — By 2021, more than 20% of Canada's population will be over 65 years old. (This age group is now less than 11%.) This "greying" of the population might be the single most important trend affecting Canada's population over the next 40 years. Problems resulting from the aging population will be most obvious in our towns and cities. What can be done to help older people to live a comfortable, productive lifestyle? How will our medical system cope? How much will it cost and who will pay? Should the design of our cities, our neighbourhoods, and our homes change to meet the needs of this rapidly growing part of our population?

- *Crime in the City* — Few topics are discussed in our urban areas as much as crime. Is crime as serious a problem as it often seems? What role can be played by innovative crime prevention strategies such as **Neighbourhood Watch**, **Block Parents**, **domestic response teams**, and **community relations police** officers (Fig. 14–4)?

- *New Designs in the City* — Are we missing opportunities to decide how our cities should look and work? Are there better ways to build cities and neighbourhoods? Could we build cities which would have fewer problems and be cheaper to live in? How do we go about putting these new ideas into existing cities?

- *Urban Living Choices* — In the natural world, plants and animals have niches in which to live. Niches also exist for the residents of towns and cities. Some people may choose to live on the 40th floor of an apartment building in the downtown area. Some might choose to live in a townhouse in the suburbs, while others want to live in a detached house on a huge lot beyond the edge of the city. What factors influence these various choices?

Fig. 14–4 Police forces in many Canadian cities are trying new crime prevention strategies, such as using community relations officers.

- *Urban Poverty* — Even in our richest cities there are people who live in the streets and find their food in garbage bins. Other people work a full week and must still rely on food banks to help feed their children. Why does such need exist in the midst of wealth? What impact does poverty have on family life and on the social services of the city? What can be done to eliminate or reduce the problem?
- *Quality of Life* — In a number of places in this book you will see the term **quality of life**. What exactly does this term mean? What determines the quality of life for an urban resident? Consider such factors as family life, job satisfaction, wealth, recreational opportunities, safety, shopping, **mobility**, and housing quality.

mobility: ease of movement

■ IN CLOSING . . .

These are only a few suggestions for you to consider. You might choose one of these urban problems to study, or you might pick something totally different. Perhaps you might wish to investigate a problem which is unique to the area where you live. Chapter 38 will give you some ideas on how to research and present your topic.

QUESTIONS

ANALYZE

1. Most public issues are complex. One method that helps you analyze the effects of urban change is to construct an organizational chart. Copy the following example (Fig. 14–5) into your notebook. Choose one of the issues listed in this chapter, and construct a similar chart to sort the issue into a number of smaller, connected issues. Use this as a basis for your study of an urban issue.

Fig. 14–5

Main Issue	Consequences	Results
rapid urban growth	more services needed	- more employment - more taxes
	more traffic	- pollution - slower traffic
	more roads and buildings	- less farmland - less food produced

WHAT DO YOU THINK?

2. When everyone in your class has completed their study of an urban problem, organize into groups of four to six students and discuss how living in Canadian cities in 20 years will be different from today.

ECONOMIC
LANDSCAPES

15 Types of Industry

Do you own a bicycle? When you bought your bicycle, did you consider where it was made? If you bought a bicycle made in Canada, you helped to support Canada's economy in many ways (Fig. 15–1). How?

In this chapter you will learn about the three types of industries that make up Canada's economy and how these three combine to produce Canada's wealth.

Fig. 15–1 When you buy a bicycle, you are involving all parts of the economy.

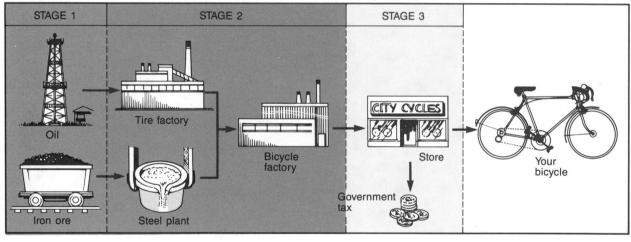

Key Terms

extractive industry   retailing   transportation
manufacturing industry   communications   personal services
service industry

■ THREE TYPES OF INDUSTRY

exploitation: development or use

Canada's wealth comes from the exploitation of its rich natural resources and from the work of its citizens. Canadians are employed in a tremendous variety of jobs. All of these jobs can be grouped into one of three categories: **extractive industries**, **manufacturing industries**, and **service industries**.

EXTRACTIVE OR PRIMARY INDUSTRIES

Industries that take raw materials from the natural environment are called extractive or primary industries. What types of extractive industries are involved in the production of your bicycle?

Canada has a wealth of natural resources. The extractive industries that have been developed to exploit these natural resources make an important contribution to the wealth of our economy. Without these extractive industries, and the money they bring from other countries, Canada's economy could not exist in its present form. Yet only a small percentage of Canada's labour force works in extractive industries (Fig. 15–2). Extractive industries rely on labour-saving machines instead of human labour.

Extractive industries include hunting, fishing, forestry, mining, farming, and production of hydroelectricity.

Extractive industries contribute 10% ($55 400 million) to Canada's Gross Domestic Product (GDP)

Fig. 15–2 Employment in Canada, 1988

Type of Industry	% of Canada's Labour Force
Extractive	
Agriculture	3.6
Forestry	0.7
Fishing and Trapping	0.3
Mining	1.5
Manufacturing	
Manufacturing	17.1
Construction	6.2
Service	
Finance, insurance and real estate	5.7
Trade (buying and selling goods)	18.2
Transportation, communications (radio, television, newspapers, magazines)	
Utilities (e.g. sewage disposal, fresh water, electricity)	7.3
Government Services	6.4
Other Services (health, education, entertainment, personal)	33.0
TOTAL	100.0

MANUFACTURING OR SECONDARY INDUSTRIES

Manufacturing and construction industries process the products of extractive industries into finished products. Manufacturing industries transform raw materials into many different forms to be used by consumers or by other companies. This processing may be done in one or more stages. For example, iron ore is transformed into steel in factories. This is called primary manufacturing. The steel is then sent to companies for further processing into cars, mining equipment, machines, nails, and other products — such as bicycle frames. This is called secondary manufacturing.

transform: change

Making the paper for this book is an example of primary manufacturing, while the printing of the book is secondary manufacturing.

Manufacturing represents 23% ($127 400 million) of Canada's GDP.

Manufacturing industries are located in many towns and cities across Canada. Companies try to build their factories in densely populated areas because they want to be near the people who buy their products. If they locate near their customers, then they save money on shipping costs. Accordingly, if you know where most Canadians live, you will know where most manufacturing is done.

Manufacturing industries provide more jobs to Canadians than do extractive industries. Yet the number of people employed in manufacturing is still small in comparison to the third category, services. As with extractive industries, manufacturing processes use many machines that require relatively few workers.

This is a good reason for you to **Buy Canadian** when possible.

SERVICE OR TERTIARY INDUSTRIES

Service industries provide services needed by the extractive and manufacturing industries, and by society in general. Without these services, society could not operate (Fig. 15–3). What service industries were involved in providing you with your bicycle?

Services represent more than 67% ($371 200 million) of Canada's GDP

The majority of Canadian workers do not produce "goods" in their jobs. Instead, they provide "services" for others. The range of services is very great and includes such things as **retailing**, office work, education, health care, **communications**, government, **transportation**, and **personal services**.

Service industries in one form or another are spread over the entire country. In every community there are stores, banks, schools, police forces, and dozens of other services. The majority of service industries are found in towns and cities because services are provided for people and there are many more people in urban areas.

In some regions of the country, one service industry dominates. Think for a moment about Ottawa and one service industry should come to mind. Can you think of other examples?

■ IN CLOSING...

Canada's economy depends upon the creation of jobs in all three types of industry. By purchasing a bicycle made in Canada you help to provide jobs for people in each of these types of industries. Who knows, you may be helping to ensure that, in a few years, you will be able to find the kind of job you want.

Fig. 15–3 Retailing is just one example of a service industry. Name others.

QUESTIONS

CHECKBACK

1. Define, in your own words, the meaning of:
   a) extractive industries
   b) manufacturing industries
   c) service industries
2. **a)** In Fig. 15–1, what type of industry is shown at each stage?
   b) Select a product with which you are familiar. Describe what steps it went through before you got it. Use the following headings: extractive industries, manufacturing industries, service industries.
3. In your notebook, match each item in Column A with the three terms in Column B most closely related to it.

Column A	Column B
1. Extractive industry	a) raw materials
2. Manufacturing	b) secondary
3. Services	c) factory
	d) mine
	e) tertiary
	f) processing
	g) primary
	h) golf course
	i) civil servant

4. Give at least two reasons why the importance of extractive industries is not shown by the number of workers employed in them.

ANALYZE

5. Examine the isodemographic map in Fig. 12-1. In which areas of the country would you expect to find large numbers of manufacturing companies? Explain why.
6. Make a chart similar to Fig. 15–4 and fill in the missing figures, using the information given in this chapter.

	Extractive	Manufacturing	Service	Total
% Contribution to Canada's GDP				
Dollar Value				

Fig. 15–4

7. Draw a chart similar to Fig. 15–5 in your notebook.
   a) Using Fig. 15–6, calculate the percentage of workers in the extractive industries in Atlantic Canada. (Add the percentages of extractive industry workers in each province of the region: 2% (Nfld.) + 1% (P.E.I.) + 4% (N.S.) + 3% (N.B.) = 10%.) Write the answer in the appropriate place on your chart.
   b) Similarly, calculate the percentage of workers in each type of industry for each of the three main regions of Canada.
   c) Nine percent of Canada's population lives in Atlantic Canada, 62% in Central Canada, and 29% in western Canada. Place these figures in the appropriate spaces on your chart.
   d) Compare the percentage of Canada's population in each region to the percentage of workers in each industry in that region. If the figures are close to each other, then the region has a fair share of jobs in that category. If not, then the region does not have a fair share of jobs in that category. What significant patterns do you see?

Workers in the Yukon and N.W.T. are included in the B.C. total.

INVESTIGATE

8. Name three typical jobs in each of the following fields:
   a) financial services
   b) trade
   c) education
   d) health care
   e) transportation
   f) communications
   g) utilities
   h) personal services
   i) business services

9. a) In this exercise you will determine the percentages of people in your community employed in the three types of industries. To do this, interview students in your school. Ask each student what job is done by each of two close relatives or family friends. List these jobs in your notebook and classify each job as extractive, manufacturing, or service. Interview enough students so that you can list 50 jobs.
   b) Calculate the percentage of people employed in each of the three types of industries.
   c) Compare the results obtained in b) to the national average (Fig. 15–2) and to your regional average (Question 6). Explain the reasons for any significant differences that appear.

WHAT DO YOU THINK?

10. A geographer once said that service industries are at the same time the most important and the least important segment of Canada's economy. What do you think was meant by this statement?

	% of Extractive Workers	% of Manufacturing Workers	% of Service Workers	% of Canada's Population in Each Region
Atlantic Canada (Nfld., P.E.I., N.S., N.B.)				
Central Canada (Qué., Ont.)				
Western Canada (Man., Sask., Alta., B.C.)				

Fig. 15–5

Fig. 15–6 Distribution of workers within each type of industry

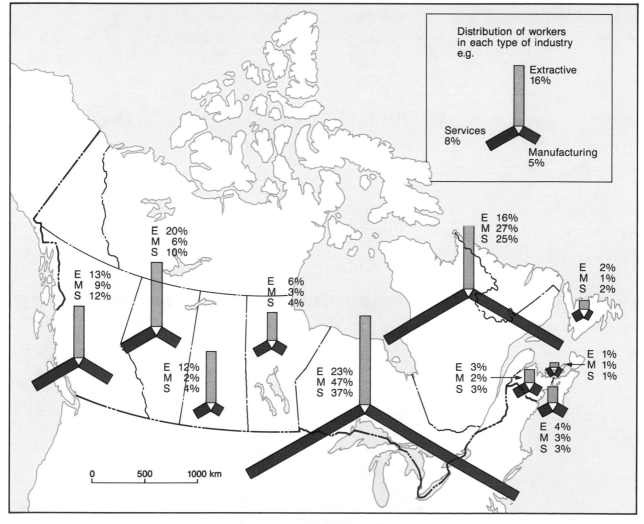

Portrait of a Manufacturer

Nancy and Marc worked together on an economic geography project about Canada's **aerospace industry**. They started by examining the aerospace industry in general and then interviewed an executive of one company, de Havilland (Fig. 15–7). Here is their report.

Key Terms

aerospace industry   STOL aircraft   privatization

■ THE CANADIAN AEROSPACE INDUSTRY

Aerospace manufacturers in Canada design, build, and repair aircraft and aircraft engines. They also make related products such as airport control systems and equipment for use in space such as satellites. There are about 160 aerospace companies in Canada. Many of these are subsidiaries of American firms. Canada ranks fifth in the world's aerospace industry, with total sales in 1986 of $2 375 000 000.

Fig. 15–7 Nancy and Marc tour the de Havilland factory with the plant manager.

Structure of Canada's Aerospace Industry

First Level:	Large companies that design, develop, manufacture and market complete aircraft and engines. For example, de Havilland: Toronto, Ontario. Canadair: Montréal, Québec.
Second Level:	Companies that manufacture parts of aircraft, engines and control systems for aircraft and space vehicles. Almost all of them are located in Montréal and Toronto. Most are subsidiaries of U.S. companies. For example, McDonnell-Douglas (wing and tail assemblies); Pratt and Whitney (engines); Litton Systems (electronic systems); Spar Aerospace (satellites).
Third Level:	There are over 80 smaller businesses that do machining, parts manufacture, sheet metal work and repair work.

Fig. 15–8

Canada's aerospace industry can be divided into three levels according to the type of production carried on (Fig. 15–8). Although Canada is the second-largest user of airplanes in the non-Communist world, only 12% of all the commercial aircraft in Canada were made in this country. This is because Canadian companies do not make the large commercial aircraft most commonly used. Most make only aircraft parts. Those that do make aircraft concentrate on specialized planes for use by the military, for work in the bush, and for carrying passengers and freight.

Our aerospace industry cannot be self-sufficient because the market in Canada is so small. Companies rely heavily on government contracts and grants to continue their research and to update their equipment in order to remain competitive in world markets. This last point is important because between 70 and 80% of Canada's aerospace production is for export. Canadian planes and aerospace products are sold throughout the world. The U.S. is our best customer, but we also sell airplanes to countries such as Australia, Saudi Arabia, Brazil, and Zaire, which need the specialized kinds of aircraft that we build.

■ INTERVIEW WITH DE HAVILLAND PLANT MANAGER

Nancy: How old is de Havilland?

Manager: The de Havilland Division of Boeing Canada has a long history. The company was founded in England in 1920 by Sir Geoffrey de Havilland. In 1928 a branch plant was set up in Toronto. We first began by building British-designed aircraft in a very small workshop and an old shed.

Marc: What types of planes has de Havilland built?

Manager: During the 1920s and 1930s we produced the Gypsy Moth, the Tiger Moth, and other planes for the military. During World War II we built the Mosquito, and other fighter and bomber planes used by the British and Canadian air forces.

Fig. 15–9 The de Havilland Beaver and Otter (shown) have been workhorses in the development of Canada's north.

The other innovation was the Bombardier snowmobile.

Commuter airlines usually operate between cities that are no more than 600 km apart.

After the war we switched from building military to building civilian planes. In deciding what kinds of planes to build we considered two factors:

- what kinds of plane would be needed in Canada in the years to come; and
- what kinds of plane were not being built by our competitors.

A plane was needed to fly into the Canadian bush under tough conditions. It had to be able to land on wheels on rough landing strips or on floats or skis. To meet this need we developed the Beaver in the late 1940s. The Beaver was one of the most successful small planes ever built. We built hundreds.

In 1987, the Canadian Engineering Society honoured the Beaver as one of the two most important transportation innovations of the past century in Canada. This award was given for the Beaver's contribution to social and economic change in remote regions of Canada and elsewhere. It indicates the role that de Havilland has played and continues to play as a pioneer in developing aircraft for special needs.

A plane larger than the Beaver was needed for bigger hauling jobs in the north, so we developed the single-engine and later the twin-engine Otter in the 1950s and 1960s (Fig. 15–9). The Otter was Canada's first **STOL** (short take-off and landing) **aircraft**. The Twin Otter is used for such things as ambulance duties, photographic surveys, paratroop training, ice patrols, and search and rescue work, as well as being used as a small commuter plane.

During the late 1950s we developed more powerful engines and built a bigger cargo-handling aircraft called the Caribou. By using rear loading doors we increased the cargo capacity tremendously. Most of these aircraft were bought as military transports.

In the early 1960s we designed a STOL transport plane mainly for military transport. It was called the Buffalo and is excellent for heavy work.

Because of our experience in building sturdy, reliable planes for tough jobs and our knowledge of STOL technology, we decided to build STOL aircraft for commercial use — the Dash 7 and 8. They are quiet and fuel-efficient and ideal for city-to-city transportation, especially if a short runway is built close to a city's downtown (Fig. 15–10).

Nancy: We've heard a lot in the news about these STOL airplanes. Tell us more about them.

Manager: The Dash 7 came first and it was not easy to get off the ground, so to speak! The problem with any new design is that you must first spend hundreds of millions of dollars on research and development several years before you get any sales income from the project. Money for the project was hard to find and we had to go to the federal government for help. In 1974, de Havilland was taken over by the government and became a crown corporation. The Dash 7 was ready for sale in 1977 and was produced until 1988.

crown corporation: an independent company owned by the government

Marc: How is the Dash 8 different from the Dash 7?

Manager: When we started selling the Dash 7, some of our customers told us that they had need of a smaller, cheaper aircraft than the "7". Using this information, we developed the Dash 8, Series 100. It has two engines and seats 37 to 40 depending on the interior arrangement chosen. We sell four per month to regional airlines around the world: Europe, Caribbean, U.S.A., Canada, New Guinea, and New Zealand.

In 1987, we started production of the Dash 8, Series 300. This model seats 50 to 60 passengers and is more luxurious than the Series 100. It was designed to meet an identified market need and we hope that it will be very successful.

Fig. 15–10 The Dash 8 is being used by smaller airlines in many parts of the world.

Nancy: Are you still a crown corporation?

Manager: No, we are not. The government decided that it would sell crown corporations that were attractive to the private sector. This process is called **privatization**. De Havilland was sold in 1986, to the Boeing Corporation of the U.S.

Nancy: Has your sale to Boeing helped de Havilland?

Manager: Without a doubt. Boeing is the largest producer of large commercial aircraft in the world. They have been able to contribute money so that we have been able to modernize our equipment. In addition, they have an unmatched reputation in the aircraft industry. This has made selling our planes much easier. Combine this with our knowledge of STOL technology and you have a winning combination.

Some people criticized the government for selling de Havilland to an American company; but without Boeing we would not be where we are today. A good indicator of this is that in the first year after the purchase, our work force increased by 1000.

Marc: What must de Havilland do to continue its success in the future?

Manager: It isn't easy. Our product must be better than the competition's product and our sales staff must be aggressive. We must know what kind of airplane the world needs — five to ten years before the buyers actually want the planes.

■ IN CLOSING...

Remember that most sales are outside Canada.

The Canadian aerospace industry currently employs over 40 000 highly skilled workers. Its future success depends upon being able to compete in a highly competitive world market. To do this we must have innovative products, a highly skilled labour force and the capital needed for research and development.

CHECKBACK

1. Define the following terms:
   a) aerospace   **b)** subsidiaries   **c)** STOL
2. **a)** Why is Canada's aerospace industry not self-sufficient?
   b) How does this industry survive in spite of this?

ANALYZE

3. Create a magazine advertisement that could be used to help sell Dash 7 and Dash 8 aircraft.
4. What does Canada's aerospace industry need to be successful in the future? How could these things be achieved? Be specific.

INVESTIGATE

5. Why has de Havilland been expanding at a time when other makers of large commercial aircraft have been cutting back?
6. Research the history and present situation of Canada's other first level aerospace company, Canadair of Montreal.

WHAT DO YOU THINK?

7. **a)** The plant manager suggested that de Havilland must be able to predict five to ten years ahead what the airplane buyers of the world will need. Why is this long lead time needed?
   b) What would be the probable result if de Havilland miscalculated the demand for a new kind of airplane and only a few were sold?
8. **a)** Define "privatization".
   b) Describe the advantages and disadvantages of privatization for:
        i. de Havilland
        ii. Canada in general
   c) Do you think the sale of de Havilland to Boeing was a good idea? Why or why not?

16

Transportation

If Canada is compared to a living organism in which the cities, towns, rural areas, and industries are parts of the body, then the **transportation** system would be the circulatory system. Without an efficient transportation system, the country would die. In the crossword puzzle (Fig. 16–1), you will be introduced to some of the features, facts, and definitions of transportation in Canada.

Key Terms

transportation	deregulation	unit train
mobility	hub and spoke	piggyback

Fig. 16–1   Transportation cross-word puzzle

Across

1 trailers carried by train
2 large metal boxes used for moving freight
7 abbreviation for short take-off and landing airplanes
8 movement of goods or people
9 ■ ■ ■ materials
10 removal of regulations
11 used for moving oil and gas
14 ■ ■ ■ ■-Canada Highway
15 ■ ■ ■ ■ ■ ■ jams
17 passenger rail company
19 train carrying only one cargo
22 Japanese car built in Canada
23 ease of movement
24 limited-■ ■ ■ ■ ■ highway

Down

1 someone who travels
3 ■ ■ ■ ■ ■-city: between cities
4 1000 kg (of cargo)
5 the answer to 6 Down is an example of this
6 Air ■ ■ ■ ■ ■ ■
10 "Can I ■ ■ ■ ■ ■ the car?"
12 second largest railway: Canadian ■ ■ ■ ■ ■ ■ ■
13 a bulk cargo: ■ ■ ■ ■ ore
16 used to get to Newfoundland or Vancouver Island
18 another name for car
20 ■ ■ ■ and spoke air route pattern
21 most widely used form of public transportation

■ INTRODUCTION

Without the development of transportation routes across its vast land mass, Canada could not exist as it does today. At each stage in Canada's development, various forms of transportation have taken settlers to their new homes, brought raw materials from the wilderness to the cities, shipped products across the country, allowed Canadians to travel from coast to coast, and provided a link with the outside world (Fig. 16–2).

Every day Canada's transportation system faces an immense task. Millions of people travel tens of millions of kilometres. Thousands of tonnes of goods must be moved from one place to another as quickly and as cheaply as possible. This must be done in spite of

Fig. 16–2 In a country as large as Canada, modern transportation methods are extremely important. When was each of these methods introduced?

Fig. 16–3 Railway line through the Fraser Canyon in British Columbia. Can you imagine how difficult it must have been to build this line?

great distances, harsh climates, and landforms that present real obstacles to travel (Fig. 16–3).

Canada's transportation network is composed of many parts: waterways, roadways, railways, airways, and pipelines. Each of these plays a role in the movement of people and goods, and each competes against the others for business. By linking nearly all regions of the country, the transportation network helps the development of Canada's economy.

The transportation methods used, and the problems faced, vary enormously in different parts of Canada. Perhaps the single most important difference that exists is access to land transport. Although most Canadians have easy access to rail lines or roads, there are some people who have no access to land transport. Examine Fig. 16–4 and answer the following questions.

1. a) Describe the pattern of ground transport in Zone A.
    b) Why is this pattern not surprising?
    c) Why are there gaps in this pattern in the following areas:

      i. along coastal British Columbia
      ii. along the British Columbia-Alberta border
      iii. in northern Ontario and Québec
      iv. in northern New Brunswick, western Nova Scotia, and Newfoundland?

2. a) Describe the pattern of surface transport in Zone B. Why do gaps exist?
    b) With the help of an atlas, explain why surface transport exists to each of the following places:

      i. Inuvik   v. Churchill
      ii. Yellowknife   vi. Moosonee
      iii. Fort McMurray vii. La Grande Rivière
      iv. Lynn Lake   viii. Schefferville

3. a) Why does surface transport not exist in Zone C?
    b) What alternatives might be used here?

We will study Canada's transportation network to see how it links different regions of the country, and how it helps develop the country's economy. We can do this best by dividing transportation into two parts: the movement of people, and the movement of goods.

■ MOVEMENT OF PEOPLE

When people select a method of transportation, they make their choice based on a number of factors such as the distance to be covered, the cost, and the time involved. People may travel by road, rail, air or water.

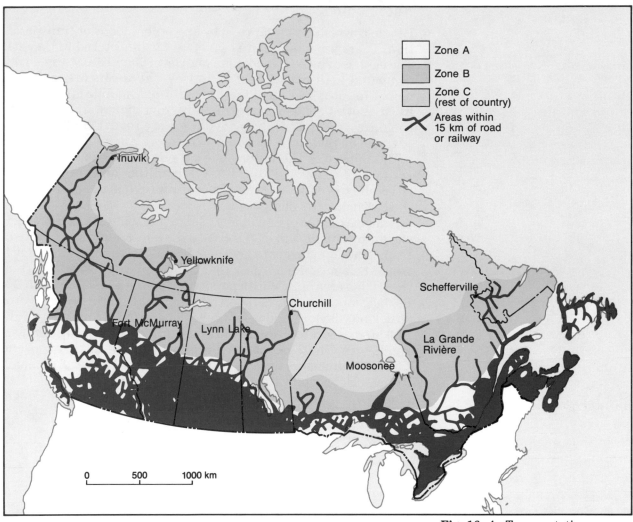

Legend:

☐ Zone A
▨ Zone B
▨ Zone C (rest of country)
✕ Areas within 15 km of road or railway

Map labels: Inuvik, Yellowknife, Churchill, Schefferville, Fort McMurray, Lynn Lake, La Grande Rivière, Moosonee

Scale: 0 — 500 — 1000 km

Fig. 16–4 Transportation zones across Canada

ROAD

Roadways are the most important means of moving people from place to place in Canada. Every year over $4 000 000 000 are spent on the construction, upkeep, and administration of roads across the country. There are more than 900 000 km of highways, roads, and streets. Over 12 000 000 vehicles, including cars, trucks, buses, and motorcycles, use the roadways to carry people from place to place.

Roads play a vital role in maintaining Canada's economy. First, they allow people to move from one region to another. A family on a driving holiday and a travelling business executive both spend money on food, accommodation, and gas. This is good for the country's economy and could not occur if the roads were not there for people to use. When regions are not linked by roads they become isolated. The two most important vehicles used to travel by road are automobiles and buses.

Automobiles

mobility: ease of movement

People travel more by car than by any other means of transportation. There are more than 11 000 000 cars registered in Canada. The car has allowed Canadians a high level of **mobility**, especially compared with residents of countries where cars are less common. The most important feature of the automobile is its flexibility. It allows people to travel directly from their starting point to their exact destination (provided there are roads). It allows them to travel on their own schedule, in comfort, and in privacy.

impact: effect

The impact of the automobile on our society has been staggering. It has changed our lifestyle and the appearance of our cities and towns. People travel more now than in the past because the car makes travelling so easy.

A good example of Canadians' ability and willingness to travel is shown by supporters of the Saskatchewan Roughriders football team. The Roughriders play their home games in Regina, but it would be a mistake to think that the team's support comes from the Regina area only. With a population of much less than 200 000, Regina alone could not support a team. A check of a typical crowd at Regina's Taylor Field would reveal many fans from Moose Jaw, Saskatoon, Yorkton, Swift Current—in fact all of southern Saskatchewan. These people are prepared to make a trip of several hundred kilometres to attend a football game. This level of mobility, which could only exist with reliable, inexpensive automobiles, allows the football team to be truly the *Saskatchewan* Roughriders.

Bus

intercity: between cities

The bus is a major method of travelling between cities and is used mainly for journeys of less than 1000 km. Each year, more than 30 000 000 passengers travel on **intercity** buses. Bus travel has several advantages over other methods of transportation. It is relatively inexpensive and comfortable. Bus operators can establish and change routes quickly and cheaply to meet changing needs.

intracity: within a city

Intracity buses are used in almost every Canadian city and in many towns. In large cities like Montréal and Toronto there might be thousands of buses in use; in a small town there might only be one. In either case, buses are a key part of the transportation system for people who either cannot drive or choose not to. Buses can move large numbers of commuters efficiently and, compared with cars, reduce traffic, noise, and pollution in the city.

RAIL

At one time, travel between Canadian cities by train was more common than travel by any other means. Trains were faster, more reliable, and more comfortable than any other form of transporta-

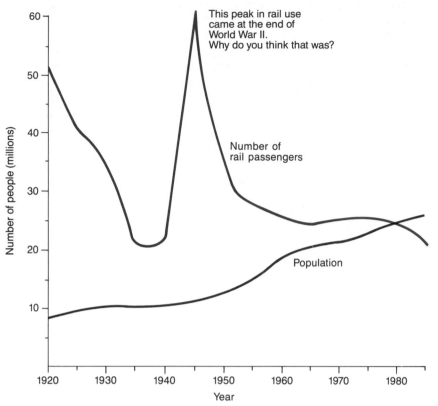

60 — This peak in rail use came at the end of World War II. Why do you think that was?

Number of rail passengers

Population

Number of people (millions)

1920 1930 1940 1950 1960 1970 1980

Year

Fig. 16–5 The drop in rail passengers is made even more dramatic if we remember that the population and the total amount of travel in Canada has increased enormously in this time.

tion. But other forms of transport rapidly became more attractive, especially after World War II. More people owned cars, and both cars and buses became more reliable. Intercity highways were improved. Travel by airplane, especially for longer trips, became cheaper and more comfortable. Fig. 16–5 illustrates the decline in the number of Canadians travelling by train since 1920.

The deterioration of the rail passenger business created a serious dilemma for the two major railway companies, Canadian National Railway (CNR) and Canadian Pacific Railway (CPR). Each company lost millions of dollars per year on its passenger operations. To reduce losses, the purchase of needed new equipment was postponed, and services such as dining and sleeping cars were often eliminated. This, of course, only made rail travel less attractive to the public.

To encourage public travel by train, the government created VIA Rail. VIA Rail is a crown corporation that provides only passenger service. It was given the task of providing passenger service on the routes formerly operated by CNR and CPR. The problems faced by VIA are the same as those faced by the private companies. Political pressures have made it very difficult to close unprofitable lines. Much of the equipment used is now more than 30 years old and obsolete, but the federal government has not provided adequate funding for modernization.

deterioration: worsening

TGV: Train à Grande Vitesse. What does this mean?

Ontario's Golden Horseshoe is the heavily developed commercial and industrial urban area stretching from Oshawa through Toronto and Hamilton to St. Catharines.

The future of rail passenger service could be getting brighter, though. High speed trains, similar to the "bullet trains" of Japan or the TGV trains of France, might one day solve the problems of Canadian rail passenger service. Travelling at speeds up to 380 km/h, high speed trains can move passengers from one downtown to another in less time than it takes to fly. This is possible because most airports are far from downtown. The rail passenger avoids time-consuming trips to and from the airport. Rail travel with such modern equipment is well-suited to distances of up to 600 km. This includes such routes as Edmonton-Calgary, Windsor-London-Hamilton-Toronto-Ottawa-Montréal-Québec City, and Halifax-Moncton-Saint John.

Trains are very important for moving commuters to work in some cities. The largest of these commuter rail systems is GO Transit—a train and bus system operated in the Golden Horseshoe area of Ontario by the Ontario government. The primary purpose of GO is to move people to and from the Toronto downtown core. Within Toronto and other larger cities, subway trains and light rail vehicles are the backbone of the mass transportation system.

AIR

The airplane has revolutionized travel. In 1850, a person travelling from eastern Canada to southern British Columbia would have travelled by ship from Halifax around Cape Horn at the tip of South America and up the west coast. This dangerous journey took at least five months! In 1885 when the CPR was completed to the West, passengers could cross the country in about seven days. The next great advance in speed came with the airplane. The first passenger flights were made across Canada before World War II (Fig. 16–2). Today, modern jet aircraft allow passengers to cross the country in just a few hours.

Today's airline industry is a very competitive one. There are several reasons for this but perhaps the most important is what is called **deregulation**. This means that there is now less government control of such things as fares and how many companies may fly on one route. Airlines are forced to become very efficient to survive. Canada's two major airlines, Air Canada and Canadian Airlines International, have moved toward a **hub and spoke** route pattern (Fig. 16–6). This pattern allows an airline to serve a large number of communities as cheaply as possible.

Increased competition in the airline industry has had other effects. Small, regional airlines using smaller aircraft have developed to provide service to smaller communities. Some of these communities used to be serviced by the major airlines. When deregulation was introduced, the major companies dropped service to these smaller communities because they were unprofitable using larger planes.

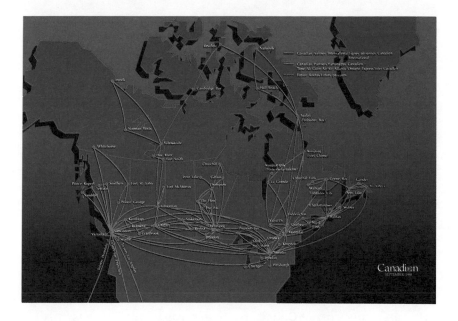

Fig. 16-6 An example of the hub and spoke route pattern. What are "hubs" and what are "spokes"? Why is this an efficient way to operate an airline?

WATER

Travel by ship is not very common in Canada, but where it is used it is of vital importance. Ferries carry tourists and island residents from the mainland to islands and back, or from island to island. Newfoundland, Prince Edward Island, and Vancouver Island are three places that rely heavily on ferry service. Attempts have been made to improve ferry service, because bad weather, labour problems, and mechanical problems can leave islanders isolated from the rest of the country.

When Prince Edward Island joined Canada in 1873, it was promised a "fixed link" — a bridge or tunnel to the mainland to replace the ferries. Plans are now underway to finally build the fixed link.

QUESTIONS

CHECKBACK

1. Why do roads play a vital role in maintaining Canada's economy?
2. What is the difference between intercity and intracity buses?
3. Why has passenger rail travel declined over the years?

ANALYZE

4. **a)** State two factors that allow the high speed trains of Japan and France to compete with airlines for intercity travel.
   b) What three routes in Canada would be best suited for these trains. Why?
5. **a)** What are commuter trains?
   b) Why are trains well-suited for this purpose?

6. What are the advantages and disadvantages of air travel compared with other forms of travel?

7. How would the deregulation of the airlines affect each of the following:
   a) the amount of service and fares between larger cities? Why?
   b) the amount of service and fares between smaller cities? Why?

8. Which parts of Canada rely heavily on ferry service? Why is this service important to these areas?

INVESTIGATE

9. Examine the maps in an atlas showing major roads, railway lines and air routes in Canada.
   a) Describe the direction of most of the roads, railways, and air routes.
   b) Explain the physical and human factors that influence the pattern of transportation routes.

10. a) Name a major Canadian city that you would like to visit.
   b) Make a chart similar to Fig. 16–7. Obtain the information you need to complete the chart from sources such as: your atlas, your parents, a travel agent, railway companies, airlines and bus companies.
   c) Which type of transportation would you select? Why?
   d) Would people who are not students make the same choices? Explain your answer.

Fig. 16–7

Type of Transportation	Distance in Km From My Home	Cost in Dollars	Time in Hours
automobile			
train			
bus			
plane			

11. Between the 1800s and today, the relative importance of different transportation methods has changed.
   a) In your notebook, complete a chart similar to Fig. 16–8 by naming the most important transportation methods in each time period.
   b) What changes have taken place in
      i. short distance transportation?
      ii. long distance transportation?
   c) Explain why these changes have occurred.

Fig. 16–8

	Short Distances	Long Distances
1800s		
1900 – 1950		
1950 – present		

12. You have been appointed Minister of Transport. You must solve some serious problems in Canada's transportation network.
   a) One form of long distance passenger transport (car, bus, train, or plane) must be eliminated to save money and fuel. Which one will you eliminate and why?
   b) It is unrealistic to talk about eliminating one method of transportation completely, but improvements are possible.
      i. Suggest three improvements to Canada's transportation system.
      ii. Describe why each improvement is needed.

■ MOVEMENT OF GOODS

Lean back in your chair and imagine that you have been miraculously transported to a railway station platform in a small town in the middle of a spruce forest. The town does not look familiar but the sign on the station reads: Armstrong, Ontario. You know that Armstrong is a town on the main CN railway line between eastern and western Canada, but you do not know which way is east and which way is west. There are two freight trains parked in the town waiting for a track to be repaired. The trains have come from different directions, but you don't know which train came from which direction. Might their cargoes tell you? You check both trains and find that one is carrying grain, plywood and Japanese cars while the other is carrying mining equipment, German trucks, and Canadian magazines.

- Which train is heading east and which is heading west? How do you know?
- List three other important commodities that might be carried on each of these trains.

Every day Canada's transportation system must handle cargoes ranging from 50 000 tonnes of coal to 100 kg of live lobsters or even a human heart for transplant. With this variety of commodities comes a range of freight-handling needs. Some cargoes must be moved as quickly as possible with little concern for cost. Other shipments can travel at any speed but cost must be kept as low as possible. Still others are very easily damaged and need special protection.

Meeting all of these needs demands a transportation network that is diverse, efficient, and up-to-date. In a country that has the problems of distance, terrain, and climate that face Canada, the problem is even greater. Over the past 100 years, Canada's transportation system has been developed to respond to all of these challenges.

RAIL

Canada's railways are the backbone of the system that moves freight from one place to another. Although the railways carry many types of products, they are particularly good for moving **bulk cargoes** such as coal, grain, wood, and oil (Fig. 16–9). Bulk cargoes have a relatively low value and large volume. The railways have developed several methods to move these cargoes as cheaply as possible. One method is the **unit train**.

Industry	Products Shipped	Number of Rail Cars
Mining	Iron Ore	398 000
	Other metal ores	138 000
	Potash	113 000
	Coal, sand, and other mine products	709 000
	Petroleum products and chemicals	204 000
Forestry	Lumber and plywood	178 000
	Pulpwood, paper	334 000
Agriculture	Wheat	240 000
	Other grains and farm products	205 000
	Prepared food products	27 000
Other	Motor parts and vehicles	134 000
	Manufactured goods	770 000
	Miscellaneous	91 000
TOTAL		3 541 000

Fig. 16–9 Rail cargoes, 1986

A unit train carries huge quantities of only one cargo along a fixed route. The train consists of specially-designed cars that can be loaded and unloaded quickly and therefore cheaply. Some of the most important unit train routes are:

- from the interior of Québec-Labrador to ports on the St. Lawrence River (iron ore)
- from the Rocky Mountains to Vancouver (coal)
- from the Prairies to Vancouver and Thunder Bay (wheat)
- from Saskatchewan to Vancouver (potash)

In the 1950s and 1960s, the railways found that they were facing stiff competition from trucks. Trucks have a major advantage over trains — they do not have to stay on tracks. They can go directly to a factory to pick up a shipment and then carry it to its exact destination. Because the shipment never has to be transferred to another vehicle, handling costs and delays are reduced.

The railways decided to combine the advantages of trucking with those of rail. They developed the **piggyback** system, which works like this:

- truck trailers are loaded with cargo at a factory

Rail still has the advantage for longer distances and bulkier cargoes.

Fig. 16–10 The Halifax container port

- trailers are trucked to a nearby railyard and loaded onto flat-cars
- a train takes trailers to a distant railyard where they are unloaded
- trailers are trucked to their final destination

The piggyback system has helped the railways to remain competitive.

The final shipping method, also used for shipping by road, water, and air, is the use of containers for non-bulk cargoes (Fig. 16–10). A container is, very simply, a large metal box of standard size and shape. Containers are loaded by the shipper and can be moved by any combination of trucks, trains, ships, and planes. Containers can be moved quickly and cheaply, and theft and damage are unlikely. Before the development of containers, freight had to be loaded and unloaded piece by piece. This was very time-consuming and costly.

ROAD

Trucking is less expensive than rail because:
- vehicles cost less to buy and maintain than railway cars and engines
- truck terminals are less expensive to build than train terminals
- trucks are better suited to carry lighter, less bulky cargoes.

Efficient intercity trucking is a fairly recent development. Before World War II, trucks were small and unreliable, and the roads were not very good. Since then, both equipment and roads have been greatly improved. Larger, more reliable trucks and a growing network of paved highways allow goods to be moved quickly and reliably.

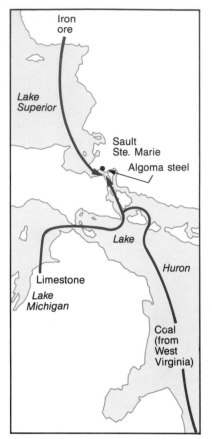

Fig. 16–11 Algoma Steel in Sault Ste. Marie

WATER

Ships have been used for Canadian commerce for more than 400 years. One hundred and fifty years ago, ships moved all kinds of cargo and passengers on all three coasts and on the Great Lakes. They were the most important part of the transportation system at the time because transportation methods on land were slow and unreliable. Even though conditions for land transport have greatly improved since then, ships are still tremendously important to Canada's economy.

Ships are best suited for the movement of very bulky, low value cargoes. These include grain, iron ore, coal, petroleum (both crude and refined), sand and gravel, and lumber. Mills, refineries, and factories are usually located to take advantage of water-borne transport. Consider the case of Algoma Steel in Sault Ste. Marie, Ont. The company was built at this crossroads of the Great Lakes because the major raw materials — iron ore, coal, and lime-stone — could all be brought to the steel mills by ship at minimum cost (Fig. 16–11).

The St. Lawrence Seaway is a system of canals and locks that links the interior of the continent with the Atlantic Ocean, via the Great Lakes and the St. Lawrence River. It allows ocean-going ships to travel 3800 km into and out of the heart of the continent.

Some ships, as well as some ports on the east and west coasts of Canada, are now designed to handle containers rather than cargo packed into small boxes. Container ships and ports allow a speedy transfer of goods from ship to shore and vice versa.

Canada's far north presents special transportation problems. The distances between the populated parts of Canada and the far north are great. Since shipping goods by plane is very expensive, air transport is usually reserved for people, perishable goods, and small items. Transporting goods to the far north by truck is impossible because there are few, if any, roads. However, in the winter when the land is frozen, convoys of tractors carry goods to some settlements.

In the spring, when the ice has broken up, barges travel down the Mackenzie River to supply settlements in the area. Ships make annual trips into the Arctic and along the coasts of Labrador and Hudson Bay. They deliver bulky cargoes such as oil products, building materials, and equipment needed by companies in the far north. They also bring the residents many of their food supplies for the coming year. This movement of goods requires careful planning because the shipping season is only six weeks long at the most.

AIR

Although shipping goods by air is more expensive than by any other method of transportation, the use of air freight has greatly increased over the years (Fig. 16–12). The amount of freight car-

Fig. 16–12   Air cargo being loaded

ried is small compared to that moved by rail and ship. Goods shipped by air tend to be specialized in nature and tend to have one or more of the following characteristics:

- light in mass and small in size
- of high value
- perishable
- needed quickly

Air transport has played a very important part in the development of Canada's frontier regions. Airplanes are ideal for transporting workers and cargoes across the northern terrain. The people who fly these planes are called bush pilots and some have become famous for their daring feats of flying. They fly with help whenever emergencies arise, even though weather conditions are often dangerous.

Air freight commonly includes such things as: fresh fish, flowers, mail, electronic equipment, and anything needed in a hurry – no matter how heavy.

A famous bush pilot, Max Ward started with one plane and developed his business into a major airline – Wardair.

PIPELINES

When we consider the ways in which goods are moved, we often forget about pipelines (Fig. 16–13). This is understandable because pipelines do their work out of sight of most people. Pipelines can move gases, liquids or even solids that have been crushed and mixed with water.

A pipeline is built only when there is

- a supply of suitable material that must be moved from one place to another and which is large enough to last for many years;
- no chance to use transport by ship (which is generally cheaper). Fig. 16–14 shows the location of Canada's oil and gas pipelines. Not shown, however, are the dozens of smaller pipelines that collect oil and gas from the fields and then move them to the main pipelines.

Fig. 16–13   Covering over an oil pipeline

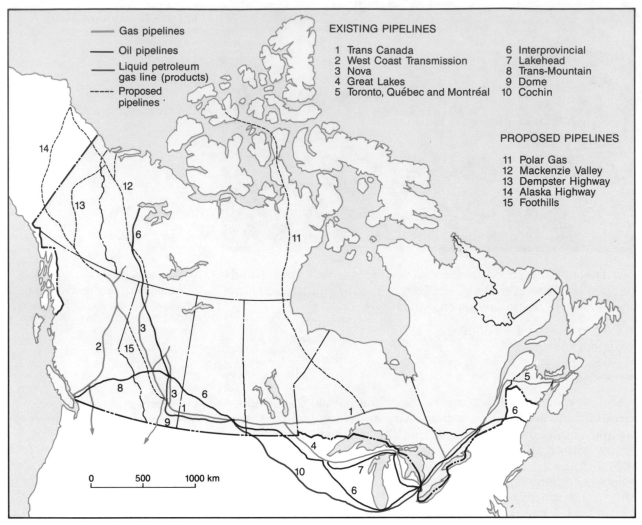

Gas pipelines
Oil pipelines
Liquid petroleum gas line (products)
Proposed pipelines

0   500   1000 km

Fig. 16–14 Major Canadian pipelines

■ IN CLOSING...

Canada's transportation network is extremely important to the country's economy. Raw materials from mines, forests, fisheries, and farms are transported to processing plants and manufactured goods are transported to markets in Canada and elsewhere. People use the many means of transportation to crisscross the country visiting, vacationing and doing business. You need look no further than your daily newspaper to understand how Canada's economy is dependent upon its transportation network. You will often see stories of pipeline and aircraft construction, highway expansion, or improvements in rail and ferry services.

Canada's transportation network performs another, perhaps less obvious, task. It links all of Canada's diverse regions, making people feel that they belong to one, unified country. Without the movement of people and goods made possible by efficient transportation, Canada could not survive as a nation.

QUESTIONS

See Chapter 33 for help with this graph.

CHECKBACK

1. What types of bulk cargoes do railways carry?
2. **a)** What is a unit train?
   b) List three unit train routes and indicate the cargoes carried on each.
3. **a)** Describe two methods which have been developed to allow easy transfer of cargo from one transportation method to another.
   b) Explain how these methods have improved the overall efficiency of moving goods.
4. Make a list of reasons describing why trucks are less expensive to operate than trains.
5. **a)** Why were ships so important to Canadian commerce more than a century ago?
   b) What types of goods do ships move today? Why?
   c) Give an example of a shipping route within Canada.
6. Describe the role of ships in Canada's far north.
7. What types of goods do airplanes carry? Why?
8. Why are some Canadian pilots called bush pilots?
9. What conditions are necessary before it is practical to build a pipeline?

ANALYZE

10. Why would grain going from Saskatchewan to Europe be loaded onto a ship at Thunder Bay rather than at Halifax?
11. A Canadian jeans manufacturer in Winnipeg has just filled a container with jeans at the factory. The container is to be sent to a clothing distributor in London, England. Describe the possible steps involved in this trip.
12. **a)** Refer to Fig. 16–9. Calculate the percentage of the total cargo made up by each of the following categories:
    i. mining products   **iv.** automobiles and parts
    ii. forestry products   **v.** manufactured goods
    iii. agricultural products
    b) Draw a pie graph to illustrate the types of cargoes carried by railways.
    c) What do these cargoes have in common? What differences are there?
13. Which method of transportation would you choose to move each of the following? Explain your choices.
    a) 100 000 t of wheat from Saskatoon, Sask. to Churchill, Man.
    b) six pianos to be shipped from Montréal: four to Ottawa, one to Peterborough, Ont. and one to Kingston, Ont.
    c) 200 000 t of oil from Alberta to Sarnia, Ont.
    d) 50 000 t of iron ore from Sept-Isles, Qué. to Hamilton, Ont.
    e) 100 kg of fresh daffodils from Victoria to Montréal.

14. **a)** Define "upbound" and "downbound" for ships on the St. Lawrence Seaway.
    b) Give one or more examples of cargoes moving in each direction on the Seaway.
    c) The table in Fig. 16–15 shows the traffic trends on the Welland Canal between Lake Ontario and Lake Erie. Calculate the average tonnage carried by each ship in 1959 and 1985.
    d) What happened to
       i. total tonnage?
       ii. number of ships?
       iii. size of ships?
    e) If a large transport truck can carry 50 t of cargo and a train with 60 cars can carry 4000 t of cargo, calculate:
       i. How many truck and train loads of cargo went through the Welland Canal in 1986?
       ii. How many truck and train loads was the average ship's cargo equal to?
    f) How do these figures help to explain why bulk cargoes are shipped by water whenever possible?

Fig. 16–15 Welland Canal shipping

	1959	1985
Number of ships	7500	3800
Cargo Tonnage (t)	27 000 000	42 000 000

Communications

17

When your grandparents were children, a long distance phone call was a rare occurrence. It might signal a happy event such as a birth or graduation, or a sad event such as a death. People could go many months or even years without making or receiving such a call. Today, long distance calls, even across oceans, are common in many families.

Have you ever thought about what actually happens when you make a long distance call? By dialing a few numbers you can make a specific phone ring in a country on the other side of the world. This involves the use of the phone systems of two (or more) countries, satellites or undersea cables, and a great deal of international cooperation. Because it is so easy to do, we often forget what a remarkable feat it is.

A famous Canadian writer named Marshall McLuhan stated that the world is becoming a **"global village"**. By this he meant that technological improvements have made communications throughout the entire world as easy as they had once been in a small village.

To demonstrate how small the world really is, complete the following exercise. You will need a telephone book containing a section dealing with long distance calls, a globe, a piece of string, a ruler, and graph paper.

1. a) For station-to-station calls in Canada and the U.S. (excluding Alaska and Hawaii), it is necessary to dial:
    $$1 + \text{area code} + \text{local number}$$
    b) For station-to-station calls overseas, it is necessary to dial:
    011 + country code + routing code* + local number
        (2-3 digits)   (1-5 digits)   (2-9 digits)
    *needed only in some countries

2. Examine the telephone numbers in Fig. 17–1, Column B. Using the information in the telephone book, match up each telephone number with a call in Column A.

Hint: Check the area codes in the long distance section of your telephone book.

Fig. 17–1 Match the call to the phone number

Column A		Column B
a)	The Prime Minister in Ottawa	i. 011–57–1–35–50–**
b)	Walt Disney World in Florida	ii. 1–202–456–****
c)	The Sydney Opera House in Australia	iii. 1–613–992–****
d)	The R.C.M.P. at Sachs Harbour, N.W.T.	iv. 011–44–01–930–****
e)	Buckingham Palace in London	v. 1–305–824–****
f)	The White House in Washington	vi. 011–65–31–***
g)	The Canadian Ambassador in Bogota, Colombia	vii. 011–7–095–205–**
h)	The Prime Minister of Singapore	viii. 1–403–690–****
i)	The Kremlin in Moscow	ix. 011–61–1–256–****

Why do you think the last few digits of each phone number have been left out?

3. Determine the cost for the first minute of a telephone call, during regular business hours, from where you live to each of the destinations in Column A. (NOTE: Your teacher may provide you with this information.) Record these costs.

4. What do you think is the relationship between the cost and distance of a telephone call? Explain.

5. On a globe, use a piece of string to measure the shortest distance between where you live and each of the telephone call destinations. Record these distances in kilometres.

6. Construct a graph similar to Fig. 17–2. Use your data on cost and distance to plot the location for each city. Write the name of the city beside each dot.

7. Do the results of the above prove or disprove your answer to question 4? Discuss your findings in a group.

Fig. 17–2

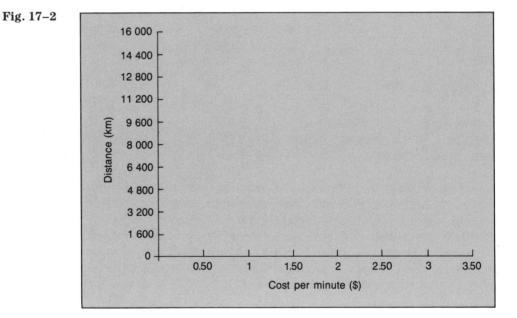

Key Terms

global village
communications
telecommunications

satellite transmission
microwave transmission
submarine cables

■ INTRODUCTION

In the previous chapter we learned that transportation involves the movement of people and goods from one place to another. **Communications** also involves movement: the movement of information. Early humans probably communicated through sounds and body language. Once written language developed, information could be recorded on materials such as stone, clay, skins and paper. In this form it could be moved easily from one place to another or from one time to another.

More recently, people have developed the technology to send information along wires and through the air, using inventions such as the telegraph, radio, telephone, television, and satellites (Fig. 17-3). The past twenty years have brought an avalanche of improvements in communications technology. We have even tried to open communications with neighbours who might exist on other planets (Fig. 17-4).

Canadians are fortunate to have access to the most advanced communications network that has ever existed. It is possible for us to conduct business, keep informed and entertained, and talk to each other quickly and easily across long distances. This is

Fig. 17-3 Communications have always been an important feature of Canadian life.
- Construction of telegraph lines in British Columbia in the 1880s
- A radio broadcast in the 1920s
- A satellite earth station in Weir, Québec today

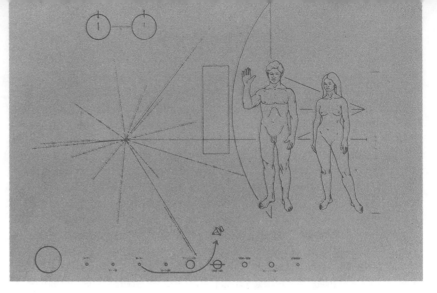

Fig. 17–4 We are already trying to communicate with beings beyond our solar system. This plate was attached to the Pioneer 10 spacecraft, which was the first object made by people to leave the solar system. Try to figure out the message on the plate. What information would you have sent?

especially important if we remember that Canada is a vast, rugged country with a relatively small population.

There are two main forms of communication:
1. printed text such as newspapers, magazines, and books
2. **telecommunications**; that is, information sent in the form of electro-magnetic waves over long distances. Telecommunications includes such things as telephone, radio, and television.

The remainder of this chapter will concentrate on telecommunications for two reasons: the importance of telecommunications to Canada; and the rapid changes in telecommunications technology.

■ COMMUNICATIONS WITHIN CANADA

How do Canadians exchange information?
• They talk to one another;
• They listen to the radio (98% of Canadian households have a radio, and there are more than 7 000 000 car radios);
• They watch television (97% of Canadian households have a television — over half of these have cable service);
• They write letters (Canada has over 8500 post offices);
• They use the telephone (Canadians make over 22 000 000 000 telephone calls each year);
• They read (Canada has 120 daily newspapers, with a total circulation of over 5 000 000).

Most of us are very familiar with these methods of communication, but few of us think very much about what happens behind the scenes. What allows you to watch a television show, receive a long distance phone call, or pick up a morning paper at the door each day?

The television show must somehow be sent from the network centre to your local station. The phone call must be correctly routed to your home. The news for your newspaper must be gathered at the newspaper office. Several systems are used to do all this.

MICROWAVE TRANSMISSION

In **microwave transmission**, information sent in the form of telephone calls, television, radio, or telex, is first converted to radio signals. These signals are transmitted over a series of radio towers. Since radio waves travel in straight lines, there must be relay towers about every 50 km because the curvature of the earth does not allow direct communication over longer distances (Fig. 17–5). At the message's destination, the signals are converted back into their original form. For example, a person on the other end of a telephone hears a voice, television viewers see a picture, and the telex prints a message. Microwave transmission is ideal for Canada because much of our terrain is too rugged to cross with wire or cable (Fig. 17–6).

Telex is a system in which messages are sent from one teleprinter (similar to a microcomputer and printer) to another. It is widely used in business.

Fig. 17–5 What differences do you see between the location of the microwave networks and of the satellite stations?

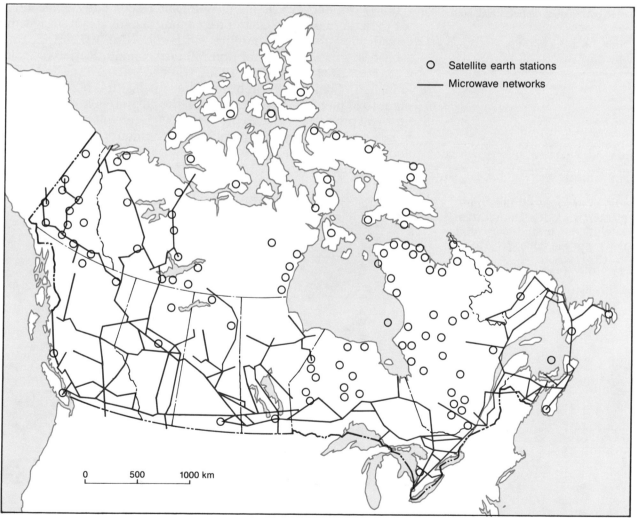

- ○ Satellite earth stations
- — Microwave networks

0   500   1000 km

Fig. 17–6 Microwave transmission can be used where a cable network could never be built.

In 1987, Telesat Canada was sold to a private company.

"Anik" is an Inuktitut word meaning "brother".

Fig. 17–7 How satellite transmission works. Communication satellites are in stationary orbit, moving at the same speed as the Earth's rotation.

DOMESTIC SATELLITE

A more recent method of sending information is by **satellite** (Fig.17–7). A single satellite can be used to transmit a message from one side of the country to the other. Many microwave towers are needed on the ground to do the same thing.

In 1969 an Act of Parliament established a company called Telesat Canada to operate a satellite communications system within Canada. The first Anik satellite was launched in 1972. Anik was the world's first satellite for non-military communications within a country. By the end of the 1970s, three more satellites had been launched, followed by another five during the 1980s. Telesat plans to launch two new satellites in the early 1990s. These satellites will provide service to the year 2000, and will be technically more advanced. They will handle greater amounts of information and cover larger areas of the country with their signals. Each new satellite will do the work of four of the older ones.

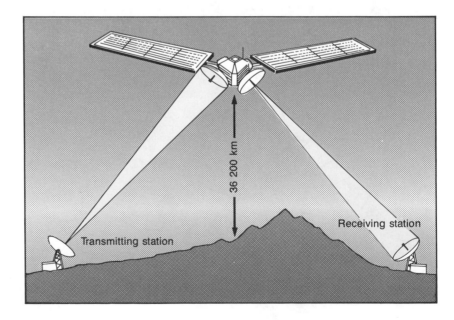

QUESTIONS

CHECKBACK

1. **a)** What is the difference between transportation and communications?
   b) How do Canadians benefit by having a good communications system?
2. **a)** Define telecommunications.
   b) Name four communication systems that are based on telecommunications.
3. Outline in a flow chart how your voice would travel by microwave transmission during a telephone call from your home to someone in another part of Canada.
4. **a)** What is an Anik satellite?
   b) How is information sent by satellite from one part of the country to another? Refer to Fig. 17–7.

ANALYZE

5. **a)** Describe in your own words what is meant by "global village".
   b) How has it come into being?
6. How did each of the developments in Fig. 17–2 affect Canadian society?
7. **a)** Examine Fig. 17–5. In what regions are most satellite earth stations located?
   b) Give at least two reasons why satellite communication is particularly important to the people in these regions.
   c) Why is satellite communication especially important to the Native peoples living in remote areas of the north?
8. Compare the locations of the microwave network and the satellite earth station network (Fig. 17–5) with the locations of Canada's railways and highways (Fig. 16–4). Which network more closely follows the railways and highways? Explain why.

INVESTIGATE

9. Canada has the most widely developed cable television network in the world.
   a) Is cable available where you live?
   b) What are the advantages of cable?
   c) What disadvantages are there?
10. **a)** What is your postal code?
    b) The first letter of your postal code is a regional or provincial designator. Check with a postal code guide book and determine what first letters are used and what areas across Canada they refer to.
    c) On a blank map of Canada, show the areas represented by each letter in part b).

11. Here are different views expressed by two Canadians:

"Communication systems join Canadians together because they enable us to learn more about one another."

"Communication systems divide the Canadian people because they allow us to see how little we have in common with one another."

Which view do you think is correct? Why?

12. In the previous chapter, Canada's transportation system was likened to the circulatory system of the body. To what part of the body would you compare the communications system? Why?

COMMUNICATIONS WITH OTHER COUNTRIES

Canada has always strived to maintain good communications with other countries. There are many reasons for this.

- Good communications are necessary to the economy. In this age of worldwide trade, it is vital for Canada to have contact with international suppliers of both finished products and raw materials. Canada must also have contact with customers who buy our exports.
- Communication links with other countries allow the exchange of cultural, medical, scientific, and other information.
- Communicating with other countries is essential to Canada's role in world politics.
- Canadians wish to communicate with relatives and friends in other countries.

Teleglobe Canada is now a private company

How do we communicate with people in other parts of the world? In 1950, the federal government created Teleglobe Canada to develop our overseas cable network. This organization was later given responsibility for our satellite links with other countries. Teleglobe Canada works with similar agencies in other countries to provide a worldwide communications network. This network allows all member countries to benefit from efficient international communications.

SUBMARINE CABLE

Canada has communicated with other countries using submarine cable for many years. The first transatlantic cable was put into operation between Newfoundland and Ireland in 1856. This cable could carry one radio message at a time. The first cable to carry telephone messages was completed in 1956. It also ran between

Newfoundland and Ireland and could carry 52 phone calls simultaneously. It was called Tat-1. The newest cable is Tat-9, scheduled for use in 1991. The cost of laying this cable is $500 000 000. Because it is a fibre-optic cable, Tat-9 can carry a staggering 80 000 phone calls at one time! It is also the first cable designed to carry television programs.

Why are Canada and other countries still laying new cables in what most people assume to be the satellite age? There are several reasons. Submarine cables last for 25 years or more, while communications satellites tend to last for only 7 to 15 years. The cable's longer life makes it economical to operate. Furthermore, cable transmissions are immune to interference from sun spots and the northern lights. A final advantage is that it is much more difficult to eavesdrop on messages sent by cable than by satellite. Cable and satellites complement one another to provide us with an effective, reliable communications system.

Tat: Transatlantic

In addition to Tat-9, the early 1990s will see the completion of a new transpacific cable.

SATELLITES

In 1964 Teleglobe Canada joined the International Satellite Organization (INTELSAT). This organization, which now has more than 100 members, was set up to control a global commercial satellite system. The first INTELSAT satellite, Early Bird, was launched in 1965. It had a capacity of 240 phone calls at one time. Today there are five INTELSAT satellites in orbit 35 900 km above the earth's equator. They each have a capacity for over 6000 phone calls, plus space for television signals. Live television programs from other parts of the world are transmitted via INTELSAT satellites to ground stations in Canada. We currently have four such ground stations.

■ COMMUNICATIONS IN THE FUTURE

The advances in communications technology today are so rapid and are occurring in so many fields that it is impossible for most people to keep up with them. The next 20 years will be an exciting time for Canadians as new methods of communication come into use. The new technology will have a major impact on our lives. In this section we can only suggest a few of the things that are likely to happen. Perhaps you know of others.

TELEVISION

For most Canadians, television is the principal source of entertainment and information. In the future, both what we watch and how we watch it will change. Television today is designed to appeal to a wide range of people. If a particular show on commercial television does not appeal to enough people it is likely to be cancelled by the advertisers who pay for the show. The term "TV broadcast" implies the idea of reaching a wide range of people.

Fig. 17–8 Television of the future will be worldwide and more varied.

Canadian families with satellite dishes already have access to several dozen stations.

Fig. 17–9 In the future, computers and television will combine to allow us to shop, learn and obtain information at home.

a)

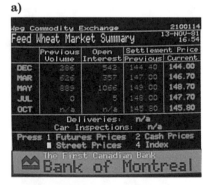

b)

| 112 | **Tai Chi** Your morning exercise direct from Beijing |
| 114 | **Sunrise Semester** Prof. Ian Clark discusses, "Dealing with the Aging Parent" |

7:00 am

2	**Learning Japanese** with Melissa Nishioka
5	**World Chess Championship** Game 13, live from Singapore
6	**Arctic A.M.** from Iqaluit
7	**M.A.S.H.** Hawkeye writes to his father
10	**Mélange** A live fashion show, direct from Paris, of the hot fashions for fall
11	**Polka Dot Door**
12	**Young and the Restless** Can Cynthia tell Brad the awful truth?
14	**Stanley Cup Hockey Final** live from Moscow, Montréal Canadiens versus Moscow Red Army
15	**Noon News** from the BBC World TV Service in London
17	**Australian Pro Tennis final** live from Perth
18	**Shopping Roma** Your chance to buy the latest products from Rome as they are displayed to you by the merchants of the Via Veneto
21	**I Love Lucy** Lucy's new job is more than she asked for
23	**Growing Orchids** with David Wallace, from the Cloud Forest of Costa Rica
24	**Brazil Today** with Lee Da Silva in Rio (in Portuguese)
26	**Computer Corner** Sandra answers your questions
27	**WakeUp Canada!** News, sports, and weather from around the corner and across the nation
29	**Movie** Rocky 9 (1998, Sly Stallone) Rocky hangs up the gloves but must return to the ring to prove he still has what it takes

17 • TV Times — Lists all 93 stations available in this area.

In the future, television will be "narrowcast". This means that shows will be designed to meet the needs of specialized groups of people (Fig. 17–8). This specialization can only happen if there are many stations available that can operate very cheaply. Recent technical advances permit this. Television experts predict that Canadians will eventually have access to 100 or more stations. Many stations mean that television will become more personal, and therefore more useful.

COMPUTERS

Many Canadian households and most schools already have computers. They can operate as information centres, giving us access to libraries and databases all over the world (Fig. 17–9a). They allow us to also communicate with other people. If we want to send a letter to someone, we can use a FAX machine and the letter will be available at the other person's location in seconds.

The computers that we will use in the future will do even more. Computers will allow us to shop from home at stores almost anywhere in the world (Fig. 17–9b). They will operate the mechanical systems of our homes, controlling such things as temperature, lights, lawn watering, and security. Furthermore, computers will become much easier to use and cheaper to buy.

FIBRE-OPTICS

Not all communication improvements will be as obvious as those mentioned above. Some will be "behind the scenes". A good example of this kind of change is the introduction of fibre-optic cables. Since the invention of the telegraph in the 1840s, copper wires have been used to transmit signals in the form of electric pulses. Although this has worked reasonably well, the quality of the message sent, especially over long distances, could be improved.

Scientists have discovered that messages can be sent in the form of light through thin strands of glass (Fig. 17–10). These fibre-optic cables not only transmit messages without distortion, but also carry 100 times as much information as a comparable copper cable. Fibre-optic cables are gradually replacing copper in many parts of Canada's phone network. It will be many years, however, before all of Canada uses fibre-optics because there are so many tens of thousands of kilometres of cable to be replaced.

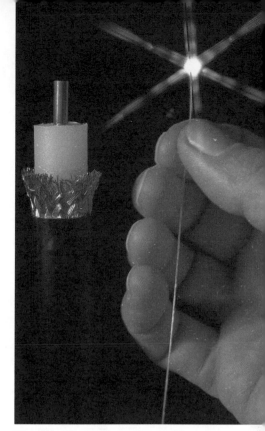

Fig. 17–10   Fibre-optic strands

■ IN CLOSING...

Our communications network lets us share information not only with Canadians in other parts of the country but also with citizens of other nations. This movement of information from one place to another is essential to the Canadian economy, to Canadian life in general, and to our understanding of the world.

Q U E S T I O N S

CHECKBACK

1. Complete the puzzle below in your notebook.

a) underwater communication lines
b) strands of glass that carry communications
c) to send a message
d) messages sent electrically
e) an information-handling device
f) Canadians use this device more than anyone else in the world
g) Canadian satellite
h) wires are currently made of this material
i) the international organization that controls world commercial satellite communication
j) what is sent by communications systems
k) a satellite of the 1960s

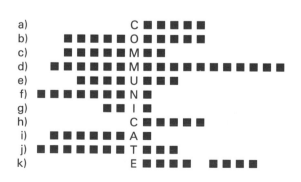

2. Provide four reasons why Canada needs good communications with other countries.
3. Construct a chart to compare submarine cables with satellites as means of communication. Describe the advantages and disadvantages of each.
4. a) What is a fibre-optic cable?
   b) What are the advantages of fibre-optics?
   c) Even though fibre-optic cables are superior to copper cables, it will be many years before they replace copper cables in our communications system. Why?

ANALYZE

5. Compare the different roles of Telesat Canada and Teleglobe Canada. Why are there two different agencies?

INVESTIGATE

6. Your parents have asked you to design a communications room in your home. Money is no object. What equipment would you want and why? Be sure to consider the communications, entertainment, and information needs of all members of your family.

WHAT DO YOU THINK?

7. "Modern communications technology will allow people to work from their homes instead of having to go to an office." Imagine that you have a job as a secretary or as a lawyer. Discuss the advantages and disadvantages of working at home and in an office. Which would you prefer? Why?
8. What roles do television and computers currently play in your life? How might these roles change in the future? What will cause these changes? How might your answer to this question differ if you lived in a small village in the Far North?
9. a) Why is it not surprising that Canada has been and remains a pioneer in communications technology?
   b) How does Canada benefit by being a pioneer in this field?

Canada's Industrial and Urban Heartland

Examine Fig. 18-1. It lists Canada's largest cities. A surprising number of these are found in the small area of Canada shown on Fig. 18-2. Use this figure and your atlas to complete a copy of Fig. 18-3 in your notebook.

Fig.18–1   Canada's largest cities

Census Metropolitan Areas, 1986 (thousands of people)			
Toronto	3427	Victoria	256
Montréal	2921	Windsor	254
Vancouver	1381	Oshawa	204
Ottawa-Hull	819	Saskatoon	201
Edmonton	785	Regina	186
Calgary	671	St. John's	162
Winnipeg	625	Chicoutimi-Jonquière	158
Québec City	603	Sudbury	149
Hamilton	557	Sherbrooke	130
St. Catherines	343	Trois-Rivières	129
London	342	Thunder Bay	122
Kitchener-Waterloo	311	Saint John	121
Halifax	296		

Fig. 18–2   Canada's industrial and urban Heartland

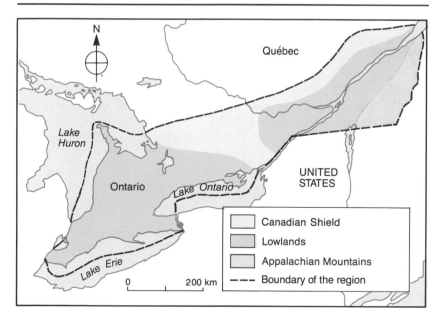

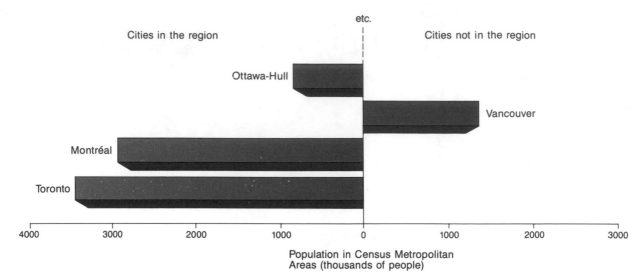

etc.

Cities in the region   Cities not in the region

Ottawa-Hull

Vancouver

Montréal

Toronto

4000   3000   2000   1000   0   1000   2000   3000

Population in Census Metropolitan
Areas (thousands of people)

Fig. 18–3   Complete this graph in
your notebook.

How many of the largest cities are in this region? What percentage of Canada's population lives in this area — which covers less than 2% of the country? What caused people to live there? What effect does this population concentration have on Canada's geography? In this chapter you will find out.

Key Terms

intensive farming
historical head start
tariff

branch plants
research and development (R and D)

■ CHARACTERISTICS OF THE HEARTLAND

In Chapter 15, you learned that where you find large numbers of people you will find large amounts of manufacturing and services. This is certainly the case in that part of southern Ontario and southern Québec shown in Fig. 18–2. Geographers call this small region the "Industrial and Urban Heartland" of Canada. Let's look at its characteristics.

LANDFORMS

At first glance, it may appear that the Heartland consists only of the Great Lakes Lowland in Ontario and the St. Lawrence Lowland in Québec (Fig. 18–2). However, the Heartland extends beyond the limits of the lowlands and includes nearby parts of the Canadian Shield and the Appalachian Mountains.

POPULATION

Approximately 13 000 000 people live in the Heartland—about half of Canada's population. People are attracted to the area because of the availability of jobs. This increases the population.

POLITICAL POWER

The Heartland elects many members to the House of Commons. During most of the 1970s and early 1980s, the Liberal Party of Canada formed Canada's government, even though relatively few Liberals from outside the Heartland were elected to Parliament. In the elections of 1984 and 1988, many people in the Heartland switched their support to the Progressive Conservative Party. This switch allowed the PCs to form majority governments in each case.

WEALTH

The residents of the Heartland earn about 60% of all personal income received by Canadians. This is not surprising, considering the large population of the region. Because of this concentration of wealth, manufacturers aim their products and advertising at the people of the Heartland.

concentration: having a larger amount than elsewhere

CULTURAL IMPORTANCE

The large population and great wealth of the Heartland support many cultural activities. In less populated and less wealthy areas it is difficult to maintain professional opera companies, full-time theatre companies, or major league hockey, football, or baseball teams. A number of cities in the Heartland have all of these.

URBAN CONCENTRATION

One of the most obvious characteristics of the Heartland is the great number of cities and towns. Lowland areas are very suitable for farming, manufacturing, settlement, and transportation. All of these activities in turn have led to the growth of many towns and cities in the Great Lakes-St. Lawrence Lowlands. About 83% of the people of the Heartland live in its cities and towns, which include Canada's two largest cities—Toronto and Montréal.

AGRICULTURE IN AN URBAN REGION

Agricultural demand is high in the Heartland for two main reasons. The region's large population must be fed, and agricultural

Fig. 18-4 How many of these food products may have come from the Heartland?

arable: capable of growing crops

products are important raw materials for factories in the area (Fig. 18-4). Only 13% of Canada's arable land is found in the Heartland but about 40% of farm sales come from this area. There are several reasons for this.

The region has an especially long **growing season**. In fact, the area of southwestern Ontario near Windsor has one of Canada's longest growing seasons (over 180 d/a). The Heartland region also has ample precipitation (more than 750 mm/a in most areas). The result is that some very specialized, high-value crops can be grown. Crops of this type, including grapes, peaches, tobacco, soybeans, and vegetables, make more money per hectare than other crops.

Heartland farming can be described as **intensive farming** because large amounts of machinery, labour, irrigation, and fertilizer are used on relatively small farms. These techniques are used to produce the largest income possible from the amount of land used. Because cities are nearby, products can be shipped to market quickly and easily.

SERVICES

Service industries employ far more people than any other type of job in the Heartland. They include government, **finance**, education, **retail** and **wholesale trade**, and business and personal services. Service industries in this region meet the needs of local people and of people across Canada. Many head offices of companies are located in the Heartland because of the area's large markets and huge labour force.

The influence of these companies may often extend across the whole nation, because decisions made by company head offices in the Heartland may create or eliminate jobs in towns thousands of kilometres away. For example, when a company locates in the

Heartland, jobs are not created in other parts of the country (such as Atlantic Canada and Western Canada). Similarly, when a company moves to the Heartland, jobs may be lost in the region it leaves. On the other hand, decisions by the head offices of large corporations can have positive benefits in other parts of the country. If an oil company decides to build an oil sands processing plant in Alberta, thousands of people and millions of dollars will flow into that part of Canada.

The decisions of financial institutions affect jobs and development throughout the country. If these institutions agree to lend money, businesses can expand; if they refuse to lend money, expansion is held back.

MANUFACTURING

The Heartland has the greatest concentration of manufacturing industries in Canada. These industries employ about 72% of the country's manufacturing workers. Almost all important types of manufacturing, such as automobiles, chemicals, clothing, and electrical goods, are found in the Heartland. Even though other areas of Canada are attracting manufacturing, the Heartland continues to draw many new industries.

QUESTIONS

CHECKBACK

1. List three ways in which the Heartland influences other regions within Canada.
2. a) Explain why agriculture remains an important activity in the Heartland.
   b) What is "intensive farming"? Why is it so common in the Heartland?

ANALYZE

3. Why are most of the Heartland's towns and cities located in lowland areas rather than in the Canadian Shield or the Appalachians?
4. Explain why the Heartland could be considered a multi-factor region.
5. Why does the Heartland extend beyond the Great Lakes-St. Lawrence Lowlands to include nearby parts of the Canadian Shield and Appalachians? Consider how the population and economy of these areas would tie them more to the Heartland than to the Canadian Shield and Atlantic Canada.

6. The decisions made by a company with its head office in the Heartland, such as the Royal Bank or Eaton's, may affect events in other parts of Canada. Explain this statement. Is this situation fair? Is it avoidable?

■ LOCATION FACTORS AND MANUFACTURING IN THE HEARTLAND

There is far more manufacturing in the Heartland than in any other region of Canada. This is a result of the combined effect of seven major **location factors**. We will examine each of the factors and look at how they have affected a company in the Heartland.

HISTORICAL HEAD START

The Heartland has always attracted large numbers of settlers. Its eastern part, along the St. Lawrence River, was first settled by French colonists during the 1600s, and by British settlers after 1763. This early settlement led to the development of towns, industries and trade. As each of these expanded, more settlers were attracted to the region.

Another part of the reason why the Heartland had a **historical head start** over the other regions of Canada is that it is located close to the industrial areas of the northeastern U.S. Many American parent companies found it convenient to set up **branch plants** in the Great Lakes-St. Lawrence Lowlands where they could take advantage of growing markets.

As settlers moved westward in the 1800s and early 1900s, they needed manufactured goods. These came from factories in eastern Canada. But why did factories not develop in the West? In these early years, western markets were too small to support local factories. It was cheaper to expand a factory in the Heartland than to build an entirely new plant in another part of the country. This historical head start is one reason why the Heartland's manufacturing developed at the expense of manufacturing in other parts of Canada.

Another advantage for the Heartland occurred when the federal government developed the National Policy in 1879. This policy involved the placing of **tariffs** on imported manufactured goods. A tariff is a tax that increases the price the consumer has to pay on imported goods. It made American goods much more expensive than Canadian-made products. Of course, people in the West and in the Maritimes bought Canadian goods because they

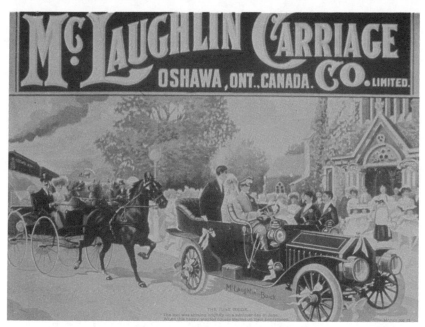

Fig.18–5 General Motors of Canada developed from this carriage-making company.

were cheaper. By purchasing goods made in the Heartland, eastern and western Canadian residents had little choice but to help provide jobs for Heartland citizens. What these residents wanted and needed was either jobs in their own region or the right to buy less expensive foreign-made goods. The National Policy helped to give the Heartland a historical head start over other regions of Canada.

General Motors

In the 1800s a carriage-making business started northeast of Toronto. A number of years later, this company moved to Oshawa, Ontario. When the "new-fangled" horseless carriage appeared on the scene at the beginning of the 1900s, the company started to make automobiles (Fig. 18–5). In a relatively short time the McLaughlin Carriage Company became General Motors of Canada. Because its carriage-making business had been established for a number of years, McLaughlin had a head start in terms of having skilled workers, a factory, and capital when the **technology** of the automobile appeared.

MARKET

With its large population, the Heartland has more purchasing power than any other area in Canada (Fig. 18–6). Such a huge market is very attractive to companies searching for places to build new factories. Furthermore, the presence of many manufacturing firms attracts new businesses to the region. It is therefore not surprising that almost three-quarters of Canada's manufacturing jobs are in the Heartland.

Fig. 18–6 The Heartland's huge population gives it more purchasing power than the rest of Canada combined.

Cooperative Agrapur Inc.

The Eastern Townships, southeast of Montréal, form one of Canada's richest farming regions. This area is also close to one of Canada's most heavily populated regions. Montréal, Québec City, and many smaller cities are within easy reach. As a result, a large local market exists for the agricultural products of the Eastern Townships. The farmers around Granby, Québec, send their milk to Cooperative Agrapur Inc. for processing before shipment to market.

Cooperative Agrapur Inc. now ships products such as yogurt to markets in many parts of Canada.

LOCATION OF RAW MATERIALS

The Canadian Shield, Canada's great storehouse of minerals and timber, extends into the northern fringe of the Heartland. It is here that raw materials such as copper and nickel are mined and forest products are produced. As we have seen, the Heartland itself is a major source of agricultural raw materials. The rich sources of raw materials have greatly helped the development of the Heartland's manufacturing industries. Before a manufacturing or processing company builds a plant, it will ask the following: "Where can we build so that we will be able to obtain raw materials easily, and yet be close to our markets?" What would be your answer to this question?

H. J. Heinz Co.

The products of the H.J. Heinz Co. are common on the tables of Canadian homes and restaurants. Heinz makes dozens of products from a variety of farm crops. You can probably name several. The Heinz Company's Canadian production is centred in Leamington in southwestern Ontario. There is one dominant reason for its location here. This region combines fertile soils with a frost-free period of more than 130 d (see Fig 6-22). Consequently, this area is suitable for growing a wide range of vegetables and fruits that are used as raw materials by Heinz and other food processing companies.

Fig. 18-7 Cheap, abundant hydro-electric power from plants like this one on the Niagara River attracted many manufacturers to the Heartland.

POWER AND FRESH WATER

One of the basic needs of industry is an abundant supply of cheap power. In pioneer times, flowing water was used to drive machinery in sawmills and grist (grain) mills. Many of the towns in the Heartland therefore grew up near waterfalls and rapids.

As time passed, hydro-electric generating stations were built at larger falls, such as Niagara Falls and those along the St. Lawrence and Ottawa Rivers (Fig. 18-7). Others were built along the many rivers that tumble from the Shield to the Great Lakes-St. Lawrence Lowlands. Because these sites were easy to develop, cheap hydro-electric power became available. This inexpensive source of power attracted industry to the Heartland.

Many manufacturing companies, such as the steel and automobile industries, need vast amounts of fresh water for cooling and cleaning purposes. The Heartland has many freshwater lakes and rivers that can be used for this.

Dominion Textiles

Dominion Textiles employs about 700 people in Drummondville, Québec to make sheets, towels and similar items. Drummondville is located on the St. François River at a point where water power is easy to harness. Two-thirds of Canada's textile industry is located in the Québec section of the Heartland. One major reason for this is that abundant power and fresh water were available here when most of these companies were established in the nineteenth century.

LABOUR

A company must consider the presence of both skilled and unskilled labour when deciding where to locate its factory. A wide variety of workers can be found in the huge labour force of the Heartland (Fig. 18–8). Many of the skilled workers in the Heartland are graduates of its various technical schools, universities, and other educational institutions. These graduates meet most of the needs of industry. In addition, the constant flow of immigrants to the Heartland has added large numbers of both skilled and unskilled workers to the labour force.

AES Data Ltd.

AES Data Ltd. of Montréal is a company with 300 employees that makes "high-tech" electronic office equipment such as word processors. The company hires engineers, designers, draftspeople, and assemblers – all skilled workers provided by the labour force of the Heartland.

Fig. 18–8 The availability of skilled and unskilled workers is an important advantage enjoyed by the Heartland.

TRANSPORTATION

Manufacturing companies need fast and efficient transportation. Water, rail and road transportation must be available for the shipment of bulky raw materials and finished goods. Airlines are needed for the fast transport of light or perishable products and for the easy movement of executives and salespeople.

Efficient and inexpensive transportation is found in the Heartland. The nation's busiest railway lines and highways are located in the region. Canada's most travelled highway stretches from Windsor to Québec City. The country's busiest airports are in Toronto and Montréal. The St. Lawrence Seaway is particularly valuable in giving the manufacturing centres access to the rest of the world.

Dow Chemical Ltd.

Dow Chemical Ltd. is a large company that makes a wide range of chemicals from petroleum. It employs about 1600 people at its plant in Sarnia, Ont., Canada's leading centre for the production of **petrochemicals**. The petroleum is transported to Sarnia from Alberta by means of the 2000 km inter-provincial pipeline. Dow and other companies refine it to produce hundreds of petrochemicals. These chemicals can be easily transported by many means to other industries located throughout the Heartland.

POLITICAL FACTORS

One way to attract and keep industry is to provide a good climate for investment. This can often be done by political decisions. Governments may make decisions that attract or discourage new businesses. For example, a government may offer a company tax reductions to encourage it to locate in a particular area.

Many government decisions that are made for the country as a whole often work to the advantage of one region (particularly the Heartland) at the expense of another. For example, the decision to build the St. Lawrence Seaway helped increase the Heartland's lead in manufacturing. At the same time, the opening of the Seaway took business away from the ports of Atlantic Canada.

Why would this happen?

Volkswagen Inc.

In recent years, sales of foreign-produced cars in Canada have grown. Canadians have realized that if these cars, or at least parts for them, were built in Canada, jobs would be created and the economy would benefit. In 1981 Volkswagen, a German automobile company, decided to build a parts plant somewhere in North America to supply its assembly plant in the U.S. The federal government offered financial aid to the company if it would locate in Canada. Volkswagen was attracted to the Heartland city of Barrie, Ont., because the provincial government and the Barrie municipal government offered the company further financial savings.

1. Briefly describe how each of the following has helped make the Heartland such an important manufacturing region:
   a) historical head start
   b) presence of markets
   c) location of raw materials
   d) availability of power and water
   e) supply of labour
   f) transportation facilities
   g) political factors.

2. Name a city in the Heartland where each of the following products is made.
   a) automobiles   d) breakfast cereals   f) records
   b) photographic film e) gasoline   g) canned food
   c) hockey sticks

3. Some cities across Canada, as well as cities in the Heartland, offer many benefits to companies locating in their areas. Some have good transportation routes, large markets, good building sites, and a good supply of trained workers. Some cities even offer tax savings.
   a) Select a city that you feel would provide a good location for a manufacturing company.
   b) Put yourself in the position of the mayor of the town you picked. You have just been asked by the president of a major company to describe the advantages of your city as the location of the company's new factory. Write a report describing why the company should locate in your city. In your report, describe at least three specific factors that favour your city.

4. "A large proportion of manufacturing in the Heartland is directly or indirectly controlled by parent companies in the U.S."
   a) List ten Canadian manufacturing companies that are **subsidiaries** of American companies. Was it easy to find ten?
   b) Describe three advantages and three disadvantages of a high level of American control in our manufacturing.
   c) Overall, are you in favour of or opposed to foreign control? Why?

SERVICES IN THE HEARTLAND

DEVELOPMENT OF THE SERVICE SECTOR

The number of Canadians employed in service industries has grown tremendously. In 1901, only about 33% of Canadian workers were employed in services; now the figure is close to 70%. Why has this part of Canada's economy grown so large? Consider the following:

- During this century, greater use of machinery in farming, mining, forestry, and manufacturing has increased productivity and revenue. As a result, workers have gained more money and leisure time. An increased demand for services has been a natural consequence of Canada's improved standard of living.
- Greater educational opportunities have helped people obtain the specialized skills needed to provide a variety of services.
- A growing and more affluent population has increased the demand for services.
- A more complex technology, particularly in handling information, has given rise to a wider variety of services.

Service industries are found mainly in urban areas, where there is a large population. The reason for this is that people moved to cities in search of work after increased **mechanization** eliminated many jobs in rural areas. As the population in cities increased, so did the demand for services for them.

affluent: wealthy

TYPES OF SERVICE INDUSTRIES IN THE HEARTLAND

The Heartland has services of all types. Most business and personal services in the Heartland exist mainly to meet the needs of the people who live there. For instance, a printing company located in Kingston finds that most of its work comes from businesses located in and around Kingston.

However, some business and personal services in the Heartland may meet the needs of people living in other parts of Canada. For example, an advertising company in Montréal may have a contract with an oil company in Calgary, or with a fish-processing company in the Maritimes. A bank with its head office in Toronto will have branches throughout the country.

Trade

The selling of goods is called "trade." Trade is divided into two categories: **wholesale** and **retail**. As you might expect, the retail activities of the Heartland exist mainly for local residents. In contrast, wholesalers may sell across Canada as well as locally. For example, a retail milk store sells its milk to local citizens; a wholesale clothing business sells its products not only to local retail stores, but also to others throughout the country.

Financial Services

Financial services are provided by banks, trust companies, stock exchanges, loan companies, insurance companies, and real estate companies. The financial institutions of the Heartland range in size from local real estate offices in small neighbourhoods to huge insurance companies and head offices of banks that do business all across Canada and throughout the world.

The Heartland's financial domination of the rest of the country can be shown by the importance of the stock exchanges in Montréal and Toronto (Fig. 18-9). The Toronto and Montréal exchanges account for between 80% and 85% of Canadian stock sales. Banks, investment dealers, insurance companies, and other financial organizations naturally try to locate near these exchanges. As a result, control over most of the Canadian economy is in these two cities.

domination: control

Government Services

The importance of the Heartland is reinforced by the concentration of government services. Toronto and Québec City are the centres of government for Canada's two largest provinces, Ontario and Québec. The capital of Canada is also in the Heartland. The federal government and the provincial governments provide many jobs, not only in the capital cities but also in smaller Heartland communities. In fact, these governments are **decentralizing** some of their operations. For example, the operations of the federal Department of Veteran's Affairs were transferred from Ottawa to Charlottetown, P.E.I. This decentralization is being done to distribute wealth and jobs to other parts of the country.

Fig. 18–9 The Toronto Stock Exchange is Canada's largest.

CHECKBACK

1. Give three reasons why service industries have become increasingly important in Canada.

ANALYZE

2. **a)** Name six examples of service activities performed by people who you know.
   b) Give two examples of service activities in the Heartland that are performed mainly for
      i. the people of the Heartland
      ii. all Canadians

INVESTIGATE

3. **a)** What is the difference between wholesale and retail trade?
   b) From the *Yellow Pages* of your telephone book, find examples of five wholesale companies and five retail companies in your area. What products does each sell?

WHAT DO YOU THINK?

4. **a)** Why are the major governments in Québec, Ontario and Canada decentralizing some of their operations?
   b) If you were a federal government official in the following departments, where would you suggest your department be moved and why? In making your choice, consider which parts of the country are most in need of economic growth as well as where the services of that department are most used.
      i. Department of Fisheries and Oceans
      ii. Department of Mines
      iii. Department of Agriculture

5. When new products are being tested for marketing, the people of Peterborough, Ont. are often chosen to represent "typical" Canadians. Why do you think this city is chosen?

■ FUTURE OF THE HEARTLAND

Even though the Heartland remains Canada's wealthiest region, it must meet many challenges if this situation is to continue. What has happened in the automobile industry illustrates some of these challenges. In the 1970s, the market for large "gas guzzling" cars declined and the large North American auto companies lost hundreds of millions of dollars. They responded by restructuring their industry. New models were designed that could compete with the best models from Japan and Europe. Old plants were closed and new ones opened. These new factories used the latest computer and robot technology to increase quality and cut costs. Many workers lost their jobs to automation. By making these enormous changes, the auto industry was able to regain its economic health.

Not all companies could make the change. An example is a company in Oshawa, Ontario, that made the steel bumpers used on large cars. This company closed because the smaller modern cars used plastic bumpers instead of steel ones. The workers lost their jobs. Similarly, a tire factory in Hamilton was closed down in 1988 because the demand for the type of tire it produced had decreased.

Since the company's experience was in making steel bumpers it did not have the equipment, nor did its workers have the skills, to make plastic bumpers.

Technological changes will eventually affect most of the manufacturers of the Heartland. The ability of traditional "**smoke-stack industries**" to respond to such changes, and the ability of the Heartland to attract new factories to replace those that close down, will determine whether the Heartland will remain as the industrial centre of Canada.

The Industrial Heartland is facing other challenges as well. In recent years, Canadian industry has fallen behind in **research and development (R and D)**. R and D is the part of industry that explores new ideas to develop into new products (Fig. 18–10). We in Canada receive most of our new technical developments second-hand from the U.S., Japan, and Europe. There are a number of reasons for this.

- Our manufacturing industries are small compared to industries in the U.S., Japan and West Germany. Therefore, we have less money available for R and D.
- The R and D of many of our foreign-owned firms is done in their home country. Thus, Canada loses out on the jobs and other advantages of doing research here.
- The Canadian government does not support R and D to the extent that governments in some other countries do.

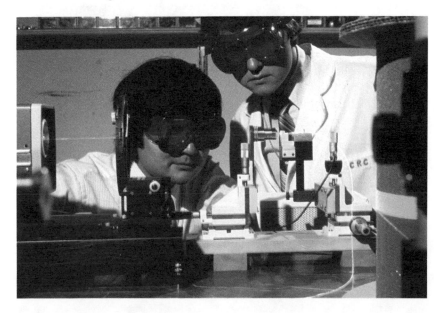

Fig. 18–10 Research and development, like this work with lasers, is important if Canada is to continue as a major industrial power.

The area around Ottawa is becoming the centre of the electronics industry in Canada. How is this location different from that of most industries in the Heartland?

Our lack of R and D is a special problem now because of recent developments in electronics. For example, a pocket calculator uses a tiny device called a microprocessor or "chip" as its "brain". Calculators using this device can do many of the things that could only be done in the 1950s by a computer as big as a room and costing many thousands of dollars. A powerful modern pocket calculator sells for less than $50. The chip revolutionized the way in which we live and work—and yet little micro-electronic R and D is being done in Canada. If the industries of the Heartland are not leaders in the electronics revolution, Canada may be unable to compete in the expanding world electronics market.

■ IN CLOSING...

In this chapter we have looked at the importance of Canada's Industrial and Urban Heartland. We have seen that it is the country's most important manufacturing region and the home of the majority of its service industries. The presence of manufacturing and service industries, along with the large population, give the Heartland an influence that extends across Canada. Some critics complain that the Heartland has developed at the expense of the rest of the country. We should remember, however, that the Heartland and the rest of Canada depend on each other and that they need each other to survive.

In the future, the relative importance of the Heartland within Canada may decline. Other parts of the country are taking over some of the roles now performed by the Heartland. But at present, and in the near future, southern Ontario and southern Québec will remain the Industrial Heartland of Canada.

QUESTIONS

CHECKBACK
1. List two problems that Heartland industries must overcome.
2. a) What is R and D?
   b) Why has Canada fallen behind in R and D?

INVESTIGATE
3. a) What is a microprocessor?
   b) List at least five inventions that use microprocessors.
4. To make companies in the Heartland more competitive, what can be done by:
   a) governments?
   b) the companies themselves?

5. **a)** What is meant by a "smokestack industry"?
   b) Give at least three examples of such industries.
   c) The challenge to smokestack industries in the U.S. Industrial Heartland has gone further and faster than in Canada. Research the U.S. situation to determine what has happened there and what we can learn from them.

6. **a)** In what ways has the Heartland grown at the expense of other regions in Canada? (Consider government policies and head office locations.)
   b) Will this change in the future?
7. The auto industry was the first major industry in Canada to restructure to meet the challenges of the future. How did being first make the process both easier and harder than it will be for other industries?
8. Will services become more or less important to the economy of the Heartland in the next 20 years? Why?

19 Regional Disparity

Examine Fig. 19–1 and complete the following tasks.

Fig. 19–1 Provincial Unemployment Rates, 1977 and 1987

Province	1977	1987
Newfoundland	15.5%	18.6%
P.E.I.	9.8	13.3
Nova Scotia	10.6	12.5
New Brunswick	13.2	13.2
Québec	10.3	10.3
Ontario	7.0	6.1
Manitoba	5.9	7.4
Saskatchewan	4.5	7.3
Alberta	4.5	9.6
British Columbia	8.5	12.0
Canada	8.1	8.9

1. a) Make two lists showing the five provinces with the highest unemployment rates in i) 1977 and ii) 1987.
   b) Which provinces are found in both lists?

2. a) Construct a chart similar to Fig. 19–2.
   b) Based on the 1977 and 1987 unemployment rates, write the names of the provinces in the appropriate column.
   c) In which columns are the provinces of Atlantic Canada found?

Fig. 19–2 Changes in Unemployment Rates between 1977 and 1987

Increase in Unemployment Rate	Decrease in Unemployment Rate	No Change in Unemployment Rate

3. Based on your answers to questions 1 and 2, what conclusions can you reach about employment opportunities and the wealth of people living in Atlantic Canada?

Key Terms

migration
regional disparity

unemployment
equalization grants

incentive grants

■ INTRODUCTION

Bill McCracken is a Maritimer. He is 27 years old and works as a shipper in a warehouse. He is typical of a large number of Maritimers. Why? Because he does not live in Atlantic Canada. He lives in Central Canada.

It has been estimated that there are more Maritimers in Toronto than in Halifax, and more Newfoundlanders in Ontario and Québec than in Newfoundland. What factors have caused this enormous **migration** of people from the Atlantic region to other parts of Canada? What effect does having to move away from home have on people? How does it affect the region losing people and the region gaining people? We can answer these questions by considering the problem of **regional disparity**.

■ BACKGROUND TO THE DISPARITY IN ATLANTIC CANADA

Regional disparity refers to the differences in wealth that exist between the regions of Canada. It is illustrated by the differences in average family income (Fig. 19–3). The largest and most permanent disparity is found in most of Atlantic Canada. The average family there earns between $3500 and $10 000 less per year than families in other regions of Canada.

The gap between the incomes of families in Atlantic Canada and those elsewhere is increasing. Over the past 10 years it has gone up by $2-3000.

Fig. 19–3 Average Family Incomes, 1985

Atlantic Canada	$30 972
Québec	34 582
Ontario	40 949
Prairie Provinces	37 635
British Columbia	36 980
Canada	37 368

Note: Provinces on the East Coast and the Prairies are grouped together because their statistics are very similar.

What makes this disparity worse is that many necessities cost more in Atlantic Canada. Most manufactured goods must be shipped in from southern Québec and Ontario. Many families have difficulty paying for necessities like housing, food and clothing, and have little money left over for luxuries.

necessities: basic needs like food, clothing, and housing

What causes this regional disparity? Compared to the rest of Canada, the agricultural, forest and mineral resources of the Atlantic provinces are not as rich. For the most part, manufacturing is less well-developed. The region is on the eastern margin of the country and is far from the major markets of central and western Canada. Shipping costs to these markets are high and this makes factories in Atlantic Canada uncompetitive with factories elsewhere. When companies have money to invest in new mines, mills, or factories, they tend to look for opportunities in parts of Canada that are closer to major markets. This means that few new jobs are created and **unemployment** grows as the population increases (Fig. 19–1).

High unemployment causes other difficulties as well. When people do not have jobs, they have little money to spend. The economy does not grow if money is not spent. Without growth, new jobs are not created. As the population increases, unemployment increases even more. Unemployed people are supported by government programs, therefore high unemployment means higher costs to government and to taxpayers.

■ WHAT CAN BE DONE?

Many attempts have been made to meet the challenge of regional disparity in Atlantic Canada. Individuals have come up with their own solutions, while governments and businesses look at strategies for the region as a whole. Here are some of the solutions that have been tried.

"GOIN' DOWN THE ROAD"

On the late show some night, you may see a famous Canadian movie called "Goin' Down the Road".

Many people in Atlantic Canada, especially young adults, have been faced with an unpleasant choice. They cannot find a steady job in their home region. But if they move to another part of Canada, like Bill McCracken did, they leave behind their families and friends and give up a lifestyle they know and enjoy.

In the 19th century, "goin' down the road" usually meant moving to Boston or elsewhere in New England.

Tens of thousands of people have chosen to leave — they have "gone down the road" to another part of Canada where the chances of a job are better. Their departure means that Atlantic Canada loses many people with useful skills and talents.

EQUALIZATION GRANTS

The federal government has organized a system to resolve issues of regional disparity. For example **equalization grants** transfer funds from provinces with higher revenues to provinces with lower revenues. Equalization grants have not solved all the problems of regional disparity, but they have helped give the Atlantic provinces more money with which to carry out government programs.

INCENTIVE GRANTS

The federal government and the provincial governments of Atlantic Canada give **incentive grants** to companies to help them build or expand factories, or to buy equipment for fishing, mining, and forestry. The purpose of these grants is to help companies in the Atlantic region compete with those in other parts of Canada and in other countries. The Atlantic Canada Opportunities Agency was created in 1987 to aid business expansion.

Grants are needed by manufacturers so that they can overcome some of the disadvantages they face. Many of the factories of the region were built before World War I and have out-of-date equipment. Replacing this equipment is costly but necessary. The steel mill in Sydney, Nova Scotia, was in danger of losing crucial contracts to make rails for CNR. The aging equipment in their mill could not produce rails of the quality that CNR demanded. New equipment, paid for by the government, had to be installed or the mill might have been forced to close.

Another disadvantage to be overcome is the small size of the local market. A manufacturer in the region must find markets outside Atlantic Canada to survive. When the products of Atlantic Canada are sold elsewhere in Canada, or in the U.S. or Europe, their price must include the high transport costs involved in moving these goods to market. This often means that the price of these goods is high and they cannot compete with goods produced elsewhere. Incentive grants have allowed companies faced with this problem to survive.

A successful example is that of the Swedish carmaker, Volvo. It received incentive grants to locate an assembly plant in Nova Scotia. The cars built there are shipped all over Canada. The workers have stable, well-paying jobs as a result, and the economy has received a boost (Fig. 19–4). A similar example is that of the Michelin tire company of France, which established a factory in Nova Scotia after receiving incentive grants from the federal and provincial governments.

Fig. 19–4 Volvo automobile parts are shipped in from Sweden and assembled in Nova Scotia.

Unfortunately, not all incentive grants have been so successful. New Brunswick invested in a plant to build Bricklin sports cars in the province. The Bricklin proved to be unreliable and too costly. The plant closed after only a few years. Newfoundland subsidized an oil refinery at Come-by-Chance. Because of technical and economic problems the refinery did not go into production for many years. A super-computer facility on Cape Breton Island in Nova Scotia opened only with the help of government grants. It closed after a few months because it was unable to secure the research contracts it needed to be successful.

Atlantic Canada, like other parts of Canada facing regional disparity, has a difficult choice: either continue the costly and only partly successful practice of paying grants, or accept that increasing numbers of people will "go down the road". The choice is not an easy one.

■ REGIONAL DISPARITY ELSEWHERE

Regional disparity does not exist only in Atlantic Canada. This area is only the most obvious and long-standing example in the country. Many other less obvious examples exist. Some of them are temporary in nature, while others are more permanent.

Although Ontario is Canada's richest province, disparities exist within it. Most of northern Ontario and parts of eastern Ontario have not experienced the kind of economic growth that the central and western parts of the province have enjoyed. As is the case with Atlantic Canada, young people from these areas often must leave their home to seek their fortunes elsewhere. The regional differences tend to be hidden because most statistical reporting is done for all of Ontario together. A similar situation exists in Québec, where people in many of the small towns and rural areas do not enjoy the same economic advantages as the residents of the Montréal-Québec City area.

Many of the people of western Canada are victims of a temporary kind of regional disparity. In the 1970s when prices for oil and farm products were high, the West was Canada's boom region. Many people from eastern Canada who were looking for opportunities went to the West. In the 1980s the economy of the West stagnated following a sharp drop in the prices of both oil and farm products. How long this situation will exist remains to be seen.

stagnated: not growing

■ IN CLOSING...

Economic disparity can occur even within the limits of one city. You can find some people living in homes worth many hundreds of thousands of dollars, while others only a few blocks away are living in the streets. Whether we are talking about the disparity involving the residents of a city, or that of a whole region, the challenge is the same — how do we change the basic economic conditions that caused the economic disparity in the first place?

QUESTIONS

CHECKBACK

1. **a)** Define regional disparity.
   b) What are the principal causes of the disparity that exists between Atlantic Canada and the rest of the country?
2. "High unemployment is usually related to many other problems." What are some of these problems?
3. Briefly describe two government programs designed to reduce regional disparity.

ANALYZE

4. **a)** What does "goin' down the road" mean?
   b) Describe at least one good and one bad effect of goin' down the road on:
       i. the people involved
       ii. the region they leave
       iii. the region to which they go
5. Analyze why some incentive programs have succeeded while others have failed.

INVESTIGATE

6. Regional disparity is a challenge in many areas of Canada that are smaller parts of the regions listed in Fig. 19–3. Their lower economic standing is "buried" in the regional or provincial figures given. Research the locations and characteristics of economic disparity within one or more of the following:
   i. Québec   **iv.** Ontario
   ii. Prairies   **v.** British Columbia
   iii. Northwest Territories **vi.** within one or more major cities

7. **a)** What is the purpose of equalization grants?

   b) Do you think it is fair that those who live in "wealthier" provinces should pay higher taxes so that grants can be given to "poorer" provinces?

8. Are the basic economic conditions that cause regional disparities so powerful that they cannot be changed? Should we give up trying to reduce economic disparity and instead encourage people to move to areas where growth is occurring and jobs are available? How would this affect areas like Atlantic Canada?

OUR NATURAL RESOURCE BASE

20 Fish: Canada's Oldest Resource

Pictured below (Fig. 20-1) are some of the major fish species caught in Canadian waters: cod, halibut, herring, tuna, salmon, lobster, shrimp, scallop, and oyster. How many can you identify?

In this chapter we will examine the habitats in which the fish live; how they are caught, processed, and marketed; and the major problems facing the fishing industry.

habitat: the area or environment in which an organism normally lives

Key Terms

continental shelf	offshore fishery	factory freezer trawler
inshore fishery	banks	200 nautical mile limit
inland fishery	sport fishing	(370 km)

Fig. 20–1   How many of these fish can you identify?

■ INTRODUCTION

Ocean fishing is Canada's first and oldest industry. Starting in the 1500s, boats from Great Britain, France, Spain, and Portugal brought people to the east coast fishing grounds for a few months each summer to catch the abundant cod and other fish. Later, colonists arrived to establish permanent fishing villages. The fish were dried or salted, and sent to Europe, the U.S., and the West Indies. Fishing continues to be an important industry in Canada today.

Canadians generally do not eat large quantities of fish. Consider your own eating habits. Think back over the past couple of weeks and count the number of times you ate beef, pork, poultry, and seafood. Chances are that you consumed less seafood than any of the other meats. The average Canadian consumes in one year 39 kg beef, 27 kg pork, 25 kg poultry, and only 6 kg fish. For much of the world's population, fish is a major part of the diet, but in Canada it is not.

While Canada is not one of the world's top ten fishing countries, it is one of the world's largest exporters of seafood. In fact, we export over 75% of our catch. This is necessary because Canada's small population cannot consume all this seafood. The large markets of the U.S., Japan, and Europe are needed. Relying so heavily on exports causes special problems for the fishing industry.

Commercial fishing is done in three locations in Canada: on the East Coast, the West Coast, and in the inland lakes. Fig. 20-2 compares the importance of the East Coast and West Coast fishing industries. The West Coast catch is much smaller than the East Coast catch, and in total is worth much less. Its value per tonne, however, is much higher. The reason for this is that the types of fish caught on the West Coast have a higher market value. Which West Coast fish is most responsible for this situation?

Some Canadians eat a lot of fish. Here is an Atlantic Canada delicacy you might like to try.

Cod Tongues
24 cod's tongues
1 egg
60 ml of milk
125 ml flour
5 ml salt

Wipe the tongues with a damp cloth. (If salted tongues are used, soak them in cold water for 10 min.) Dip the tongues in milk and egg mixture and roll them in salted flour. Fry in hot fat 4-5 min. Four to five tongues per serving.

The value of the inland fishery is much less than that of either coastal fishery.

Fig. 20-2 Value of East Coast and West Coast Catch (1985)

	East Coast	West Coast
kilograms	590 750 000	151 310 000
value	$1 624 350 000	$ 696 510 000
value per kilogram	$2.75	$4.60

About 80 000 people have commercial fishing licences and another 25 000 people are involved in the processing of fish products. The value of the fish products produced by these people amounts to over $2 400 000 000 per year. While this value is small when compared to the value of farming, mining, or forestry, the fishing industry is vitally important to the east and west coast provinces as a major source of employment and income.

Answers
1. herring
2. cod
3. scallop
4. cow
5. lobster
6. shrimp
7. tuna
8. oyster
9. halibut
10. salmon

Your score (number of correct answers)
8 to 10 – "Holy mackerel!" You must love fish!
5 to 7 – You "cod" have done better!
3 to 4 – Better review this – just for the "halibut!"
1 to 2 – You seem to be "floundering."
0 – Hint — Number 4 is a cow.

■ THE EAST COAST

By the end of the 1600s about 500 ships worked the Atlantic fisheries.

A number of favourable conditions in the waters off Canada's east coast combine to produce one of the world's great fishing areas. Why are the fish so plentiful here? Consider the following points.

- Many fish eat tiny animals called **zooplankton**. Zooplankton eat microscopic plants called **phytoplankton**. This food chain means that where there are large amounts of phytoplankton, there will be lots of fish.
- Because phytoplankton are green plants, they require sunlight to grow. Sunlight penetrates the ocean only to a depth of about 200 m. Beyond this depth there is very little plant life. In shallow areas, sunlight penetrates to the ocean floor and phytoplankton grow in abundance.
- Phytoplankton require nutrients to grow. In deep areas of the ocean most nutrients sink to the bottom and are lost. In shallow areas, however, nutrients are closer to the surface. The pres-

Fig. 20–3 Canada's East Coast fishery

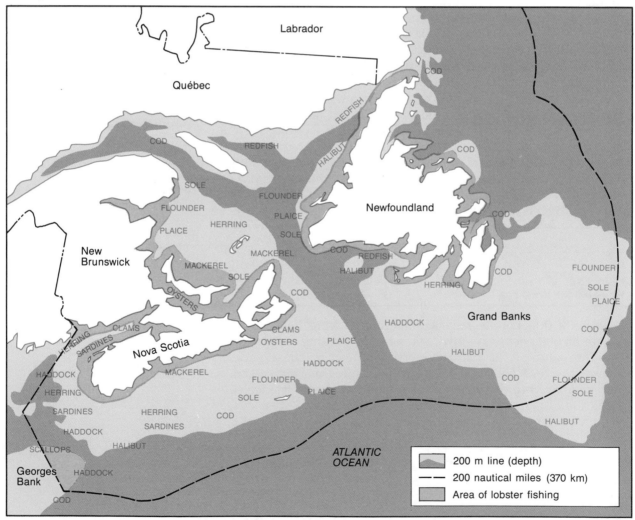

ence of both sunlight and nutrients in shallow areas increases the growth of phytoplankton.

- Shallow areas are situated next to continents and are called continental shelves. Atlantic Canada has a very wide **continental shelf**. On the shelf are large areas called **banks** that are even shallower (Fig. 20–3). The shallow banks are ideal for fish because sunlight can reach the bottom and huge amounts of phytoplankton grow in these areas. The largest and most important are the Grand Banks, which cover an area of 282 500 km². This is much larger than the island of Newfoundland. These Banks are the best cod fishing areas in the world.
- Atlantic Canada's coastal waters have one more condition that favours fish. A current of warm water flowing from the south meets a current of cold water from the north. When the currents meet, the cold Labrador current sinks below the warm Gulf Stream. The result is that nutrients that have settled to the bottom are churned up, making them more readily available for the growth of phytoplankton.

At the end of the last ice age, the banks were a chain of islands. Today, trawlers sometimes bring up parts of ancient trees that grew on these islands.

The island of Newfoundland is 111 400 km².

The meeting of the warm air and cold air above these currents produces many foggy days. Over 100 days of fog occur per year on the Grand Banks.

INSHORE AND OFFSHORE FISHERIES

Fishing on the East Coast can be divided into two main categories: inshore and offshore. The distance from shore is only one of the features that distinguishes between the two fisheries. Other differences are outlined in Fig. 20–4.

Relations between the two fisheries have not always been good. People in the **inshore fishery** complain that fish caught out at sea cannot migrate inshore to be caught. Fewer fish means that fewer people can support themselves by inshore fishing. Those in the **offshore fishery** argue that it operates in all seasons and therefore provides jobs year round.

The federal government has the difficult job of trying to help both fisheries to remain competitive. The inshore fishery must be protected because it provides many jobs for residents in small coastal towns. It is also the basis of a way of life that goes back to the time of the first European colonists in North America. The offshore fishery, on the other hand, provides well-paying jobs and a fresh supply of fish year round. The government's best approach is probably one that recognizes the needs and benefits of both fisheries.

■ THE WEST COAST

You discovered in Fig. 20–2 that the types of fish caught on the West Coast have a higher market value than those caught on the East Coast. By far the most important fish caught on the West Coast is salmon. There are five kinds of salmon: coho, chum, pink, spring (chinook) and the most valuable of all—sockeye. The Pacific harvest also includes herring, halibut, cod, flounder, redfish, clams, and oysters (Fig. 20–5).

Fig. 20–4 A comparison of inshore and offshore fisheries.

Inshore Fishery	Feature	Offshore Fishery
Within 16–25 km of shore	Location	Up to 370 km from shore, on the continental shelf and fishing banks
85%	Percentage of people who fish	15%
10%	Percentage of total catch	90%
Small boats (up to 20 m in length) with a limited amount of fishing gear	Type of boat and equipment	Large boats (from 21 to 50 m in length) with a large quantity and variety of fishing gear
Individuals and families	Ownership of boat and equipment	Large companies
Self-employed	Type of employment	Unionized employees
Mainly summer months during good weather	Fishing Season	All year round in all types of weather
Every morning the fishing boats travel the coastal waters. They return to small coastal villages before nightfall.	Fishing Procedure	The large trawlers travel the fishing grounds of the banks for two or more weeks before returning to port.
Fish are cleaned and cured by the family or taken to a processing plant in a larger community.	Processing	Fish may be partially processed on board then taken to processing plants that are able to handle large quantities.
Often live in small coastal communities. Because the catch is usually small and variable, the income is also low and variable. Many live near the poverty line and may have other jobs in the winter.	Lifestyle	Usually live in larger coastal communities. As year-round employees, the incomes are higher and more regular.

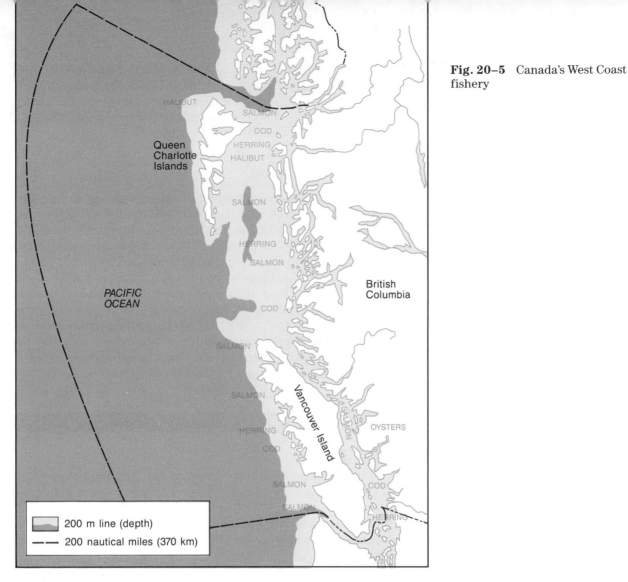

Fig. 20–5 Canada's West Coast fishery

Map labels: HALIBUT, SALMON, COD, HERRING, HALIBUT, Queen Charlotte Islands, SALMON, HERRING, SALMON, PACIFIC OCEAN, COD, British Columbia, SALMON, SALMON, Vancouver Island, SALMON, OYSTERS, HERRING, COD, SALMON, COD, SALMON, HERRING

Legend:
200 m line (depth)
--- 200 nautical miles (370 km)

Although salmon are found on both coasts, the West Coast catch is 60 times larger than the East Coast catch. Salmon hatch in gravel beds in fresh-water streams and make their way to the ocean. Here they spend their adult life before returning to spawn in the spot where they hatched. After spawning, the Pacific salmon die.

The large mature Pacific salmon leave the open sea and enter coastal waters during the summer and fall. British Columbia's modern fishing fleet is there waiting for them. Fifty-eight percent of the vessels are gill-netters, 33% are trollers, and 9% are seiners.

■ INLAND FISHERIES

Canada's **inland fisheries** are distributed throughout the Great Lakes, Lake Winnipeg, Great Slave Lake, and 600 or so smaller lakes. Ontario has the most important fresh-water fishery, followed by Manitoba. Whitefish, perch, and pickerel are the major species marketed.

spawning: producing offspring

The Atlantic salmon has a similar life cycle, except that after spawning the salmon do not die but return to the sea. They may return to their spawning ground three or four times during their lifetime.

The methods used by purse-seiners and gill-netters are shown in Fig. 20–7. Trollers are ships with many large poles. Each pole has a line containing many hooks. The ships move slowly through the water. Fish are hooked just as in sport fishing.

The inland fisheries are much less important to the Canadian economy than those of the East or West Coast. Only about 5% of the total value of the Canadian fishery comes from inland waters. Employment in these fisheries represents about 9% of the total employment in the Canadian fishing industry.

■ SPORT FISHING

It is easy to forget the importance of **sport fishing** to Canada's economy. It is estimated that five million Canadians fish for pleasure. That is about 20% of the Canadian population. Of these five million, about one-fifth are under 16 years of age! Another million anglers are visitors to Canada, mostly from the U.S.

anglers: people who fish with a hook and line

Sport fishing is big business in Canada. Anglers spend about $5 000 000 000 per year on fishing equipment, boats, motors, lodging, transportation, food, fuel, guides, and licences. A study in Québec indicated that the value to the provincial economy of the salmon caught for sport by anglers was about $73 000 per tonne. In contrast, the value of the commercial salmon catch to the provincial economy was only $8000 per tonne!

QUESTIONS

CHECKBACK

1. a) Compare the size and value of the East and West Coast fish catches. Which is larger? Which has the greatest value per tonne?
   b) Why does this difference exist?
2. Describe in detail the conditions that have produced an outstanding fishing area off the east coast of Canada.
3. Using the features in Fig. 20–4 as a guide, compare the inshore and offshore fisheries.
4. a) What is the most important species of fish caught on the West Coast?
   b) Describe the life cycle of this fish.
   c) When and how are these fish caught?
5. a) Who participates in sport fishing?
   b) "Sport fishing is big business in Canada." Explain this statement.

ANALYZE

6. a) How does Canada rank in the world as a fishing nation?
   b) How important is Canada as an exporter of fish?
   c) Why is there a difference between these two positions? How could this change in the future?
7. a) Relations between people in the inshore and offshore fisheries are not always good. Why is this conflict not surprising?
   b) Why does the federal government have a difficult role in dealing with this conflict? What should it do?

8. **a)** In your notebook, make a table like the one in Fig. 20–6. Visit your local supermarket and fill in the table using the information you find there. An example is completed for you.

b) **i.** Compare the average cost of fresh fish with the cost of fresh meat and poultry.

ii. What does this mean to a typical Canadian family when they shop?

iii. What implications does this have for the Canadian fishing industry?

c) Compare the price of fish from the East Coast with that of fish from the West Coast (and with the Inland fishery if its products are sold where you live). Is there a difference? Explain your answer.

d) Which form of fish is most expensive? Why do you think this situation exists?

Fig. 20–6

Fish/Meat Product	Form	Where Produced	Cost
cod fillets	frozen	Newfoundland	$4.99/500g

9. Discuss the following question with a group of your classmates and with your parents. "If seafood is so good for people, why do Canadians not eat much of it?" Consider both economic and non-economic factors.

HOW THE FISHING INDUSTRY WORKS

FISHING METHODS

Commercial fishing methods are being improved constantly. They must be. Today, the men and women employed in fishing have to catch many fish quickly and cheaply if they are to earn a profit. More than 50 years ago, when fishing schooners such as the famous Bluenose were used, fishing was a relatively simple business. But the methods used were time-consuming and the types of fish caught were limited. Today, a wide variety of specialized fishing boats and methods are used to catch different kinds of fish under different conditions (Fig. 20–7).

Bluenose is the sailing ship on the Canadian dime.

Fig. 20–7 Specialized methods have been developed for many kinds of fishing.

Trawling

Trawling is the "big league" of the fishing industry. Large schools of fish are located by an echo-sounding device. When a school of fish is located the trawler lowers a large net, called a trawl. This cone-shaped net is usually pulled along the ocean floor. The mouth of the net, held open by two boards, engulfs the groundfish.

Purse Seining

A long net (seine) is laid out in a circle around a school of fish. When the circle is complete, a line along the bottom of the net is pulled tight — like a purse string. The fish are then scooped out with a net. Purse seining is the most important type of salmon fishing in B.C. It is also used to catch herring near shore on both coasts.

Scallop Dragging

Scallops are the third most important product of the Atlantic fisheries. Scallops live on the ocean floor in inshore locations such as the Bay of Fundy, Gulf of St. Lawrence, and offshore banks, especially George's Bank. Power scallop draggers tow one or two drags (iron rakes) along the sea floor. Attached to the rake is a metal bag that collects the catch as it is scooped up from the bottom.

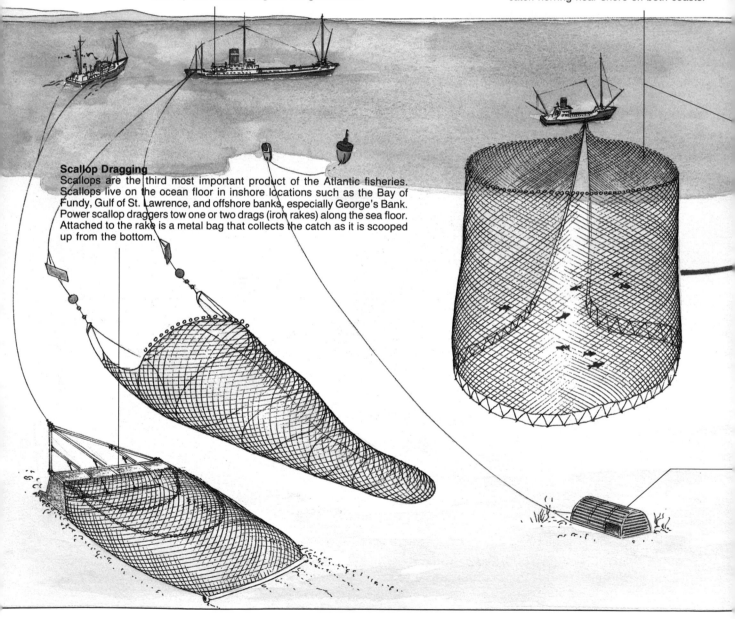

Gill Netting

Gill nets may be used near the surface or along the bottom. Gill netting is used inshore to catch a variety of species on both coasts, including herring, mackerel, and Pacific salmon. It is also the most popular method for inland fishing. The size of the mesh determines the size of the fish caught. The larger the mesh, the larger the fish. Adult fish push their heads through the mesh but cannot pass through or back out. Smaller fish swim through the mesh.

Weirs

Weirs are made of netting wrapped around poles that are fixed to the bottom. They are constructed where fish such as cod, mackerel and sardines are known to cruise near shore. A barrier forces the fish to swim into an enclosure from which escape is difficult. A small boat tows a seine net inside the weir to collect the fish. Weirs are very popular in the Bay of Fundy.

Long-lining

A rope line more than a kilometre long with thousands of baited hooks is stretched along the ocean floor. It is used both inshore and offshore to catch **groundfish.**

Lobstering

Lobsters live in both inshore and offshore locations on the east coast. They are usually caught in traps. At the lobster grounds the traps are baited, weighted with stones, and lowered to the sea floor. The lobster finds the trap easy to enter but impossible to escape from. Several traps are fastened to a coloured buoy which floats on the surface. Every few days the fishing boats return to their buoys to lift the traps, collect the lobsters, and rebait the traps.

PROCESSING

To ensure the highest quality possible, raw fish should be processed as quickly as possible after being caught. There are several ways to do this. See Fig. 20–8.

Processing is used to preserve the fish and to remove unwanted portions (about 70% of the fish). These unwanted portions, such as guts, head, skin, bones, and fins, are used as raw materials for various industries (Fig. 20–9) or made into fish meal for animal feed or fertilizer.

The unwanted portions of fish are called "offal".

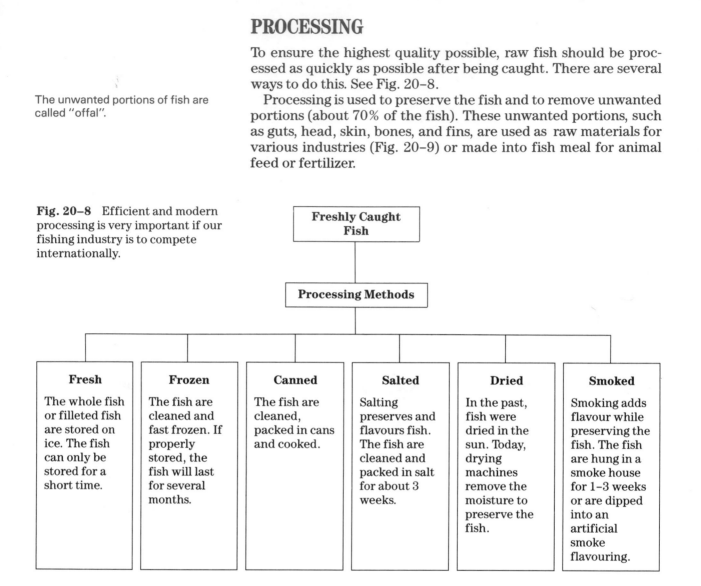

Fig. 20–8 Efficient and modern processing is very important if our fishing industry is to compete internationally.

Freshly Caught Fish
Processing Methods

Fresh	Frozen	Canned	Salted	Dried	Smoked
The whole fish or filleted fish are stored on ice. The fish can only be stored for a short time.	The fish are cleaned and fast frozen. If properly stored, the fish will last for several months.	The fish are cleaned, packed in cans and cooked.	Salting preserves and flavours fish. The fish are cleaned and packed in salt for about 3 weeks.	In the past, fish were dried in the sun. Today, drying machines remove the moisture to preserve the fish.	Smoking adds flavour while preserving the fish. The fish are hung in a smoke house for 1–3 weeks or are dipped into an artificial smoke flavouring.

MARKETING

As we have seen, fish exports are very important to the Canadian economy. In 1985 over $1 855 000 000 worth of fish products were exported. The main destinations were:
- U.S. ($1 134 000 000)
- Japan ($319 000 000)
- Western Europe ($221 000 000)

The Canadian fishing industry views the huge Japanese market as an area for growth. Fish are a major part of the Japanese diet, and much of this fish has to be imported.

The average Japanese citizen eats 66 kg of fish per year.

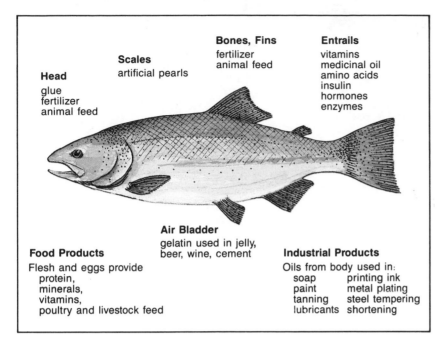

Fig. 20–9 Products obtained from fish

Head
glue
fertilizer
animal feed

Scales
artificial pearls

Bones, Fins
fertilizer
animal feed

Entrails
vitamins
medicinal oil
amino acids
insulin
hormones
enzymes

Air Bladder
gelatin used in jelly,
beer, wine, cement

Food Products

Flesh and eggs provide
protein,
minerals,
vitamins,
poultry and livestock feed

Industrial Products

Oils from body used in:
soap   printing ink
paint   metal plating
tanning   steel tempering
lubricants shortening

Since so little of the catch is consumed in Canada, external markets are very important to the Canadian fishing industry. In the past, Canadians did not compete well against other nations for these markets. Our fish was not of consistently high quality. Today, however, grading systems are used to help ensure a consistently high-quality product. Canadian frozen fish is now in high demand in the U.S.

Better marketing is also required in Canada to encourage people to eat more fish. Most people do not know what varieties of fish are available, how to prepare them properly, or the benefits of eating fish.

Fish are an important source of food because they are high in protein and low in fat.

■ ISSUES

Despite the demand for Canadian fish, the Canadian fishing industry is facing several issues that must be addressed if it is to prosper.

COMPETITION

Foreign fishing boats have come to the Grand Banks and other Canadian offshore areas for almost five centuries. The Canadian industry withstood this competition for many years because the foreign boats were inefficient and made small catches. Fishing fleets of large modern ships now come from the U.S.S.R., Japan, Spain, Portugal, Poland, and other countries (Fig. 20–10), and Canada's fishing industry faces increased competition.

Fig. 20–10 Russian trawler at St. John's

Some of these ships are **factory freezer trawlers (FFTs),** which catch, process, and freeze large quantities of fish very quickly and cheaply while still at sea. The result is a product of excellent quality that will fetch a high price. Soviet FFTs stay off Canada's coast for up to two years at a time before returning home. New crews are flown to and from Canada, and are taken on and off the FFTs by smaller ships.

Canada has only one factory freezer trawler. It made its first voyage in 1986 out of Lunenburg, Nova Scotia. Although it can compete with FFTs from other countries, there is little need for a fleet of FFTs. The fishing grounds are close enough to the fish processing factories on land for regular deep sea trawlers to provide excellent quality fish. If Canada is to compete in world markets it must have a high-quality product, and this can be achieved by processing the catch quickly.

Deep sea trawlers fishing off the East Coast may be grouped into three types:

- wet trawlers — the most common type — pack fish in ice until it is unloaded for processing.
- freezer trawlers clean and freeze fish on board.
- factory freezer trawlers clean, process, package and freeze fish.

SUPPLY OF FISH

Fish are a renewable resource. They can be harvested forever if the breeding stock is not reduced. This conservation technique is called "sustained yield" resource use. During the 1950s, 1960s, and 1970s, the Canadian and foreign fishing fleets caught too many fish. As a result, the breeding stock was reduced and the size of the catch began to decline in the 1970s. Something had to be done.

Until 1977, Canada controlled the fishing grounds for only 12 nautical miles (22 km) from shore. In 1977, a 200 nautical mile limit (370 km) was established. This allows Canada to manage all the fish stocks within an area of 1 300 000 km² on the Atlantic Coast, and 330 000 km² on the Pacific Coast. Canada can determine which nations may fish in this area, what they will catch, when it can be caught, how much may be caught, and what type

nautical mile: measurement of distance used by sailors and pilots. Equal to one minute of latitude (1/60 of a degree)

of gear can be used. But since fish migrate in and out of these areas, Canada must still work closely with other countries to ensure that over-fishing does not occur.

About 10% of the traditional Canadian fishing grounds lie beyond the 200 nautical mile limit. Canada must negotiate with other countries to protect the fishery in these areas.

HABITAT DAMAGE

It is possible to increase fish stocks through various conservation methods, such as improving water quality, preserving spawning grounds, and protecting food supplies. There will not be many fish to preserve, however, unless we stop damaging the environment in which the fish live. The problem is worse in inland and coastal areas. Freshwater lakes and rivers are being harmed by a variety of pollutants. Raw sewage from cities, soil eroded due to forestry and agricultural practices, waste wood from logging, poisonous chemicals from industry, and acid precipitation all endanger fish populations.

In Atlantic Canada, many rivers are losing their salmon because the waters are too acidic for eggs to hatch and young salmon to survive. Since World War II, over 100 000 ha along the east coast have been closed to shellfish harvesting as a result of pollution from raw sewage, fish processing plants, and industrial plants.

In British Columbia salmon are unable to reach their spawning grounds in some rivers because of hydro-electric dams and flood control barriers. Although fish ladders have been built to help the salmon around these barriers, many do not make it. As well, over 50 000 ha of shellfish grounds in British Columbia's coastal waters can no longer be fished because of sewage contamination.

fish ladders: structures built to allow fish to swim around obstacles like hydro-electric dams

The water quality in many of Canada's inland lakes, including the Great Lakes, has been improving since the 1970s. For example, in 1970, fish such as walleye in Lake St. Clair were found to contain high concentrations of mercury. This mercury was being discharged into the lake by a chemical plant. Commercial fishing in Lake St. Clair was stopped and anglers were told to fish only for sport, not for food. That same year, the mercury discharges were halted. Since then, the mercury levels in walleye have declined. There are still some restrictions, however, on the consumption of sport fish in Lake St. Clair due to the presence of mercury and other toxic substances. (Fig. 20–11.)

The levels of mercury in walleye in Lake St. Clair have dropped from over 2 parts per million (ppm) in 1970 to less than 0.5 ppm in 1985.

Toxic substances are still being discharged from Canadian and American sources throughout the Great Lakes and on both coasts. The control and investigation of these substances is necessary to prevent further damage to aquatic life. Laws now require new industrial development to provide environmental impact assessment studies to avoid future problems.

HIGH COSTS AND LOW INCOMES

Those who work in the inshore fishery and the inland fishery cannot fish in the winter and must rely on other sources of income.

Today, the costs involved in inshore and offshore fishing are enormous. Bigger boats are being used together with larger, more

Fig. 20–11 The Ministry of the Environment for Ontario publishes a *Guide to Eating Ontario Sport Fish*. It gives information on recommended levels of consumption of sport and game fish from lakes and rivers throughout Ontario. Examine the chart describing consumption levels for some of the fish from Lake St. Clair.

Fish Species	Fish size in centimetres									
	<15	15-20	20-25	25-30	30-35	35-45	45-55	55-65	65-75	>75
Walleye [5, 8]				▢	▢	▢	▢	▢	▢	
White Bass [5, 8]		▢	▢	▢	▢	▨				
Channel Catfish [5, 7, 8]		▢	▢	▢	▢	▢	▢	▨	▨	
Smallmouth Bass [5, 8]			▢	▢	▢	▢	▢			
Yellow Perch [5, 8]		▢	▢	▢	▢					
Carp [5, 7, 8]			▢	▢	▢	▢	▢	▨		
Rock Bass [5, 8]	▢	▢	▢	▢						
Northern Pike [5, 8]			▢	▢	▢	▢	▢	▢	▢	▢
Largemouth Bass [2, 8]	▢	▢	▢	▢	▨	▨				
Bluegill Sunfish [1]		▢								

Contaminant identification

The type of laboratory tests carried out on each species listed in the table can be determined by noting the number that appears after each species name and then checking this number against the following:

Key to Analysis:
1 — Mercury.
2 — Mercury, PCB, mirex and pesticides.
3 — PCB, mirex and pesticides.
4 — Mercury, PCB and mirex.
5 — Mercury, other metals, PCB, mirex and pesticides.
6 — Mercury, other metals.
7 — 2, 3, 7, 8 – TCDD (Dioxin)
8 — Toxaphene.
Example: A species name followed by a 2 has been analysed for mercury, PCB, mirex and pesticides.

The fact that testing for a particular contaminant was carried out does not necessarily mean that the fish will contain this substance.

Consumption Guidelines

	One week	Two weeks	Three weeks	Long-term consumption
(fish icon)	No restrictions	No restrictions	No restrictions	No restrictions
(fish icon)	10 meals per wk. 2.3 kg./wk.	5 meals per wk. 1.3 kg./wk.	4 meals per wk. 0.95 kg./wk.	0.226 kg./wk.
(fish icon)	7 meals per wk. 1.54 kg./wk.	4 meals per wk. 0.86 kg./wk.	3 meals per wk. 0.63 kg./wk.	0.136 kg./wk.
(fish icon)	1 or 2 meals/wk. 0.45 kg./wk.	1 or 2 meals/wk. 0.45 kg./wk.	1 or 2 meals/wk. 0.45 kg./wk.	1 or 2 meals per month 0.45 kg./mo.
(fish icon)	None	None	None	None

Children under 15 and women of child-bearing age should eat only (fish icon)

costly nets and expensive electronic equipment. Getting started in inshore fishing requires an investment of between $10 000 and $1 000 000; offshore fishing requires between $2 000 000 and $20 000 000. The costs of setting up in offshore fishing make it very difficult for individuals to run their own fishing operations. As a result, companies rather than individuals own most offshore boats. The federal and provincial governments have special loan and grant programs to help purchase new vessels.

Although some people who fish have very good incomes, most do not. A government study in Atlantic Canada showed that the incomes of almost one-third of the households that fished were below the poverty line! And this is for work that is physically hard and has been rated as the most dangerous in Canada.

■ IN CLOSING...

The ocean and fresh-water fisheries of Canada are an important industry. The natural resources of our waters are used for food, as a source of employment, and as a product for export. The way of life associated with fishing is an important part of our cultural heritage. The future of the fishing industry depends upon preserving fish stocks by not over-fishing and by protecting our waters. The next few decades will be critical in determining the future health of our oldest industry.

QUESTIONS

CHECKBACK

1. Copy a table similar to the one in Fig. 20–12 into your notebook. In this table, summarize each of the fishing methods described in Fig. 20–7.

Fig. 20–12

Method	Species Caught	Inshore or Offshore	Description

2. **a)** Briefly describe the various methods used to process fish.
   b) What products are produced from fish?
3. **a)** Define "renewable resource".
   b) Why can fish be called a renewable resource?
4. **a)** Why did the size of the fish catch begin to decline in the 1970s?
   b) In your own words, describe what is meant by "sustained yield".
5. Describe some of the ways in which fish habitats are being damaged.

ANALYZE

6. **a)** Using the statistics given on p. 270, construct a pie graph to show Canada's customers for fish. On the graph show the U.S., Japan, Western Europe, and Other Countries.
   b) Why is this distribution of sales not surprising? How might it change in the future?

7. **a)** What is the 200 nautical mile limit?
   b) What effect did Canada's extension of its control of the seas to 200 nautical miles have on foreign fishing fleets?
   c) Is this limit necessary? Should it be expanded? Explain.

INVESTIGATE

8. Investigate five methods by which damage to fish habitats may be corrected, and write a short report.

9. Although Canada has a 200 nautical mile limit, it still has disagreements over resource use inside parts of this zone. Investigate one of the disagreements that currently exists (or has existed) between Canada and a) the U.S., b) another country.

WHAT DO YOU THINK?

10. Describe at least three ways in which running a fishing operation is very much like running a family farm. (See the Complementary Study in Chapter 22 for information about operating a modern farm.)

11. If you had the opportunity to fish for a living, would you? What would be the advantages and disadvantages?

Water: An Abundant Resource?

How much water do you and your family use each day? To find out, record the amount of water used in your home for all uses for one day. You will have to estimate how much you use for some activities. Here are some figures to help you (Fig. 21–1). Don't forget the water that is lost because of dripping faucets. Studies suggest that as much as 10% of the water piped into a home is lost this way. For each dripping faucet in your home, add 75 ℓ/d.

After you have collected the data, form groups to compare your family's use of water to that of your classmates' families.

1. Construct a graph like the one in Fig. 21–2 and complete it using information provided by each student.

Fig. 21–2 Graph of water use

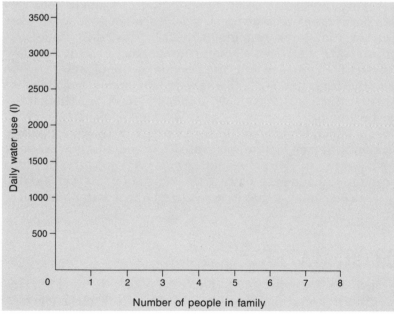

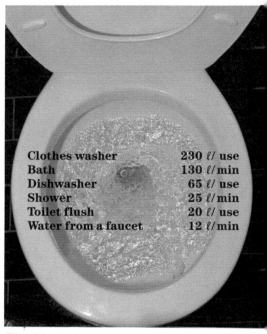

Clothes washer	230 ℓ/ use
Bath	130 ℓ/min
Dishwasher	65 ℓ/ use
Shower	25 ℓ/min
Toilet flush	20 ℓ/ use
Water from a faucet	12 ℓ/min

Fig. 21–1 Average water use for various activities

These figures are averages. Your appliances and water fixtures may have higher or lower rates of flow.

2. Does the graph show a relationship between the number of people in a household and the consumption of water? Explain this relationship.

3. a) What is the total water consumption for a household with four members?
   b) Divide the answer in a) by 4 to obtain the consumption per person.

4. What factors other than family size affect the amount of water a family uses?

5. What things could you and your family do to reduce the amount of water you use?

Key Terms

water use

drainage basin

toxic chemical

water consumption

water diversion

■ INTRODUCTION

The earth is located 150 000 000 km from the sun. If the earth were much closer, the water would boil away. If it were much further away, the water would freeze.

In most parts of Canada, we take water for granted. But many people in the drier parts of the world view water as a resource more important than gold. Without water we could not survive. About two-thirds of the human body is water, all our crops and livestock need water to survive, and most human activities require water.

Studies show that the average Canadian uses about 300 litres of water per day for personal use. How does this figure compare to the one that you calculated at the beginning of this chapter? We could try to calculate the total amount of water Canadians use by multiplying this figure by the population of Canada. But this would not come close to giving us the total amount of water used in Canada. Agriculture, mining, manufacturing, electrical generation, and other activities all require great amounts of water. If all these are taken into account, the per person use of water rises to about 4000 litres per day! Canadians are the second-largest users of water in the world. Which of our neighbours do you think is the largest water user?

The fact that we use water does not mean that we actually consume it. In many situations water is used and then put back into a lake or river. In total, about 120 000 000 000 litres of water are used in Canada each day. Of this only about 10 000 000 000 litres are consumed — that is, not returned to a water body after use.

■ WATER, WATER...

The earth is sometimes called the "blue planet". This is not surprising since more than two-thirds of the earth's surface is covered with water.

Of the 40 000 000 km³ of freshwater, 37 000 000 km³ are in the form of ice or are underground.

1. Using the information in Fig. 21–3, calculate the percentage of the earth's water that is
   a) freshwater
   b) freshwater available for use
   c) freshwater in Canada
   d) the remaining water in the world.

Amount of water on earth	135 000 000 000 km³
Amount of freshwater	40 000 000 km³
Amount of freshwater available for use	135 000 km³
Amount of freshwater in Canada	20 400 km³

Fig. 21–3 Distribution of water on the earth

2. Draw a pie graph showing the different percentages of the earth's water that you calculated in question 1.

3. Why is so much water unavailable for use?

About 755 180 km² of Canada's total area of 9 970 610 km² is covered by lakes and rivers. The water bodies of Canada drain into the Pacific Ocean, Hudson Bay, Atlantic Ocean, Arctic Ocean, and, surprisingly, the Gulf of Mexico (Fig. 21–4).

Fig. 21–4 The rivers in these five drainage basins carry the water that is available for use in Canada.

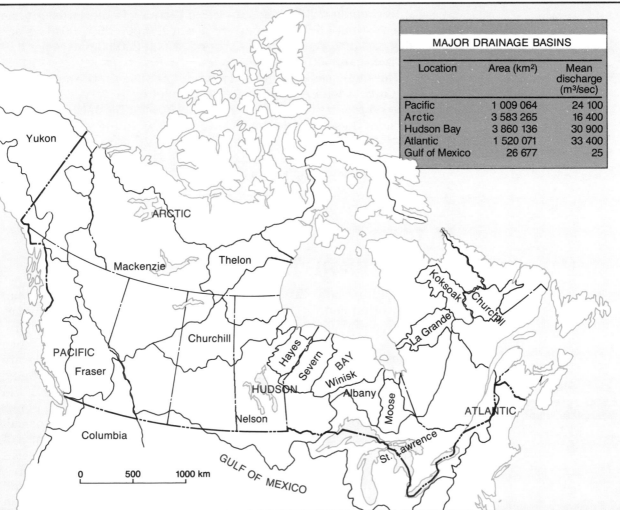

MAJOR DRAINAGE BASINS		
Location	Area (km²)	Mean discharge (m³/sec)
Pacific	1 009 064	24 100
Arctic	3 583 265	16 400
Hudson Bay	3 860 136	30 900
Atlantic	1 520 071	33 400
Gulf of Mexico	26 677	25

FUTURE CANADIAN NEEDS

Today, Canadians have more water available than we need. But the demand for water in the future is likely to increase, for the following reasons:

- As Canada's population increases, there will be greater demand for water.
- Expanding industries will require more water. For example, one tar sands plant uses more than 80 million litres of water per day!
- People will have more leisure time for fishing, boating, and swimming. This will increase the demand for clean water.
- Large amounts of water will be needed to protect and improve the natural environment. For example, water is critical for maintaining marshlands and for diluting the treated sewage wastes from cities.
- More water will be needed to irrigate land so that agricultural production can be increased.

How much will the need for water increase in the future? It has been estimated that the current use of 120 000 000 000 litres per day in Canada could jump to over 250 000 000 000 litres per day by the year 2000.

This increased demand will not be a problem for the many areas of Canada where there is a **water surplus**. However, there are several regions of Canada where there could be shortages in the future. These include the Okanagan Valley in the southern interior of British Columbia and some southern portions of Alberta, Saskatchewan, Manitoba, and Ontario. These regions receive relatively little precipitation and stream flow is often irregular. The answer to shortage problems may be to divert or transfer water from other drainage basins to those in need.

WATER DIVERSIONS

Canada already diverts more water between drainage basins than any other country. But these diversions are over short distances only, and the water is used primarily for large hydro-electric projects. The James Bay project has many such diversions. Since these diversions are far from populated areas, few people are even aware that they exist. The water diversions that are being suggested for the future are entirely different in both size and purpose.

The shortages that drier parts of Canada may face appear small when compared to the **water deficits** that may occur in parts of the U.S. There are predictions that there will soon be a water crisis in the western and southwestern U.S.. For almost half a century, these dry states have been using large amounts of underground water to irrigate crops and support urban growth. This **ground**

The ancient Romans built aqueducts to move water to places that were short of water.

water is being used up faster than precipitation can replace it. It is becoming increasingly obvious that there will be severe water shortages in these regions by the year 2000. But what does this have to do with Canada?

When American regions have faced water shortages in the past, they have brought water in from elsewhere. For example, Los Angeles pipes water a distance of 400 km from the Colorado River and 800 km from northern California over surrounding mountain ranges. The problem is that the U.S. has few drainage basins with large surpluses of water. Because of this, the U.S. may put pressure on Canada to sell its water.

As early as 1963 the first proposal was made for a large "transborder" **water diversion**. The North American Water and Power Alliance (NAWAPA) is a truly gigantic scheme to divert rivers in Alaska, the Yukon, and British Columbia to the southwestern U.S. and the Great Lakes region (Fig. 21–5). A major feature of this proposal was to flood 2100 km of the Rocky Mountain Trench from Montana to the Yukon.

Fig. 21–5 The North American Water and Power Alliance (NAWAPA) Plan, showing source, storage and distribution areas.

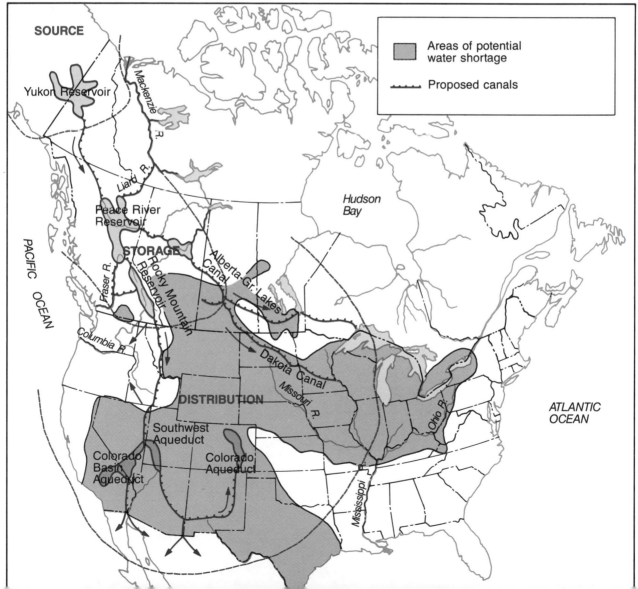

NAWAPA could cost between $150 billion and $300 billion. To justify the enormous cost, great benefits were promised. More than 30 American states, 7 Canadian provinces and territories, and 8 Mexican states would benefit from increased water supplies, hydro-electric power, and irrigated land.

Another major diversion scheme has been proposed by Canadian engineers. It is called the GRAND (Great Recycling and Northern Development) Canal and would cost $100 billion (Fig. 21–6). This scheme calls for a dam to be built across the mouth of James Bay. The fresh water flowing in from the many rivers surrounding James Bay would eventually replace the salt water. Water from this huge fresh-water lake could then be pumped southward into the upper Ottawa River. From there it would be diverted into Lake Nipissing, Georgian Bay, Lake Huron and Lake Michigan. Water from the Great Lakes would then be sent by rivers and canals into the American Midwest and Southwest and the Canadian West.

The benefits of diverting large amounts of fresh water to regions with shortages are obvious. But what are the true costs involved in these massive diversion projects? Thousands of mil-

Fig. 21–6 The source, storage and distribution areas of the GRAND Canal concept.

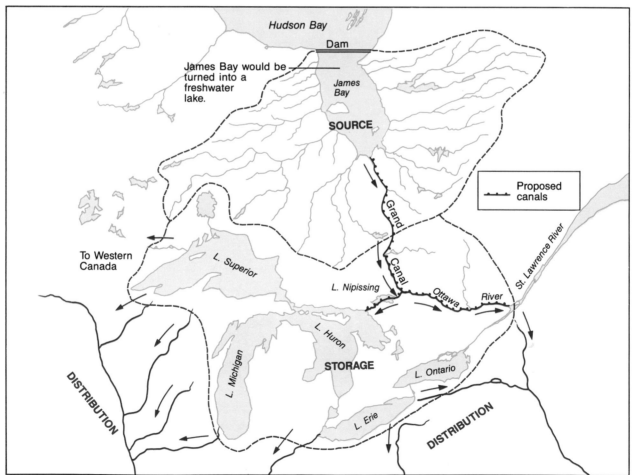

lions of dollars would be needed to construct these diversions and each one would take 15 or 20 years to build. Large amounts of land would be flooded for reservoirs and canals. Since these would be in valleys, some of our best land would be lost. Wetlands that are used as nesting and breeding grounds for birds would be affected, as would fish spawning grounds. The damage to the environment would be extreme and largely unpredictable. For example, if water was diverted from James Bay and Hudson Bay, would these bodies of water freeze over for a longer portion of the year? If this occurred, what effect would it have on the climate of North America? Could winters be extended and Prairie grain-growing be harmed?

Canadians would also lose some control over their own affairs. Once the projects were built and the Americans had come to rely on Canadian water, the flow could not be turned off easily. Thus if Canadian demand were to increase in the future, we might not have access to the water that we need.

What alternatives are there to massive water diversion schemes? Canada and the U.S. are the largest per person users of water in the world. More attention to **conservation** practices would make current supplies last longer. (Remember the dripping faucet!) One way to force people to use water more carefully is to charge more for it. Another is to research new methods to reduce water use. For example, we could reduce irrigation of crops by growing crops that require less water. There are many possibilities that should be investigated before irreversible damage is done to our environment.

QUESTIONS

CHECKBACK

1. a) What is the difference between **water use** and **water consumption**?
   b) What percentage of the water used in Canada is actually consumed?
2. a) With the help of an atlas, estimate what percentage of Canada's area is covered with fresh water.
   b) Use the information in the text to calculate the actual percentage of Canada's area that is covered with fresh water.
3. List four reasons why the demand for water will probably increase in the future.
4. a) Which regions of Canada may experience water shortages in the future?
   b) Why might this happen?
   c) Why might there be severe water shortages in some parts of the U.S. by the year 2000?
   d) Briefly state how this would affect Canada.

5. **a)** Define **drainage basin.**
   b) On a drainage map of Canada (provided by your teacher), draw the borders of the five major drainage basins in Canada. Shade in each with a different colour.
   c) Label each with:
      i. name
      ii. area (km²)
      iii. mean discharge (m³/s)
   d) Rank the drainage basins in terms of i) area and ii) mean discharge. Explain the difference in rankings.
   e) How would the rate of flow vary during the year? Why would this happen? How would northern rivers (e.g. the Mackenzie) and southern rivers (e.g. the St. Lawrence) differ in this regard?
   f) **i.** In what direction does most of Canada's water flow?
      ii. What percentage of the total flow goes in this direction?
   g) Where is most of Canada's population located? Compare the pattern of population with the pattern of water flow. What does this suggest about our ability to meet growing water needs in the future?

Answer questions 6 and 7 in a group

6. **a)** On a map of North America (provided by your teacher), show the water diversions that are the basis of the NAWAPA and GRAND Canal schemes. Label the map fully to explain the two proposals.
   b) How does North America's physical geography contribute to these schemes?
   c) Draw a chart with two columns labelled "Benefits" and "Costs". List the positive features of these schemes in the "Benefits" column and the negative features in the "Costs" column.
   d) Do you think that the benefits of these schemes outweigh the costs? Explain your answer.
7. What are some of the alternatives to large-scale diversion projects?

8. Using the resources of a library, select an existing water diversion project, such as the James Bay Project, and examine:
   a) why the project was undertaken
   b) what was done to divert water
   c) the benefits of the scheme
   d) the negative effects of the scheme on the environment and people
   Give your opinion on whether this was a necessary project.

These questions may be done individually or in a group.

9. **a)** Should the waters of North America belong to the country of origin or should the waters be considered a North American resource and be shared accordingly?

   b) How do differences of opinion on this question contribute to water being a political issue between Canada and the U.S.?

10. If the U.S. were to pressure Canada to share its water, how should Canada respond?

■ WATER POLLUTION

We have seen that Canada is a land with abundant fresh water. In the past it may have seemed that our fresh water resources were limitless. Over time, however, water pollution has damaged this resource and we now realize that we must take greater care of it.

There are three main types of water pollution: physical, biological, and chemical. Perhaps the least harmful but most obvious form of pollution is the physical variety. Floating garbage, old tires, pieces of paper, pop cans and bottles are not pleasant to look at. But this pollution is easily seen and its clean-up and prevention are relatively simple.

Biological contamination refers to bacteria and algae that enter lakes and rivers from a variety of sources. Sewage from cities and towns is the largest source of biological contamination. While most sewage is treated, not all treatment is adequate. Some human sewage enters water bodies without any treatment at all.

Some bacteria that occur naturally in rivers and lakes are able to cleanse biological pollution from the water over time. We are, however, overloading many water bodies to the point where there is too much waste for the natural purification process to be effective.

The most dangerous form of water pollution results from the dumping of poisonous chemical wastes into our lakes and rivers (Fig. 21–7). These wastes are often colourless, odourless, and tasteless in our water but they can be deadly! What makes things worse is that the water bodies where these chemicals are dumped are often the source of drinking water for millions of people.

Many Canadian cities have old sewage systems. During heavy rainfalls, these systems are unable to handle the volume of water produced and raw sewage flows into rivers, lakes, and oceans. These systems are currently being repaired but this is a long and costly process.

Some people say that there is no safe level for these chemicals in our water supplies because many of them build up in the body over time.

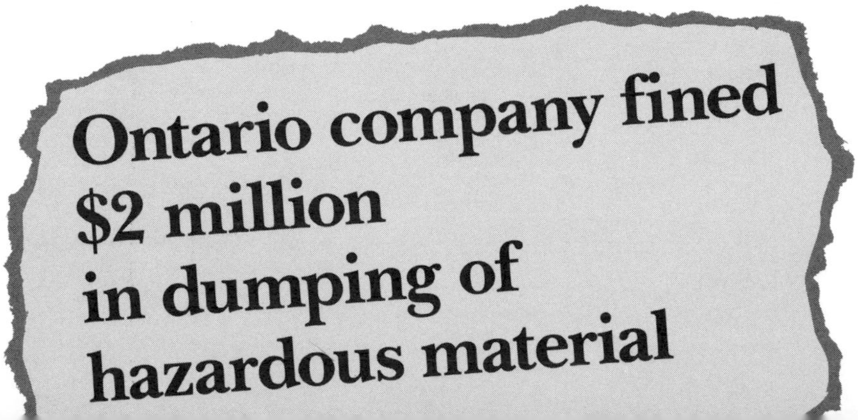

Fig. 21–7 Newspaper headlines, such as this one, illustrate a serious problem that must be overcome.

Ontario company fined $2 million in dumping of hazardous material

Some of these chemicals are considered harmful in quantities measured in parts per *trillion*.

The winner of a Lake Ontario fishing contest was disqualified because the salmon he claimed to have caught in Lake Ontario was found *not* to contain toxic chemicals. The contest judges knew that this fish could not have come from Lake Ontario.

Some industries have been dumping **toxic chemicals** into our water supplies for years. The Great Lakes have been referred to as a "chemical soup" because of the number of chemicals dumped into them. In fact, 42 "toxic hot spots" have been identified in the Great Lakes where there are particular problems with the accumulation of toxic chemicals. Thirty-two percent of Canadians and thirteen percent of Americans live in the Great Lakes basin. These 40 million people are exposed to hundreds of potentially dangerous chemicals produced by industries. Many of these chemicals have been found in the bodies of fish and gulls that live in and around the Great Lakes. This proves that the chemicals are in the food chain (Fig. 21–8).

The quality of our water is also threatened by pesticides used on farms. These chemicals, which protect our food supply from animal pests, disease, and weeds, are washed from farmers' fields into rivers and lakes.

Fig. 21–8 How toxic wastes move through the food chain

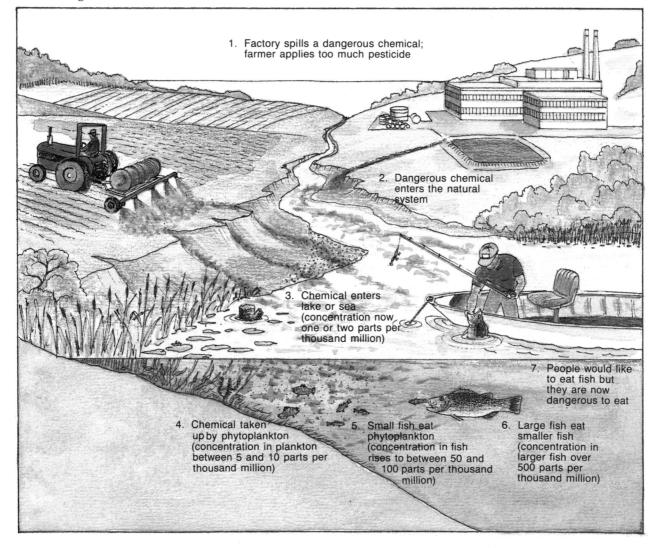

1. Factory spills a dangerous chemical; farmer applies too much pesticide

2. Dangerous chemical enters the natural system

3. Chemical enters lake or sea (concentration now one or two parts per thousand million)

7. People would like to eat fish but they are now dangerous to eat

4. Chemical taken up by phytoplankton (concentration in plankton between 5 and 10 parts per thousand million)

5. Small fish eat phytoplankton (concentration in fish rises to between 50 and 100 parts per thousand million)

6. Large fish eat smaller fish (concentration in larger fish over 500 parts per thousand million)

There is, however, some good news. Government studies indicate that the levels of many **contaminants** in the Great Lakes have been declining since the 1970s. Restrictions on the manufacture and use of mercury, many pesticides, and PCBs have resulted in reduced contaminant levels in fish.

We currently face two major problems in trying to rid our water supply of toxic chemicals. First, we do not know how to completely stop dangerous chemicals from reaching water bodies. Some chemicals seep into lakes and rivers from contaminated underground water sources, some may be illegally dumped, and others may be accidently spilled from factories. Second, we do not have the technology in place to remove chemicals once they are in the water. Large-scale water purification plants treat only biological pollution. They do not eliminate hazardous chemicals that may be in local drinking water supplies.

Sources of chemicals do not have to be located near a water body for pollution to occur. Consider the example of the American national park, Isle Royale, a remote island in Lake Superior. Scientists were shocked in the mid-1970s to find PCBs and a banned insecticide called toxaphene in fish caught on the island. There were no sources of these chemicals on the island. Apparently these chemicals were brought to the island by the wind.

The sources of chemical pollution in the Niagara River are no secret (Fig. 21–9). For many years chemical companies along the American side of the Niagara River buried their waste chemicals in a number of dumps near the river. At the time that this was done, the dangers associated with the chemicals were not fully realized. In one case, an unused canal, the Love Canal, was used as a waste chemical dump. Later the dump was covered with soil and became a residential area. Years later, in the 1970s, it became apparent that the residents of the Love Canal district suffered higher than normal rates of cancer and birth defects. All of the

PCBs (polychlorinated biphenyls) are often used as insulators in electrical transformers. You may have them in your school building.

Fig. 21–9 Sources of hazardous wastes

Source	Major Pollutants
Auto making	Oil, lead, other metals and chemicals
Farming	Manure and chemical fertilizers (promote algae growth in lakes and rivers), silt (clouds water), toxic pesticides
Glassmaking	Oil, fluoride
Iron and steel production	Toxic chemicals, tin, zinc, chromium
Mining a) base metals	Copper, lead, zinc, mercury, etc.
b) uranium	Radioactive products, heavy metals
Pesticides	Toxic chemicals such as dioxin
Chemical industry	Toxic chemicals such as PCBs
Petroleum refining	Chemicals, sulphur dioxide and nitrogen oxides (cause acid rain)
Refining of aluminum	Fluorides, large amounts of red mud
Refining of base metals	Heavy metals, sulphur dioxide
Pulp and paper making	Ammonia (promotes algae growth in water), other chemicals and metals
Thermal electric a) coal	Thermal pollution (temperature rise in nearby water body), sulphur dioxide, nitrogen oxides
b) nuclear	Thermal pollution, radioactive products

homes in the area were torn down and Love Canal became a fenced-off wasteland.

Canadians looked sympathetically at their neighbours but thought that Love Canal was an American problem until an ominous discovery was made. Chemicals, including deadly dioxins, were leaking from the Love Canal and other chemical waste dumps into the Niagara River and then into Lake Ontario and the St. Lawrence River. These are water bodies that supply drinking water to millions of Canadians.

A decision has yet to be made about what to do with these dumps. Should the chemicals be removed or should the dumps be sealed so that they cannot leak? Both methods involve enormous costs and considerable risks. Neither method offers any guarantee for success.

Over 200 000 chemicals are used in industry and most are thought to be hazardous in some way to human health. In only a few cases has the risk of these chemicals been fully determined, and new chemicals are being developed daily. How can chemical wastes be made safe? In Alberta, some companies are disposing of wastes in deep wells. In Ontario, a provincial crown corporation is building a multi-million dollar treatment plant in the Niagara Peninsula. Acids can be neutralized, and many dangerous chemicals can be destroyed by burning them at very high temperatures. Many people, however, fear that it is impossible to guarantee that such treatments will be 100% effective. Whenever a dump site or incinerator is proposed for a certain area, the local residents usually mount a campaign to stop the project. The attitude of most people is "Yes, we need disposal sites – but Not In My Back Yard!" This attitude has even resulted in a new term, the "NIMBY Syndrome".

neutralized: when alkaline substances are combined with acids, the acidity is eliminated. This is what happens when you take an antacid to combat heartburn or an "acid substance".

■ IN CLOSING...

If we do not take measures to curb the pollution of our environment, the words from the poem *The Ancient Mariner* may predict our future:
"Water, water, everywhere
Nor any drop to drink."

QUESTIONS

CHECKBACK

1. **a)** Describe three ways in which the contamination of water supplies may occur.
   b) Which form of pollution is most obvious? Which form is most dangerous?

2. The Great Lakes have been called a "chemical soup". Explain the meaning of this expression.
3. How does farming contribute to water pollution?
4. **a)** Describe how toxic wastes move through a food chain up to and including people.
   b) Draw your own diagram to describe this process.
5. Describe a specific example of industrial water pollution.

ANALYSIS

6. Why is the storage and dumping of chemicals on land discussed in a chapter on water resources?
7. **a)** Why do people not want storage or disposal sites near where they live?
   b) Why is this reaction not surprising? What, if anything, could be done about this?

INVESTIGATE

8. Investigate one of the 42 "toxic hot spots" in the Great Lakes basin (or another major water pollution site). Write a short research paper to include the following:
   a) the nature of the problem
   b) the cause of the problem
   c) the effects on Canadians
   d) the possible solutions (or solutions already tried)
   e) your opinion on the problem
9. Investigate the approved methods for the disposal of hazardous waste. (If your school library has a clippings file, it would be helpful for this task.) If satisfactory disposal methods exist, why is so much waste disposed of in a dangerous manner?

WHAT DO YOU THINK?

10. The public puts pressure on the government to stop pollution of the environment. The government in turn puts pressure on industry by developing laws to stop pollution. Industry responds by saying that it wants to stop pollution, but pollution controls are enormously expensive. Installation of pollution controls would drive many companies out of business and eliminate many jobs. How can this "vicious circle" be broken?
11. The government has announced plans for a $300 million, state-of-the-art, toxic waste treatment plant to be built 4 km from where you live.
    a) List at least two arguments in favour of this plant and at least two arguments against it.
    b) What questions would you have for the planners of the plant if they came to speak at your school?
    c) Given local public opinion, do you think the plant will eventually be built?
    d) Do *you* think the plant should be built?

Acid Rain

It is more properly called acid pre-cipitation and acid deposition since rain, snow, fog, dew, and dry gases may be acidic.

Acid rain is one of the most serious environmental problems facing Canada and other industrialized countries today. It is not a new problem, having first been studied by English scientists as early as the late 1600s. The term "acid rain" was first used in England during the 1850s. What is new about this problem is its large scope in the industrialized countries of North America and Europe.

Key Terms

acid rain   pH scale
neutralize   acid shock

■ FORMATION

The first stage in the formation of acid rain occurs when sulphur dioxide and nitrogen oxides are released into the atmosphere (Fig. 21–10). These chemicals are released from coal-burning electrical generating stations, metal smelters, and automobiles (Fig. 21–11). Acid rain forms when these oxides combine with water in the atmosphere to form sulphuric and nitric acids.

Fig. 21–10 How acid rain is produced.

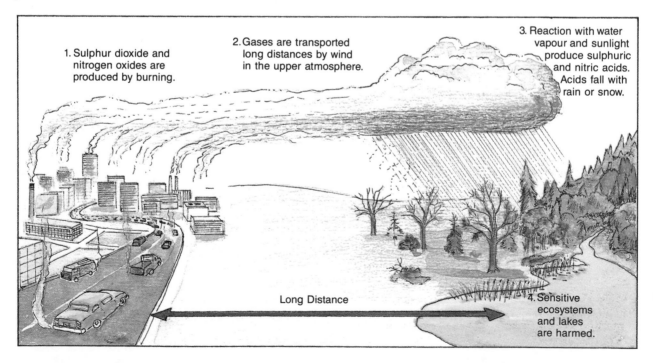

1. Sulphur dioxide and nitrogen oxides are produced by burning.

2. Gases are transported long distances by wind in the upper atmosphere.

3. Reaction with water vapour and sunlight produce sulphuric and nitric acids. Acids fall with rain or snow.

Long Distance

4. Sensitive ecosystems and lakes are harmed.

Gases	Sources	Amounts (in million metric tonnes)		
		Canada	U.S.	Total
Sulphur Dioxide	thermal power stations factories ore smelting plants burning of combustible products for home and commercial use	5*	26	31
Nitrogen Oxides	cars, trucks, buses, etc. thermal power stations other fuel burning operations	2	22	24

Fig. 21–11 Sources of gases that produce acid rain.

INCO in Sudbury alone produces over 900 000 t/yr. It is North America's largest single producer.

■ IMPACT

The impact of industrial pollution has been evident since the beginning of the Industrial Revolution. It is only since the Second World War, however, that new developments have made the damage more widespread. Forests are dying, aquatic life is disappearing, building exteriors are being dissolved, metal objects are being eaten away, and people are suffering from respiratory diseases. The increased number of automobiles has greatly increased the amount of nitrogen oxides in the atmosphere, and industrial expansion has meant more sulphur oxides in the air. The building of tall smokestacks has also spread the effects of acid precipitation over wider areas. These smokestacks, often over 150 metres tall, have been built to remove pollution from the local environment. But this has created invisible rivers of pollution high in the atmosphere. This pollution must come down some time, and it does – in the form of acid rain and snow. The acidity of the precipitation can be measured on a pH scale (Fig. 21–12).

The impact of acid rain on forests is discussed in Chapter 23.

Fig. 21–12 Acid rain on the pH scale

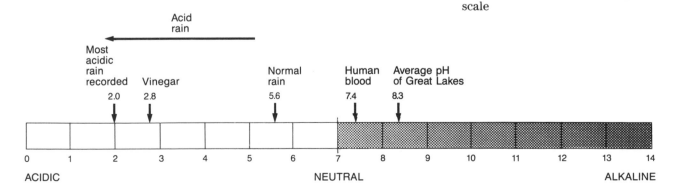

■EFFECTS OF ACID RAIN

Atmospheric pollutants can be carried up to 1000 km by prevailing winds from the highly industrialized areas of the U.S. and southern Ontario and Québec. One report indicates that about three to four times as much sulphur dioxide crosses from the U.S. into Canada as from Canada to the U.S. (Fig. 21–13). Not all areas are equally affected by acid rain. Obviously, locations that are downwind from major pollution sources are at risk. Less obviously, areas that have non-acidic bedrock, like limestone and sandstone, have the natural ability to **neutralize** acid rain. More acidic rocks, such as igneous and metamorphic rocks, lack this ability. These two characteristics mean that areas of the Canadian Shield and the Appalachians in both Canada and the U.S. are most affected (Fig. 21–13).

Acid rain and snow can make lakes and rivers too acidic to support fish and plant life. In spring, the acidic snow that accumulates over winter melts. The acidic meltwater flows into water

Fig. 21–13 Areas in the shaded parts of the map are most affected by acid rain. The dots show sites where gases that produce acid rain are formed. The prevailing storm paths carry these gases northeast.

Sources of gases that cause acid precipitation in Eastern U.S. and Canada

Areas containing lakes that are most subject to damage by acid rain

Storm paths

bodies where fish eggs are ready to hatch. This **acid shock** causes many of these eggs to die. Those that do hatch may produce deformed fish. Larger fish are also affected by water that is too acidic for their systems to tolerate.

Acid rain can cause problems in other ways. When acid rain falls onto the ground it sinks toward the water table. On this journey it can dissolve metals from the soil and the rock that would not be dissolved by normal rain. Aluminum, mercury, lead, and other toxic metals are carried into the water table and then into rivers and lakes where aquatic life is affected. For example, dissolved aluminum coats the gills of fish and causes them to suffocate.

Some of Canada's most beautiful recreation spots are threatened by acid rain. Many think that polluted lakes must look dirty. But although a lake in the final stages of dying from acidification may contain algae that smell like rotten cabbage, a fully dead lake is crystal clear! Many lakes in the Canadian Shield are becoming like this, a sure sign that few organisms are alive in them.

Scientists have conducted experiments in which huge amounts of crushed limestone have been dumped into threatened lakes. The limestone neutralizes excess acidity, but this solution is far too expensive to be considered for the large number of lakes affected. In Ontario alone, it would cost one billion dollars a year ($126/ha of lake surface area) to lime the lakes in danger.

It is estimated that in Canada, over 14 000 lakes have become acidified and that 300 000 more lakes are nearly at this stage. Numerous rivers are similarly affected. The recreational fishing industry, which brings millions of dollars to the economy of the central and eastern provinces, may soon be a thing of the past.

■ CONTROLLING ACID RAIN

If the acid rain problem is so severe, why is it not stopped? Part of the difficulty lies in the fact that the Canadian and U.S. governments have not been able to come to an effective agreement on the matter (Fig. 21–14). The only agreement now in force is one for detailed research on the causes and effects of acid rain.

American utility companies say that the cost of cleanup would make electricity from American coal-fired plants very expensive. Then Canada would be able to sell its hydro-electricity more cheaply in the U.S. The U.S. government says that there is not enough evidence to show that sulphur dioxide from coal-burning plants is the main cause of acid rain. It also feels that the link between acid rain and the death of trees and the acidification of lakes has not been proven. The U.S. also says that Canada does not have strict enough controls on the release of nitric oxides from vehicles.

Canada decided it could not wait for the U.S. to help control acid rain. In 1984, the federal and provincial governments decided to spend enough money to reduce Canadian emissions of sulphur dioxide by 50% by the year 1994. How much money will

In 1988, researchers reported that acid-loving algae has been found floating in highly acidified lakes in Ontario. In addition, a thick green moss (sphagnum moss) thrives in acidic lakes. It eventually falls to the lake bottom and decomposes.

Fig. 21–14 Acid rain has become a serious problem between the United States and Canada. Although no timetable to stop acid rain has been established, President Bush told Prime Minister Mulroney in February 1989 that the U.S. was serious about dealing with the acid rain problem.

Canada gets another slap from U.S.: acid rain will keep falling

this take? Nobody really knows, but a recent estimate by Environment Canada suggested an expenditure of more than $500 million per year. Can we afford to spend this much money? A better question is, can we afford not to spend it?

QUESTIONS

CHECKBACK

1. **a)** What does the term "acid rain" include?
   b) Describe the harmful effects of acid rain.
2. Why is acid rain more widespread today than it was before World War II?
3. How is acid rain formed and deposited? Use a diagram to help answer this question.
4. Why are lakes in some areas more affected by acid rain than those in other areas? Where are these lakes?
5. **a)** In what ways does acid rain affect lakes and aquatic life?
   b) How can one tell when a lake is acidified?
   c) How many lakes have been affected?

ANALYZE

6. Why have the Canadian and U.S. governments not been able to work together to solve the acid rain problem?

WHAT DO YOU THINK?

7. Should Canada spend a lot of money to reduce our contribution to acid rain even if the U.S. does not reduce its air pollution? Explain your answer.
8. What should Canada do to change the views of the U.S. government about reducing the emissions that create acid rain?
9. How would *you* convince a U.S. citizen that he or she should help pay for the costly controls to stop the acid rain that is affecting Canada?
10. Debate:
    One portion of your class will represent people who live in an area that produces acidic emissions and is seriously affected by acid rain. The other part of the class will represent those who live in an area that creates acid rain but is not affected by it. In each group there should be representatives of:
    a) government
    b) environmental groups
    c) industry that releases acidic emissions
    d) health organizations
    e) ordinary citizens
    Research the opinions of people who belong to these five groups in the area you represent. Prepare arguments for a debate on the topic: "Acid Rain — What's the Problem?"

Land:
A Scarce Resource

The American writer Mark Twain once wrote: "Buy land, they've stopped making it!" His humorous advice has a serious side. Most Canadians, especially farmers, value ownership of land. But why is land so important? Land is a **renewable resource** in the sense that, properly used, it can support new crops year after year (Fig. 22–1). On the other hand, land is a non-renewable resource because, as Mark Twain reminds us, its amount is limited. If it is seriously damaged because of bad farming practices, or is paved over to build a town or highway, it can no longer be used for agriculture. Before we change land from a renewable into a **non-renewable resource**, we should be sure to consider the consequences.

renewable: a resource that replaces itself unless badly mismanaged

non-renewable: a resource that can be used only once

Key Terms

renewable resource   erosion   intensive agriculture
non-renewable resource   land capability   extensive agriculture

■ INTRODUCTION

What is land? We often use the word without realizing that it has many meanings. Consider the following:

- To a farmer, land is the basic resource of farming.
- To an artist, land is the subject for a painting.
- To a map maker, land is an area to be shown on a map.
- To an environmentalist, land is a resource to be protected.
- To a real estate developer, land is something to be bought and sold.
- To a geologist, land is a storehouse of valuable minerals.
- To a geographer, land is many things. . .as you will discover in this chapter.

Fig. 22–1 Good soils allow farmers to produce high yields year after year.

A

B

Fig. 22-2 On these two photos, the numbers refer to capability classes while letters refer to the reasons for limitations. (T stands for topography or hilliness; W stands for wetness; and, E stands for erosion)

surveyed: examined and measured the quality of the land for agriculture

Other surveys were done to determine the land capability for forestry, outdoor recreation, and wildlife.

grazing: animals such as cattle and sheep feeding on growing plants

■ LAND CAPABILITY

During the 1960s and 1970s, the federal and provincial governments surveyed much of the land of southern Canada. The object of this study was to determine the **land capability** for agriculture. The results were published as part of the Canada Land Inventory. The survey divided Canada's agricultural land into seven classes.

Class 1 land is excellent for farming. It has no climatic or land limitations.

Class 2 land is very good farmland. It has no serious climatic or land limitations.

Class 3 land is good farmland but has some climatic or land limitations that make some farming activities impossible.

Class 4 land is at the "break-even" point for commercial agriculture because of a short growing season, poor soil conditions, or other significant limitations.

Class 5 land has serious limitations for agriculture, such as a very short growing season, hilly landscape, thin soil, or poor drainage. Class 5 land may be used for grazing or producing hay.

Class 6 land is similar to Class 5 except that the limitations are more severe. These lands can only be used for rough grazing; crops cannot be grown successfully.

Class 7 land has no capability for farming.

The land capability classification system is invaluable for land-use planning. Fig. 22-2 shows how this system can be applied to typical farming areas.

■ THE NATIONAL PICTURE

Canada has a total land area of 922 000 000 ha – a vast amount of land. Yet according to the Canada Land Inventory, only 11% of this area is capable of being used for any form of agriculture (Fig. 22-3). In fact, the amount of good farmland in Canada is about equal to the amount of good farmland in the state of California!

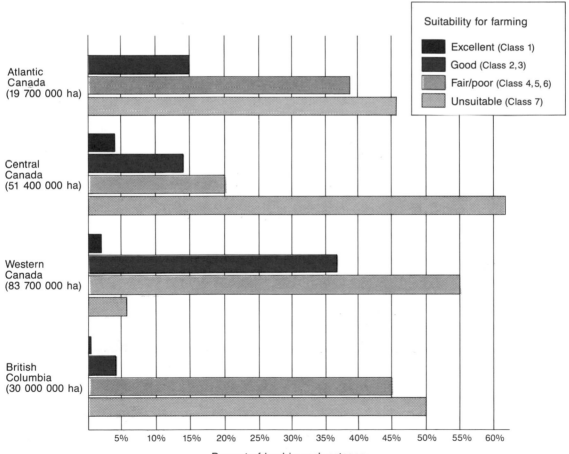

All of Canada
922 000 000 ha

Farmland of
all types
126 000 000 ha

Good farmland
46 000 000 ha

Excellent farmland
4 200 000 ha

Fig. 22–3 The amount of excellent farmland in Canada is very small.

Fig. 22–4 illustrates the distribution of land capability across Canada. This graph tells us several interesting things. Notice that Atlantic Canada has no Class 1 farmland and that British Columbia has very little. On the other hand, the Prairies have very little Class 7 land.

Fig. 22–4 The distribution of farmland of different qualities across Canada.

Suitability for farming

- Excellent (Class 1)
- Good (Class 2,3)
- Fair/poor (Class 4,5,6)
- Unsuitable (Class 7)

Atlantic
Canada
(19 700 000 ha)

Central
Canada
(51 400 000 ha)

Western
Canada
(83 700 000 ha)

British
Columbia
(30 000 000 ha)

5% 10% 15% 20% 25% 30% 35% 40% 45% 50% 55% 60%

Percent of land in each category

APPROACHES TO FARMING

There are essentially two approaches to farming in Canada: extensive agriculture and intensive agriculture.

Extensive Agriculture

When land is cheap, available, and plentiful, farms tend to be large. These farms are usually highly mechanized and require relatively few workers. Farmers raise crops or animals, or both. Major types of **extensive farming** include cattle ranching, grain and oil seed growing, mixed farming, and dairying. Most Canadian farms are of this type.

Intensive Agriculture

Intensive agriculture is carried on in areas where land is of outstanding quality but is in short supply. Farms are small, but require large investments of labour and money to produce crops. Intensive agriculture is most commonly used for the production of fruits and vegetables in such areas as the Annapolis Valley of Nova Scotia, the Niagara fruit belt of Ontario, the Okanagan Valley of British Columbia, the Holland Marsh of Ontario, and the lower Fraser Valley of British Columbia.

Fig. 22–6 shows the regional farming pattern across Canada.

QUESTIONS

CHECKBACK

1. How can land be considered both a renewable and non-renewable resource?
2. **a)** What is the Canada Land Inventory?
   b) In your own words, outline the characteristics of each of the seven classes of land.
3. In your notebook, construct and complete a chart similar to Fig. 22–5.

Fig. 22–5

	Intensive Agriculture	Extensive Agriculture
Size of Farms Use of Labour/ Machines Types of Farming		

ANALYZE

4. The term "land" has many meanings. What might it mean to each of the following:
   a) a regional planner

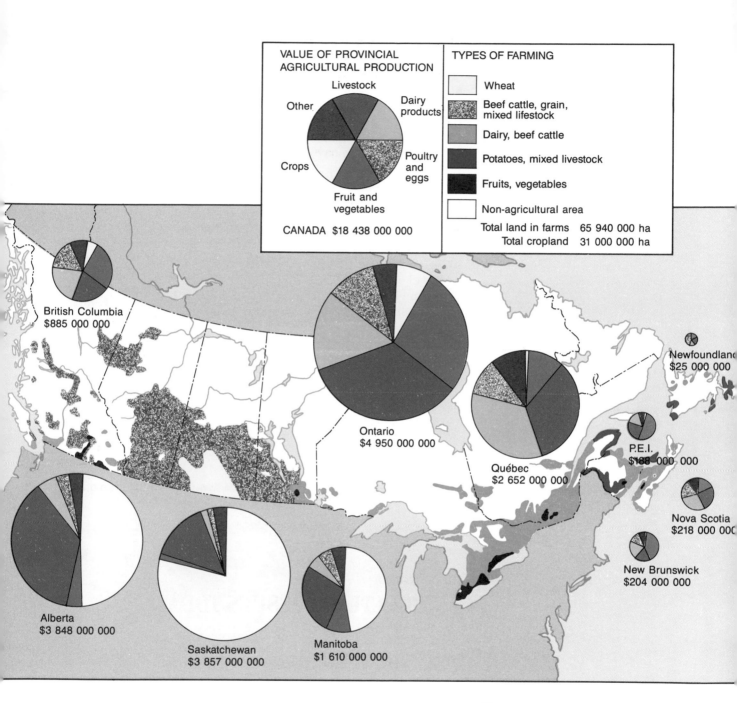

VALUE OF PROVINCIAL AGRICULTURAL PRODUCTION

Livestock
Other
Dairy products
Crops
Poultry and eggs
Fruit and vegetables

CANADA $18 438 000 000

TYPES OF FARMING

- Wheat
- Beef cattle, grain, mixed lifestock
- Dairy, beef cattle
- Potatoes, mixed livestock
- Fruits, vegetables
- Non-agricultural area

Total land in farms 65 940 000 ha
Total cropland 31 000 000 ha

British Columbia
$885 000 000

Ontario
$4 950 000 000

Québec
$2 652 000 000

Newfoundland
$25 000 000

P.E.I.
$188 000 000

Nova Scotia
$218 000 000

New Brunswick
$204 000 000

Alberta
$3 848 000 000

Saskatchewan
$3 857 000 000

Manitoba
$1 610 000 000

Fig. 22–6 Distribution of types of farming across Canada.

  b) a biologist
  c) a hiker
  d) a Native person?
5. Examine photograph A in Fig. 22–2.
  a) What is meant by a 2T and a 3W classification?
  b) Explain why one part of the field has a 3W classification while the other has a 2T classification.
  c) Why does the land in the distance have a 5T classification?

Examine photograph B in Fig. 22–2.

d) Why does the land in the foreground have a 6TE classification?

e) Why is some of the land classified 7T? What could this land be used for?

f) Farmer A owns the land in photograph A while Farmer B owns the land in photograph B. What type of farming could each do with the land they have? Which one would find it easier to farm their land?

6. Examine Fig. 22–4.

    a) Rank the regions in terms of the amount of good and excellent farmland found in each.

    b) Rank the regions separately in terms of the amount of land that is fair or worse.

    c) What do these rankings suggest about the agricultural potential of each region?

7. Construct a chart similar to Fig. 22–7 in your notebook. Complete it using Fig. 22–6 as a source of information.

Fig. 22–7

Province	Value of Farm Production	Location(s) of Farming Area(s)	Major Types of Farming

WHAT DO YOU THINK?

8. What would life be like for a family whose farm consisted only of Class 6 and 7 land? What options would they have?

AGRICULTURAL ISSUES TODAY

THE CHANGING FARM

In the 1880s, about 80% of Canadian families farmed the land. Today, less than 4% do! What has caused this staggering change?

A hundred years ago, farming was a labour-intensive activity. In other words people, not machines, performed almost all farming tasks. Today, one or two people can operate a large farm with the help of modern equipment. This increased **mechanization** has brought about an increase in the size of farms and a decline in their number (Fig. 22–8).

The long, irregular hours and low incomes associated with farming have caused many people – especially the children of

Do you think this trend will continue?

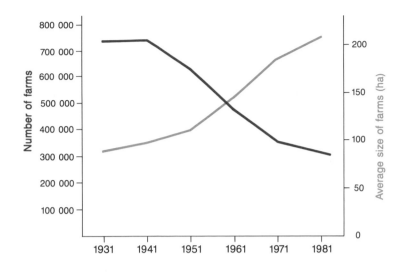

Fig. 22–8 Changes in the number and average size of farms. Are these trends continuing today?

farmers – to leave farms and look for better opportunities elsewhere. The result is that the average age of farmers is higher than that of workers in most other jobs. More than half of Canada's farmers are over 45 years of age. As they reach retirement, who will buy their farms? Young people wishing to become farmers may buy some; but few young people can afford the enormous costs of buying a farm. Most of the rest will be bought by other farmers who wish to expand, or by **agribusiness** companies.

When compared to most other Canadians, farmers have low incomes. Much of what they carn goes back into the farm in the form of new machinery, new buildings, or more land. Incomes are so low that many farmers must take jobs away from their farm. They work at these jobs, often in the winter, to earn needed cash.

DAMAGING THE LAND

Over the past century, much of our farmland has been damaged by poor farming practices (Fig. 22–9). This damage can be classified under three headings.

Fig. 22–9 Soil erosion is a common problem in many parts of Canada.

- **Erosion:** The loss of soil through the action of water and wind.
- Chemical damage: Soils may become **alkaline,** or contaminated with salts, chemicals, or dangerous **heavy metals** as a result of excessive irrigation or pollution.
- Physical damage: The repeated use of heavy equipment can compact the soil so that it loses its ability to hold the water and air needed for plant growth.

Of course, farmers do not intentionally destroy the soil. But soil conservation methods are expensive, and farmers must operate as cheaply as possible if they are to survive. Farmers have the difficult task of balancing the short term costs of soil conservation against the long term benefits.

Damage to farmland is an important issue in all regions of the country, but the type of damage varies from place to place. In British Columbia, erosion is a particular problem. On the Fraser River Delta, near Vancouver, soil is exposed to heavy winter rains. Because the soil does not freeze in the mild winter weather of the region, it is easily washed away. Greater use of winter cover crops would reduce this soil loss.

In the dry interior of B.C., the orchards are heavily irrigated and fertilized. This makes the soil very acidic, a condition that is harmful to many crops. Spreading lime on the soil reduces the **acidity**, but this is an expensive solution.

The forest industry in several parts of the country can harm land by cutting down trees, especially using the clear-cutting method. This removal of trees from a single large area exposes the soil to water erosion. The problem can be reduced by reforesting soon after cutting.

In the semi-arid southern Prairie provinces, where most of Canada's grain is grown, the soil is easily damaged by harmful farming practices. During the early 1900s farmers developed the **wheat-fallow system**. They cropped the land one year and left it fallow the next. This summer fallowing was supposed to help the soil store scarce water, control weeds, and restore soil fertility. However, recent studies indicate that this method causes increased soil erosion, a reduction in fertility, and a buildup of harmful salts. During the fallow season winds can blow the soil away, and the salts deep in the earth are drawn upward as the surface water evaporates. Today, many fields are white from salts that have made the soil infertile.

There is a new method of farming that seems to hold promise. It is called **conservation tillage**. With it, the farmer disturbs the soil as little as possible. Deep ploughing is not used. Instead, chemicals are used to control the weeds. The stubble left from the previous year's crops forms a cover that holds the soil in place and protects it from wind erosion. Stubble also traps the snow in the fields and helps build up soil moisture. This moisture helps reduce the buildup of salts.

In southern Ontario and Québec, many of the problems are similar to those elsewhere: water erosion, loss of organic matter, compaction from heavy farm machinery, high soil acid levels, and wind erosion. In central Canada, however, the land is also exposed to other forces. Harmful chemicals from smokestacks and vehicles fall onto the land. Some farmers use processed sewage and industrial waste as fertilizer. These contain heavy metals that contaminate the soil. **Insecticides** and **herbicides** have gradually built up in the soil after many years of application. Fortunately, a greater awareness of these problems has made farmers more careful about the use of sewage and chemicals.

In the Atlantic provinces, the most serious threat to good soil conditions is water erosion as a result of a wet climate. Proper cultivation practices such as contour plowing can reduce this damage.

fallow: a field that has been plowed but not planted with crops

fertility: richness of minerals needed for plant growth

contour plowing: plowing around a hill so that water cannot run down-hill as easily

LOSS OF FARMLAND

Most of Canada's best farmland is located near its largest cities. About 57% of Canada's Class 1 land and about 29% of its Class 2 land are located within 80 km of the 23 largest cities. This is not surprising if we remember that most of our large cities grew because they were located in excellent agricultural areas. In fact, if you looked around from the top of the CN Tower in Toronto, you would be able to see about 37% of Canada's Class 1 land and about 25% of its Class 2 land!

For the loss of each hectare of this excellent land, farmers must develop several hectares of poorer quality land elsewhere to produce the same quantity of crops. Some of the land we have used for orchards and vegetable-growing cannot be replaced because suitable land and climate conditions just do not exist elsewhere in Canada.

As a city expands, the surrounding farmland becomes very valuable. Farmers must choose between continuing a business that pays poorly, and making a great deal of money by selling their land to **speculators**. Speculators buy land in the hope that they will make money by selling it to people who wish to build homes and factories (Fig. 22–10).

Some people have suggested that land use be restricted so that farmland remains in production. This would maintain our present level of farmland. It would also keep the price of agricultural land more stable since it could not be used for urban purposes. But the farmer who holds on to the land would never benefit by its rising value. Land often represents a farmer's retirement savings. If farmers are prevented from selling their land at the higher value, how will they survive in their retirement?

Since the Inventory was done in the 1960s, much of this land has been urbanized. It is estimated that for every 1000 people who are added to a city, 72 ha of land are used.

speculator: a person who buys farmland near a city to make a profit when the land is needed for urban growth

Fig. 22–10 Much of our best agricultural land is being lost as our cities expand.

■ IN CLOSING...

How important is agriculture to Canada? Yearly, agriculture adds more than $10 000 000 000 to the economy. The food and beverage industry contribute another $8 000 000 000. When all the people involved in the growing, processing, transportation, and selling of food are counted, about one job in five is related to the agricultural sector of the economy. Agricultural products play an important part in our trade with other countries. Canada has a large surplus in agricultural exports. Much of this surplus is based on the export of grains from the Prairies.

At home, we rely on farmers to produce our food so that it remains relatively inexpensive. In the 1950s, Canadians spent about 25% of their income on food; today we spend only about 20%. This trend may not continue. There are many problems facing Canadian agriculture that could force us to spend a greater percentage of our income on food. Whether we can solve these problems depends on the attitudes that Canadians have toward this vital industry.

Only the Prairie provinces export a greater value of agricultural products than they import.

Canadians spend a smaller percentage of their income on food than people in most countries.

Solutions to all problems have not been provided.

QUESTIONS

CHECKBACK

1. Why are there so few families farming today compared to 100 years ago?
2. Why is it so difficult for young people to go into farming?
3. Read the section "Damaging the Land". Construct a chart similar to the one in Fig. 22–11 in your notebook. Fill in the available information under each heading.

Fig. 22–11

Location	Kind of Damage	How Caused	How Prevented/Corrected
British Columbia	1. 2. 3.		
Southern Prairies			
Southern Ontario & Québec			
Atlantic Canada			

4. Describe the importance of the agricultural sector to our economy. Give at least two pieces of evidence to support your answer.
5. Is food today a better value for consumers than it was in the 1950s? Explain.

6. "When our best farmland is lost to other uses we can develop land elsewhere to replace it." What is wrong with this point of view?

7. a) As urban areas expand, why does the surrounding farmland become more valuable?
   b) What effect does urban growth have on farmers?

8. Examine Fig. 22–8.
   a) How many farms have disappeared between 1931 and 1981?
   b) What percentage of the 1931 total does this decrease in farms represent?
   c) How many times larger are farms in 1981 compared to 1931?
   d) Why has there been a decrease in the number of farms but an increase in the size of farms?

9. Examine Fig. 22–12. For maps A and B, perform the following activity. In each military grid square determine whether the land use is mainly rural (white, green space) or mainly urban (red background, large buildings).
   a) How many squares were used for rural activities in 1965 (Map A) compared to 1980 (Map B)?
   b) What has happened to the pattern of land use in this part of southern Ontario?
   c) Examine the Land Capability Map (Map C). What type of land is mainly being used for urban expansion? Why is this happening?
   d) The recreational land along the Niagara Escarpment (left part of map) is protected from urban growth.
      i. Why do you think this land is protected?
      ii. Why isn't farmland also protected?

If a square is more than half rural, consider the whole square as rural.

10. Research one of the following issues. Your teacher will tell you whether you are to do a written report, an oral presentation, a blackboard display or some other kind of project.
    a) Precious soil is being lost through poor farming practices.
    b) Much of our best farmland is being lost to urban growth.
    c) Farmers do not receive adequate compensation for their investment of time and money.
    d) Our transportation and distribution systems for food are not efficient enough.
    e) Canada has a food surplus while others in the world are desperately short of food.
    f) World food prices are low because of overproduction. As a result, Canadian farmers do not receive enough income to pay their costs of production.
    g) Agricultural chemicals (fertilizers, insecticides, and herbicides) cause unacceptable environmental damage.

See Chapter 38 for help on research skills.

Fig. 22–12 A topographic map of the Burlington area in 1965.
B topographic map of the same area in 1980.
C agricultural capability map of the Burlington area (based on the 1965 topographic map).

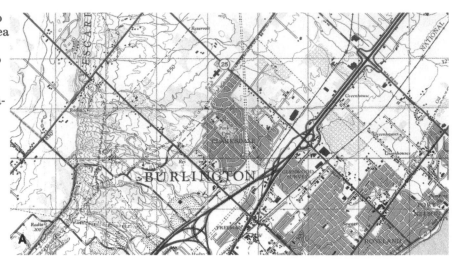

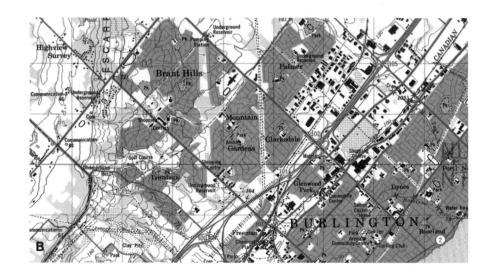

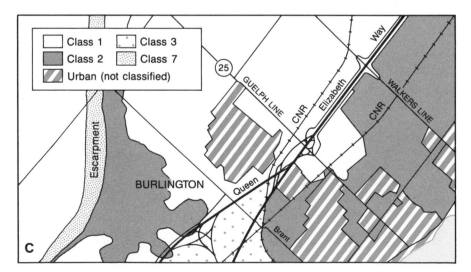

11. During the period of one week keep track of the food you eat.
    a) Make two lists:
        i. food from Canadian sources
        ii. food from non-Canadian sources
    b) Which list is longer? Does this surprise you? Why?
    c) Would your lists change throughout the year? Explain.

WHAT DO YOU THINK?

12. "If Canadian farmers were unable to grow enough food to feed Canadians, we could become dependent on other countries for our food supplies." What do you think about this possibility? Fully explain your opinions.

13. A government committee is examining a proposal for the development of a new subdivision on the outskirts of a city. The site is currently occupied by several farms. Several interest groups are appearing before this committee to present their views. What arguments would each of the following put before this committee?
    a) an aging farmer
    b) an environmentalist
    c) a transportation planner
    d) a real estate developer
    e) a local government official
    f) a local resident who does not farm

The Business of Farming

At one time, most Canadians lived on farms. Almost all of these farms were small and operated by members of a single family. Each farm produced several different crops and had a few cows, pigs, and chickens. Most of the food needed by the family was grown on the farm. Other needs were provided for with money earned from selling farm products. As a result, the "family farm" was a self-supporting unit, and the people who owned it had a distinctive style of living.

Although most farms are still family owned, their methods of operation have changed. In the 1950s many farmers began finding it more difficult to make ends meet. Competition was increasing, and the cost of everything was going up. Farmers needed more money to buy more land, modern machinery, fertilizers, expensive animal feeds, and other products. As a result, farmers found that they had to change their approach if they wished to stay in business. We will see how the family farm has changed by looking at the N.H. Culp and Son Ltd. farm near Vineland, Ontario.

A recent trend is the ownership of farms by large companies. These companies often process and market farm products. This type of farming is called "agribusiness".

Key Terms

soft fruits   capital

■ BACKGROUND

The Culp farm is located in the heart of the famous Niagara Fruit Belt (Fig. 22–13). This area is Canada's most important region for growing grapes and **soft fruits** such as peaches, pears, and cherries. It originally started as a wheat growing area and later changed to mixed crop and livestock farming. In the early years, the Culp farm followed this pattern. Fruit growing was only a small part of the farm's whole operation. On the Culp farm, as elsewhere in the region, the farmers noticed that the special soil and weather conditions were excellent for the growing of soft fruit. The sandy loam and clay loam are ideal, and the coolness caused by Lake Ontario tends to delay the opening of buds on the fruit trees until the risk of frost is gone. In the autumn the warm water of Lake Ontario delays the first frost. This gives farmers time to harvest their crops. The farmers gradually began to use

loam: soil with a mixture of particle sizes: sand, silt, and clay. Sandy loam contains an extra mixture of sand; clay loam an extra mixture of clay.

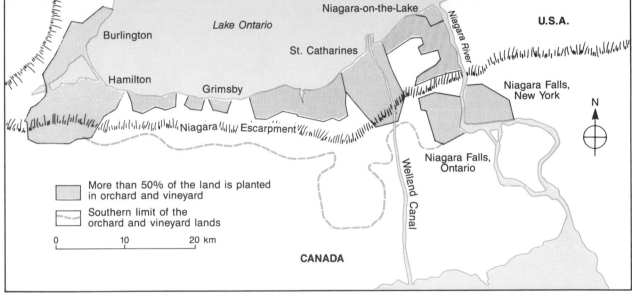

More than 50% of the land is planted in orchard and vineyard

Southern limit of the orchard and vineyard lands

0   10   20 km

more land for growing soft fruits and grapes. By 1950, the Culps and most other farmers in the Niagara region were specializing in fruit growing.

Between 1950 and 1970, the Culp farm was a typical Niagara family fruit farm. During this period most Niagara fruit farms ranged in size from 8 to 16 ha. The Culp farm was about 14 ha and produced a wide variety of soft fruit crops and grapes.

In 1970, the farm began to take on its present form. It became a limited company with three shareholders: Russell Culp, son of N. H. Culp, the original farmer; Don Culp, Russell's son; and Craig Gillespie, Russell's nephew. As a company, the Culp farm was better able to borrow money to expand its operation. And expand it did. The farm now consists of 46 ha of owned land and 10 ha of rented land. The new land was originally part of seven other farms. There are only a few farms larger than this in the Niagara Fruit Belt.

Fig. 22–13 Can you identify the location and extent of the Niagara fruit belt on the satellite image, using the map that accompanies it?

shareholders: people who own part of a company

■ FARM OPERATION

Three things are required for any farming business: land, labour, and **capital**. We will look at each of these three factors to establish what is involved in operating a modern farm.

LAND

The Culps' 56 ha farm is divided equally into two parts: one half has sandy loam soil, and the other has clay loam soil. Land with sandy loam can be used for all types of crops and is worth about $20 000/ha. Land with clay loam is less suitable for fruit trees, but is very good for grapes. This land costs about $12 500/ha. (If the land was **zoned** for urban use it would be worth much more.) The Culps' farmland is used as shown in Fig. 22–14.

Fig. 22–14 Land use on the Culp farm.

Peaches	24	ha
Grapes	18	ha
Pears	6	ha
Strawberries*	3.5	ha
Cherries	2	ha
Plums	2	ha
Tomatoes	1	ha
Apricots	0.5	ha
Houses, ponds, roads, bush, etc.	2.5	ha
Total	59.5	ha

* planted between rows of fruit trees

LABOUR

Farming is a seasonal business and as a result the farm's labour force changes from month to month.

a) Year round: 5 workers
   i. 3 partners in the farm
   ii. 1 office worker
   iii. 1 truck driver

b) Seasonal, April to October: 14 extra workers
   i. 2 truck drivers/general labourers
   ii. 12 field hands brought from the West Indies each year under a government program

Why would this program be needed?

c) Seasonal, mid-July to mid-September: about 130 more workers
   i. 14 packing-house workers for two months
   ii. 15 pickers for cherries and strawberries for five weeks
   iii. 100 pickers for strawberries for two weeks

In 1988, the cost of labour was $220 000. This included the salaries of the three partners who, as well as being owners of the company, are also employees. Not included in this total is the cost of housing provided for the three partners and 14 other employees (including the West Indian workers). Because the farm is made up of seven original farms, there are several houses on the property.

CAPITAL

The capital investment on the farm includes all the machinery, buildings, and land improvements. The farm uses a total of 46 different machines. Included in this number are five tractors, six trucks, and a wide variety of very specialized machines, such as one that thins peaches by grabbing the tree trunk and shaking some of the young fruit from the tree. The cost of these machines ranges from $2500 for a strawberry planter to $40 000 for a tractor-trailer truck. In addition, the equipment for sorting and packing fruits cost about $70 000. The total value of all equipment and buildings (not including the houses) is about $450 000.

■ THE COSTS OF DOING BUSINESS

The old-fashioned family farm was a relatively simple operation that produced little cash and seemed to survive well enough without it. The modern farm is totally different. Fig. 22–15 shows the costs of operating the Culp farm in 1988.

Labour	$220 000
Purchase and repair of machinery	105 000
Fertilizer, straw, manure, chemicals	44 000
Fuel and electricity	40 000
Building repairs	24 000
Baskets and boxes for fruit	67 000
Interest on operating loans	15 000
Miscellaneous (such as office costs)	11 000
TOTAL	**$526 000**

Fig. 22–15 Yearly cost of running the Culp farm (not including land costs).

Notice that this table does not include the cost of buying new land. The Culp farm has grown 400% since 1970. A serious problem facing farmers is the high interest charged on loans (mortgages) needed to purchase land. Farmers are helped in this by the government's Farm Credit Corporation, which lends money at reduced rates.

A second problem farmers face is high land prices. Land in the Niagara region has a high value because developers want to use it to build homes and factories. Craig Gillespie feels that this makes the land about twice as costly as it would be if it were only used as farmland. As a result, the new land they buy does not provide enough income to pay for itself. The money that pays for this new land must come from income provided by the old land.

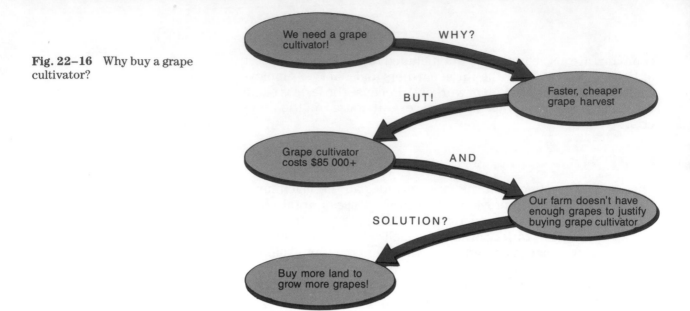

Fig. 22–16 Why buy a grape cultivator?

We need a grape cultivator!

WHY?

Faster, cheaper grape harvest

BUT!

Grape cultivator costs $85 000+

AND

Our farm doesn't have enough grapes to justify buying grape cultivator

SOLUTION?

Buy more land to grow more grapes!

Why buy more land if it does not pay for itself? A larger farm is needed for other reasons. One of them is illustrated in Fig. 22–16. You can see why Don Culp says that the farm will continue to grow and develop in the future as finances allow.

■ FARM INCOME

The Culp farmers sell both retail and wholesale to a large number of customers. Like most fruit farmers, they sell to fruit wholesalers. These wholesalers, in turn, sell to supermarkets, fruit stores, and other buyers. In addition, the Culps sell directly to supermarkets in Toronto, Ottawa, and elsewhere. They can do this because they have their own refrigerated trucks. The trucking service itself does not make a profit but it gives the Culps access to markets they would not have otherwise. They also use their trucks twice a week to take produce to sell at the Kitchener farmers' market. The fourth destination for the Culp fruit is a number of local factories where wine, jams, and preserves are made.

Manufacturing companies tend to have fairly stable incomes from year to year; farms do not. Here are two factors that can affect the Culp farm's annual income:

- Bad weather: late spring frost and summer hail reduce fruit yield and the income from it.
- Poor market conditions: good weather in fruit growing areas throughout North America can cause an oversupply of fruit. The result will be lower prices and reduced income.

The Culps are forced to make plans for the year without knowing future weather, labour, and market conditions. They always hope that they will have a profit at the end of the year. If they find they have a larger profit than predicted, they re-invest most of it to improve their business.

■ IN CLOSING...

The Culp farm is typical of the Canadian farm of the 1980s. It is large (for its locality) and is still growing. It is highly mechanized (Fig. 22–17) and produces crops for sale, not for the sole use of people on the farm. The farm is a business in every sense of the word. It has stockholders, employees, profits, and long-term planning. It faces the problems of any modern business: high interest rates, foreign competition, labour problems, lack of capital for expansion, uncertain markets, and new technical development.

Young people wanting to be farmers today must be special. They must have all of the following:

Fig. 22–17 A grape cultivator.

a) Technical farming skills to understand such things as a choice of crop varieties, use of fertilizers and pest sprays, machinery operation and repair, simple veterinary medicine (on livestock farms).

b) Business skills to hire and handle employees, understand and arrange financing, understand complicated government laws and programs, do long- and short-term planning.

c) Access to a large amount of money to invest in the farm. In most parts of Canada the minimum amount of capital needed to start commercial farming is about $400 000.

d) Traditional farming attitudes toward working 70-hour, 7-day weeks during the summer, accepting bad years, making generally low wages, having short vacations (or in some types of farming, none at all).

The surprising thing about all this is not that Canadian farmers are leaving the business. The surprising thing is that there are any farmers left at all!

QUESTIONS

CHECKBACK

1. a) Compare the characteristics of the traditional family farm to the modern farm.
   b) Why was the change from one to the other necessary?
2. Briefly describe the history of the Culp farm. Why did changes occur on this farm?
3. The following ideas are used in this study but the exact words are not. Define the following terms:
   a) **cash crops**
   b) **farm consolidation**
   c) **farm specialization.**
4. State four characteristics that make operating the Culp farm similar to running a business.
5. Describe the kinds of business and technical skills a farmer must have.

Hint: strawberries are ready for market several weeks before other crops.

ANALYZE

6. Some activities of the Culp farm do not produce a profit but they are necessary to support other parts of the farm's operation. Explain the purpose of the following activities, none of which makes money by itself:
   a) the trucking business
   b) continued expansion of the farm's area
   c) growing strawberries.

7. a) Draw a pie graph to illustrate the costs of running the Culp farm for one year. Shade each segment in the graph a distinct colour and be sure to label the graph correctly.
   b) The costs in this chapter refer to the year 1988. How much would they be today? Your teacher will give you guidelines for determining these.

8. Rented land is likely to be an increasingly important part of the Culp farm in the future. Suggest at least two advantages and two disadvantages of renting land for farming.

INVESTIGATE

9. Fruit farming is a type of farming that is labour intensive and land intensive.
   a) Explain the meaning of both these terms.
   b) Give an example of a type of farming that is land and labour extensive (that is, the opposite of intensive).

Hint: discuss this with a law or business teacher.

10. a) What is a "limited company"?
   b) What advantages are there for a farmer making a farm into a company?

11. Like many modern farms, the Culp farm uses a lot of energy. Why are its energy needs so high?

12. Determine the average sizes of other types of farms. Consider such types as Prairie wheat farms and cattle ranches, and southern Ontario mixed farms. Compare these to the size of the average Niagara fruit farm. Why do these differences exist?

WHAT DO YOU THINK?

13. a) Calculate the total value of land, equipment, and buildings of the Culp farm.
   b) Assume that you invest this money. How much would you earn in interest per year? Assume an interest rate of 10%.
   c) Put yourself in the position of one of the owners of the Culp farm. You have two choices. You can sell your farm and live on invested interest, or you can continue to work for considerably less money. Which would you choose? Why?
   d) Most farmers stay in farming, but not for financial reasons. Suggest at least three other reasons why farmers stay in the business.

Marketing Boards — An Efficient Way to Feed Canadians?

Could you explain what a marketing board is? Some of you may never have even heard of a marketing board! Nevertheless, they play an important role in your life. **Marketing boards** also create strong feelings among Canadians. Consider these statements about them:

"Marketing boards give Canadians a steady supply of food at affordable prices."

"They prevent our farm industry from operating in an efficient manner."

"They make Canadians pay much more for food than they should."

"Marketing boards allow farmers to survive bad economic times."

Key Terms

marketing boards	supply management	supply
demand	cycles of boom and bust	free market

■ WHY HAVE MARKETING BOARDS?

The easiest way to understand what a marketing board does is to examine the situation before marketing boards existed. Picture yourself as a chicken and egg farmer. You have enough hens to produce 400 dozen eggs on a typical day. You can produce these eggs at a cost of 70¢ per dozen and you can sell them for 80¢ per dozen.

- What is your profit for each dozen eggs sold? What is your total profit each day?
- Calculate your profit if you were to sell:
  a) 600 dozen eggs per day
  b) 800 dozen eggs per day
  c) 1000 dozen eggs per day

Fig. 22-18 Egg production, like most kinds of farming, is a big business.

economist: someone who studies the production, distribution, and consumption of goods

Obviously it would be to your advantage to expand your operation and sell more eggs. However, many of the other egg producers in your region (your competitors) will reach the same conclusion since their costs and selling price will be similar to yours. If all the egg producers expanded, there would be many more eggs to be sold (Fig. 22-18). Economists call this an increase in **supply**. However, the number of eggs required by stores, restaurants, and food processors (called the **demand**) will not increase. If the supply exceeds the demand, the price of eggs will drop from 80¢ to perhaps 65¢ per dozen.

Those who buy eggs will be pleased with the drop in price. But producers will be devastated because the money they receive for their eggs will be less than the cost of producing them. What would you do now? Most likely you would get rid of a substantial number of your hens, since they are not producing enough income to pay for themselves.

By the way, since your competitors will also reduce the size of their flocks, the price paid for chickens is likely to fall drastically so you will lose there too.

If all the producers dispose of their surplus chickens, the supply of eggs may then fall below the demand. As you might expect, this will drive up the price of eggs – to perhaps $1.10 a dozen. Consumers will be angry about the high cost of eggs. Producers who were badly hurt by **overexpansion** in the past will be left wondering what to do.

Such **cycles of boom and bust** tend to occur, on average, about once every 12 to 18 months. They affect all kinds of farming and can destroy a farmer's future. Chaotic market conditions like these were responsible for the creation of marketing boards.

■ THE ROLE OF MARKETING BOARDS

Marketing boards fall into two categories. Some help farmers by organizing the selling of agricultural products and are therefore true "marketing boards". Others go much further and actually control the production of crops and livestock. These agencies, which properly should be called "supply management boards", are what most people think of when they hear the term, "marketing board".

Let's see how eggs are produced under **supply management** compared to the **free market** system described above. If you want to produce eggs you must have a licence from the egg marketing board. This licence, called a quota, allows you to sell a certain number of eggs each day. By controlling the supply of eggs in this way, the marketing board is able to maintain a price high enough to ensure an adequate income for egg farmers.

When the marketing board was established, these licences were given to existing egg farmers.

If the demand for eggs grows, the marketing board will increase the number of eggs that farmers may produce. On the other hand, if the demand should fall, the marketing board can reduce the number of eggs being produced so that prices do not drop. If farmers want to leave the business, they can sell their quota to someone else because it is a very valuable commodity.

Excess eggs are sold to food manufacturers at reduced prices.

■ ADVANTAGES AND DISADVANTAGES OF MARKETING BOARDS

There are four major supply-managed marketing boards in Canada. They control the production of dairy products, chickens, turkeys, and eggs. The importance of these four boards is shown by the fact that they control 23% of Canada's total agricultural production or about $4 400 000 000 per year! Three main criticisms have been levelled against these marketing boards.

1. They artificially increase the cost of food for Canadians. Critics point out that the cost of milk, chickens, turkeys, and eggs is higher in Canda that it is in the U.S. where these products are not supply-managed.

2. Since the amount of production is restricted, there is a large demand for quotas. As a result, the price of a quota is so high that only rich farmers and large companies can get into these kinds of farming. For example, a milk quota to produce only one litre per day can cost $300 or more.

3. Consumers complain that marketing boards exist only to serve the needs of farmers and that the needs of consumers are ignored.

Supporters of marketing boards counter by arguing that:

1. Erratic price changes have been avoided for marketing board products.

erratic: unpredictable

2. Prices for these products have gone up more slowly than those of non-managed goods.

In view of this success, there has been pressure to expand supply management to other products such as beef and grain. Will this happen, or could pressure from opposing groups cause the existing boards to disappear? The debate continues.

1. **a)** Define supply and demand.
   b) Describe how supply and demand interact to determine the price of an agricultural product.
2. Explain the difference between supply-managed marketing boards and "true" marketing boards.

ANALYZE

3. **a)** Define quota.
   b) How does a farmer obtain quota?
   c) What problems are caused by the quota system?
4. Copy Fig. 22–19 into your notebook and complete the information.

Fig. 22–19

Situation	Effect on prices paid for product	Why?
1. Early frost damages peaches on trees in Niagara Fruit Belt 2. Perfect growing conditions for corn in the U.S. 3. Deep-fried chicken wings become a fad food across Canada 4. Soviet Union's wheat crop fails 5. Increasing numbers of people quit smoking 6. Drought strikes Ethiopia		

INVESTIGATE

5. Choose one of the four supply-managed products mentioned in this chapter. Investigate, in detail, how price and production levels are determined.
6. There are other, less important, agricultural products that are supply-managed. Determine what at least one of these is and why this form of marketing was chosen.

WHAT DO YOU THINK?

7. **a)** Are supply-managed marketing boards a good idea? Explain your answer.
   b) Should other products such as grain and beef be supply-managed? Why or why not?
8. Should consumer needs be considered by marketing boards? If so, how?

Forests:
A Resource at Risk

The Past

"A Canadian settler hates a tree, regards it as his natural enemy, as something to be destroyed, eradicated, annihilated by all and any means."

> –Anna Jameson, Canadian settler in the 1830s

eradicated/annihilated: eliminated

The Present

"Somehow we must learn to manage the forest in the same way that farmers manage their land. We must cease to be merely exploiters of the forest resource and become instead cultivators and nurturers.

> –Ken Drushka, writer and logger, 1985

The Future

Either

"What was done to our forests is a national scandal and disgrace. We went from a world forestry leader to a has-been and it was all preventable!"

> –Prime Minister Rosemary St. Clair, May 12, 2040

Or

"All Canadians can take pride in the manner in which they have rescued their forest resources from the grave threats faced half a century ago."

> –King William V, May 12, 2040

The first quote illustrates a historical view of forests. The second hints at the problems faced by the forest industry today. The final two quotes, both fictional of course, suggest what could happen over the next several decades.

To understand the importance of our forests, we will look at their characteristics, how they are used, and the major problems in forest management.

Key Terms

boreal forest	hardwood	broad-leaved forest
mixed forest	clear cutting	commercial forest
softwood	selective cutting	sustained yield management
logging		

◼ NATURE OF THE RESOURCE

Most Canadians find it hard to imagine how large Canada's forests really are. This should come as no surprise, since few Canadians have the opportunity to see more than a tiny part of the forests in their lifetime. Most city dwellers rarely leave built-up areas, and many others travel only through the southern fringes of our forests.

How large are the forests? Imagine driving at 100 km/hr for 12 hours per day. It would take you more than four days to cross the continuous band of forest that stretches from British Columbia to Newfoundland. Thirty-seven percent of Canada, more than 3 500 000 km², is forest. This is an area greater than the total land area of 15 western European nations combined! Only two countries, the Soviet Union (9 200 000 km²) and Brazil (5 000 000 km²), have more forest than we do.

Examine Fig. 23–1. It shows the extent of Canada's forests and introduces the useful idea of **commercial forest** and non-commercial forest. The commercial forests are those that have been or could easily be harvested for timber. In contrast, the non-commercial forests are those that are unlikely ever to be cut down for industrial use. This could be true for two main reasons.

marginal: only just able to grow trees

1. Some parts of the non-commercial forest are marginal for the growth of trees. In these areas, either temperatures or precipitation levels are too low to allow trees to grow quickly or thickly. In parts of the non-commercial forest, a 100-year-old tree might be less than 3 cm in diameter. In contrast, a tree could grow to this size in only a few years further south.

2. These poor growing conditions tend to be found on the northern fringes of the forest region. They are a very long distance from the Canadian and export markets to the south. Therefore transportation costs are very high.

◼ CHARACTERISTICS OF THE FOREST

It would be a serious mistake to think that all parts of the Canadian forest are much alike. In fact, the diversity that exists allows Canada's forest industry to produce a wide range of products. Fig. 7–1 shows Canada's main forest regions. Each is quite distinctive.

The **boreal forest** is by far the largest region. The most common species here is the black spruce, which dominates huge tracts of land. Other important species include white spruce, balsam fir, jack pine, and tamarack. Because of the long winters and low precipitation, tree growth tends to be slow. Very large trees are not as common as in other parts of Canada. As a result, pulp and paper production, which uses smaller logs, tends to be more important than lumber production.

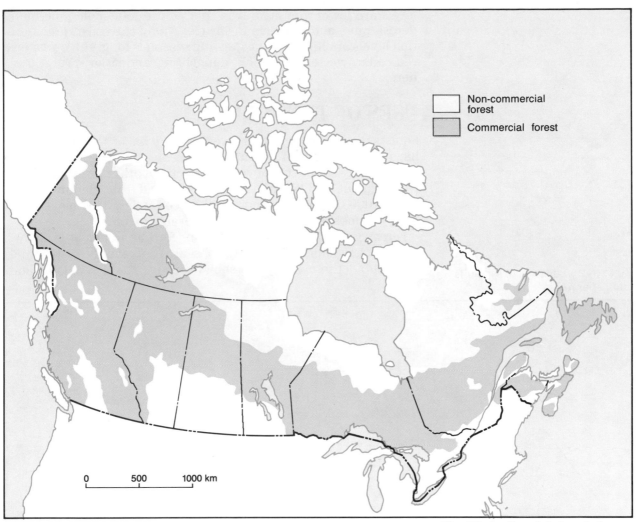

0   500   1000 km

Fig. 23–1 Canada's forested areas

The **broad-leaved** forest is the smallest and least important of Canada's forest regions. It is located within an **intensively farmed** and highly urbanized area. Very little of this forest remains and commercial forestry is not common. Broad-leaved species such as the black walnut, maple, and cherry are usually cut individually from farmers' woodlots. Sawmills in the area tend to be small and specialized. They process local, high-value trees into veneers for furniture-making.

veneer: a thin layer of wood

The **mixed forest** region is a **transition zone** between the broad-leaved forest to the south and the boreal forest to the north. In the southernmost parts of the region, broad-leaved species such as maple, beech, and oak dominate. Most of Canada's maple syrup is produced in this region. Further north, needle-leaved species such as white pine, hemlock, and red pine are more common. Pulp and paper and lumber production are both important.

The many different landforms and climates of British Columbia cause a diverse forest pattern. In the interior, where precipitation levels are lower, the main tree species are lodgepole pine, ponderosa pine, and Engelmann spruce. Along the coast, precipitation levels are high and the growing season is long. Huge western red cedar, western hemlock, douglas fir, and sitka spruce grow here.

■ USES OF THE FOREST

Forests play very important roles in the lives of Canadians. Perhaps the single most important one is economic. The forest industry produces shipments of wood, paper, and other forest products worth about $23 000 000 000 per year. Of this amount about $8 000 000 000 is exported to other countries. This makes forestry our most important earner of foreign income.

Forestry provides over 300 000 jobs for Canadians. It is important to remember that these jobs are not evenly distributed throughout the country. As shown in Fig. 23-2, saw mills and

Fig. 23-2 Location of sawmills and paper mills

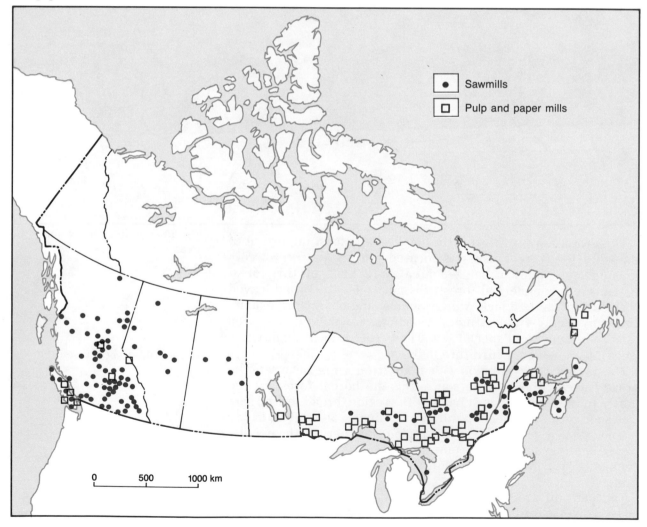

paper mills are located near the forest but close to transportation routes. The economic health of a town with a paper mill or large saw mill depends on the continual operation of the mill. Should it close, the town's future is threatened.

Canadians who live far from the forests owe a significant part of their economic well-being to the forest industry. Many of the administrative jobs and sales functions of the forest industry are carried out by employees in large cities. The goods and services produced far from the forests are bought by customers in the forest industry.

Forestry can be divided into **logging** operations and **manufacturing** operations.

LOGGING

About 20% of the forestry jobs in Canada are in logging. There are two main types of harvesting. **Clear cutting**, which is used in about 80% of logging operations, is much cheaper. An area that has been clear-cut can be totally replanted so that the new forest will be of uniform size and type. However, if replanting is not done, or if it is not successful, the soil may erode and the land may be ruined.

Selective cutting is much less disruptive to the forest environment. Only trees of a desired size, type, or quality are cut. Selective cutting tends to be a costly process because of the extra care and time taken to cut the trees, and because it does not allow the replanting of a new uniform forest.

In most of Canada, the trees are small enough to be cut by large tree-harvesting machines (Fig. 23–3). On the west coast of B.C., however, a special method of cutting is used. Because of the huge trees and often difficult terrain, the **high lead** system is used (Fig. 23–4).

Why is clear cutting cheaper?

Fig. 23–3 Trees of the boreal forest are easily harvested by machines like this.

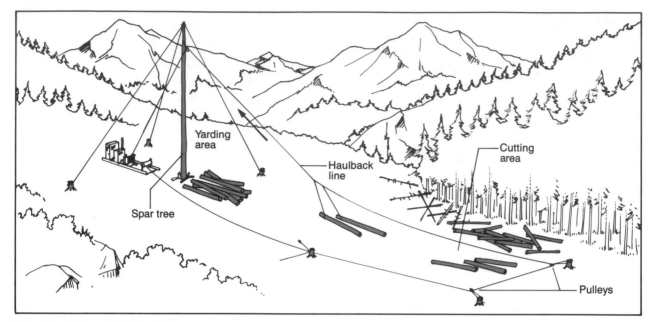

Fig. 23–4 The "high lead" logging system is used to harvest the large trees of British Columbia.

MANUFACTURING

Canada's forests produce products of great value, but the two most important are pulp and paper and lumber.

Pulp and Paper

Most kinds of paper are made from cellulose fibres. Cellulose comes from a wide variety of sources, but since the nineteenth century most has come from wood pulp. Today, about 95% of Canada's paper comes from wood pulp.

It is very easy to make paper. The challenge is to make papers with a wide variety of properties (for example, compare newsprint and paper towel) and to make them as cheaply and efficiently as possible (Fig. 23–5). In order to produce hundreds of different paper products, the Canadian pulp and paper industry has become highly specialized and costly.

Fig. 23–5 Different types of paper have different characteristics and cost.

Kind of Paper	Appearance/ Texture	Low Cost	Absorbency	Strength
newsprint	uniform, white	important	moderately absorbent	unimportant
paper towel	several colours, soft to touch	moderately important	very absorbent	unimportant
magazine paper	glossy, white	unimportant	non-absorbent	moderately important
cardboard	light brown	moderately important	unimportant	very important

Today, Canada is the world's second largest producer of pulp and paper (after the U.S.) and the largest exporter. More than three quarters of our production is exported. The U.S. is Canada's most important customer, buying more than half the total. The two most important products for export are newsprint and wood pulp.

Pulp and paper plants are found in every province except Prince Edward Island (Fig. 23–6). The industry is concentrated in three provinces: Québec, Ontario, and British Columbia. If we compare the size of trees common in Québec and Ontario with those found in B.C., we can understand why central Canada is the leading pulp and paper producer. The forests of central Canada contain mostly second growth (and even third growth) forest. These trees are much smaller than those that they replaced and are only suitable for use as pulp logs. The larger B.C. trees, while they could be used for pulp and paper, are more valuable when used for lumber production.

There are about 140 pulp and paper mills in Canada. Pulp and paper mills tend to be large, multi-million dollar installations (Fig. 23–7).

Ten percent of our exports are pulp and paper products

second growth: the forest that grew up after the original forest was cut down

Fig. 23–6 Provincial pulp and paper production

Québec 6 400 000 t	Ontario 4 400 000 t	British Columbia 5 400 000 t	Other Provinces 4 400 000 t

Fig. 23–7 A paper machine like this one costs millions of dollars.

Lumber

One province dominates Canada's lumber industry. British Columbia produces more than 60% of Canada's lumber. Québec is far behind in second place (Fig. 23–8). Lumber products take many forms. These include lumber, plywood, veneers, particle board, cedar shingles, and chip board. In B.C., cut lumber is the major product. But the province is also Canada's leading plywood producer because its tall, knot-free logs are easily unrolled or "peeled" to make the thin layers that are then glued together to make sheets of plywood.

particle board: sheets of building material produced by gluing together small chips of wood under pressure

Fig. 23–8 Provincial lumber production

Québec 6 890 000 m³	Ontario 4 600 000 m³		British Columbia 30 900 000 m³

New Brunswick
1 100 000 m³

Alberta
2 400 000 m³

Other Provinces
1 200 000 m³

About 95% of the wood used in the Canadian lumber industry is from **softwood** species such as fir, pine, and spruce. The rest, which is used primarily for veneers, furniture and panelling, comes from **hardwood** species such as maple, oak, and walnut.

Saw mills tend to be much smaller operations than pulp and paper mills (Fig. 23–9). The **technology** used in saw mills is much simpler. Some small mills can be operated by only two workers. This means that many small saw mills can be built in an area, rather than one big one. Each can take advantage of the characteristics of the forest that supplies it to specialize in a particular market. For a large mill in coastal B.C., this might mean concentrating on the production of lumber for house construction in the U.S. For a much smaller mill in southwestern Ontario, it might mean concentrating on processing the valuable hardwood trees for the fine furniture manufacturers of the region.

Saw mills in Canada, however, are changing. Since 1970, the number of saw mills has decreased by almost 600 to about 1250. This has occurred because of the need for more efficient mills. In particular, better methods to process smaller logs have been developed. This has become necessary because there are fewer large trees available. In addition, ways are constantly being sought to reduce waste when logs are cut up. Parts of the log that would have been thrown out 30 years ago are now being used to make paper, particle board or chip board. Even the bark and sawdust can be used: they are burned to help power the mill.

There is a triple benefit from this careful use of each log.
1. Production is increased and costs reduced.
2. Pollution is reduced. Elimination of forest wastes used to be a serious problem. Most were either burned or thrown in lakes and rivers.
3. Less of the forest is used.

RECREATION

Not all our uses of the forest involve cutting trees. For many Canadians, especially those from cities, the most important use of the forest is for recreation — as a place to get away from it all.

Forests, with their lakes and rivers, provide opportunities for a wide range of activities including camping, hiking, hunting, fishing and cottaging.

The importance of these activities is clear if we consider the number of people involved. For example, 27% of Canadian families own camping equipment. Each year more than 5 000 000 Canadians enjoy sport fishing, along with another 1 000 000 foreign visitors (mainly from the U.S.). Activities like these also contribute greatly to our economy.

Fig. 23–9 In the sawmill, the round logs are squared and cut into lumber of various sizes.

QUESTIONS

CHECKBACK

1. You have 1000 logs, each 1 m in diameter. You could sell them to either a saw mill or a paper mill (both are nearby). Which would likely offer you a higher price? Why?
2. What are the major characteristics of each of the four forest regions mentioned?
3. Describe the effect of the forest industry on:
   a) people who live in the forest regions
   b) people who live elsewhere in Canada.
4. List the advantages and disadvantages of:
   a) clear cutting
   b) selective cutting.
5. Complete a chart in your notebook, similar to Fig. 23–10, to compare the forests of the west coast of B.C. to those of central Québec and Ontario.

Fig. 23–10

Forest	West Coast	Central Canada
Size of Trees		
Logging System Used		
Major Products		

6. Compare pulp and paper mills and saw mills in terms of size and technology.
7. How do mill owners ensure that the whole log is used?

ANALYZE

8. a) Describe the difference between commercial and non-commercial forest.
   b) The boundary between the commercial and non-commercial forest moves over time. Is it more likely to move north or south? Why?

See Chapter 33 for instructions on how to draw a proportional circle graph.

9. a) Fig. 23–11 gives the total area and percentage of land covered by forest in some of the world's largest forest nations. Draw a circle proportional to each country's area and shade in part of the circle to show the percentage of the country that is forested.
   b) Why are proportional circles used rather than circles of the same size? Why is this important?

Fig. 23–11 Comparison of major forest–producing countries

Country	Area (km²)	Forest Land (%)
Brazil	8 512 000	68
Canada	9 976 000	35
China	9 597 000	13
India	3 288 000	23
USSR	22 402 000	41
USA	9 363 000	31
Zaire	2 345 000	78

10. Those of you who have been paper carriers know how heavy the weekend paper can be. A recent copy of the Sunday New York Times (which is made from Canadian trees) weighed 1.6 kg. About 1 400 000 copies of this paper were produced.
    a) How many kilograms of paper were used to produce this day's newspaper?
    b) One black spruce tree 13 m high and 20 cm in diameter can produce about 130 kg of newsprint. How many trees were cut down to produce this edition of the Times?
    c) What are the advantages and disadvantages of this use of our forests?

INVESTIGATE

11. a) Check your furniture and kitchen cabinets at home. Are they:
    - solid wood
    - wood core with veneer surface
    - particle board core with veneer surface
    - non-wood construction?

    What are the advantages and disadvantages of each kind of construction?
    b) If your cabinets are wood or veneer, is it likely that the wood was grown in Canada? How could you tell?
12. Go to a local lumber store and find out the following:
    a) the kinds of wood used to make chip board, plywood, particle board and lumber
    b) the difference in construction and use between chip board, particle board and plywood
    c) the cost of plywood and lumber made from different woods
    d) why these differences exist

■ CONSERVATION

conservation: wise use

Canadians are faced with a difficult problem when it comes to using our forests. We want to enjoy the economic and recreational benefits of the forest. At the same time we must protect the forest environment from damage.

THREATS TO THE FOREST

There are many reasons for protecting our woodlands. Some are economic. A forest fire or insect pests can destroy millions of dollars worth of timber. Other reasons for protecting our forests are not quite so obvious. The forests provide habitats for hundreds of kinds of mammals and birds. The trees hold back moisture during the spring run-off. This prevents flooding, and in drier seasons helps maintain stream flow.

All is not well in our forest industry. For more than 200 years, forestry has been one of the major contributors to Canada's wealth. Now we are faced with several serious threats to this situation (Fig. 23–12).

Fig. 23–12   Threats to the forest

Fig. 23–13 Seedlings are started in greenhouses to ensure early growth. They are then planted in areas from which trees have been cut.

TREE is a fictional company, but the situation described is one faced by real forest companies.

Poor Forest Management

Forests should be treated as a renewable resource. This means that for every tree that is cut, steps should be taken to ensure that another tree reaches maturity (Fig. 23–13). If this is done, the forest stock never decreases.

Unfortunately, this **sustained yield management** has not been a routine practice in the forest industry in most parts of Canada. The result is that we have gradually been eating away at our forest stocks. In many areas we now cut smaller trees, because the bigger ones are all gone. Loggers must travel further into the forest to find suitable trees. This greater distance from mills and markets increases costs and makes the industry less competitive on the world market.

Why have we allowed this to happen? Why are we, even today, still not doing very much to solve this problem? The reasons are fairly clear if we examine how our economic and political systems work. Consider the case of Transcanada Resource Exploitation Enterprises Ltd. (TREE for short). The company has just cut the trees on a tract of land near one of their pulp and paper mills. TREE must make a decision about what to do with the land now that it has finished cutting (Fig. 23–14). If TREE is like most forest companies in Canada, it will choose Option A. To understand this decision, consider the pressures that TREE's managers face.

- Option B would seriously reduce TREE's profits. The shareholders would want an explanation.
- The benefits to be gained from Option B would not be seen until at least the year 2040.
- TREE's Canadian competitors are generally choosing Option A. If TREE chooses Option B it will have higher costs and be at a disadvantage. Worse still, foreign competitors have access to faster-growing forests in places such as the southern U.S. and Brazil. Their costs of operation are often lower than Canadian costs, even using Option A.
- The government's forest management requirements are not very strict. Option A will satisfy them.

Option A	Option B
• Do as little cleanup and replanting as possible • Move to forests in other areas to meet future needs	• Research and develop new trees which grow quickly, resist disease and insects • Clear land of logging debris so new tree growth is not harmed • Replant with seedlings from tree nurseries • Fertilize, prune, and thin growing forest over next 40 years or more • Guard forest from loss to insects and forest fire

Fig. 23–14 Options for the TREE corporation

• Any extra capital that TREE has could be spent on improvements to its 60-year-old mill. Without these technological and pollution-control improvements, this old mill would have to close in a few years.

The problem can be summarized very simply. How do we strike a balance between long-term and short-term needs? The needs of the forest must be considered over a 50- or even 100-year period. Business must be most concerned with keeping profits up over the next few years. Governments do not seem to look much beyond the next election. Obviously some sort of compromise between these needs must be found if we are to have any forest and forest industry in the future.

Foreign Competition

The Canadian forest industry faces one disadvantage that it cannot overcome — Canada's climate. Canada is a northern nation with a short growing season. Most of our competitors have the great advantage of warm weather all year, so their forests grow much faster than ours. In Brazil, for example, experiments have produced pulpwood-sized trees in less than ten years. Since we cannot change our climate, we must find other ways to keep our forestry industry a world leader.

Sweden offers an example of how to be competitive in the world market in spite of having less favourable climatic conditions. For many years the Swedish government and forest companies have agreed on the need for careful forest management. This means that when a forest is cut down it must be carefully replanted with seedlings that will grow quickly, resist disease, and produce the kind of timber needed. As the forest grows, it is thinned and pruned. Insect pests are controlled by spraying, and great efforts are taken to minimize forest fires. The result is that Sweden has a highly competitive forest industry today; an industry that competes successfully with Canada for customers in western Europe. Sweden's approach is costly, but in the long run it pays off because the forest is maintained on a sustained yield basis.

Canadian forest companies realize the need for better forest management to help the industry in the future. At the same time, they must remain competitive today. The solution lies in a cooperative effort by industry and government.

Environmental Hazards

The problems considered in the previous sections were largely economic in nature. Our forest industry faces a number of environmental problems as well. Two in particular stand out.

Acid rain is becoming a very serious problem in some forest areas. So far, the worst problems are in the maple syrup-producing areas south of Québec City. In this area, more than 80% of the maple trees have been affected. Sap production is down and trees are experiencing symptoms like those seen when very old trees die of natural causes. Leaves yellow and drop, and within 2 to 5 years a healthy tree is dead and only good for firewood. Needle-leaved trees are affected as well. Their needles yellow and the tree weakens. Those that are not killed outright grow much more slowly than normal.

Insect pests, such as spruce budworm and gypsy moths, cost forest companies hundreds of millions of dollars each year. To fight them, aerial spraying of the worst infected areas is done each year (Fig. 23–15). With more attention to forest management in the future, even more spraying would be likely. This spraying is not without risks.

Aerial spraying has been linked to increased numbers of cancers and birth defects among forest workers and people who live near sprayed areas. While all the evidence is not in, most people would agree that the chemicals being used are potentially very dangerous.

There are several options to consider with respect to spraying:

1. Continue as at present and accept any risks.

2. Stop spraying and accept the losses to insects.

3. Spray more carefully. Use less dangerous chemicals and only spray far from populated areas. This option would mean more insect losses than today but reduced risks.

4. Intensify research into new methods of insect control. This could include safer chemical methods or biological controls. Biological controls include using insects that eat only one thing — a pest insect. The control insects are released into an infested area. After they have eaten the pests, the predators would die off because they would have nothing left to eat. Other researchers are investigating ways of using genetic engineering to develop "birth control for bugs".

Fig. 23–15 Aerial spraying to control pests is a very common sight in many parts of Canada's commercial forests.

■IN CLOSING...

In the first chapter of the Bible, God instructs Adam and Eve to "... replenish the earth, and subdue it . . . ." Many people would say that Canadians have concentrated too much on subduing the forests and not enough on replenishing them! (Check the first quote in this chapter.) Do we have a responsibility to ensure that the forests we leave to our children are at least as rich as those that were left to us by our parents? Whether the quote from "Prime Minister St. Clair" or from "King William" (p. 319) comes true remains to be seen. Either is possible. Canadians must decide which outcome they want, and then do the things that are needed to obtain it.

QUESTIONS

CHECKBACK

1. Define sustained yield management. How is this concept related to the idea of a renewable resource?
2. **a)** Why must Canada worry about foreign competition?
   b) What does the example of Sweden teach us about meeting the foreign challenge?
3. Describe the effect of acid rain on Canada's forests. What parts of Canada are most affected? Why?

Fig. 23–16 Examples of managed and unmanaged forests. What are the obvious differences?

ANALYZE

4. **a)** In what ways are forests like an agricultural crop? In what way(s) are they different?
   b) How does this affect the way that business and government treat the forest?
5. Examine Fig. 23–16. One photo shows a managed forest and one an unmanaged forest. Which is which? For what use is each best suited?

INVESTIGATE

6. Investigate how business and government could cooperate to improve forest management in Canada.
7. Learn how biological controls work. What kinds are being used now? Which ones are now being developed?

WHAT DO YOU THINK?

8. Which of the alternatives on p. 332 would you choose for controlling insect pests? Why did you make this choice?
9. A forested area of 5000 ha could either be used for logging or could be added to an adjacent provincial park. The park is very heavily used and would benefit from expansion. On the other hand, the local saw mill is gradually running out of local trees to process. How should the best use for this area be decided? Which use would you choose?
10. Every year, thousands of trees are destroyed by insects. This means a loss of millions of dollars to the Canadian economy. One way of controlling insects is by spraying insecticides over infested areas. Some people believe that these insecticides are poisoning the environment and damaging peoples' health.
    a) Obtain information about this issue from newspapers, magazines, and books.
    b) Make lists of the benefits and risks of spraying.
    c) What would your reaction to the spraying be if you were:
       i. the owner of the forest
       ii. a fish biologist in the area
       iii. a forest worker who lives in the area
    d) Having completed questions 10 a) through c), explain why this is a difficult issue to settle.
11. Why is it not surprising that Canadians have concentrated more effort on "subduing" the forest than on "replenishing" it? What changes in attitude are necessary before we alter the way that we treat our forests?

Mineral Wealth

Do you have a little bit of Canada with you today? Chances are that you do.

Check in your pocket or purse for coins. What are they made of? Now examine your clothing. Is the cloth made of synthetic fibres such as nylon or polyester? If so, you may be wearing materials derived from oil that came from Canadian rocks. The same may be said for glasses with plastic frames. Metal buttons or zippers are most likely made from minerals mined in Canada. If you are not carrying coins or wearing any of the items mentioned, consider this: the building you are sitting in is probably supported by steel made from Canadian iron ore. Canadian minerals are much more a part of your life than you may have realized (Fig. 24-1).

Fig. 24-1 Items made from Canadian minerals

In this chapter we will examine the types of minerals found in Canada, where they are found and why, and how they are extracted from the earth. We will also examine their economic importance to the country and some of the issues surrounding their use.

Key Terms

mineral   structural material   open pit mining
ore   metallic mineral   surface strip mining
fossil fuel   non-metallic mineral   underground mining
mineral reserves

■ TYPES OF MINERALS

A **mineral** is a naturally occurring, pure, non-living substance found in the rocks of the earth. Canada's valuable minerals can be divided into four groups on the basis of their composition (Fig. 24–2).

The minerals we use today have not always been important to us. A mineral becomes valuable and is considered a resource only when a use is found for it. For example, uranium was not considered a valuable resource until ways were found to unlock the energy contained within it. Perhaps, in the future, new uses will be found for some of our common minerals. Then they too will become valuable resources.

Fig. 24–2 Examples of minerals that are mined in Canada

Metallic Minerals	Non-metallic Minerals	Fossil Fuels	Structural Materials
cobalt	asbestos	coal	clay products
copper	feldspar	natural gas	cement
gold	gem stones	oil	lime
iron ore	gypsum		sand
nickel	potash		gravel
silver	quartz		slate
uranium	salt		granite
zinc	soapstone		fieldstone

■ FINDING MINERALS

Minerals are useful to our industrial society only if we can obtain them at a reasonable cost. In other words, a company will not develop a mineral deposit unless it is profitable to do so. Mineral deposits that are economical to mine are called **mineral reserves**.

Gold is found in many rocks and even in sea water. However, the cost of recovering this gold is many times its value.

Canada's mineral reserves are being used up very quickly. Reserves are increased, however, if known deposits turn out to be larger than originally thought, or if new deposits are discovered. Discovering new deposits is not as easy as it may seem. Mineral deposits that are economical to develop are found in very few places on the earth. It is the job of a geologist to narrow the search so that there will be a good chance of finding the desired mineral (Fig. 24–3). Geologists must know how mineral deposits are formed, and which minerals are found in specific types of rocks (Fig. 24–4). There are several techniques geologists use to locate areas for exploration.

Some **ore** bodies, such as nickel, iron, and copper, create a powerful magnetic field compared to the surrounding areas. This magnetic field can be detected by an instrument called a magnetometer, which is towed behind an airplane. The magnetometer shows the approximate location of an ore body by measuring its magnetic field as the airplane flies overhead. Geologists then travel to the region to check the findings of the magnetometer.

Some minerals, such as uranium, emit radioactivity. Geologists use geiger counters to locate radioactive minerals in rock.

Geologists test the soil in river beds for chemicals that have been eroded from nearby ore bodies.

No matter which method is used, the aim is to discover a difference from the surrounding rock patterns. This difference may indicate the presence of a mineral deposit.

Once an ore body is discovered, its size and shape must be determined to see whether it would be economical to develop.

Fig. 24–3 Once a promising site is found, geologists must study the deposit to determine if it is worthwhile developing.

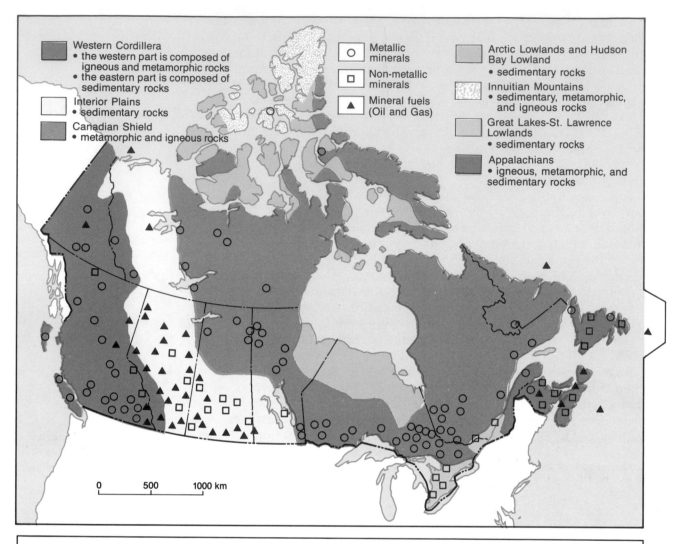

Western Cordillera
• the western part is composed of igneous and metamorphic rocks
• the eastern part is composed of sedimentary rocks

Interior Plains
• sedimentary rocks

Canadian Shield
• metamorphic and igneous rocks

○ Metallic minerals

□ Non-metallic minerals

▲ Mineral fuels (Oil and Gas)

Arctic Lowlands and Hudson Bay Lowland
• sedimentary rocks

Innuitian Mountains
• sedimentary, metamorphic, and igneous rocks

Great Lakes-St. Lawrence Lowlands
• sedimentary rocks

Appalachians
• igneous, metamorphic, and sedimentary rocks

0   500   1000 km

Questions

1. a) Compare the types of minerals found in the western part of the Cordillera with those in the eastern part.
   b) Why does this difference exist?

2. a) In which physical regions are mineral fuels found?
   b) What type of rocks make up these regions?

3. Why are all three types of minerals found in the Appalachians?

4. a) In which region of Canada are most of Canada's metallic minerals found?
   b) What type of rocks make up this region?

5. Why are both metallic minerals and mineral fuels found in Canada's Arctic region?

6. Mineral fuels have been found in some places off Canada's coastline. What type of rocks underly these areas?

Fig. 24–4 In what types of rock are various minerals found?

MINING MINERALS

After an ore deposit has been discovered, geologists must map its underground location and test its quality. This information is often obtained by taking core samples of the ore body from deep below the surface. Core samples are extracted by drilling a series of deep holes across the area with a hollow drill bit. Samples of rock brought up from below are analyzed. If there is enough ore of good quality, the company will develop the site.

Many mining sites on the Canadian Shield are located far away from populated areas and transportation routes. If the world price for the mineral is high enough to permit the mining company to make a profit, then the company will begin to develop the site. It must build a railway line or road to ship equipment in and the product out. It must build mine facilities and a mill to separate the ore from the rock. It may build housing for the people who work in the mine. Fresh water and electric power for workers and for the mining operation must also be supplied.

The type of mining operation needed to obtain the ore varies according to where the deposit is located in the earth (see Fig. 24–5).

This is called diamond drilling because a diamond drill bit is needed on the very hard rock. Few substances are harder than diamond.

PROCESSING METALLIC MINERALS
MILLING

After the ore has been removed from the mine, it is placed in a storage area until needed at the mill. At the mill, the mineral (e.g. nickel, silver, gold, copper, zinc) is separated from the waste rock. The metal, although far from pure, is now in a concentrated form. For example, a concentrate of copper contains 30% copper and 70% other materials. Concentrates are sent to a smelter for further processing.

A slightly different procedure is used to separate iron ore from waste rock. Many iron ore deposits in Canada do not have a very high iron content. Since it would be very expensive to ship huge amounts of this low-grade ore to factories for processing, the metal is concentrated into higher grade pellets near the mine. The pelletizing process removes a great deal of waste rock and increases the iron content from about 40% to 60%. The pellets are shipped to steel mills in southern Canada, the U.S., Europe, and Japan.

SMELTING AND REFINING

At the smelter, the ore concentrate and a flux are heated in a furnace. The metal sinks to the bottom of the furnace, and the waste material, called slag, floats to the top. The almost pure metal is then poured into molds. Some metals require further refining before use by industry.

flux: a substance needed to help separate the mineral from waste rock in the smelting process

Fig. 24–5 a) Strip mining
b) Open pit mining
c) Underground mining

STRIP MINING

— is used to extract minerals, such as coal and oil sands, that are located in horizontal layers near the surface.

1. Overburden (trees, earth, rock) is removed.

2. Blasting may be necessary for some mineral deposits.

3. Material is loaded onto trucks or conveyor belts by shovels or draglines.

4. Material is taken to storage area for shipment to market or processing.

OPEN PIT MINING

— is used to extract minerals that are located near the surface but that may extend deep into the earth.

1. Overburden is removed.

2. Holes are drilled 10-15 m deep and filled with explosives. The rock is blasted apart.

3. Ore is loaded into large trucks (which may carry 90 to 250 t) by huge shovels.

4. Ore can now be taken to a storage site near the mill.

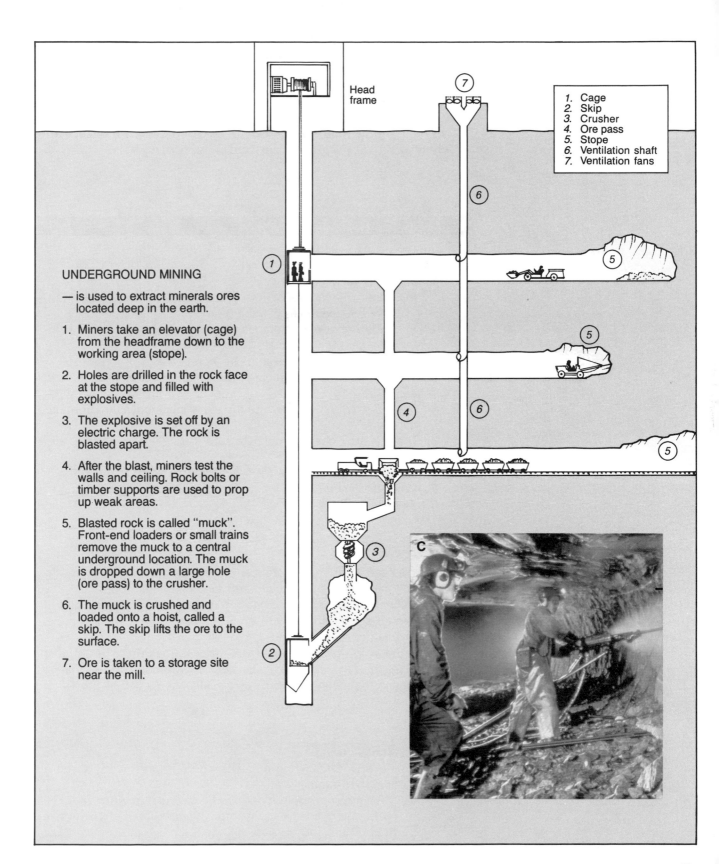

Head
frame

1. Cage
2. Skip
3. Crusher
4. Ore pass
5. Stope
6. Ventilation shaft
7. Ventilation fans

UNDERGROUND MINING

— is used to extract minerals ores
located deep in the earth.

1. Miners take an elevator (cage)
from the headframe down to the
working area (stope).

2. Holes are drilled in the rock face
at the stope and filled with
explosives.

3. The explosive is set off by an
electric charge. The rock is
blasted apart.

4. After the blast, miners test the
walls and ceiling. Rock bolts or
timber supports are used to prop
up weak areas.

5. Blasted rock is called "muck".
Front-end loaders or small trains
remove the muck to a central
underground location. The muck
is dropped down a large hole
(ore pass) to the crusher.

6. The muck is crushed and
loaded onto a hoist, called a
skip. The skip lifts the ore to the
surface.

7. Ore is taken to a storage site
near the mill.

dikes: walls built to hold back a liquid

In Timmins, Ont., a tailings area has been transformed into a park.

Waste materials, called tailings, are produced during the processing of the ore. Tailings – a mixture of water, chemicals, and rock – are poisonous to plants and animals, and must be carefully handled. They are dumped into tailing ponds surrounded by dikes made of earth. These keep the tailings from seeping into rivers and lakes. The liquid wastes eventually evaporate, leaving solid waste behind. Solid waste can be treated with fertilizers and chemicals to allow grass, trees, and flowers to grow.

QUESTIONS

CHECKBACK

1. a) What are minerals?
   b) Name the categories into which minerals may be divided. Give two examples of each type.
2. a) Under what circumstances does a mineral become a valuable resource to society? Give an example.
   b) How may mineral reserves be increased?
3. What techniques do geologists use to discover new mineral deposits?
4. Draw a chart to demonstrate the steps involved in underground mining.
5. Draw a flow chart to demonstrate the milling, smelting, and refining sequence.
6. How is low-grade iron ore prepared for shipment to markets?
7. What is done with the waste products from the processing of metallic minerals?

ANALYZE

8. Why are some mineral deposits obtained using open-pit methods while others require underground mining methods?
9. What conditions must exist before a company will develop a mining site? Consider ore body, transportation, market price, and demand.
10. If the world price of a metallic mineral goes up, what effects might be felt in Canada? Consider exploration, size of mines, jobs in the mining industry, and businesses (such as stores) in nearby towns.

WHAT DO YOU THINK?

11. Which of the following opinions do you agree with? Write a paragraph to explain why.
    a) "Tailings areas do not need to be cleaned up when they are no longer needed. A few small areas covered in waste will not hurt the countryside."

b) "Tailings areas should be cleaned up and replanted or covered over so plants will grow again. The environment must be protected against permanent damage."

12. How can companies that smelt ore be encouraged to reduce pollutants that cause water and air pollution?

OIL AND GAS

FORMATION OF OIL AND GAS

About 500 000 000 years ago, a shallow sea covered Canada's Interior Plains region. Over millions of years, the remains of marine plants and animals fell to the ocean floor. They accumulated and were gradually covered by layers of sand, silt, and clay – referred to as sediments. The animal and plant remains gradually decomposed. Over time, the immense weight of the sediments compressed the lower layers into sedimentary rock. Bacterial action, heat, and pressure converted the compressed organic remains into oil and gas.

Oil and gas today are found in tiny spaces called pores in porous sedimentary rock. They tend to move through the pores, sometimes reaching the earth's surface. They may become trapped, however, in a layer of porous rock that is "sandwiched" between two layers of non-porous rock (Fig. 24–6).

FINDING OIL AND GAS

Finding oil and gas in large enough quantities to make their extraction economical is not an easy task. Geologists spend a great deal of time trying to reconstruct a region's geologic structure and history to discover clues to the location of these resources. They know that all oil and gas traps have two common

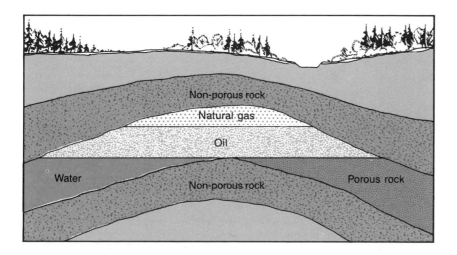

Fig. 24–6 Anticlinal trap containing oil and gas

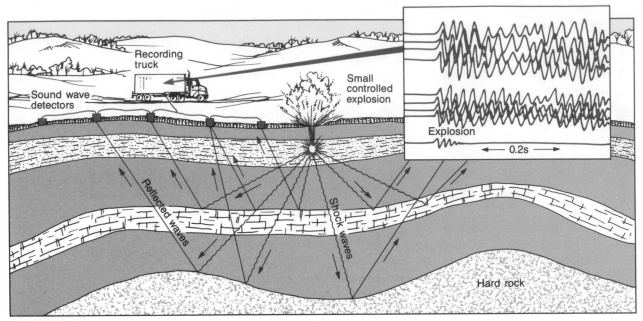

Fig. 24–7 Seismic surveys are used to locate oil- and gas-bearing rock structures. The depth of the different rock layers is measured by the number of seconds it takes for the shock waves to return to the surface.

features: i) porous sedimentary rock that was formed under an ancient sea, and ii) non-porous rock that traps the oil and gas.

Geologists can make predictions about the presence of oil and gas by looking at

- oil-bearing rock outcrops
- fossils in the sedimentary rock that indicate conditions for the formation of oil and gas existed millions of years ago
- drill cores that contain oil-bearing rock
- the seismic survey. A small explosion is set off underground. The shock waves created behave differently in different types of rock. Rocks and rock structures can be identified by the patterns created by the reflected shock waves (Fig. 24–7).

An oil company decides where to drill after analyzing the information obtained by some or all of these methods.

DRILLING FOR OIL AND GAS

Whether drilling takes place on land or sea, the object is the same: to find large enough resources of oil and gas to justify development.

The oil rig is really just a very large drilling platform. Once drilling has begun, interruptions occur only when workers must add more pipe or replace the drill bit. Although coated with diamonds, the drill bit wears out after only a few hours' use in hard rock. The drilling crew must remove the drill pipe piece by piece in order to replace the worn-out drill bit.

If no oil or gas is discovered, the "dry holes" are plugged up. If oil or gas is discovered, tests are conducted to determine how much is present. If there is not enough to make production worthwhile, the hole is sealed up.

RECOVERING OIL AND GAS

Removal of oil and gas proceeds in one of two ways, depending on the type of well.

Flowing Wells

Some wells have enough natural pressure to force the oil or gas up out of the hole. The flow is controlled by a series of valves, called a "Christmas tree".

Non-flowing Wells

If there is not enough pressure to make the oil or gas flow to the surface, workers use pumping equipment powered by a gasoline or electric motor. This pump is called a "nodding horse" or "grasshopper".

As oil is removed from the earth, recovery of the remainder becomes increasingly difficult. In the past, when wells reached this difficult stage, they were abandoned. Since we can no longer afford to do this, scientists have developed methods referred to as secondary or enhanced recovery, which remove a greater percentage of the oil from the ground. These methods include:

- flooding: water or gas is injected into the well to increase pressure.
- fracturing: fluid is injected into the rock at great pressure, causing the rock to crack or fracture. Oil then moves more freely through the rock and can be pumped to the surface.
- fire-flooding: some of the oil in the rock formation is set on fire. This heats the remaining oil which then flows more easily and can be pumped to the surface.

The oil industry exists to provide the needed energy supplies for Canadians and to make profits so that it can continue to explore for oil and gas. Both of these goals require conservation – that is, a careful use of our oil and gas. Conservation will be even more important in the future if energy prices increase and reserves become smaller.

QUESTIONS

CHECKBACK

1. Using your atlas and this book, locate four regions in Canada where oil and gas have been discovered.
2. What characteristics of an oil and gas trap allow it to hold these two fossil fuels?
3. What are the three possible outcomes for any well that is drilled?

ANALYZE

4. **a)** Define "secondary recovery".
   b) Secondary recovery involves doing something to either the rock structure or to the oil itself. What do all secondary recovery methods have in common?
   c) Why have secondary recovery methods become increasingly important?

INVESTIGATE

5. **a)** What offshore or Arctic areas are currently being explored?
   b) Who is exploring these areas?
   c) What has been the result of this exploration?
   d) How are these searches being financed? Consider corporate and government contributions.
6. Use the resources of your school or public library to find the differences in purpose and operation among the various types of offshore drilling rigs. Construct a table or write a short report outlining these differences.

◼ IMPORTANCE OF MINING IN CANADA

Canada ranks third in the world behind the U.S. and the U.S.S.R. in the production of minerals. It is, however, the world's largest exporter of minerals. Canada exports about 80% of what it produces.

How important are minerals to the Canadian economy? In 1985 the total value of mineral production was $44 700 000 000; in 1986 it was $33 800 000 000. The amount of money from each mineral category is shown in Fig. 24–8.

The significance of each mineral category to the incomes of the provinces and territories is shown in Fig. 24–9.

The mining industry has contributed greatly to the development and use of transportation routes in Canada. Since the mid-1940s, almost all railway construction was developed to help exploit mineral resources.

Federal and provincial governments have helped the mining industry by offering incentive programs that encourage exploration and research and development. Governments have helped mining companies build port facilities, power projects, roads, railways, and urban mining communities. Some governments even have part ownership of some mining companies. The federal government created the crown corporation known as Petro-Canada; the Saskatchewan government is a major owner of potash mines; the government of Québec is a major owner of asbestos mines.

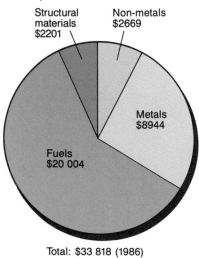

Fig. 24–8 The value of minerals produced in Canada (in millions of dollars)

Structural materials $2201
Non-metals $2669
Metals $8944
Fuels $20 004

Total: $33 818 (1986)

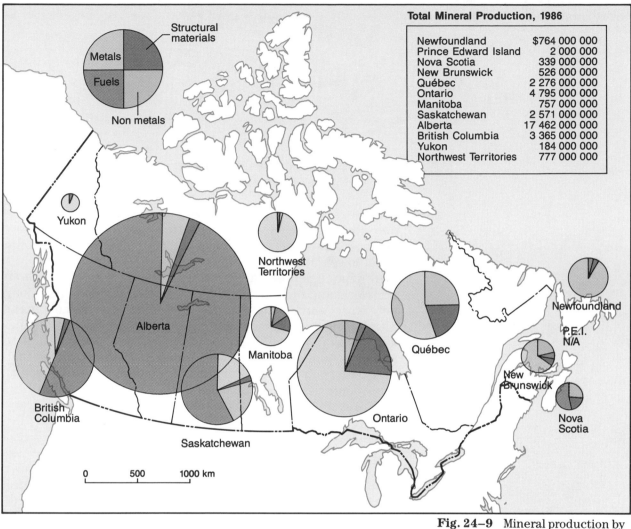

Fig. 24–9 Mineral production by province

◼ ISSUES

There are several controversial issues related to the development of Canada's mineral resources.

- About 50% of the minerals mined in Canada are exported before any smelting/refining or manufacturing is performed. Since most of the jobs are in the manufacturing sector of the industry, Canada is exporting jobs along with the minerals.
- Canada has very little control over the price received for its minerals. The Canadian mining industry cannot set prices in international markets. The prices are set by international competition and often change. If the price increases, mines can develop their resources and create more jobs. If the price drops, the industry cuts back production and jobs. The lower value of

Mine's closing spells disaster for town

mineral production in 1986 was due to price decreases in the fuel sector. In extreme cases, mines may shut down (Fig. 24–10).

- As high-grade ore deposits are used up, companies will have to mine lower-grade deposits. The final product will be more expensive unless new technologies are developed to make mining of lower grade ores more economical.

- New mineral deposits are continually being found throughout the world and more nations are producing minerals that compete with Canadian minerals. Many countries, especially in the Third World, have lower costs of production because of cheaper labour and fewer pollution controls. They are therefore able to sell their minerals on the world market at lower prices than Canadian companies. If Canada is to remain competitive with these countries, it must achieve lower costs of production. This will probably mean more mechanization of the mining and milling processes.

- Towns that have developed at the site of a mining operation are dependent on the mine for their existence. If the mine closes down because the mineral has run out or because markets have disappeared, the town will close down. This occurred during the early 1980s when the market for iron ore decreased. The mine at the town of Schefferville, on the Québec-Labrador border, had to close. The town found it very difficult to exist without its economic base and the Québec provincial government provided money to help the residents move to other communities. In 1988 this former mining town was turned over to the Montagnais Indian band.

- One of the most serious issues facing the mining industry is its impact on the environment. Over the past 20 years, more than $1 000 000 000 have been spent on research, design, and equipment for controlling harmful emissions from mines and processing plants. But despite the many successful efforts to reclaim land ruined by mining, and to reduce water and air pollution, millions of tonnes of waste still find their way into the air and water. Scientists will have to develop new technologies to restrict air and water pollution.

The very serious problem of acid rain is directly related to the mining and smelting industry. Canada produces more sulphur dioxide pollution per person than the U.S. Six of Canada's top ten

The impact of acid rain is discussed in detail in the complementary study in Chapter 21.

Fig. 24-11 Environmental damage in the Sudbury area is a result of air pollution from the metal smelters in the region.

industrial producers of waste sulphur dioxide are smelters and refineries in Ontario, Québec, and Manitoba. INCO's nickel smelter in Sudbury is the world's largest single source of sulphur dioxide (Fig. 24–11). There are plans to cut back this pollution, but the cost to industry and government will be very high. Companies must reduce pollution in such a way that they are still competitive in international markets. If they cannot accomplish this, they will have to close and jobs will be lost.

Any mining operation will scar the landscape. The removal of minerals from open pit mines and the storage of wastes result in some environmental damage. Industries can minimize and correct this damage to a large extent once their operations are finished. They can flood open-pit mines and landscape them for recreational use. They can neutralize acidic tailings, and then plant grass or clover on them. An experiment by INCO in Sudbury used ryegrass as a cover crop on tailings. This has come to be known as "rye on the rocks".

■ IN CLOSING...

What does the future hold for the development of mineral resources in Canada?

Canadian mining companies will have to adjust to international competition and pricing. As a result, they will suffer from periods of boom and bust. They must continue to explore for mineral deposits in the millions of square kilometres of northern Canada. Certainly there are significant deposits to be developed, but this may have to wait until Native land claims have been settled. Mining minerals such as oil, gas, manganese, copper, and nickel from the ocean floor is another possibility. Some exploration and development have taken place in Canadian offshore locations, but much remains to be done. One of the important concerns the mining industry will have to address in the future is, "Will the minerals currently necessary to our industrial society be as important in the 21st century?"

1. Summarize the major issues facing the mining industry.

ANALYZE

2. Why is Canada well-off in the quantity and value of its mineral storehouse compared to other countries?

3. Demonstrate the importance of mining to the Canadian economy.
4. Examine Fig. 24–9.
   a) Choose the four most important provinces for each of the following categories.
      i. metals
      ii. non-metals
      iii. fuels
      iv. structural materials
   b) What type of minerals are most important in Ontario, Québec, and Manitoba but less important in Alberta and Saskatchewan? Why?
   c) Why does British Columbia have both metals and fuels?
5. How might Canadian mining companies react to foreign competition?
6. What can mining companies do to reduce environmental damage?
7. What might the future hold for the Canadian mining industry?

WHAT DO YOU THINK?

8. Put yourself in the position of the union president at a mine in the Canadian Shield. The president of the company that owns the mine has told you that the cost of production must be cut or the mine will be closed. The mining company is developing a new mine in a Third World country which could replace your mine.
   a) What options are open to your union?
   b) What alternatives could you suggest to keep the mine open and your union members employed?
   c) Which one will you select? Why?

Potash: A Special Canadian Resource

If your family has a garden or farm, you are probably familiar with fertilizers. On a bag of fertilizer there is a set of three numbers, such as 7-7-7 or 3-10-10. These numbers are the percentages in the fertilizer of three elements that plants need to grow. In order, they are nitrogen, phosphorus, and potassium. The name given to potassium compounds is **potash**. The most common form of potash in Canada is potassium chloride.

After reading this complementary study, answer the questions that follow. Then check your answers by decoding the secret message.

Key Terms

potash   shaft mining   solution mining

■ WHAT IS POTASH?

Canada is one of the world's leading producers of potash. Saskatchewan and, to a much lesser extent, New Brunswick, are the suppliers for much of the world.

Potash was formed in the Mesozoic era when the area now known as the Prairie provinces was covered by shallow seas. As the waters of these seas evaporated, deposits of potash were left behind.

The first clue to the potash wealth lying below the earth's surface came in 1943. Drilling crews looking for oil found potash instead. This proved to be a very valuable discovery for Saskatchewan and for Canada (Fig. 24–12).

See Chapter 4 for a review of geological events in the Mesozoic era.

■ HOW POTASH IS MINED

Potash, in the form of potassium chloride, is mined in two ways. If the deposit is less than 1000 m below the ground, **shaft mining** is used (Fig. 24–13). Shaft mining requires the digging of vertical shafts and horizontal tunnels. Huge machines dig the potash as quickly and cheaply as possible. Then it is moved to the surface where the potassium chloride is separated from the waste rock.

If the potash is too deep for shaft mining, **solution mining** is used. In solution mining, people do not go underground. Instead, boiling water is pumped through a pipe into the potash deposit. The hot water dissolves the potash. The resulting solution is then pumped to the surface. This method of mining is easy and inexpensive. Drying the potash solution, however, is expensive since much natural gas is used in the process.

Fig. 24–12 Potash deposits in Saskatchewan

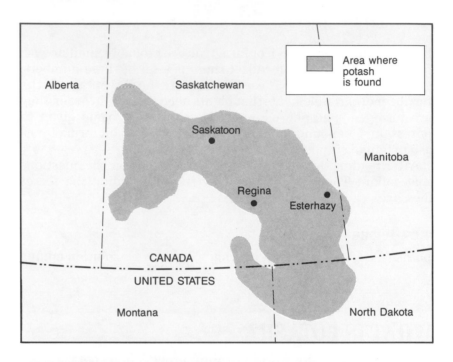

Fig. 24–13 Potash mining equipment

■ THE IMPORTANCE OF POTASH

Potash is very important for several reasons. Without potash in fertilizers, world food production would be lower and more people would face starvation. For Canada, and especially for Saskatchewan, potash is a major industry providing many jobs. Canada is the world's second leading producer of potash after the U.S.S.R. We export more potash than any other country.

Canada sells potash all over the world. Our main customers are the U.S., Japan, Korea, China, India, Malaysia, Brazil, Australia, and New Zealand. We do not sell very much potash in Europe, the Middle East, or Africa. The shipping distances are great, and there is competition from potash producers in Europe.

■ POTASH IN THE FUTURE

It has been estimated that there are about 151 000 000 000 t of potash available to be mined in the world. Of this total, Canada has almost half (74 000 000 000 t). This suggests a great future for our potash industry. In fact, Canada could meet the world's present need for potash for more than 2000 years! Unlike some other non-renewable resources, such as oil, we will not run out of potash for a long time.

Canada's potash industry must overcome several serious problems, however. Canadian deposits are deep and difficult to shaft mine because of flooding. Mining improvements must be made constantly to keep costs as low as possible. High transportation costs must be minimized. In many cases the cost of moving the potash to market is greater than the value of the potash itself. Many other potash-producing countries are closer to their markets than Canada. An overproduction of potash has kept prices low. The Saskatchewan government has tried to limit production to keep prices up.

Canada currently supplies about 25% of the world's potash. In the future, demand is expected to increase as the countries of Latin America and Asia import fertilizer to improve their food production. The potash industry hopes to develop new markets in these countries.

The Potash Corporation of Saskatchewan, a publicly-owned company, is now Canada's largest producer. In the future, Canada's potash production could overtake that of the U.S.S.R.

QUESTIONS

CHECKBACK

To find the secret message on the next page, answer questions 1-10 and transfer the numbered letters to the correct space(s) in your notebook. Question 1 is already answered as an example.

Secret Message

■■■■__S__■ ■__S__■ ■■■■■■■
12 5 11 3 1 8 4 1 3 7 2 5 13 4 10 7

■■■■__S__■■■
4 10 6 9 1 11 2 14

1. The leading province for potash production is
   __S__ __A__ __S__ __K__ __A__ __T__ __C__ __H__ __E__ __W__ __A__ __N__
   1

2. The main use of potash is in farming as
   ■■■■■■■■■■■.
   2

3. Potash was formed when Saskatchewan was covered by a shallow ■■■■.
   3

4. Potash was found by mistake when drilling crews were looking for ■■■■.
   4

5. Some shaft mines have problems with
   ■■■■■■■■.
   5   6   7

6. If you were mining a potash deposit 700 m deep, you would use ■■■■■ mining. If the deposit was 1300 m down, then
   8
   you would use ■■■■■■■■ mining.
   9   10

7. Without Canadian potash, world food production would be much lower and ■■■■■■■■■■ would increase.
   11

8. Most of our potash customers are located along the edges of the ■■■■■■■ Ocean because we have less competition
   12
   in this area.

9. Because our potash will eventually run out, it is called a non-■■■■■■■■ resource.
   13

10. There has been much disagreement over what role the Saskatchewan government should have in what was a private ■■■■■■■.
    14

ANALYZE

11. What percentage of the world's total supply of potash is found in Canada?
12. What problems are faced by the potash industry?
13. How does the future look for this industry? Explain.

Canada's Energy Future

Some years in history, such as those listed in Fig. 25-1, have such significance that we need only hear the year and we know what event is being referred to. When the history of the twentieth century is written, the year 1973 may be added to this list.

Fig. 25-1

. . . 1492	. . . 1867	. . . 1945
. . . 1812	. . . 1914	. . . 1973?

Key Terms

wind power
tidal power
solar energy
biomass

nuclear fusion
conserver society
nuclear fission

hydro-electric power
hydrogen-based economy
oil sands

■ INTRODUCTION

Why was 1973 so important to Canada and other developed countries? It was the year when people all over the world faced an energy crisis for the first time. How did this happen?

Until the 1960s, energy was rarely mentioned in the newspapers or on television. That is not because energy was unimportant, but because it was easily and cheaply available. Gasoline could be bought for less than ten cents per litre. (How much is it now?) Few people worried about a time when the cost of energy might affect the kinds of cars we drive, the design of our homes, and the way our industries operate. Fewer people still could imagine a time when we might run short of any major energy source.

In 1973, a series of events occurred that showed Canadians and people in other countries just how fragile our energy situation is. To understand what happened, you must understand something of the world's oil supply system.

■CANADA'S ENERGY TODAY

The industrialized countries of North America, Western Europe, and Asia rely, at least partly, on oil imports to meet their needs. Most of these imports come from the Arab countries of the Middle East and North Africa. In 1973, Israel fought a war with its Arab neighbours. The Arab oil-producing countries decided, for political reasons, to limit oil exports to countries that supported Israel. This caused an oil shortage that resulted in a huge increase in world oil prices. The world's oil exporters realized how much power they had and pushed oil prices even higher. In less than ten years, the world price of oil increased by more than 1000% ... yes, that's right, 1000%!

The effect on Canada was dramatic. People drove less and bought smaller cars. They added more insulation to their homes and switched to alternative heating fuels to replace oil. People had to spend a larger portion of their income on oil-related products. As a result, they had less money to spend on other things. The wise use of energy products suddenly became a preoccupation of industry, government, and individuals in Canada and elsewhere.

An unexpected, and for most Canadians, financially rewarding result came from all the attention paid to energy conservation. As the demand for oil products declined significantly, the world price fell to less than 40% of what it had been only a few years previously. This meant cheaper energy for industry and lower gasoline costs and heating bills for individuals.

While most Canadians benefited from these lower prices, those who worked in the oil industry and those who lived in oil-producing regions faced hard times. Also harmed were efforts to develop new energy reserves in Alberta, Atlantic Canada, and the North.

These countries (with a few others) form OPEC, the Organization of Petroleum Exporting Countries.

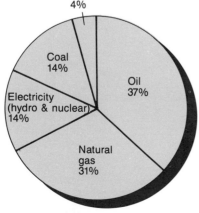

Fig. 25-2 Canada's major energy sources (1985)

Wood 4%
Coal 14%
Electricity (hydro & nuclear) 14%
Oil 37%
Natural gas 31%

■WHAT ARE THE PROSPECTS?

As long as the sun shines we will never run out of energy. But what we do have to worry about is running out of the cheap energy sources on which our whole lifestyle is based (Fig. 25-2). Some experts say that the oil reserves of Alberta could be used up in as few as 20 years. Furthermore, nearly all of the best hydro-electric sites have been developed and major new energy projects will require ten or more years and billions of dollars to complete!

When we think about our energy future, we must keep three important points in mind. First, many types of energy are not interchangeable. For example, cars and trucks operate on gasoline, diesel fuel, natural gas, and propane, which are all products of the oil and gas industry. Coal-powered cars do not exist and electric cars are only at the experimental stage. Fig. 25-3 shows how we use energy in Canada.

The second factor is that Canadians use an enormous amount of energy. Canadians use about 10 times as much energy per person as the world average and about 1200 times as much as a resident of Nepal. Nepal is a poorly developed country by Canadian standards, but even in the developed world we use more energy than anyone else! The average Japanese citizen uses less than one-third as much, and the average Briton less than one-half as much. Only the Americans come close to using as much energy as Canadians do.

Why do Canadians use so much energy? There are several good reasons. Distances between places are large. Our cold climate causes us to use a great deal of energy to keep warm. Our standard of living is high, and is based on cheap, available energy. In addition, it would be fair to say that many Canadians waste energy. Since 1973, however, this tendency has been gradually changing.

The third point to remember is that we can improve our energy supply for the future. We can further develop the energy sources that we already use. In addition, we can develop completely new sources of energy. Some of these could be in use within ten years. Others are unlikely to be important before the year 2010 or even later.

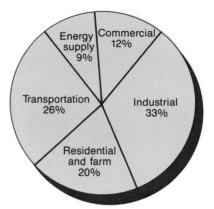

Fig. 25–3 How energy is used in Canada (1985)

■ENERGY FOR THE FUTURE

What sources of energy might we use in the future? Some will be the same as those we use now. Energy will also come from newly-developed alternative sources.

WELL-DEVELOPED SOURCES

Oil and Natural Gas

Location   Most of Canada's oil and gas is currently produced in Alberta, Saskatchewan and B.C.

Now   Oil, natural gas, and natural gas by-products such as propane make up about 68% of our total energy supply. They are used mainly for transportation, heating, and industry.

Future   Likely to be less important in future as sources of cheap oil and gas run out. Future sources (Fig. 25–4) will be costly to develop because they are located so far from where they are needed. Even with oil sands products, this energy source may drop to one-third of the total energy we use.

Technology   Further research is needed to ensure that we recover as much oil from each well as possible. Only 60% of the oil in the ground can be recovered with current **technology**.

Costs   Likely to rise rapidly. In future, oil and natural gas may be used only when no other fuels are practical. They may be reserved as raw materials for manufacturing (e.g. for plastics, clothing, and chemicals).

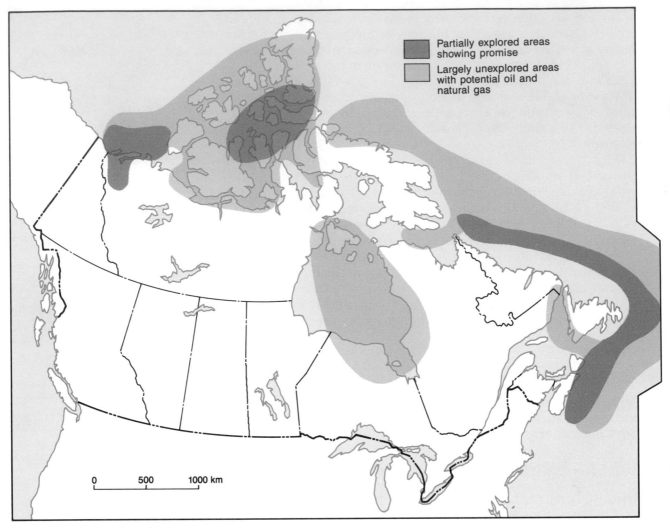

Fig. 25–4 Areas where future Canadian oil and gas may come from

Hydro-electric Power

Location Highly developed in the Western Cordillera, southern part of the Canadian Shield and Great Lakes-St. Lawrence Lowlands. Québec produces almost half of Canada's hydro power.

Now Few countries have as much **hydro-electric power** as Canada.

Future Major undeveloped sites are not near areas where electricity is needed.

Technology Production methods are well-developed. Improvements in the transmission of electricity over long distances will allow the development of more remote sites.

Costs Building costs are high but operating costs are very low. Often valleys must be flooded and natural stream flows disrupted.

Coal

Location   Large deposits of coal are located in British Columbia, Alberta, Saskatchewan, and Nova Scotia.

Now   Less than 15% of our total energy supply comes from coal. Coal is used mainly in thermal-electric power stations and for steel-making.

Future   Coal should increase in importance as new uses are developed. For example, coal can be liquefied or gasified and used instead of oil and natural gas.

Technology   Research is being conducted on liquefication and gasification and on improving ways to burn coal while reducing pollution that causes acid rain.

Costs   Likely to increase more slowly than oil and gas costs; therefore should become economically more desirable. Surface mining scars large areas.

Oil Sands

Location   The oil sands are located in northeastern Alberta.

Now   Considerable synthetic crude oil is being produced.

Future   Reserves of **oil sands** are many times greater than those of conventional oil.

Technology
1. Surface (strip) mining is used for deposits within 60 m of the surface (Fig. 25–5).
2. Steam extraction is used for deeper deposits. Steam or hot water is forced into the earth to separate the **bitumen** from the sand. The bitumen is then pumped to the surface.

Costs   More expensive than conventional oil costs, but likely to rise more slowly. Large areas are scarred by surface mining.

Fig. 25–5   a) Cross-section of oil sand particles
b) Cross-section of oil sands deposits
c) Huge bucket-wheel excavators remove the oil sands.

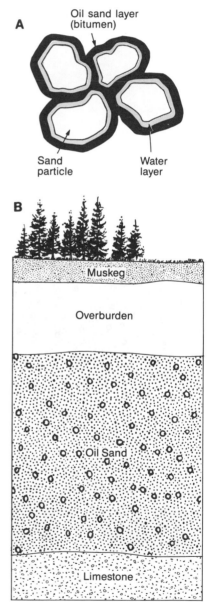

Nuclear Fission

Location   Ontario has multiple reactors at three locations, while Québec and New Brunswick each have one reactor. Uranium, the fuel used, is produced in Ontario and Saskatchewan.

Now   Canada ranks fifth in the world in the nuclear generation of electricity. Important only in Ontario where it provides 30% of the province's electricity.

Future   Because of high building costs and environmental concerns, no new plants are planned at this time. One large plant in Ontario is under construction.

Technology   The CANDU reactor system is well-developed, but concerns exist about plant breakdowns and the disposal of dangerous waste products.

Costs   Building costs are extremely high; operating costs are relatively low. Accidents that cause the release of nuclear materials could have catastrophic results.

ALTERNATIVE SOURCES

Some scientists and geographers have suggested that we should be looking at entirely new alternatives for meeting at least some of our energy needs. In particular, they stress that we should be expanding our use of renewable energy sources. Energy sources such as the sun, wind, and the tides are free – at least in terms of fuel costs. They also tend to be relatively free of harmful effects on the environment.

Wind Energy

Wind-generated electricity could help Atlantic Canada overcome energy costs that are the highest in Canada (Fig. 25–6). **Wind power** experiments are currently being carried on in P.E.I. and Québec's Iles de la Madeleine. These experiments have suggested that wind power is too expensive today but would be feasible as oil and other energy sources become more expensive in future.

Solar Energy

Solar heating of homes is a good example of the use of a renewable energy source. There are two methods of solar heating: active and passive. Active heating involves the installation of solar panels, a system of pipes, and heat storage facilities. With current energy and construction costs, the use of active heating systems in homes is not economical.

Passive solar heating, on the other hand, is much simpler and cheaper. If you have ever sat in a sunny room on a cold day and noticed how warm it was, then you have experienced passive

uranium: a metal that gives off energy as it decays into a lighter material

The CANDU reactor (Canada Deuterium-Uranium) is a Canadian-designed system.

Fig. 25–6   Harnessing the power of the wind

solar heating. A home owner can save hundreds of dollars per year in energy costs if a few simple changes are made to the design of the house before it is built. A particular advantage of solar heating in Canada is that parts of the country with the highest solar potential are also those with the greatest demand for energy.

Tidal Energy

Tidal power is an excellent example of using a local resource to meet local needs. A demonstration plant opened in 1984 near Annapolis, N.S. (Fig. 25–7). Its purpose was to show that the very high tides of the Bay of Fundy (as high as 17 m – the highest in the world) could be used to generate electricity. This small plant produces enough electricity to meet the needs of about 1000 families. Two larger plants further up the Bay of Fundy, where tides are higher, could produce more electricity than is currently generated by all means in New Brunswick, Nova Scotia and P.E.I. The cost of these plants, if they were built today, would be more than $30 000 000 000. This makes them uneconomical with energy costs at their current level, but possible in the future as energy prices increase.

Fig. 25–7 Demonstration tidal power plant on the Bay of Fundy. The map shows possible tidal power sites. Higher tides means more potential power.

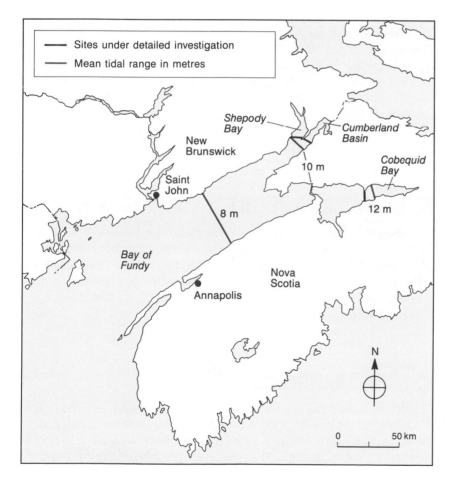

Biomass Energy

Biomass energy comes from plant or animal sources. Two different types of biomass energy are being used in Canada today and the use of each could be expanded in future. In forested areas, a significant number of homes are heated using wood stoves. This makes economic sense only where a reliable, inexpensive source of wood is available.

Biomass conversion to alcohol is a less common form of energy use now, but offers greater potential for expansion. Agricultural or forest wastes, coal, urban garbage, or even sewage can be converted to alcohol, which can be used as a motor fuel. At present, costs are prohibitive but this energy source could become common in the future.

Gasohol (gasoline plus alcohol) is a major motor fuel in Brazil where alcohol is made from agricultural waste.

Nuclear Fusion

Imagine an energy source that would meet all our energy needs, be pollution-free, and use water as its raw material. Sounds too good to be true? It might not be. **Nuclear fusion** is the process that occurs inside the sun. It has been produced on earth in an uncontrolled fashion in the hydrogen bomb, and more recently in a controlled manner in the laboratory. Experiments point toward the possibility of nuclear fusion generating plants in the future. The technical problems and costs involved in fusion generation are staggering. In fact, it has been called the toughest task ever tackled by science. If these problems can be overcome, however, fusion-generated electricity could be available starting in about the year 2020.

How old will you be in 2020?

■ ENERGY TRANSPORT AND STORAGE

It is essential that we find new energy sources. However, we must also find better methods of storing and shipping energy. Energy is often available at the wrong place, or at the wrong time, or at an uneven rate. More efficient transport and storage methods would allow Canadians to use their energy resources in the most efficient manner.

Examples of these problems:
wrong place – Beaufort Sea oil and gas
wrong time of day or year – solar heating
uneven rate – wind power

ENERGY TRANSPORT

Energy sources that are located close to areas of need have, for the most part, already been developed. New sources of oil, natural gas, and electricity are almost all in remote locations. In some cases, the cost of transporting the energy makes development of the resource uneconomical. More efficient ways must be found to move the energy. For oil and natural gas, this usually involves some combination of ships and pipelines. In either case, the costs are enormous, but are necessary if we are to enjoy the benefits of the energy produced.

The transmission of electricity is in some ways an even more difficult task than the movement of oil and gas. While pipelines are usually buried, electric transmission lines are above ground and take up valuable land. Many people consider them to be an eyesore.

A longer pipeline simply means more pipe and more pumping stations. In contrast, there is a limit to the length of an electric transmission line. Beyond a certain length, losses of energy to heat and friction make the line impractical. Canada was a world leader in the research of long distance transmission lines from the Churchill Falls and James Bay projects to markets in the south. Now we must expand our research to let us bring power from even more remote sites. Research in superconductive materials suggests that we may be able to transmit electricity over long distances with very little loss.

ENERGY STORAGE

Some forms of energy, such as coal and oil, are easily stored until they are needed. Electricity, on the other hand, must be used as it is generated. This prevents the most effective use of generating plants, which produce equal amounts of electricity at all times — even in the middle of the night when demand is low (Fig. 25–8). If we could more easily store electricity at times of low demand, we would reduce the amount of generating capacity needed to meet peak demands. A number of proposals have been made to store energy.

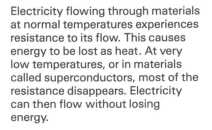

Electricity flowing through materials at normal temperatures experiences resistance to its flow. This causes energy to be lost as heat. At very low temperatures, or in materials called superconductors, most of the resistance disappears. Electricity can then flow without losing energy.

Fig. 25–8 Energy use throughout a typical day

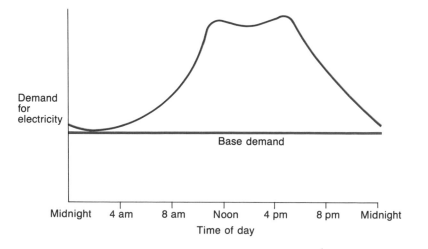

Demand for electricity

Base demand

Midnight   4 am   8 am   Noon   4 pm   8 pm   Midnight

Time of day

Batteries

Batteries store electrical energy in the form of chemical energy. The basic design of the lead-acid battery (the kind found in cars) has not changed for a century. A great deal of research is being done to develop better batteries. Existing batteries are not entirely satisfactory for several reasons. They tend to be expensive, very heavy, and are unable to hold large amounts of electricity. More efficient batteries could be used to power cars or to store electricity produced by solar or wind generators.

Pumped Storage

Ontario Hydro operates a pumped storage facility near Niagara Falls.

Often the demand for energy is lower than the supply available. This situation might occur with a wind-powered system on a windy day, or with a hydro-electric plant in the middle of the night. The extra energy can be stored by using it to pump water to an elevated storage basin. Later, when demand is high, this stored water can be used to power a hydro-electric plant (Fig. 25–9).

Hydrogen

Fig. 25–9 Pumped storage
a) When excess electricity is available (during the night) water is pumped from a lower to a higher reservoir.
b) When extra electricity is needed, the water stored in the upper reservoir is used to power the hydro-electric generating station at the bottom of the hill.

The storage of hydrogen gas may become the ultimate method of energy storage. In time, hydrogen may replace petroleum in a **hydrogen-based economy**. Hydrogen gas is produced by breaking down water with electricity. The hydrogen gas can be moved by pipeline, ship, truck or rail and stored until it is needed. Hydrogen can be used as a fuel in vehicles or factories. It can be burned to heat homes or to generate electricity. When burned, hydrogen produces only water, which causes no pollution. By the year 2020, hydrogen gas may be as common a fuel as gasoline is today.

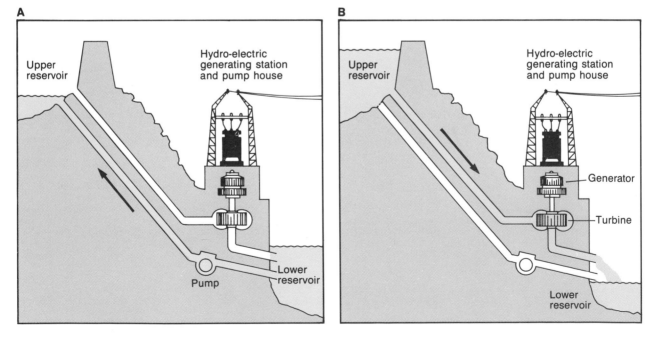

IN CLOSING...

People first began farming and living in towns 6000 years ago. They started building factories and using steam power 200 years ago. The automobile and airplane revolutionized the way we live less than 100 years ago. We now face a change in way of life every bit as great as these. We are moving toward a lifestyle that emphasizes the careful use of energy and other resources. We are slowly learning this new approach to living, and are becoming a **conserver society**

QUESTIONS

CHECKBACK

1. What significance does the year 1973 have in Canada's (and most of the world's) history? Why?
2. What happened to world oil prices between 1970 and today? Explain why these changes occurred.
3. What effects did rising oil prices in the 1970s have on Canada?
4. **a)** "When we think about our energy future, we must keep three important points in mind." What are they?
   b) Why are they important?
5. **a)** What are the differences between nuclear fission and nuclear fusion?
   b) Which method appears to have a brighter future? Why?
6. Copy this word puzzle (Fig. 25–10) into your notebook. Use the clues to fill in the blanks.

Clue	
Used to produce light	C
Energy from the earth's interior	O
Canadian nuclear reactor	N
Source of synthetic crude oil	S
A device used to store energy	E
Could be a motor vehicle in the future	R
What we should all do with our energy sources	V
Most common motor vehicle fuel used today	A
May be used to produce electricity in Nova Scotia	T
How c) produces electricity	I
Gasoline + Alcohol =	O
The type of society we are becoming	N

Fig. 25–10

ANALYZE

7. "We don't face an energy shortage, we face an oil shortage." What is meant by this statement?
8. **a)** The oil sands of Alberta are estimated to contain the equivalent of 152 000 000 000 m^3 of oil. Of this, about 4 000 000 m^3 can be extracted using current technology. What percentage of the total is this?

b) In 1986, Canada used about 103 000 000 m³ of oil. At this rate, how long could the oil sands meet Canada's needs?

c) Describe two ways in which the oil sands could be made to last longer.

9. In future, Canada's energy supply pattern will change. In your notebook, draw and complete a table similar to Fig. 25-11.

Fig. 25-11

	Now	1995-2010	2010-2050
Major Importance	oil natural gas coal hydro-electric		
Some Importance	oil sands nuclear fission		
Little or No Importance	sun biomass wind tides nuclear fusion		

10. Our present energy system consists of a number of energy sources that are basically independent from each other. For example, you cannot use gasoline in an oil furnace in your home. In contrast, in a hydrogen-based society all parts of the energy system would be linked. Hydrogen could be produced in a number of ways and could then enter a common storage and shipping system and be used for any purpose. Complete a chart like the one in Fig. 25-12 to show your understanding of this concept.

Fig. 25-12

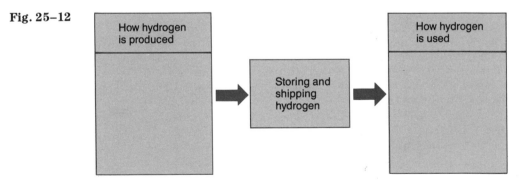

INVESTIGATE

11. Discuss with your family the energy-conservation measures that they have undertaken or are planning. Why were these measures taken?

12. **a)** Why do Canadians use so much energy? Describe at least three factors that explain this use.

   b) Canadians waste much valuable energy. List at least three places where you see energy being used wastefully in your home, school, or community. Suggest how these wasteful practices could be eliminated.

13. **a)** Talk to an auto-shop teacher, mechanic, or other knowledgeable person to determine at least five design changes in cars over the past 15 years that were meant to save fuel.

   b) How much fuel was saved by these changes?

   c) What effect did these changes have on Canada's economy? Consider such factors as who makes the cars and the amount of fuel sold.

14. Research, prepare, and report on one of the newer methods of energy production. Your choices are:

   i. solar-generated electricity   **vi.** tidal power
   ii. solar heating   **vii.** peat
   iii. wind power   **viii.** nuclear fusion
   iv. biomass heating   **ix.** ocean waves
   v. biomass conversion   **x.** geothermal

   Research in detail:
   a) how the technology works
   b) what problems must be overcome
   c) what the costs of development are likely to be
   d) when the method is likely to be available for use
   e) how well-suited the method is to Canadian use

WHAT DO YOU THINK?

15. Canada imports oil and coal to the eastern part of the country and exports oil and coal from the western part of the country. For both energy sources, our exports are large enough to allow us to eliminate our imports. Why has this not been done? Could this change in the future?

16. **a)** List, in order of importance, ten electrical devices that you consider essential to your life.

   b) List, in order of least importance, ten electrical devices you use now that you could do without.

   c) What do your two lists say about the role of cheap, readily available energy in *your* life?

17. How old will you be in the year 2010? In view of what is happening to Canada's energy situation, how will your life in 2010 be different than it is today?

Electrical Generation

Electricity is something that most Canadians take for granted. When we turn on a light switch, we rarely consider what is actually happening to make the light come on. And yet electricity is vitally important to the way we live. In fact, Canada ranks behind only Norway as the highest per capita producer of electricity.

Remember what it was like the last time you experienced a power failure, especially if it was at night in the winter. Your first reaction was probably one of annoyance, particularly if you were watching a favourite television show. Then came the cautious search for candles or a flashlight that worked. Next came that strange feeling that you cannot do very much without electricity. Finally, as your home started to cool off and you went to look for a sweater (by candlelight), you appreciated the importance of electricity.

The purpose of this complementary study is to acquaint you with the ways that electricity is produced and with the methods used to move it from where it is produced to where it is needed.

Even if you have a gas or oil furnace, it requires electricity to operate.

Key Terms

generator	power grid	nuclear electricity
reservoir	hydro-electricity	transformer
thermal electricity	turbine	

■ PRODUCTION OF ELECTRICITY

Electricity is produced by a **generator**. Generators range in size from the kind you might use to power your bicycle light to those in a power station, which could be bigger than a house. In either case, the basic idea is the same. The generator changes mechanical energy to electrical energy. In the case of the bicycle, the turning of the wheel turns the generator, which produces electricity.

Now consider the situation of a power company that wants to produce massive amounts of electricity as cheaply as possible. It must find the most efficient way to turn its huge generators. In Canada there are three ways in which this is commonly done:

- by running water in a hydro-electric generating station
- by steam produced by burning a fuel like coal, oil or natural gas in a thermal-electric generating station
- by steam produced from nuclear fission in a nuclear-electric generating station.

Fig. 25-13   The Manic 5 dam on the Manicouagan River in Québec

HYDRO-ELECTRICITY

Hydro-electric generating plants are built where there are rivers with large changes in elevation. The force of water moving from a higher to a lower elevation drives the generator.

The water is frequently stored in a **reservoir** created by a dam (Fig. 25-13). This ensures that there will always be an abundant supply of water for the plant – even in winter when natural stream flow is low. The reservoir may be near or some distance away from the generating station. Tunnels called penstocks carry the water to the **turbines**, which turn the generators (Fig. 25-14).

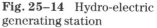

Fig. 25-14   Hydro-electric generating station

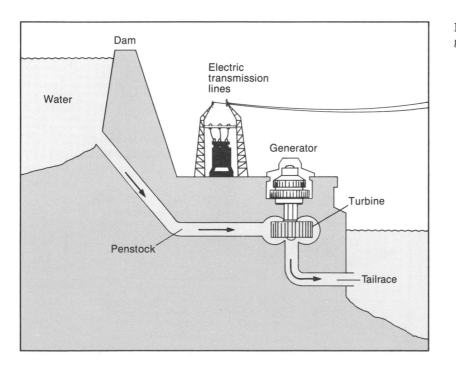

Hydro-electric plants have a number of important advantages over other kinds of generating stations.

- They are cheap to operate.
- Since they do not burn a fuel like coal or oil, they do not cause air pollution.
- Water, unlike uranium, oil, and coal, is a renewable resource.
- The reservoir created behind the dam can be used for recreation.

Hydro-electric plants also have disadvantages.

- They are costly to build.
- Suitable sites are often far from the site where the electricity is needed. This means that costly and unsightly transmission lines must be built.
- When dams are built, valleys must be flooded. Whatever was in the valley will be destroyed.

THERMAL-ELECTRICITY

In a thermal-electric plant, steam rather than moving water is used to produce electricity. The steam is produced by burning a fuel such as coal, oil, natural gas, wood, or even garbage. The expansion of this steam causes the turbine to rotate. This in turn causes the generator to turn and produce electricity (Fig. 25–15).

There are two main advantages to thermal-electric plants.

- They can be built near the site where electricity is needed or where fuel is cheaply available.
- Because they do not need costly dams and reservoirs, they are less expensive to build than hydro-electric plants.

Fig. 25–15 Thermal-electric generating station

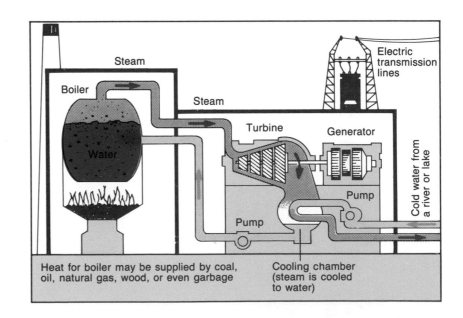

Steam

Boiler

Steam

Electric transmission lines

Turbine

Generator

Water

Pump

Cold water from a river or lake

Pump

Heat for boiler may be supplied by coal, oil, natural gas, wood, or even garbage

Cooling chamber (steam is cooled to water)

There are disadvantages as well.

- Fuel costs, especially for plants using oil and natural gas, are high and continue for the life of the plant.
- Although it is cheaper than oil and natural gas, coal is a major contributor to air pollution when burnt in coal-fired thermal plants. Unless costly pollution controls are in place, acid rain will result.
- Oil, natural gas, and coal are non-renewable and will eventually run out.

NUCLEAR-ELECTRICITY

Nuclear fission plants are similar to thermal plants in most respects except for the source of heat. The heat comes from the radioactive decay (fission) of uranium. As with thermal plants, the heat is used to boil water to produce steam that turns the turbines (Fig. 25–16).

Nuclear plants have several advantages.

- They have low operating costs because fuel costs are low compared to thermal stations.
- They can be built close to cities where the energy is needed.
- In normal operation, they do not produce air pollution.
- Canada has an abundant supply of uranium.

As you might expect, there are disadvantages as well.

- Construction costs are very high.
- The radioactive materials used in the plant are very hazardous to human health and must be handled very carefully.

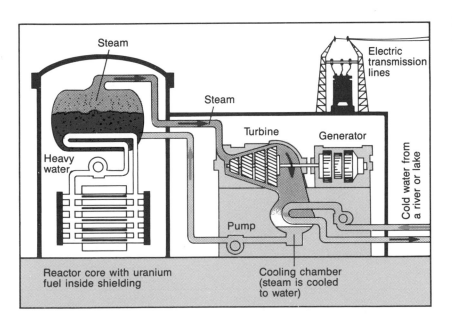

Fig. 25–16 Nuclear-electric generating station

- The waste products of a nuclear plant remain dangerous for 100 000 years. No method has been agreed on to provide long-term storage of these wastes.
- Terrorists could take over a nuclear plant or steal radioactive materials. They would then be in a position to blackmail the country.
- Accidents can release radioactive material into the atmosphere.

■ ELECTRICAL PRODUCTION IN CANADA

Where is electricity produced in Canada? Fig. 25–17 shows the electrical generating capacity of the three types of plant in each province. There is a wide variation across the country. Some provinces, such as British Columbia, Manitoba, and Québec, rely mainly on hydro-electric plants. Others, like Alberta, Saskatchewan, and the Atlantic provinces, depend heavily on thermal-electric plants.

Newfoundland's large generating capacity needs further explanation. Most of the province's hydro-electric capacity is in Labrador. The power produced there is sold to customers in the U.S. The island of Newfoundland, like the other Atlantic provinces, uses mainly thermally-generated electricity.

The situation in Ontario is also unique. Ontario uses large amounts of electricity generated by all three types of plant. Few undeveloped hydro-electric sites are left. Future increases in demand will have to be met by new thermal or nuclear plants.

Once electricity is produced, it must be moved to where it will be used. Often this means that electricity must be transmitted over hundreds of kilometres. Each province has a **power grid** into which the producing plants direct the electricity that they make.

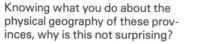

Knowing what you do about the physical geography of these provinces, why is this not surprising?

Fig. 25–17 Provincial generating capacities (1986)

Province or Territory	Hydro (%)	Thermal* (%)	Nuclear (%)	Total Generating Capacity (Kilowatts)
Newfoundland	90	10	–	7 316 000
Prince Edward Island	–	100	–	122 000
Nova Scotia	16	84	–	2 373 000
New Brunswick	26	54	20	3 479 000
Québec	92	4	4	26 991 000
Ontario	25	47	28	29 081 000
Manitoba	88	12	–	4 141 000
Saskatchewan	21	79	–	2 694 000
Alberta	10	90	–	7 602 000
British Columbia	87	13	–	12 451 000
Yukon	67	33	–	123 000
Northwest Territories	26	74	–	190 000

* includes internal combustion and gas turbine

Major customers such as large industries and cities and towns take electricity from the provincial grids. Within North America, a larger grid allows electricity to be sent from province to province and to American states. In fact, electricity is one of Canada's most important export commodities.

Long-distance transmission requires voltages measured in the hundreds of thousands. This reduces losses of electricity due to heat and friction. In your home you use mainly 110 volt current. A series of **transformers** in your local community reduces the voltage to what you need. The smallest and last of these transformers is the large box that you might see on the utility pole outside your home. From this transformer electricity is brought by wires into your home. This brings us back to what happens when you switch on the lights!

QUESTIONS

CHECKBACK

1. Describe in your own words how each type of generating station works. In each case relate your answer to the need to turn turbines.
2. What is a power grid? How does one work?

ANALYZE

3. In your notebook, make and complete a chart, similar to Fig. 25–18, to show the characteristics of each of the three ways of producing electricity.

	Hydro	Thermal	Nuclear
Cost to Build			
Cost to Operate			
Pollution Potential			
Flexibility of Location			
Availability of Fuel			
Other Advantages			
Other Disadvantages			

Fig. 25–18

4. a) Using the statistics in Fig. 25–17, calculate the electrical production capacity by each method in each province or territory. For example, in B.C., hydro produces 87% of the total: 0.87 x 12 431 000 = 10 815 000 kW
   b) On a base map of Canada, draw a triple bar graph for each province and territory.

c) What information does this map portray that was not shown well in Fig. 25–17?

5. a) At what time of the day does your family use the most electricity? When does it use the least?

b) In what season does your family use the most electricity? When does it use the least?

c) What do your answers to a) and b) suggest about the overall demand for electricity on a daily and yearly basis? What effect would this pattern have on the need for new generating stations?

INVESTIGATE

6. A transformer is a device that changes electrical voltages. High voltage (as much as 750 000 volts) is used to move electricity for long distances. Much lower voltages are needed for home use. The most commonly used are 110 volts and 220 volts. Several transformers in different locations are used to convert from high to low voltage. Try to determine where high voltages enter your community and where the transformers are that change voltages. Also try to determine what the voltage changes are.

WHAT DO YOU THINK?

7. Some Canadian provinces have long-term contracts to sell electricity to the U.S. Give at least one advantage and one disadvantage of such contracts. Overall, do you think such sales are a good idea? Explain.

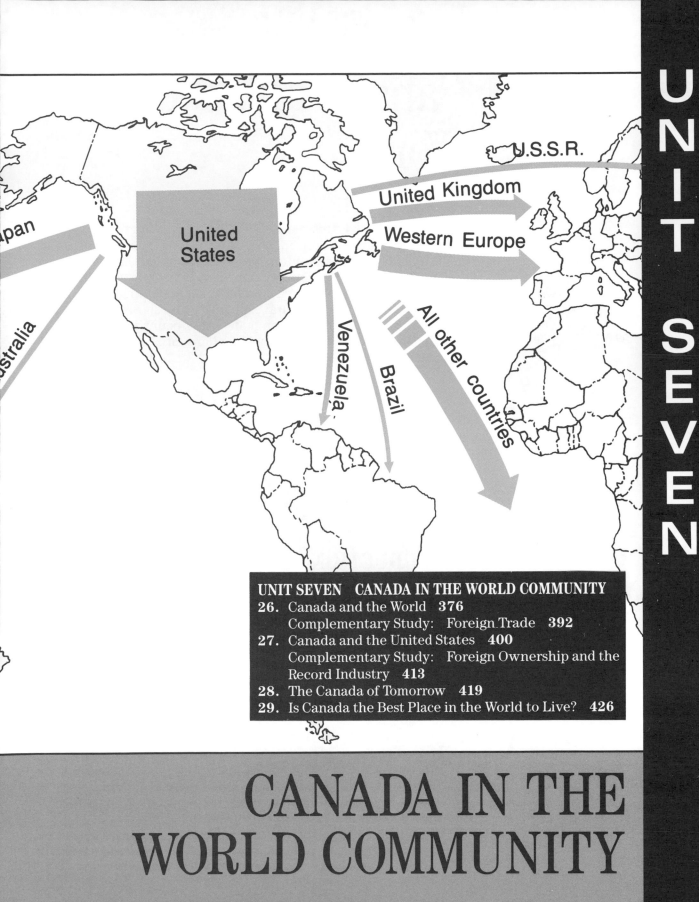

U.S.S.R.

United Kingdom

Western Europe

Japan

Australia

United
States

Venezuela

Brazil

All other countries

UNIT SEVEN

CANADA IN THE
WORLD COMMUNITY

26 Canada and the World

Canada does not exist in isolation. We look beyond our borders for many things, such as certain raw materials and manufactured goods, military support, and people with the skills that Canada needs. On the other hand, other countries also look to us because they know that we have much to offer them, including products for export, **foreign aid**, cultural exchanges, and sporting events. We are a nation that depends on many other countries, and is in turn depended upon. This makes Canadians citizens not only of Canada but also of the world.

cultural exchanges: visits by performers, orchestras, dance companies and so on from one country to another

Key Terms

foreign aid	capitalist	military alliance
First World	communist	multinational corporation
Second World	developed country	informal relationship
Third World	developing country	formal relationship

■ INTRODUCTION

The different relationships that exist between nations may be more easily understood if the countries of the world are arranged into groups. There are many different ways to do this, but we shall look at just three. These groupings classify countries into "three worlds", "two worlds", and "one world". In this chapter, we will examine Canada's relationships within each group to see how Canada is linked to other countries.

■ THREE WORLDS

concept: idea

The "Three Worlds" concept groups countries together on the basis of economic and political differences under the headings First World, Second World and Third World (Fig. 26–1).

First World countries tend to be **capitalist** countries that are rich and have highly developed economies. All have high standards of living and a great deal of industry. They also use most of the world's natural resources. In First World countries raw materials, manufacturing companies, and businesses are usually owned by individuals or groups of private citizens.

Canada, the U.S., Japan, Australia, New Zealand, and the countries of Western Europe all belong to the First World. The most influential of these countries is the U.S. because it has the largest population, the richest economy, and the greatest military power.

The **Second World** consists of those countries that we usually call **communist**. Second World countries can also be described as countries with centrally planned economies. This means that their governments control natural resources and plan how and when they will be used. They control industries by setting production quotas, standards of quality, and prices.

quota: limitation on the production of a commodity

Citizens of Second World countries tend to be less wealthy than those of First World countries. They have fewer material goods such as television sets and automobiles. This situation has developed because Second World governments tend to put more emphasis on developing the agricultural, industrial and military parts of their economies rather than on producing goods for consumers.

It is only in recent years that the Soviet Union has started to stress the production of consumer goods.

Fig. 26-1 Countries identified as the First, Second, and Third World

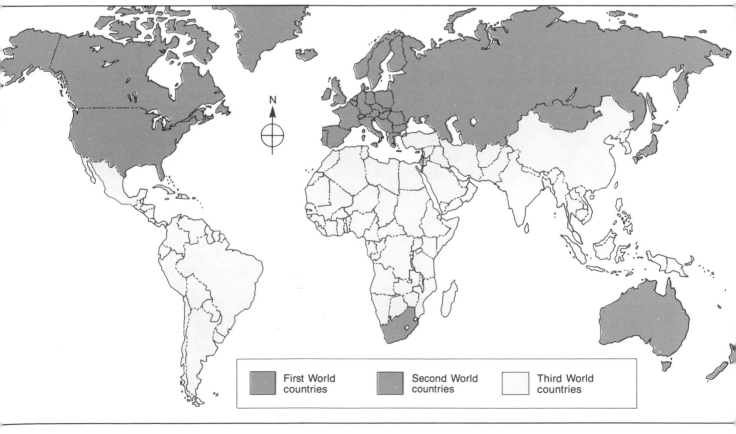

| First World countries | Second World countries | Third World countries |

The Union of Soviet Socialist Republics (U.S.S.R.) is the most influential member of the Second World, with the largest population, greatest land area, richest economy, and strongest military power.

The majority of the world's countries belong to the **Third World**. They have less wealth and less developed economies than First or Second World countries. The manufacturing and service industries in these countries are not fully developed. There are several reasons for this. These countries lack modern technology, have a scarcity of educated people, and a shortage of money to purchase goods and services. Most Third World countries have many difficulties for their governments to overcome. This also hinders their ability to provide education, health care, and money for economic growth.

Third World countries have varying amounts of natural resources and wealth. For example, Saudi Arabia has huge deposits of oil and gas that bring it a great deal of money, while Bangladesh has few natural resources and is a very poor country. Yet both countries belong to the Third World because they have a relatively low level of industrial and economic development. Third World countries have many types of government, from democracies to dictatorships. They are located in Africa, Asia, Central America and South America. China, with its massive population, is the most influential member of the Third World.

Third World countries have a wide variety of government types, such as democratic, communist, and dictatorships.

FORMAL AND INFORMAL RELATIONSHIPS

Relationships develop between countries to meet various needs. These relationships are classified as either formal or informal. **Formal relationships** are agreements made between governments and between companies and governments. **Military alliances** between countries are examples of formal relationships. Many First World countries, including Canada, belong to the North Atlantic Treaty Organization (NATO). This organization exists because its member countries have a common political and military goal, namely the defence of Europe and North America. The Second World also has a military alliance, called the Warsaw Pact, which exists for the defence of eastern Europe and the U.S.S.R. Countries of the Third World also make military alliances with other countries.

Although formal relationships exist between countries in all three groups, most are between countries in the same world group. This is because these countries have similar interests. Formal relationships have developed between countries to deal with such things as trade, economic development, communications, and other global concerns (Fig. 26-2).

Informal relationships are made between individuals, not governments. Family contacts are one of the most important.

Organization	Members
Trade	
European Economic Community	Many western European countries
Council for Mutual Economic Assistance	Many eastern European countries
Caribbean Community and Common Market	Twelve island nations in the Caribbean
Central African Economic and Customs Union	Four countries in central Africa
Economic Development	
Organization for Economic Cooperation and Development	Twenty-four First World countries (including Canada)
Islamic Development Bank	Thirty-eight Islamic countries
Communications	
International Telecommunications Satellite Organization	Eighty-three countries of the First and Third Worlds
Global Concerns	
The United Nations	More than one hundred and fifty nations from the First, Second and Third Worlds

Fig. 26–2 Examples of formal organizations

Many people have relatives living in "worlds" other than their own or they make friends while travelling in other countries. **Cultural exchanges** between countries, as well as medical, scientific, and sports links are informal relationships that bring citizens of all worlds together.

CANADA'S FORMAL AND INFORMAL RELATIONSHIPS

The majority of Canada's formal and informal relationships are with other First World countries. This is not surprising considering our capitalist economy, geographic location, and historical development. For example, formal trade agreements link Canada to its biggest trade partner, the U.S. Most Canadian immigrants originally came from First World countries, and they keep up their informal contacts with relatives back home.

Canada has formal and informal relationships with Second World countries as well. There are formal trade relations, but the amount of trade is small compared to that with First World countries. For example, Canada supplies the U.S.S.R. with grain, and the U.S.S.R. exports some manufactured goods, such as Lada cars and farm tractors, to Canada. Informal cultural and sports exchanges exist between Canada and Second World countries, but they occur less often than similar exchanges with First World countries. The Canada Cup hockey tournament is one example.

Canada also has formal and informal links with Third World countries. Many of these countries have tropical climates and can grow crops that Canada cannot. Formal trade agreements exist so that Canadians may buy tropical produce such as coffee and bananas. Bauxite, a mineral not found in Canada, is imported from

bauxite: a raw material used to make aluminum

Jamaica and Guyana by means of formal trade agreements between the Aluminum Company of Canada and the governments of these Third World countries. Canadian manufacturing companies have set up factories in Third World countries to take advantage of low wages, low taxes, and large markets. For example, Alcan has a factory in Brazil. Bell Canada developed much of Saudi Arabia's telephone system. Canadian banks such as the Royal Bank and the Bank of Nova Scotia play important roles in the economic life of the West Indies. These companies provide jobs and job training for residents. This investment benefits the economy of such countries and improves manufacturing and service industries.

Canada provides aid to Third World countries through various United Nations organizations, and the Canadian International Development Agency. These will be discussed in more detail later in this chapter.

QUESTIONS

CHECKBACK

1. Why does Canada need contacts with other countries?
2. What do other countries look to Canada for?
3. In your notebook, construct a chart like Fig. 26–3 and fill in the information on the Three Worlds.

Fig. 26–3

	First World	Second World	Third World
Level of Development			
Wealth of Average Citizen			
Who Controls the Economy?			
Sample Countries			

4. Describe the differences between formal and informal international relationships.
5. Define the following in your own words:
   a) foreign aid
   b) capitalist country
   c) communist country
   d) cultural exchange
   e) military alliance

ANALYZE

6. Why are Canada's main trading partners members of the First World rather than of the Third World?

7. Examine Fig. 26–1.
   a) With the aid of an atlas, identify eight countries in each of the Three Worlds.
   b) We have seen how the countries of the world can be grouped into Three Worlds. In the second part of this chapter we will see how countries can also be grouped into Two Worlds called "developed" and "developing".
      i. What do you think the terms "developed" and "developing" mean when referring to countries?
      ii. Which worlds (First, Second, and Third) would you put in the "developed" category?
8. In which of the three "worlds" is each of the following countries?
   a) Thailand   e) Jamaica
   b) Poland   f) Pakistan
   c) Zimbabwe   g) Ecuador
   d) Italy   h) South Africa

WHAT DO YOU THINK?

9. Should Canada develop closer relations with Second World countries? Explain your answer.
10. "It is not necessary for Canada to belong to military organizations such as NATO, because if there is a war the U.S. will protect us." Comment on this statement.

■ TWO WORLDS

The "Two Worlds" concept is based on the differences in economic development between the world's countries. Some people have suggested that the world should be divided into two parts: the **developed** and the **developing**. It is important to remember that this concept is based only on economic development. Many "developing" countries, although poor, have rich cultures and histories.

Which are the developed, wealthy countries, and which are the developing, poor countries? We can decide by looking at certain factors that measure a country's well-being. These factors are listed in Fig. 26–4.

Can you think of other factors that could be used to measure a country's economic wealth?

Factor	How Measured
Wealth	Average annual income (in dollars)
Population Growth	Annual growth (%)
Food Supply	Kilojoules consumed daily (per person)
Education Level	Literacy level (% of population that can read and write)
Health Care	Population per hospital bed
Life Expectancy	Average age at death

Fig. 26–4 Each of these factors can be used to measure the level of a country's development.

Now examine Fig. 26–5. You will notice that developed countries have certain characteristics in common, as do developing countries. What are these characteristics? How does Canada compare?

The differences between the developed and developing countries are quite obvious. We shall look at them under the headings given in Fig. 26–4.

WEALTH

When people have more income available they can buy the necessities of life and some of the luxuries. In the developed world, most people have money available for some luxuries. In the developing world, even the most basic needs such as food, clothing, and health care, may be out of the reach of most people. Sometimes the economy is so poor that an average income might be only $1.50 per person per week.

POPULATION GROWTH

The rapid rate of population growth is one of the most serious problems facing the world today. Although it may not appear to be very large, the difference between Canada's growth rate of 0.8% and Guatemala's 3.2% is very significant indeed. At this rate, Canada's population will double in 87 years, while Guatemala's population will double in size in only 24 years. The effect of this explosive population growth on a country is devastating. In only 24 years Guatemala must provide twice the housing, twice the food, twice the schools, and twice the doctors and health care facilities it now has. Is it possible for a developing country to double all these facilities in such a short time?

FOOD SUPPLY

The food supply available in each of the two worlds differs greatly. In Canada, when we talk about watching our diet it usually means that we are trying to cut down on what we eat. In the developing world, many people have difficulty just finding enough food to stay alive. Try this. What did you have for dinner last night? Imagine that you did not eat that dinner, and did not have breakfast this morning either. Imagine that today you will eat only a little rice, some meat or fish, and a few small pieces of bread. This is what a teenager in a developing country might face.

When people do not have enough to eat, they are more likely to catch diseases. People cannot work without food. In some developing countries, hundreds of children die of hunger every day. Many people would say that the shortage of food in developing countries is the greatest problem facing the world today.

The lack of food creates a circular problem. The lack of food means that farmers do not have enough energy to work hard. This, in turn, means that even less food is grown.

Fig. 26–5 These graphs indicate some of the differences between "developed" and "developing" countries.

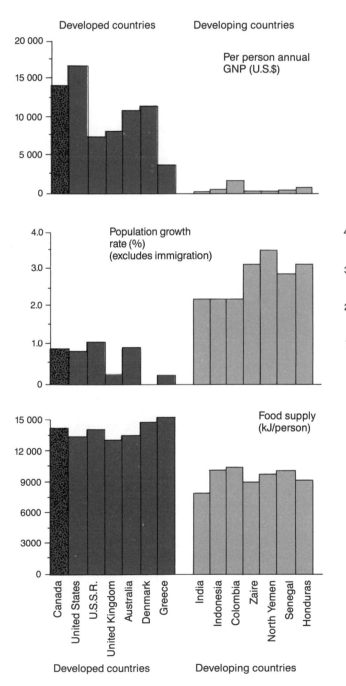

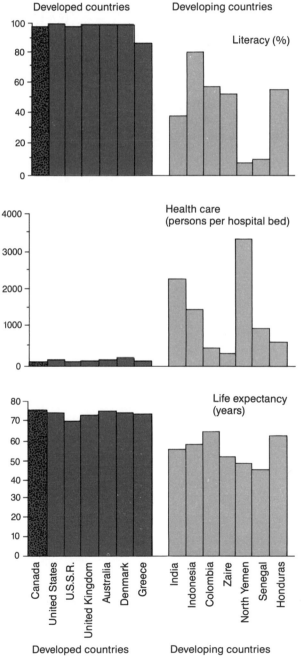

EDUCATION LEVEL

Some people have suggested that one solution to the problems of the developing world is improved literacy. They suggest that if more people could read and write it would be easier to spread information about better farming methods, family planning, and health care. When people can read they are able to become better informed and can make wiser decisions.

HEALTH CARE

In most developing countries, health care is inadequate. Many people die of diseases that in Canada could be prevented or cured. In Fig. 26–5 the availability of health care is suggested by the number of people there are for each hospital bed. You will see that in India, for example, there is one hospital bed for every 2255 people, while in Canada there is one bed for every 90 people. When Canadians need hospital care urgently, they can get it; this is not true in many countries.

LIFE EXPECTANCY

All these factors combined produce a low life expectancy for the people of developing countries. Years of inadequate food, poor health care, and crowded living conditions prevent people from living much past the age of 40 in some countries.

■ CANADA AND THE DEVELOPING WORLD

From what you have just read about these six factors, you can easily see that Canada is a developed country. Our government, through foreign aid, has made efforts to help citizens in developing countries improve their incomes, food supply, literacy level, health care and life expectancy. We have set up organizations such as the Canadian International Development Agency (CIDA), through which money and goods are given to countries in need. In 1985, CIDA gave over $2 000 000 000 to developing countries. This aid was given in response to the suggestion made by the United Nations that each developed country give an amount equal to 0.7% of its GNP for foreign aid. Denmark, France, Netherlands, Norway and Sweden are the only developed countries that have met this goal. In 1986, Canada gave about 0.48% of its GNP.

CIDA also sends human aid to developing countries. Skilled people such as teachers, transportation and agricultural experts,

Much of this aid comes from Canadian farms and factories. Thus Canada's economy benefits from foreign aid.

and doctors and nurses are sent to countries in Asia, Africa, Latin America and the Caribbean. Through the efforts of Canadians involved in activities such as these, we continue to build relationships with people in the developing countries.

Perhaps you may work for a Canadian development agency some day.

QUESTIONS

CHECKBACK

1. Why are some countries called developed and some developing?
2. Why do people in developing countries have a low life expectancy?
3. What is the purpose of CIDA? How does it try to achieve this purpose?

ANALYZE

4. **a)** Using the information found in Fig. 26–5, complete Fig. 26–6 in your notebook. The first two steps are done for you.
   b) Briefly describe the importance of each characteristic to a country's well-being.

Fig. 26–6

Developed	Characteristics	Developing
$1000-$3400	Annual Income (per person)	$60-$230
0.5–1.9%	Population Growth Rate	2.2–3.4%
	Food Supply	
	Literacy	
	Health Care	
	Life Expectancy	

5. In Question 4 you examined some of the characteristics that could be used to identify developed and developing countries. In this question you will look at four more factors to find out if they too can be used to distinguish between countries (Fig. 26–7).
   - Infant Mortality Rate (per 1000 babies) – a high rate means that modern medicine is not widely available.
   - Population under 15 years of age (%) – represents the number of children in the population who must be supported and educated.
   - Population over 64 years of age (%) – represents the number of older people who may have to be supported by their families or by the state.
   - Urban Population (%) – most developed countries have few farmers and a high proportion of people who live and work in towns and cities.

infant mortality rate: the number of babies that die before the age of one for every 1000 that are born

Country	Infant Mortality Rate (per 1000)	Population under 15 (%)	Population over 64 (%)	Urban Population (%)
1	15	26	10	76
2	160	46	3	36
3	89	45	3	58
4	12	23	13	74
5	45	28	9	81
6	126	40	4	22
7	35	44	3	58
8	149	48	3	8
9	16	30	9	81
10	97	48	3	42
11	28	26	9	60
12	45	39	4	22
13	75	45	3	27
14	12	24	14	70
15	16	26	10	74

Fig. 26–7

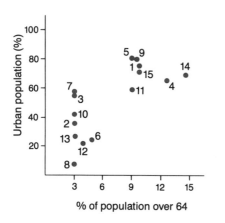

Fig. 26–8 A scattergraph showing the urban population against the population over 64 years of age.

a) Examine Fig. 26–8. It was drawn by graphing the urban population for each country against the population over 64 years of age, using the figures listed in Fig. 26–7. As you can see, two distinct clusters of dots appear on this "scattergraph". One cluster represents developed countries and one represents developing countries. Which is which?

b) Choose any other pair of factors from Fig. 26–7. Prepare a similar graph for these factors. Explain the relationship that exists between the pair of factors. For example, in Fig. 26–8, countries with a high percentage of people living in urban places also have a high percentage of their population that is over 64 years of age, and vice versa.

c) Circle the developed and developing countries on your graph. Explain the relationship that exists between each factor in your graph and the state of development of a country.

d) From a classmate, find out what relationship, if any, exists for two factors that you did not graph. Your teacher will tell you which countries are developed and which are developing. Did you classify the countries correctly?

INVESTIGATE

6. Some authors have described the difference between developed and developing countries as being a north/south difference. What do they mean? In what way(s) is this description inaccurate?

WHAT DO YOU THINK?

7. Why have so few countries met the aid goal of 0.7% of GNP set by the United Nations? Is this likely to change in the near future?

8. "Canada should not give away $2 000 000 000 in foreign aid a year to other countries when it has so many economic problems at home." Discuss this statement in two or three paragraphs by giving the arguments for and against the statement and indicating your view of the issue.

ONE WORLD

The "One World" concept views the world as one large whole, populated by people who have more similarities than differences. We are similar because we all have the same basic needs such as food and shelter, and the same desire to live healthy, happy, peaceful lives. It is sometimes hard to accept this idea of One World when we read of the numerous conflicts that occur around the globe every day. Nevertheless, many people think we would be better off working together to solve the problems that we all face. Can you think of any examples of how countries do co-operate to solve world problems?

The One World view is demonstrated by the activities of the **United Nations**. The UN was formed at the end of World War II to help promote world peace. Since 1945 the organization has grown to include more than 150 countries. It is often not successful in solving world crises because of the political differences among its many members. It does, however, provide a forum for discussion and has helped to prevent a world war for over 40 years.

If we view the globe as one world, then we should try to reduce the conflict among its member countries. The UN often acts as peace-keeper. It can organize a military force made up of troops from member nations. This military force may be sent to scenes of conflict to make sure that truces are being observed. Canada has been one of the major contributors to peace-keeping forces, and Canadian troops have served in Korea, the Middle East, Cyprus, Southeast Asia, Iran and Iraq (Fig. 26–9).

Canada is also a member of a worldwide organization known as the **Commonwealth**. The Commonwealth joins together countries that were once colonies in the British Empire. It includes India, Australia, Nigeria, and more than two dozen other nations in the Americas, Asia, Africa, and the Pacific. The Commonwealth provides a forum where discussion can occur and where minor problems may be prevented from becoming major ones. In addition, the Commonwealth encourages many economic, cultural, social, and athletic exchanges.

An organization called the **Francophonie** provides links between countries that have a French tradition in their culture. Although this organization is not as well developed as the Commonwealth, the governments of Canada, Québec, and New Brunswick send representatives to its educational and cultural meetings.

Fig. 26–9 Canadian peacekeeping troops, like these in Cyprus, have helped maintain order in various parts of the world for more than 40 years.

Québec and New Brunswick were included because they are officially bilingual provinces.

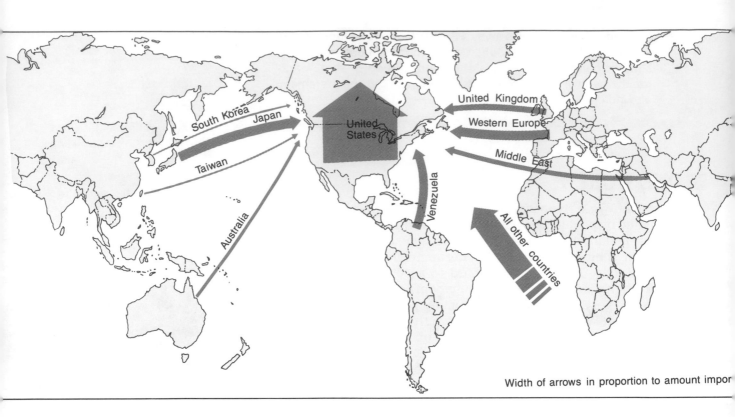

Width of arrows in proportion to amount impor[...]

Fig. 26–10 Major sources of Canada's imports

Sporting competitions may also play an important role in international relationships. Athletes who have competed internationally speak of an experience that helped them to understand the peoples and cultures of other countries. Those of us who never get any closer to international sports than our television screens can learn about the talents and personalities of athletes from other countries by watching these programs.

Another reason for viewing the globe as one world is that the economic systems of Canada and other countries are closely linked. Some companies carry on their business in many countries around the world. Some of these are so large that their budgets are greater than those of the countries they operate in. The operations of these **multi-national corporations** tie the economies of countries in the First and Third Worlds together.

Canada is linked to other countries of the world by its international trade. This trade is critical to the country's economy and to your standard of living as an individual Canadian. Because of our rich natural resource base we export many raw materials. We import mainly manufactured goods. Figs. 26–10 and 26–11 illustrate the sources of our imports and the destinations of our exports. You can see that our chief trading partners tend to be the other developed countries. But as the economies of developing countries improve, we may find that these countries become more

Multi-national corporations now operate in a limited way in some Second World countries.

Some experts have said that the economic differences between the developed and developing countries are increasing in spite of foreign aid. How could this affect Canada's future relations with these countries?

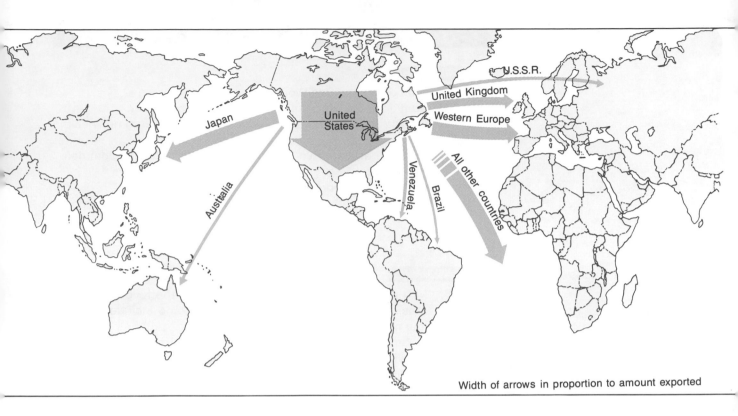

Width of arrows in proportion to amount exported

Fig. 26–11 Major destinations of Canada's exports

attractive as trading partners. The job that you hope to have when you finish school may depend upon these important foreign trade links.

■IN CLOSING . . .

Many relationships, both formal and informal, link Canada to other nations. As part of the world's community of nations, Canada has a role in making the world a better place in which to live. Whether the world is viewed as Three Worlds, Two Worlds, or One World, we all share the same planet. The problems that affect some of the world's people will eventually affect us all. To solve the problems of hunger, disease, war, poverty, and environmental destruction, much more co-operation is needed. *You* will play a role in determining how Canada will face these challenges in the future.

CHECKBACK

1. What does the "One World" concept mean?
2. What does the UN do to help developing countries?
3. a) What background do the countries of the Commonwealth share?
   b) Name at least five countries that belong to the Commonwealth.
   c) What is the purpose of this organization?
4. How can athletic events lead to better international relationships?

ANALYZE

5. With a group of your classmates, discuss the following questions. Take notes during your discussion and include them in your notebook.
   a) Describe three world problems that require united action.
   b) What contributions can Canada make to solve these problems?
   c) Describe three examples of international co-operation being used to solve world problems.
6. a) Examine Figs. 26–10 and 26–11. Use a ruler to determine:
      i. the seven most important sources of Canada's imports
      ii. the seven most important destinations for Canadian exports
   b) What differences are there between the two lists? How do you explain these differences?

INVESTIGATE

One UN agency, the International Civil Aviation Organization, has its headquarters in Canada.

7. a) To how many UN organizations does Canada belong?
   b) Name four UN organizations that give aid to developing countries. State the type of aid that each provides.
   c) What has Canada done to help achieve the goals of the UN organizations to which it belongs?
8. Research one UN organization in depth and obtain information under the following headings:
   a) when was it established
   b) what is its purpose
   c) what is the location of its headquarters
   d) what countries belong to it
   e) what are its official languages
   f) how is it structured
   g) what activities does it carry out
9. Why are multinational corporations not very active in Second World countries? Give one or more examples of a multinational that operates in a Second World country.

10. a) What is the Francophonie and what is its purpose?
  b) Why is this particularly important for Canada?

11. Canada is not one of the world's superpowers like the U.S. or the U.S.S.R. On the other hand, Canada is a more powerful nation than Senegal or New Zealand. Where do we rank as a nation in world affairs? Give evidence to support your answer.

12. "As a person who has seen the Earth as few others have seen it, from the vantage point of an orbiting space shuttle, I can tell you that it is a beautiful planet, a gem full of light and colour against the backdrop of cold dark space. More than anything else, you are struck by its fragility ... knowing that mankind has it within its power to destroy all life upon it. And there is nowhere else to go!

"Distinctions such as race, religion and nationality are lost on you as you glide smoothly over the Earth's surface ... Down below is Earth, HOME, and every human being walking upon that earth is your fellow human being. Every spot below you is equally inviting from your perspective high above it. Here is a perspective which makes you realize just how precious human life really is."

— Captain Marc Garneau
(the first Canadian in space)

  a) Why is Marc Garneau's view of the world an unusual and important one?
  b) At the moment, we can't all travel in space. How else can we try to develop this type of feeling for the earth and its people?

Foreign Trade

Look carefully at Fig. 26–12. All the objects shown have one important characteristic in common. Can you guess what it might be? If you need a hint, consider the topic of this study.

You were probably able to determine that all of these objects were imported into Canada from other countries. The source of some of these products is given in the caption. Perhaps you know where others might have come from.

To buy **imports**, we must export the goods and services that are produced by Canadians. These **exports** provide us with the money we need to pay for imports. In this complementary study, you will have the chance to learn about the fascinating and complex business of international trade and how it affects the quality of life that you enjoy.

Key Terms

imports	free trade	surplus
deficit	exports	tariffs

Fig. 26–12 Imports like these are an important part of Canadian life. Sources include the following: bananas from Costa Rica, board game from Spain, child's jacket from Taiwan, man's jacket from the United Kingdom, fruit cocktail from Thailand, mandarin oranges from China, and computer software and lettuce from the United States.

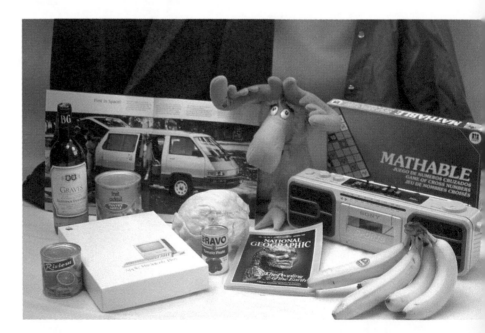

WHY TRADE?

More than 300 years ago, a famous English poet named John Donne observed that: "No man is an island, entire of itself." He meant that no person could exist independently of others. A similar situation exists among the nations of the world; no nation exists independently of other nations. One measure of this interdependence is the enormous trade that exists in the world.

Each year, Canadians import goods worth more than $110 000 000 000. This is an amount so large that it is difficult to picture what it means. Consider the following comparison. You have just won the ultimate "Super-Duper Lottery" grand prize. The prize is this: you must spend $3000 every *second*, 24 hours per day. If you did this for one year without stopping, you would approach the amount of our import bill. The value of our exports is even greater.

$$\$3000 \times 86\ 400\ \text{s/d} \times 365\ \text{d/y} \simeq \$95\ 000\ 000\ 000$$

WHAT WE IMPORT

An examination of Canada's ten leading net imports is revealing (Fig. 26–13). Three main groups of imports stand out.

- Some goods are imported because our climatic and geologic limitations mean we cannot produce them ourselves. This group includes such products as citrus fruits, fresh vegetables (especially in winter), sugar, coffee, tea, chocolate, spices, tropical woods like teak and mahogany, tin, and gem-quality diamonds.

Fig. 26–13 Canada's major net imports (Net imports = imports minus exports for each commodity)

Leading Net Imports (Figures in millions of dollars), 1983			
Commodity	Exports	Imports	Net
1. Motor vehicle parts	7 666	11 410	- 3744
2. Computer, telephone, telecommunications and office equipment	2 988	6 632	- 3644
3. Machinery	3 403	6 805	- 3402
4. Cloth and clothing	478	2 771	- 2293
5. Fruits and vegetables	404	1 770	- 1366
6. Sugar, coffee, tea, chocolate and spices	249	1 172	- 923
7. Books, magazines and newspapers	375	1 214	- 839
8. Synthetic rubber and plastics	733	1 361	- 628
9. Photographic equipment and supplies	328	939	- 611
10. Medical equipment and supplies	224	794	- 570

- A second group of imports could be called "hi-tech" products. These include computers, communications equipment, machinery, photographic equipment, and medical supplies. Only a few countries in the world, including the U.S., Japan, and West Germany, make these products in great numbers and they supply the needs of the entire world.

- Some products are imported because they are cheaper than Canadian-made ones. Included in this category are clothing, footwear, plastics, and books and magazines. Most frequently they are cheaper because labour costs may be much cheaper abroad – especially in newly-industrialized countries such as South Korea, Mexico, and Brazil. Also the Canadian market is much smaller than those of our main trading partners, the U.S., Japan, and the European Common Market. Production in quantity for a larger market allows lower prices for goods.

■ IMPORTANCE OF EXPORTS

We have seen why imports are important to Canadians. Why do we need to export?

- To pay for imports – If we want to import the necessities and luxuries that we now enjoy we must be able to pay for them. The easiest way to earn money for this is by exporting.

- To help our economy to grow – Almost 50% of the goods and services we produce are exported. With fewer exports, unemployment would be much higher and we would all be poorer.

- To lower prices of Canadian-made products – The larger market resulting from exporting means that Canadian production costs can be kept lower. This results in lower prices for Canadians who buy these products.

■ WHAT WE EXPORT

Examine Fig. 26–14. This figure lists Canada's ten leading net exports. What do most of these exports have in common? Most are either raw materials, or the processed or partly processed products of our natural resources. Critics of our trade and industrial policy would say that we export jobs by not doing more processing and manufacturing in Canada.

Only one export commodity, motor vehicles, involves a finished product that is not directly based on our resources. This exception to the rule can be at least partly explained by two factors. The first is that cars and trucks are exported under the special conditions

Leading Net Exports (Figures in millions of dollars), 1983			
Commodity	Exports	Imports	Net
1. Pulp and paper	8 096	675	+ 7321
2. Motor vehicles	14 144	7 904	+ 6240
3. Grain (mainly wheat)	6 003	284	+ 5719
4. Lumber products	4 783	523	+ 4260
5. Natural gas	3 958	insignificant	+ 3958
6. Metals and metal products	7 222	4 939	+ 2829
7. Crude petroleum, coal and products	7 587	5 161	+ 2426
8. Metallic ores	2 825	411	+ 2414
9. Electricity	1 228	3	+ 1225
10. Fish	1 566	418	+ 1148

Fig. 26–14 Canada's major net exports (Net exports = exports minus imports for each commodity)

of the U.S.-Canada Auto Pact which requires that a percentage of auto manufacturing be done in Canada. The second factor is that much of our trade surplus in automobiles is offset by large net imports of the parts used to make these cars and trucks.

TRADE IN SERVICES

When Canadians discuss trade they often consider only trade in goods. If we do this our trade picture appears rosy. In 1987, for example, we exported goods worth over $120 000 000 000 and imported goods worth about $110 000 000 000. This gave us a trade **surplus** for goods of about $10 000 000 000.

When we consider trade in services the picture is not so bright. In 1987 we had a **deficit** in trade in services of almost $20 000 000 000. When we combine the surplus in trade in goods with the deficit in trade in services we get a total deficit of about $9 000 000 000.

What exactly are these services and why does Canada have such a poor record in exporting them? To most of us, trade in services is, with one important exception, something over which we have little control. Let's look at the exception first. If we are fortunate, we may be able to take a winter trip to Florida or a summer trip to Europe. When we do, we are contributing to our huge deficit in trade in services, because most of the money we spend leaves the country. If we were to vacation in Canada this would not be the case (Fig. 26–15).

Tourism is just one way by which money leaves Canada to pay for a service. Another way is when we pay for the shipping of our

Between 1960 and 1987, our current accounts balance (which includes both goods and services) has shown a surplus in only five years.

Fig. 26-15 When Canadians vacation in other countries they increase our deficit in trade in services. If the Turks and Caicos Islands in the Caribbean, shown here, form some type of association with Canada, it would help this situation.

merchant marine: commercial shipping

dividends: profits

exports and imports of goods. We have almost no merchant marine of our own. Thus we must pay foreign shippers to carry our cargoes. A great deal of money also leaves Canada each year to pay dividends on investments and interest on loans made by foreigners in Canada.

Remedies to this problem have been suggested but all have their price. How would you feel if you were told that you could not go on a trip to Europe for which you had saved? What might happen to Canada's ability to develop its economy and create new jobs if foreign investment was restricted? Canadians disagree on what would cause the bigger headache – the services deficit or the solutions to this deficit.

■ TRADE IN THE FUTURE

International trade is a major reason why most Canadians enjoy a high standard of living. If we are to ensure that this standard of living is maintained, we must answer some major trade-related questions.

- Can we keep our traditional markets? – As we have seen, most of our exports are the products of our rich natural resource base. Our traditional markets for these resources are being invaded by forest, mineral, fish and other products from Third World countries. We must find ways to keep our customers in the face of this new competition.

- How can we export more manufactured goods? – Should we continue to import technology or should we concentrate on developing new products so that we can create new markets for ourselves? Many Canadians are surprised to learn that the telephone, snowmobile, zipper, snowblower, hydrofoil, and newsprint were invented in Canada. New commercial developments are possible only if inventors are given financial support by private industry and government.

- Can we decrease our trade reliance on the U.S.? – No two nations have ever had as much trade as Canada and the U.S. do today. This bilateral trade has contributed to the rich standard of living that both countries enjoy. But there are dangers in relying too heavily on one trading partner. We are easily harmed by fluctuations in the U.S. economy and by changes in U.S. government policy designed to reduce their large trade deficit. If we were able to expand our trade with other countries, we would not be so dependant on trade with the U.S.

bilateral: between two nations

Since the mid 1980s, the U.S. has had the largest trade deficit of any country in history.

- Should we have freer trade with the U.S.? – In early 1988, Canada and the U.S. signed a Free Trade Agreement. The purpose of this agreement is to eliminate **tariffs** on trade between the two countries. Even before this agreement, 70% of our trade with the U.S. was done without tariffs. The purpose of the Free Trade Agreement is to eliminate tariffs on the remaining 30%.

■ IN CLOSING...

The world's economy operates very differently than it did even 30 years ago. A few examples will help demonstrate this.

- Thirty years ago, the world price for oil was about $2 per barrel. Since then it has gone to over $40 before dropping back to the $15-$20 range. Each of these price changes has meant the redirection of thousands of millions of dollars.

- Thirty years ago, Japan had a reputation as a country that produced cheap, poorly-made copies of American and European goods. Now, Japanese inventions and products are the standard of excellence for the world in many fields.

- Thirty years ago, India depended on food imports to feed tens of millions of people. Now India is able to export food to its neighbours.

Many examples are possible, but they all lead to the same conclusion. Canada faces a very different competitive situation than in years gone by. We must learn to be more competitive in a world where many countries have enormous economic advantages. World trade issues are rarely straightforward and easily understood. Canadians, however, must understand and deal with them. If we cannot, then we will see our share of world trade decline dramatically. If this happens, it will mean a big change in the lifestyle that we now enjoy.

QUESTIONS

CHECKBACK

1. **a)** Describe three reasons why Canadians import products.
   b) State three ways that exports help us.
2. **a)** What is "trade in services"? Give a definition and at least two examples.
   b) What is a "current accounts balance"? How is Canada's current account balance affected by our trade in goods and our trade in services?

ANALYZE

3. **a)** Define trade surplus and trade deficit.
   b) One way to decrease a trade deficit (or increase a trade surplus) is by replacing imported products with Canadian-made ones. This is called "import substitution". Describe how this could be done for any five imported products that you buy.
   c) How would import substitution affect Canada's economy?
   d) How could import substitution be applied to trade in services?
4. **a)** Canada has been described as a nation of "hewers of wood and drawers of water". What does this mean?
   b) Why is this a problem with respect to the kinds of things that we import or export?

INVESTIGATE

5. **a)** What is the difference between gross imports and exports and net imports and exports?
   b) Consult a table of gross imports and exports in an atlas. Compare this information to Figs. 26–13 and 26–14. What differences do you see between gross and net trade?
   c) Which figures describe Canada's trade best? Why?
6. **a)** What is the Pacific Rim?
   b) Why do trade opportunities exist here?
7. Research the ways in which the world's economy has changed since 1960. You might consider one or more of the following:
   - developments in agriculture
   - changes in forestry, mining, or fishing
   - technological changes in manufacturing
   - wages paid around the world.
   In each case, indicate how these changes affect Canada's trade.

8. **a)** What kinds of "hi-tech" goods do we import?
   b) How could we reduce this amount? Consider both short-term and longer term (more than 10 years) solutions.

9. Laurentide Industries, a 70-year-old manufacturing company that employs 600 workers, is having difficulty competing with large U.S. manufacturers. It needs $20 000 000 to modernize and expand so that it can stay in business.
   Infotech Resources, a seven-year-old company with 45 employees, needs $20 000 000 to expand its operation so that it can increase production to meet the growing demand for its products in the North American market.
   a) Where might each company find the money it needs?
   b) Which would likely be more successful in its search? Explain.
   c) What options would the less successful company have?

10. Should morality play a role in Canada's trade policies? Consider the following cases.
    a) Canada's tobacco farmers have suffered financial losses in recent years as more and more Canadians quit smoking. At the same time, demand for tobacco products is increasing in the Third World. Should the Canadian government promote the sale of Canadian tobacco in other countries?
    b) South Africa, which has an official policy of racial segregation called "apartheid", is being isolated more and more by other countries. Because of this isolation, growing trade opportunities for Canadian business exist in South Africa. This trade would help our economy and create jobs in Canada. Should the federal government allow (or even encourage) this trade? What is the Canadian government's current policy on trade with South Africa?

27 Canada and the United States

Some people think that the map of North America should be labelled like Fig. 27–1. They say that the U.S. has such an enormous influence on Canada that our country is no more than a colder version of its neighbour – a place where more people play hockey than basketball in the winter and say "eh" instead of "huh". Is this true? How strong is American influence? Does Canada have an economy and culture distinct from those of the U.S.? These questions are the subject of a continuing debate among Canadians.

Fig. 27–1 What is this map suggesting about American influence on Canada? How do you react to this suggestion?

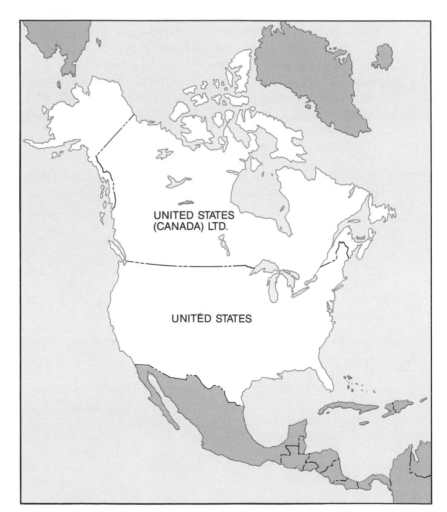

Key Terms

tariff   nationalist   culture
foreign investment   branch plant   continentalist
subsidiary   parent company

■ INTRODUCTION

You might be asking: "Why does *Canada: Land of Diversity* include a separate chapter on Canada-U.S. relationships? Were these relationships not covered in the previous chapter?" To a certain extent they were, but the U.S. plays such a critical role in our life as a nation that a closer look is needed.

critical: very important

It has been said that when the U.S. catches a cold, Canada sneezes. This represents, in a symbolic way, the close relationship between the two countries. Our culture is greatly affected by American culture. We listen to American music, watch American television programs, drive American cars, and use American expressions in our speech. Furthermore, our economic well-being depends to a large extent on the economy of the U.S. When the American economy is booming, the Canadian economy flourishes. If business slows and unemployment is high in the U.S., Canada will almost certainly face similar problems.

Canadian influence on the U.S. is much less important. There are several reasons for this. The U.S. has about ten times the population of Canada. It has ten times the economic power and is the richest country in the world. It is the largest producer of English-language books, movies, and television programs in the world. Is it any wonder that our closest neighbour has such a great influence on us?

In recent years, an increasing number of Americans have begun to complain about too much Canadian influence on the U.S. in areas like trade, investment, and cable television ownership.

■ HISTORICAL BACKGROUND

Canada and the U.S. have not always been close friends. For many years after the U.S. was formed in 1776, the British colonies, which later became Canada, were on distinctly unfriendly terms with their southern neighbours. The Americans tried to conquer Canada on two occasions. Later, many Americans wanted to establish an American nation from Mexico to the North Pole.

The U.S. invaded Canada during the American War of Independence and the War of 1812.

Canada-U.S. relationships gradually began to improve when both Canadians and Americans realized that they had more common interests than differences. Common cultural and economic ties won out and a very close relationship was the result. In the years to come this friendship, despite the occasional disputes that are bound to arise between friends, seems likely to continue.

■ ECONOMIC RELATIONSHIPS

The U.S. has not always been Canada's most important economic contact. Part of the land that is now Canada was a colony of France until 1763. This meant that Canada supplied France with needed raw materials, at that time mostly furs. In return, Canada acted as a market for products made in France. After 1763, when Great Britain took control of France's North American possessions, Canada played the same economic role for Britain. Many British companies operated in Canada and for over a century Canada's economy was dominated by the British. By the 20th century, however, it was becoming obvious that British dominance of Canada was being replaced by American dominance.

dominance: control

FREE TRADE

Free trade has been a recurring theme of U.S.-Canadian economic relationships for more than 100 years. Free trade means that goods may be shipped from one country to another without taxes, called **tariffs**, being added to the cost of the goods (Fig. 27–2). With free trade, Canada and the U.S. would each tend to specialize in the production of those goods that it could produce most cheaply. The result would be greatly increased trade. In 1988, a Free Trade Agreement was signed between the two countries.

The Reciprocity Treaty (1854–66) established free trade in natural products between Canada and the U.S. Reciprocity (free trade) with the U.S. was an issue in the 1911 national election, but was defeated.

Not all Canadians favour or would benefit from free trade. Consider the case of the blue jeans shown in Fig. 27–2. Which of the students described in Fig. 27–3 would likely be for tariffs and which would be against? Obviously your views on tariffs and free trade will vary depending on your circumstances. Those who favour free trade make three main arguments. They feel that free trade brings lower prices, especially for manufactured goods. They also argue that tariffs merely serve to protect inefficient businesses from competition. Finally, they ask how Canada can expect greater access to the U.S. market for our exports when we do not offer the U.S. freer access to our market.

Those who oppose free trade contend that free trade will cause much of the diversity of our economy to be lost. They feel that Canada could only compete with the U.S. in the natural resource field where we have a comparative advantage.

comparative advantage: Canada can produce and sell these products more cheaply than the U.S.

For Canada, free trade is meant to guarantee access to the American market for our goods. This is especially critical because there is so much pressure in the U.S. to cut imports. Canadian critics of the Free Trade Agreement point out that it does not assure absolute access to U.S. markets and that Canada is still subject to U.S. trade restrictions.

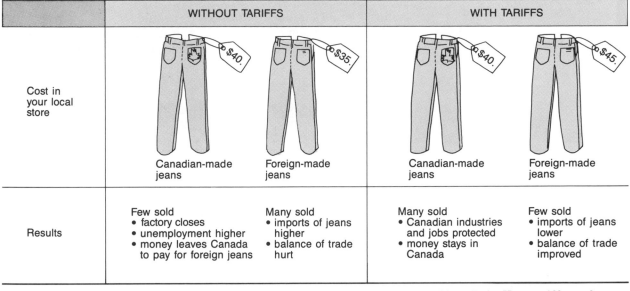

	WITHOUT TARIFFS		WITH TARIFFS	
Cost in your local store	Canadian-made jeans	Foreign-made jeans	Canadian-made jeans	Foreign-made jeans
Results	Few sold • factory closes • unemployment higher • money leaves Canada to pay for foreign jeans	Many sold • imports of jeans higher • balance of trade hurt	Many sold • Canadian industries and jobs protected • money stays in Canada	Few sold • imports of jeans lower • balance of trade improved

Fig. 27–2 How tariffs work

Fig. 27–3 Student opinions regarding the impact of tariffs

	For Tariffs	Against Tariffs
Student A: wants the best price when buying jeans in the store	?	?
Student B: parent works in a jeans factory	?	?
Student C: parent sells new cars in a town which has a large jeans factory	?	?
Student D: cousin operates foreign jeans factory	?	?

While Canadian products would have access to the rich U.S. market, the reverse is true as well. Many Canadians fear that Canadian manufactured products could not compete in Canada with the cheaper products of giant American companies. There are also fears that Canada's culture would be even more swamped by American influences than has been the case without free trade.

The benefits of free trade may prove to be uneven across the country. It would mostly benefit consumers and those who work in export industries. The benefits would be greatest in the parts of Canada that produce the things that Americans want – such as forest and mineral products. It would harm those who work in the manufacturing industries, which are concentrated in southern Ontario and Québec.

Even though a Free Trade Agreement has been signed, it does not mean that free trade is an accomplished fact. The phase-in period for the Free Trade Agreement is ten years. Since it has many opponents in both countries, future governments in either country could choose to end the Agreement. The future of the Free Trade Agreement is one of the most critical questions in Canadian political and economic life as we approach the next century.

FOREIGN INVESTMENT IN CANADA

Over the past century, many foreign companies found a way around Canadian tariffs. They realized that if they built factories in Canada, they would not have to pay tariffs on the products manufactured in these plants. Such factories are called **branch plants** of foreign companies. They are very common in Canadian business. In some important industries, such as automobile manufacturing and oil and gas, the great majority of our companies are branch plants. You can often (but not always) spot a branch plant company by its name. Some examples are:

- General Motors *of Canada* Ltd.
- McDonald's Restaurants *of Canada* Ltd.
- Shell Oil *Canada* Ltd.

In the early days, most **foreign investment** in Canada was British. Gradually, more and more American money came to Canada to be invested in branch plants. Then came World War II. The results for business in Canada were dramatic. After the war, much of Great Britain, Europe, the U.S.S.R. and Japan were in ruins and in need of food and materials to rebuild. The industries of Canada and the U.S. were undamaged and booming. Canada's economy had a tremendous potential for expansion, but there was a shortage of money for investment. America's economy had capital available for investment and needed the raw materials that Canada could supply. The result was massive American investment in Canada. This investment continues today.

Suddenly, Canada was in an era of enormous prosperity. The demand for Canadian products was great both at home and abroad. As a result, the economy grew rapidly. People had jobs and money to spend. Immigrants from Europe and elsewhere poured in. They were weary of war and prepared to work hard in a country that promised peace and prosperity. You may know someone who came to Canada during this post-war period.

During the 1950s, Canadians welcomed this investment with open arms. It allowed us to develop our economy at a much faster rate than we could have afforded ourselves. Hundreds of thousands of new jobs were created. This growth meant that millions of dollars in extra taxes were paid to the government. The money was used to provide valuable new services in fields such as health care, education, and social welfare.

As the years passed, however, many Canadians started to see problems caused by this enormous American investment. There were two major sources of concern.

capital: money

While one of your geography classes is in progress, more than $100 000 in new U.S. investment is coming into Canada (approximately $100 000/hr).

1. What happens to the profits earned? There are two possibilities. First, the money may be sent back to the **parent company** in the U.S. (or elsewhere), with the result that this money is lost to the Canadian economy. Second, the profits may be reinvested in Canada. Often this means that more Canadian-owned companies are taken over by American companies.

2. Who controls our industry? The president of an American-owned company can sometimes be in a difficult position. Canadians expect all businesses in Canada, including foreign-owned ones, to follow our laws and to operate in Canada's best interests. At the same time, the parent company expects its Canadian branch plant to follow U.S. laws and act according to U.S. interests. The problem is that Canadian and U.S. laws and interests are not always the same.

An example of conflicting interests occurred when the Canadian **subsidiary** of an American company signed a deal to sell merchandise to Cuba. The deal would clearly have helped Canada's economy. At that time, however, the U.S. had a law that did not allow American companies to trade with Cuba. The American parent firm ordered its Canadian subsidiary to call off its deal with Cuba. In a situation like this what should the company do? Is the company's first loyalty to its parent company or to Canada?

What should be done about foreign investment? Our two largest political parties, the Liberals and the Progressive Conservatives, had very different policies when each formed the government in recent years. The Liberals had definite reservations about foreign investment and passed laws that restricted it. In the 1980s, when the PCs replaced the Liberals as the government, they announced to the world that Canada was "open for business". By this they meant that foreign investment would be encouraged as it had been in the 1950s and 1960s. It is interesting to compare what each party did about foreign investment in three main areas.

The Liberals were in power for most of the years from the 1960s until 1984, when the Conservatives came into power. Who forms the government now?

Control of Takeovers

The Liberals were very concerned that so many Canadian companies were being taken over by foreign interests, mainly American. As a result, they established FIRA, the Foreign Investment Review Agency. FIRA's job was to examine proposed foreign takeovers to ensure that Canada would benefit in some way. FIRA approved about 95% of all takeovers, so it was not very restrictive. But it sent a message to the world that Canada was concerned about foreign investment.

When the Conservatives won the election of 1984, they quickly moved to replace FIRA with Investment Canada. The purpose of this agency was very different. Its main job was to encourage foreign investment in Canada.

Fig. 27–4 Petrocan is a government-owned oil company. Why does the government feel that Canada should own some of its key industries?

Government Ownership of Industry

The federal and most provincial governments own companies (called crown corporations) in key industries. Government ownership ensures that the companies operate in Canada's best interests. Examples are the federal government's ownership of CNR and the CBC. The government of Saskatchewan owns the largest potash mines in the province, and the government of Québec owns part of the province's asbestos industry.

The Liberals, when they were in power, expanded this role of government. The most obvious example was in the petroleum industry. The Liberal government established and expanded Petro-Canada so that Canadian ownership in this vital industry would be greater (Fig. 27–4).

The Conservatives, when in power, took an entirely different approach. They felt that government's role in the ownership of companies should be limited to those companies that are necessary but could not exist under private ownership. An example of such a company is Canada Post. Other crown corporations were sold to the private sector, or "privatized". The Conservative government privatized de Havilland Aircraft and Telecom Canada. In addition, attempts were made to sell such major crown corporations as Air Canada and Petro-Canada.

Foreign Ownership Laws

There is not much difference between the Liberals and Conservatives when we consider foreign ownership laws in industries considered vital to Canadian interests. These include transportation, radio and television, and uranium production. The Conservatives, however, did relax restrictions in the areas of publishing and banking. The Free Trade Agreement also eliminates many restrictions.

CANADIAN INVESTMENT IN THE U.S.

In recent years the government of the U.S. has been examining the effect of foreign investment on its own economy. Many foreign companies, including Canadian companies, are investing heavily in the U.S. Canadian investment is between 15% and 30% of all foreign investment in the U.S. Canadian real estate development companies are very active in many American cities. For example, an Edmonton-based company owns about 40% of the office space in Minneapolis and a Toronto-based company is the largest office landlord in New York City. Other companies are investing in mines, railways, cable television, and entertainment. The dollar amount of Canadian investment in the U.S. is roughly equal to that of American investment in Canada. The difference is that the huge U.S. economy is better able to absorb this amount of investment.

CHECKBACK

1. Define in your own words the meaning of each of the following terms:
   a) free trade   **c)** branch plant
   b) protective tariffs   **d)** foreign investment
2. List arguments for and against free trade.
3. Why did Canada encourage so much foreign investment after World War II? How did this investment help the country?
4. What problems can arise from large amounts of foreign investment in Canada?

ANALYZE

5. From the list below, choose three people who would probably favour free trade and three who would probably be opposed. Give reasons for each of your choices.
   a) Saskatchewan potash miner
   b) owner of a large Canadian boat factory
   c) Nova Scotia fishing captain
   d) person wanting to start a sporting goods company
   e) person wanting to buy a private plane
   f) a Montreal shoe-factory worker
6. Some regions benefit more from free trade than others. Choose one region of Canada that benefits a great deal and another that does not. Justify your choices by describing the main types of industries in each region and how free trade either helps or hurts the region.
7. **a)** Describe the different reactions in Canada to U.S. investment in the 1950s and early 1960s compared to the late 1960s and 1970s.
   b) Why did this change occur?
   c) What is the attitude to foreign investment now?

INVESTIGATE

8. Using a vertical file, indexes, or data bases, research the history of free trade negotiations between Canada and the U.S. What is the current status of free trade?
9. The St. Lawrence Seaway and Columbia River projects could only be completed with the cooperation of the U.S. and Canada. Use the resources of your school library to research either of these projects and describe how they came into being. Are there similar large, cooperative projects under way today?
10. **a)** How do the policies of the Liberal and Progressive Conservative parties differ with respect to foreign ownership? Why are the views of these two parties particularly significant over the past 25 years?
    b) Investigate the foreign ownership policies of the New Democratic Party. How do they differ from the other parties?

■ CULTURAL RELATIONSHIPS

Culture is a simple word that describes a very complex idea. Culture basically includes all of the characteristics of our way of life. It involves such things as language, religion, values, behaviour, education, food, entertainment, and the arts. These characteristics may be combined in many ways. Each combination of characteristics creates a unique culture.

People frequently ask whether or not Canada's culture is distinct from that of the U.S. Because culture is made up of so many elements, this question has no simple answer. Certain features of American and Canadian culture could be quite different, even though people from both countries might enjoy the same books, movies, or music.

The word "culture" is also used to mean only the arts, entertainment, and the media. Does Canada have a distinctive culture in this sense? Consider the following information.

Some Examples of Canadian Culture

- Some authors write about the experiences of various groups of people living in Canada. These writers include Pierre Berton, Farley Mowat, Gabrielle Roy, Robertson Davies, Austin Clarke, and Margaret Atwood.
- Canadian artists of all backgrounds depict Canada from various viewpoints. Some examples of Canadian artists are the Group of Seven, the Inuit sculptors of the North, Ken Danby, Robert Bateman, Norval Morisseau, Emily Carr, and Christopher Pratt.
- Public and private television and radio networks broadcast in French, English, Inuktituk, Cree, Chinese, Italian, Ukrainian, and many other languages.
- Singers, actors, orchestras, theatre companies, and dance companies perform in a wide variety of languages and traditions.
- Canada has an active film and video production industry. The French-Canadian film industry developed first, followed by the English-Canadian industry. In addition, movie theatres show films in many other languages.
- Many magazines, newspapers, and other publications are printed in a wide variety of languages to illustrate and keep alive the multicultural traditions of their readers in a Canadian setting.

These examples of Canadian culture convince many people that we are not the same as Americans. For example, student David Barzick has this to say: "It's nonsense to say that Canada's culture is the same as that of the United States. Our culture is distinct from anything else in the world. The culture of French Canada is not the culture of France. Nor is it the culture of English Canada or the United States translated into French. Similarly, the culture of English Canada is different from that of the United States or Great Britain. Canada's culture has also been influenced by our Native people and by the people who have come to Canada from all over the world. We have combined all of these influences to produce Canada's culture.''

Another student, Linda Davis, disagrees. She says: "Although Canada does have outstanding writers, artists, and performers, the majority of Canadians are unaware of their work, and are more familiar with American culture.'' Linda gave a quiz to a group of her friends (Fig. 27–5). She found that all of them scored less than 12 points. She thinks that this proves her point that although we have our own culture, its impact is not very significant compared to the cultural influences we receive from the U.S. Try Linda's quiz and see how you do.

Although David and Linda are fictional, their opinions summarize two commonly held views on Canadian culture.

Fig. 27–5

1. Name the last novel you read
   a) in English class.
   b) for enjoyment.
2. Name the members of the Group of Seven.
3. List your five favourite television shows.
4. List your five favourite singers or groups.
5. List the last five movies you have seen.
6. List up to three magazines that you read regularly.

Now work out your score. Give yourself one point for
a) each Canadian novel in 1
b) each correct answer in 2
c) each Canadian answer in 3, 4, 5 and 6. (Your teacher will help you score these.)

If you scored
20 to 27 points: You are a Canadian culture vulture.
11 to 19 points: You take advantage of Canadian culture.
5 to 10 points: Living in Canada makes little difference to your cultural life.
0 to 5 points: You might as well live in St. Louis!

It is easy to understand why American culture has such a great influence in Canada. Most Canadians receive U.S. television either directly or on cable. In addition, Canadian stations carry many American shows. In fact, few Canadian shows are among the favourites of Canadian viewers (Fig. 27–6). Most Canadian radio stations sound the same as their American counterparts: many use pre-packaged formats from the United States. American movies, books, and magazines are almost as available here as they would be anywhere in the U.S.

Even Canadians who live thousands of kilometres from the border can receive American television by satellite.

Fig. 27–6 The most popular television programs on Canadian TV

1. Disney Sunday Movie (U.S.)
   (3 067 000 viewers)
2. Cosby Show (U.S.)
3. MacGyver (U.S.)
4. Hockey Night (Can.)
5. Matlock (U.S.)
6. Newhart (U.S.)
7. Golden Girls (U.S.)
8. CBC National News (Can.)
9. Jake and the Fatman (U.S.)
10. W5 (Can.)

(Toronto Star; Dec 31, 1987–Jan 6, 1988)

■ OTHER RELATIONSHIPS

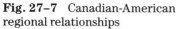

Retired Canadians often go to live in the warmer climates of Florida or Arizona.

Canada has other kinds of relationships with the U.S. Many Canadians live in the U.S. and thousands of Americans live in Canada. Perhaps you have relatives who live in the U.S. In addition, millions of Americans and Canadians visit each other's country as tourists every year.

Canada is in a unique military position. At the end of World War II we had one of the world's largest military forces, numbering over 300 000 people. Today, even with a much larger population, our armed forces number only about 80 000. What do we do about our defence? One element of our defence system is a military alliance with the U.S. Under NORAD (North American Aerospace Defence Command), both countries share the defence of North America against air attack. The U.S. has about 20 times as many military personnel as Canada, and has more sophisticated equipment. As a result, the Americans supply most of the defence.

Geography has much to do with a Canadian dilemma. Canada has been described as an east-west country existing on a north-south continent. This means that physical patterns and related economic patterns run north to south in North America while the political boundary runs east to west. The same could be said about the U.S. Examine Fig. 27–7. It shows the strong regional relationships that exist between parts of Canada and adjacent parts of the U.S. If you live in Atlantic Canada you may have more in common

Fig. 27–7 Canadian-American regional relationships

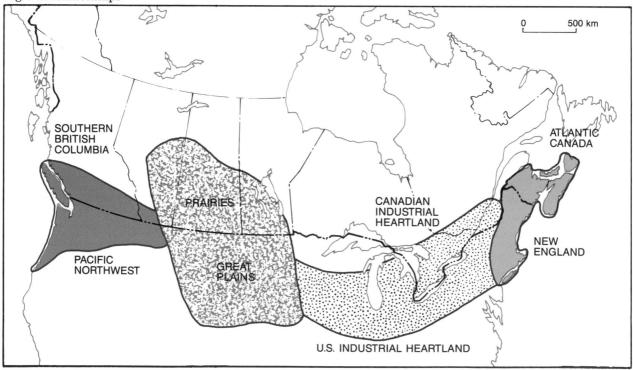

with a resident of New England than with an Albertan. Similarly, a farmer in southwestern Ontario has a lifestyle very much like that of a farmer in nearby Michigan. In some areas, these regional ties are combined with family ties. The result is that Canadians sometimes feel that these regional ties can be stronger than national ties.

■ IN CLOSING . . .

Some Canadians feel that Canada and the U.S. have so much in common that the best approach would be to work together. This cooperation could involve such things as increased trade, free movement of workers, and the sharing of natural resources. People who believe in this common approach are called **continentalists** because they view all of the North American continent as a unit.

A second, larger group of Canadians is fearful of having too close a relationship with the U.S. They feel that Canadians can make their country a better place by staying as independent of the U.S. as possible. These people tend to oppose foreign ownership and support measures to encourage Canadian cultural activities. These people are called **nationalists**.

It is up to you to decide which side of this question you support. Do you side with continentalists who stress the similarities between Americans and Canadians? Do you agree with nationalists who want to maintain or even increase the differences? Or is your position somewhere in the middle?

QUESTIONS

CHECKBACK

1. Why do Canadians often feel that regional ties are stronger than national ties?
2. Contrast the ideas of continentalism and nationalism.

ANALYZE

3. a) What makes North America a north-south continent?
   b) How does this fact affect Canada?

   Hint: check the landform and economic maps in your atlas.

4. a) The following quotations come from an American president and a Canadian prime minister. Explain the meaning of each quotation in your own words.

   "Geography has made us neighbors. History has made us friends. Economics has made us partners. And necessity has made us allies. What unites us is far greater than what divides us."
   – President John F. Kennedy

"Living next to the U.S. is in some ways like sleeping with an elephant. No matter how friendly and even-tempered is the beast ... one is affected by every grunt and twitch."

– Prime Minister Pierre Trudeau

b) Which quotation expresses a continentalist view and which a nationalist view?

c) Why would an American spokesperson be unlikely to support the Canadian nationalist view?

INVESTIGATE

5. The English language as it is spoken and written in Canada is different in small ways from American or British English. Investigate these differences (your English teacher may be able to help you) and prepare a summary of your findings. You should consider the spelling, pronunciation, and meaning of the words.

6. Mexico also shares a long border with the U.S. The American economic and cultural influence in Mexico is important but not as great as in Canada. Suggest at least two reasons for this.

WHAT DO YOU THINK?

7. You probably heard the story about the American tourist arriving at the Canadian border in July with skis on top of the car, eager to see the igloos and polar bears. This probably never happened, but it does illustrate the fact that most Americans know little about Canada.

a) Why is this so?

b) Why should this not be surprising?

8. When Canadians travel abroad they are often confused with Americans. When this happens, some Canadians become quite upset. Why do you think some Canadians do not want to be thought of as Americans?

9. Are Canadians really different from Americans? Give evidence to support your answer.

Are the differences between Canadians and Americans similar to those between, say, Germans and French?

Foreign Ownership and the Record Industry

In our interdependent world, foreign investment can provide valuable support for a nation's economy. It can, however, also create problems.

Key Terms

multi-national corporation   multiplier effect

■ INTRODUCTION

Fig. 27–8 shows some of the largest companies operating in Canada. But how Canadian are they? There are two types of Canadian companies. Some companies are owned and controlled by Canadians. Examples of these are Eaton's and Canadian Pacific. Other companies operate in Canada but are owned by foreign companies. These companies operate in many countries at the same time and are called **multi-national corporations** (MNCs). Most MNCs are owned in the U.S. Examples are General Motors, Exxon, and Sears. A few, such as Bata Shoes and the Bank of Nova Scotia, are Canadian-owned MNCs. Although MNCs operating in Canada may have their headquarters in other countries, such as Britain or Japan, in this chapter we are most interested in American MNCs operating in Canada.

Depending on whom you ask, MNCs may be described either as sensible and efficient organizations or as a threat to Canada's independence. The middle view is that MNCs can be beneficial but they can also have negative impacts on Canada. We will examine the various arguments.

Fig. 27–8 Some of the multi-national corporations that operate in Canada. Which ones are Canadian?

IN SUPPORT OF MULTI-NATIONALS

- MNCs provide vital goods and services to Canadians very cheaply. Because of their large size, MNCs are able to operate in a much more efficient way than smaller companies.
- MNCs provide millions of dollars of capital investment which Canada needs to develop new mines, factories, mills, oil and gas reserves, and other businesses. This is very important because Canada does not have enough capital available to develop its own resources as quickly.
- The growth of MNCs provides thousands of new jobs every year. Without this job creation, unemployment would be much worse.
- MNCs bring the latest inventions and technical developments to Canada. Without the MNCs, Canada would have to do without these advances. Canadian industries often cannot afford to do their own research in such costly fields as the automobile industry, the electronics industry, and the chemical industry.
- Canada, along with such countries as the U.S., Great Britain, and Japan, operates under a free enterprise system. This system allows competition between companies. To oppose multi-nationals would be to oppose a basic part of free enterprise.

AGAINST MULTI-NATIONALS

- Because MNCs are owned and controlled outside Canada, these companies do not necessarily operate in Canada's best interests. MNCs operate to serve their home country first. This means that if an issue arises over which Canada and the U.S. disagree, an American MNC would tend to follow the American policy.
- MNCs take thousands of millions of dollars of profit out of Canada. These profits should stay in Canada to be reinvested here.
- New jobs will only be created in Canada when it suits the MNCs. If a MNC has to choose between closing a factory in its home country and closing one here, Canada and Canadian workers will end up the losers.
- Many MNCs are mainly interested in Canada as a source of raw materials such as iron ore or wood pulp. Thus Canadians lose the jobs that would be created if those materials were processed into finished goods in Canada.
- MNCs do little research and development of new products and methods in Canada. New technical developments are brought to Canada from the MNC's home country. This policy keeps Canada from receiving the benefits of doing more research here, such as jobs for scientists. It also means that Canadians do not get the advantage of having the new development first.

We are left with a difficult problem. Are multi-national corporations good or bad? Should something be done about American ownership of Canadian industries? If so, what? To help you clear up this issue in your own mind, let us study a sample industry.

■ THE RECORD INDUSTRY IN CANADA

The record production industry is similar to many others in Canada. A small number of large American companies (the MNCs) dominate the industry. Many more small Canadian-owned companies (the independents) try to compete. The independents favour government action to help them. The MNCs are happy with the way things are now. To see the case for government action, let us listen to John Simpson, a Canadian record producer.

"As we (Canadian independent record producers) see it, the record industry is vital to Canada. Sales in 1985 were over $348 000 000. The actual economic value to Canada is higher, however, because of the **multiplier effect** (Fig. 27–9). This means that when money is spent for a record, tape or compact disc, there

The record industry refers to companies that produce records, tapes, compact discs, and music videos.

Fig. 27–9 How the multiplier effect works in the Canadian record industry. All shaded sections would be lost if the record was produced in another country.

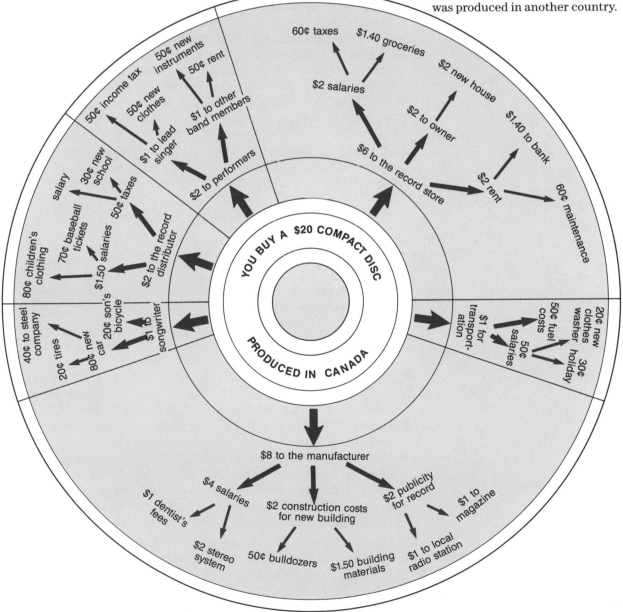

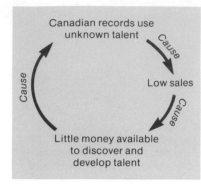

Fig. 27–10 The problems of using Canadian talent

Diagram labels: Canadian records use unknown talent — Cause → Low sales — Cause → Little money available to discover and develop talent — Cause →

are benefits for related industries responsible for things such as album design, printing, advertising, video-production, and concert tours.

"There are over 100 record companies in Canada. Of these, the 12 foreign-owned companies do 90% of the total business. At the other extreme, the 47 smallest companies do less than 1% of the total business. These companies are all Canadian-owned.

"Canadian independent companies cannot compete against the multi-nationals for several reasons. MNCs can share many costs of production with their American parent companies. The independent companies have to pay all the costs of production for their records. The MNCs use mainly foreign talent; less than 10% of their records have Canadian content. The independents discover and develop Canadian talent; their records have over 90% Canadian content. Since they use unknown talent, Canadian record companies tend to be high-risk businesses. Less than one in ten albums makes money. Fig. 27–10 illustrates the problem.

"More independent record production in Canada would be desirable for many reasons. We could reduce imports and increase exports. A country can make a great deal of money from the record industry. For example, in the late 1970s more money flowed into Sweden because of the international success of the pop group ABBA than because of Volvo exports. A final advantage of more independent production is that cultural decisions would be made in Canada by Canadians. More Canadian talent would be recorded and we would have the choice of a wide range of Canadian artists. Today only a few Canadian stars are recorded by the MNCs."

■ WHAT CAN BE DONE?

There are a number of ways in which the government could help the Canadian record industry. It could:

- Require at least 51% Canadian ownership of all record companies. This would mean that important decisions about Canada's culture would be made here.
- Restrict imports of foreign records and master tapes from which records are made. This would give independent producers a chance to grow large enough to compete with MNCs.
- Require a higher number of Canadian-produced records to be played on Canadian radio stations.
- Encourage investment in independent record companies by allowing large income tax deductions for the money invested. These deductions are already allowed for investments in Canadian movies. This is one reason why the motion-picture industry has grown so quickly.

Any of these actions would limit the freedom of some companies to operate in the most efficient way possible. In recent years, the trend has been in the opposite direction, as fewer restrictions have been placed on business rather than more.

■ IN CLOSING...

The question of whether or not to restrict foreign ownership in Canadian industry is not easy to resolve. The following questions will help you draw your own conclusions.

QUESTIONS

CHECKBACK

1. Try to answer the questions below without looking back through the chapter. What is
   a) a large company that operates in more than one country?
   b) the growth of other parts of the economy caused by growth in one industry?
2. Describe two disadvantages that Canadian independent record producers face in trying to compete with multi-national corporations.

ANALYZE

3. Copy Fig. 27–11 into your notebook.
   a) Fill in the arguments for each side.
   b) Which side seems to have stronger arguments? Explain.

Fig. 27–11

For Multi-Nationals	Topic	Against Multi-Nationals
	Research and development of new products	
	Number of new jobs created	
	Supply of capital for growth	

INVESTIGATE

4. From your own knowledge and from newspapers or magazines, list ten large corporations. Indicate whether each one is Canadian or foreign owned.
5. a) List as many record labels (manufacturers) as you can.
   b) Determine if these are Canadian independents or MNCs.
   c) Were you surprised by your results? Why or why not?
6. a) List your five favourite musical performers.
   b) Compare your list to a classmate's list. How many Canadian artists did each of you list?
   c) Do any of the artists you listed record for a Canadian independent company? Why would they have chosen this record company?

7. The government from time to time appoints a Royal Commission to study some particular problem that exists in Canada. In this project, assume that you have been appointed to form a Royal Commission on the Record Industry in Canada. Working in a group of three or four students, prepare recommendations on the problems of the independent producers. (Your teacher will tell you whether you will be making an oral or written presentation of your results.)

You should decide

a) whether or not anything *should* be done.

b) what *could* be done. (How practical are each of the proposals on page 416? Are there other things that could be done?)

c) what are the good and bad effects of each measure?

Be sure to give reasons for all your decisions.

The Canada of Tomorrow

We often do not realize that countries are constantly changing. The map of Canada has certainly not remained constant. Compare the Canada of 1867 to the Canada of today (Fig. 28–1). Some provinces have grown in size, and new provinces and territories have been added. The most recent change was the addition of Newfoundland and Labrador in 1949.

In 1867, other names were considered for the new country. These included: Mesopelagia, Cabotia, Laurentia, Boretta, and Ursalia. What do these names mean?

Fig. 28–1 Canada in 1867 and today

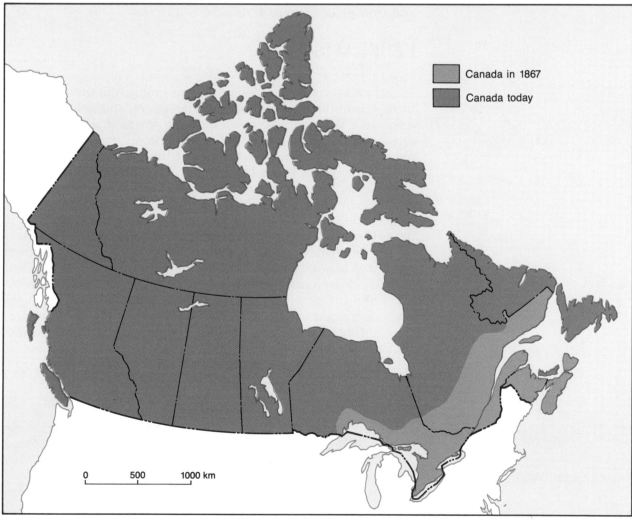

Canada in 1867

Canada today

0   500   1000 km

The obvious question is, "Are major changes in Canada's political form needed now? If so, what should they be?" In the following sections you will learn how Canada is changing, and what forces are encouraging more change for the future. Perhaps you will then be able to determine how Canada should be changed to meet the needs of the 21st century.

Key Terms

federalism   separatism   continentalism
regionalism

FORCES FOR THE FUTURE

There are four political forces at work today that will help determine what Canada will be like in the future: **federalism**, **regionalism**, **separatism**, and **continentalism**. These forces are not of equal strength. They also vary in importance from time to time and from place to place across the country.

FEDERALISM

Canada has a federal system of government. This means that the country was created as a federation, or union, of individual provinces. Powers are divided between the federal and provincial governments. For example, the federal government has powers in areas such as international affairs and defence, while the provinces have power over such things as education and health care.

In recent years, there has been much talk about "renewed" federalism. This means changing the existing federal system to meet the needs of Canada's people in the future. Most discussion has centred on giving more power to the provinces. For example, in the Constitution Act of 1982, the provinces gained more control over resource development, and the agreement of at least seven provinces is now needed to make amendments to the Constitution. The Meech Lake Accord of 1987 between the federal government and the provinces continued this process. Provinces were given increased powers in areas such as amending the Constitution, opting out of federal programs, immigration, and the selection of Supreme Court judges and Senators. The process of renewed federalism is on-going.

REGIONALISM

ethnicity: ethnic classification

In some parts of Canada, people tend to identify more with their local region than with the country as a whole. These regional feelings have developed as a result of history, economic patterns, natural resources, ethnicity, and culture. Examples of strong regional feelings are found in French Canada, Western Canada, the North, and Atlantic Canada.

An increase in regionalism does not mean that Canada would cease to exist. It does mean that Canada would have to change a great deal. Eventually, the provinces we know today might be replaced by regional governments, for example in Atlantic Canada, French Canada, and the North. The regional governments would control most powers, and Canada would become a loose union of these regions. The federal government would only look after international affairs and national defence.

SEPARATISM

When Canadians use the word "separatism" they are most often referring to the desire of some people in Québec to have their province leave Canada and become an independent country. Separatist feelings in Québec grew during the 1960s and 1970s to the point where the separatist Parti Québécois formed the provincial government after the election of 1976. In 1980, a referendum was held to determine whether the majority of people in Québec wanted their government to negotiate a form of separatism with the government of Canada. The voters' decision was "non", and the separatist cause was badly hurt. That decision does not mean that another referendum could not be held in the future. The result of a new vote would depend largely on whether the people of Québec felt that they were being treated fairly within Canada.

referendum: a vote by the people of a country, province, or city on a proposal by their government

What do you think would cause the residents of a province or region to want to separate? Clearly, they must feel that they would be better off not being part of Canada. In the case of Québec, supporters of separatism feel they do not have enough control over their culture's future.

In recent years, there has been talk of separatism involving one or more of the western provinces. Support for western separatism has grown with the feeling that Central Canada treats the West unfairly. Similar feelings have been expressed by some people in Atlantic Canada. Only time will tell how serious the threat of separatism may be to Canada in the future.

CONTINENTALISM

A totally different option for Canada is suggested by those supporting continentalism. Those who support this idea would like to see Canada gradually join with the U.S. to form a huge, new country. They argue that Canada and the U.S. are so closely related – economically, culturally, and socially – that any political division between the two countries is artificial and unnecessary.

Most people who favour a "marriage" with the U.S. see such a union developing gradually. Free trade might be the first step in the process. Later, immigration barriers might be eliminated.

Fig. 28–2 The North American dollar

Eventually, we might use the same currency (Fig. 28–2), combine our armed forces, and elect representatives to a shared parliament or congress. In some ways, the European Economic Community (the Common Market) has united western Europe in this way. The final step would be the creation of a new country, perhaps called the United States of North America (U.S.N.A.) with a new flag and national anthem.

Opponents of continentalism say that Canadians would be the big losers in any union with the U.S. They say that we would lose our culture, and that we would receive few economic benefits. At this stage in our history, most Canadians oppose the idea of closer ties with our American neighbours. Whether or not opinions on this issue will change remains to be seen.

■ WHAT WILL THE NEW CANADIAN MAP LOOK LIKE?

When we consider what Canada may be like in 20, 50, or 100 years, we must keep three things in mind:

1. Some type of change is very likely.

2. The results of a change could seem positive or negative depending on who we are and what our interests are.

3. The way in which the change is achieved is very important.

The number of possible forms for Canada is virtually endless. In this section we will examine only four options.

Changes must occur in such a way that people in different parts of the country are not left angry with one another.

A FEDERAL FUTURE

There are plans to divide the Northwest Territories into two separate parts: a First Nations territory in the west and an Inuit-controlled territory in the east. These, along with the Yukon, could become new provinces.

If Canadians choose a federalist solution for their future, the map of Canada will not change very much. The Territories may become provinces. Another change might be in the balance of power between the federal and provincial governments.

A REGIONAL FUTURE

If Canadians choose a future based on regionalism, the map of the country would be totally different. Fig. 28–3 shows one possible Canada of the future. Canada has been divided into seven provinces. Each province has been created on the basis of regional similarities of population patterns and economic activities.

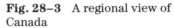

Fig. 28–3 A regional view of Canada

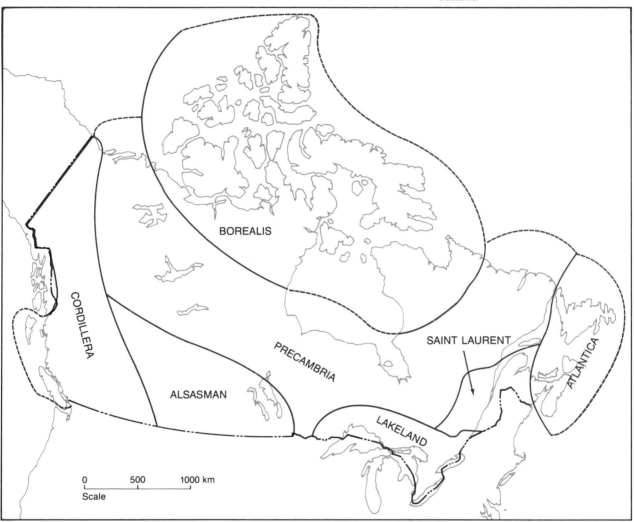

A SEPARATIST FUTURE

The subject of Québec separatism was first widely discussed in the 1960s. Since then there has been much discussion about the possible effects of separatism on Canada. If Québec were to become a separate country, then Canada would be divided into two parts. There are serious problems with a physically divided country. What might some of these be? The problems would be similar if another part of Canada were to separate.

Pakistan is an example of a country that was physically divided. It did not survive a divided existence. One part broke away to form the new country of Bangladesh.

A CONTINENTAL FUTURE

The map of a continent-wide country would be a fairly simple one. Our larger provinces could function well as states. The smaller provinces might be combined to form states.

■ IN CLOSING...

Thinking about Canada's future can be an interesting and thought-provoking experience. In order to shape that future in the best way possible, it is vital for all Canadians, whether ordinary citizens or political leaders, to be well informed about the issues involved. Our concern and awareness will increase the chances of success for the Canada of tomorrow.

QUESTIONS

ANALYZE

1. a) Define "federalism".
   b) What is "renewed federalism"?
   c) How could renewed federalism help solve Canada's future problems?
2. a) Define "regionalism".
   b) Give the economic and cultural characteristics of each of the regions shown in Fig. 28–3.
   c) List at least two advantages and two disadvantages of the regional solution.
3. a) Name three parts of Canada where separatism has been considered.
   b) Why might the people of a province or region become interested in separatism?
   c) Describe the problems of a country that is divided into separate parts.
   d) How successful would each of the following be in the case of separation? Consider such factors as population patterns, possible transportation problems, and major industries and resources.
      i. Québec alone
      ii. Canada without Québec
      iii. Western provinces
      iv. Canada without the Western provinces
      v. Atlantic provinces
      vi. Canada without the Atlantic provinces.

4. **a)** Define "continentalism".
   b) Describe three advantages and three disadvantages for Canadians if Canda were to form a union with the U.S.
   c) How would the U.S. benefit from such a union?
   d) How would you, personally, feel about being part of a United States of North America?

5. Assume that the Prime Minister and the provincial premiers have met. They have decided to produce a new map of Canada that will accurately reflect what Canada is like today. You have been given the job of suggesting the plan to be used. You should do two things:
   a) Prepare a map of the new provinces or political regions.
   b) Explain the reasons for your choice in a report.
   c) Why is the method of deciding on a new form for Canada almost as important as the new form chosen?

6. Should there be more provinces in Canada? Several suggestions have been made. One is that the Territories should be made into provinces. Another is that Northern Ontario and Northern Québec should be provinces. A third possibility is that Canada's major cities, such as Toronto, Montréal and Vancouver, should become provinces.
   a) What arguments support the establishment of new provinces in these three cases?
   b) What problems might result if these new provinces were created?
   c) Suggest a different new province which could be created. Explain your choice.

7. Canadian writers have viewed the existence of different regional feelings as either very positive or very negative. Read the two quotations below and write a two to three paragraph essay in support of one view or the other.

   Quotation 1 "Regionalism need not mean the break-up of Canada. It may mean healthy diversity. As long as the diverse regions remember that they need each other, regionalism can actually add to Canadian unity."

   Quotation 2 "As a people we don't like each other very much. We tend to feel that our region is being "taken" by some other region."

29 Is Canada the Best Place in the World to Live?

Perhaps it is not surprising that many Canadians think that their nation is the most desirable place in the world to live (Fig. 29–1). But is there an objective way to determine what is the best place in the world to live? The following activity will give you an opportunity to do this.

objective: unbiased

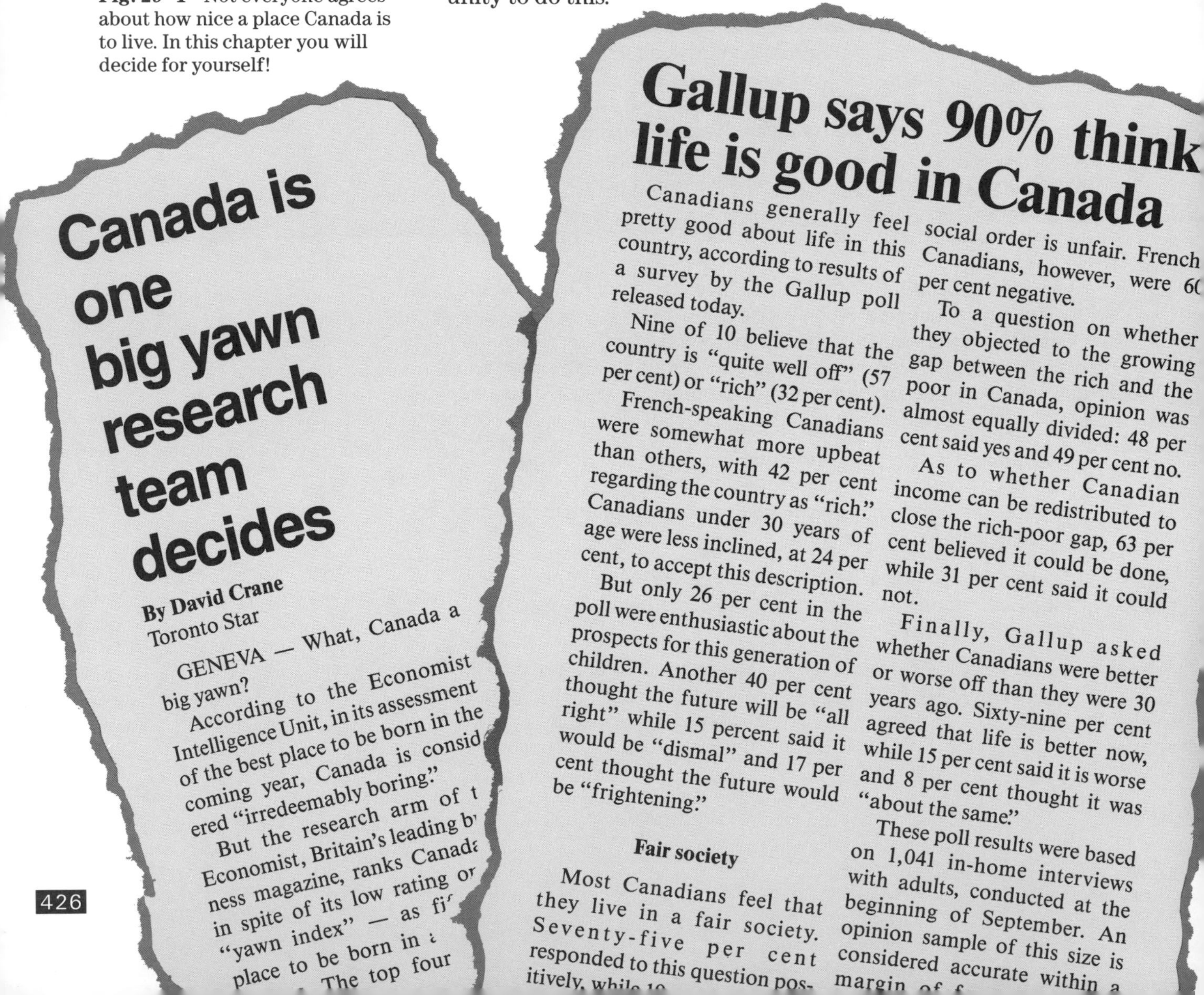

Fig. 29–1 Not everyone agrees about how nice a place Canada is to live. In this chapter you will decide for yourself!

Canada is one big yawn research team decides

By David Crane
Toronto Star

GENEVA — What, Canada a big yawn?

According to the Economist Intelligence Unit, in its assessment of the best place to be born in the coming year, Canada is considered "irredeemably boring."

But the research arm of t Economist, Britain's leading b ness magazine, ranks Canad in spite of its low rating o "yawn index" — as fi place to be born in

The top four

Gallup says 90% think life is good in Canada

Canadians generally feel pretty good about life in this country, according to results of a survey by the Gallup poll released today.

Nine of 10 believe that the country is "quite well off" (57 per cent) or "rich" (32 per cent).

French-speaking Canadians were somewhat more upbeat than others, with 42 per cent regarding the country as "rich." Canadians under 30 years of age were less inclined, at 24 per cent, to accept this description.

But only 26 per cent in the poll were enthusiastic about the prospects for this generation of children. Another 40 per cent thought the future will be "all right" while 15 percent said it would be "dismal" and 17 per cent thought the future would be "frightening."

Fair society

Most Canadians feel that they live in a fair society. Seventy-five per cent responded to this question pos- itively, while 19

social order is unfair. French Canadians, however, were 60 per cent negative.

To a question on whether they objected to the growing gap between the rich and the poor in Canada, opinion was almost equally divided: 48 per cent said yes and 49 per cent no.

As to whether Canadian income can be redistributed to close the rich-poor gap, 63 per cent believed it could be done, while 31 per cent said it could not.

Finally, Gallup asked whether Canadians were better or worse off than they were 30 years ago. Sixty-nine per cent agreed that life is better now, while 15 per cent said it is worse and 8 per cent thought it was "about the same."

These poll results were based on 1,041 in-home interviews with adults, conducted at the beginning of September. An opinion sample of this size is considered accurate within a margin of

Key Terms

quality of life   cost of living   index value
purchasing power   civil disorder   social progress
consumption growth

■ HOW DOES CANADA COMPARE?

In Fig. 29–2, Canada is compared to 13 other countries. Each of these countries could be regarded as a leading candidate for "best place to live" within its own part of the world. For each country, 13 measures of the **quality of life** are presented. Study each measure and answer the questions that follow.

MEASURES OF THE QUALITY OF LIFE

1. Incidents of civil disorder (1948-1977). **Civil disorder** includes assassinations, government crises, general strikes, guerilla incidents, purges, riots, revolutions, and anti-government demonstrations.
BEST: Saudi Arabia 14; WORST: United Kingdom 5136; CANADA: 260

civil: non-military

Fig. 29–2 Some measures of the desirability of a country as a place to live. Countries are ranked for each measure in order from 1 (best) to 14 (worst).
(na = not available)

	ARGENTINA	AUSTRALIA	CANADA	DENMARK	FRANCE	JAPAN	NETHERLANDS	SAUDI ARABIA	SWEDEN	SWITZERLAND	USA	USSR	UK	WEST GERMANY
Civil Disorder	11	6	7	4	12	8	5	1	2	3	13	9	14	10
Defence Expenditure	6	5	2	4	10	1	9	14	8	3	12	13	11	7
Purchasing Power	12	7	2	6	4	10	9	8	3	na	1	na	11	5
Energy Consumption	13	4	2	8	10	12	3	14	7	11	1	6	9	5
Work Week	na	10	3	2	7	6	8	na	1	12	4	5	11	9
Number of Cars	12	2	3	10	6	11	8	13	7	5	1	14	9	4
Consumption Growth	13	6	3	7	4	2	9	1	12	10	8	na	11	5
Living Space	11	4	1	6	9	8	7	na	5	na	3	10	2	12
Physical Quality of Life	13	6	7	4	8	1	2	14	3	5	9	12	10	11
Social Progress	na	4	5	1	9	7	3	na	2	8	10	12	11	6
Number of TV Sets	14	6	3	7	8	2	12	13	5	10	1	11	4	9
Cost of Living	6	3	2	11	10	13	8	7	12	14	1	5	4	9
Museum Visits	11	9	3	2	10	6	5	12	1	na	4	8	na	7

2. Defence expenditures per person. This measure indicates how much of a country's financial resources are spent for military purposes.
BEST: Japan $83; WORST: Saudi Arabia $1837; CANADA: $174

3. Purchasing power. This is a measure of how much money the average person has available to spend on day-to-day needs. It is an **index value** compared to the U.S. which has a value of 100.
BEST: U.S. 100; WORST: Argentina 46.4; CANADA: 90.4

4. Energy consumption per person. A high level of energy consumption indicates that the residents of a country have access to many of the amenities of modern life. Units are kilograms of coal. (Other energy forms have been converted.)
BEST: U.S. 10 410 kg; WORST: Saudi Arabia 1479 kg;
CANADA: 10 241 kg

5. Work week. Indicates the average number of hours worked per week for non-agricultural employees. Suggests how much time the average person has available for leisure and family activities.
BEST: Sweden 33.3h; WORST: Switzerland 44.4h;
CANADA: 38.8h

6. Passenger cars per person. The number of cars in a country is generally considered to be a good indicator of economic prosperity.
BEST: U.S. 0.53; WORST: U.S.S.R. 0.03; CANADA: 0.42

7. Consumption growth. An index value which indicates the increase in consumption of all types of goods and services between 1970 and 1980. This index suggests how rapidly a country's economy is growing. (1970 = 100)
BEST: Saudi Arabia 276.7; WORST: Argentina 105.8;
CANADA: 133.5

8. Living space per person. This measure indicates the average number of persons per room in all of the dwellings in the country.
BEST: CANADA 0.6 persons/room; WORST: West Germany 1.5 persons/room

9. Physical quality of life index. An index value which combines three factors: life expectancy, infant mortality, and literacy.
BEST: Japan 98; WORST: Saudi Arabia 35; CANADA: 96

10. Index of net social progress. This is a very complex measure of the overall quality of life. It includes 55 items ranging from spending on education, to inflation, to the number of natural disasters that occur in a country.
BEST: Denmark 196; WORST: U.S.S.R. 113; CANADA: 174

11. Television sets per person. In most of the developed world, television is the single most important element of culture.
BEST: U.S. 0.62 sets/person; WORST: Argentina 0.19 sets/person;
CANADA: 0.47 sets/person

12. Cost of living. This is an index indicating the relative cost of living in the major cities in each country. The costs are those for living a North American lifestyle.
BEST: U.S. 100; WORST: Switzerland 184; CANADA: 105

Washington, D.C. = 100

13. Museum visits per person. Museums act as a storehouse for culture and as a major means of communicating artistic and cultural values. The number of museum visits is an important measure of cultural influence in a country.
BEST: Sweden 1.92; WORST: Saudi Arabia 0.004; CANADA: 1.60

■ IN CLOSING...

If you would like more information on these and other measures of the world situation consult a fascinating book entitled *The New Book of World Rankings* by George Thomas Kurian (Facts on File Inc., 1984). Now on to the task of determining if Canada is the nicest place in the world to live.

QUESTIONS

ANALYZE

1. To make your choice of the "best place to live", consider the following points:
   a) Be sure that you completely understand each of the 13 factors.
   b) Decide whether all of the factors are of equal importance. If not, how will you ensure that more important factors receive more weight in your decision-making process?
   c) Will you use all 13 factors? Why or why not?
   d) Will you group related factors? If you do, on what basis?
   e) What will you do in cases where information for some countries is not available?
   f) Will you do some form of numerical analysis, or a descriptive summary, or a combination of both? How will you decide?
2. Which country do you consider to be the "best place in the world to live"? Defend your choice.
3. Now let's consider the analytical process you have just gone through.
   a) Should some of the factors in Fig. 29-2 not have been included on the list? Why not?

You may find it helpful to discuss these questions with your classmates or with your parents.

If you decide to do a numerical analysis, you might wish to use a spreadsheet program on a microcomputer.

b) Comment on the usefulness of the following factors for this analysis:

　　i. percentage of the national income going to the richest 10% of the population

　　ii. crime rate

　　iii. attractiveness of the country to tourists.

c) Can you suggest other factors that would have been useful in this analysis?

Hint: don't forget some very small countries.

INVESTIGATE

4. Are there countries not included on this list that are candidates for "best place to live"? Give two reasons why some of these countries were not included on this list.

SKILLS FOR THE GEOGRAPHER

30 Types of Maps

Carpenters or dentists need good tools to do their jobs properly. Similarly, geographers need good tools to study the world. One of the best of these is the map. Maps have been used for over 4000 years for a variety of purposes such as exploring, finding directions, fighting wars, and describing the shape of the world.

In your study of Canada, you will find that maps are very useful tools. They help you visualize the shape of the country and locate features within it. There are many different kinds of maps and each has certain advantages and uses. In this chapter we will examine the key features of maps, and learn how some specific maps are used.

Key Terms

map	thematic map	general purpose map
scale	legend	topographic map
small-scale map	large-scale map	

■ WHAT IS A MAP?

A **map** is a representation of the earth's features drawn on a flat surface. Unlike photographs, maps cannot show us what the land actually looks like. Instead, maps use symbols and colours to represent the features of an area. Examine a map in your atlas. How are cities shown? How are lowlands shown?

A map also simplifies the real world. For example, not every tree, sign post and telephone pole are shown on a map. A map concentrates on only a few important features. This simplicity allows us to focus our attention on specific characteristics within an area.

■ MAP REQUIREMENTS

Cartographer: professional map-maker

Whenever you (or a cartographer for that matter) draw a map, certain features should always be included. These features help the map reader understand the purpose of the map.

a) Title: Describes the area shown on the map and, if it is not obvious, the topic(s) of the map.

b) Legend: A **legend** explains the meaning of the symbols and colours used on the map.

c) Scale: The **scale** compares the distance between points on the map with the actual distance between the points on the earth's surface. It allows the reader to measure distance and to calculate area.

d) Direction: North, south, east and west are usually indicated on maps to allow users to orient themselves. Direction is recorded in two ways:
  i. by a direction arrow or symbol
  ii. by the use of latitude and longitude.
Latitude and longitude also show the location on the globe of the area represented by the map.

e) Borders: Borders or margins set the map apart from other information.

Many maps also have a date so that the reader can tell whether or not the information shown is current.

Map scale is examined in more detail in Chapter 32.

If a map doesn't indicate direction, assume the top of the map is north.

Fig. 30–1 A large-scale map (A) and a small-scale map (B)

A

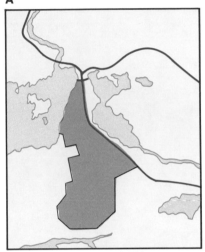

1:50 000

B

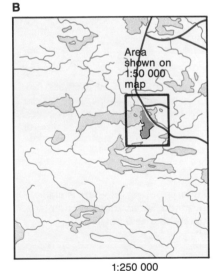

1:250 000

  Town
  Lake
  Road
  River

■LARGE- AND SMALL-SCALE MAPS

The scale of a map will vary according to the amount of detail required. Maps may be classified according to two general categories (Fig. 30–1). **Large-scale maps** show a large amount of detail of a small area. Maps with scales of 1:50 000 and 1:25 000 or less are large-scale maps. Maps with these scales are used whenever detailed information about a small area is required for such things as residential planning, hiking, and military purposes.

On the other hand, **small-scale maps** show a small amount of detail of a large area. Maps with scales of 1:250 000 and 1:500 000 or more are small-scale maps. These maps are used when general details, such as political, physical, and economic information, are needed for large areas.

■SIZE OF MAPS

The size of a map varies according to the purpose for which it is designed. If you want to use a map to illustrate the physical structure of Canada to your class, a large map like a wall map would be best. However, if you wanted a map to guide you on a hike, a small map such as a topographic map would be needed. You might find a wall map a bit inconvenient to carry! A smaller map that could be folded and put in your pack would be more practical.

1. a) What is a map? Use your own words.
   b) Why are maps useful tools?
   c) How do maps help us to focus our attention on just a few specific things?
2. a) List the essential features that are included on a map.
   b) Draw a sketch map of your school classroom. Make sure that all the essentials listed above are included on your map.
3. Construct a chart, similar to Fig. 30–2, to compare large-scale and small-scale maps.

Fig. 30–2

	Large-scale Maps	Small-scale Maps
Definition Typical Scales Used for		

TYPES OF MAPS

Geographers and cartographers make many types of maps. Some examples are political maps, navigational maps (or charts), topographic maps, vegetation maps, and weather maps. Since there are too many maps to study all at once, we will examine only a few. We can classify these under three broad headings: general-purpose maps, thematic maps, and topographic maps.

GENERAL-PURPOSE MAPS

General-purpose maps provide many types of information on one map. Atlas maps and road maps usually fall into this category. Some of the things that might be shown on general-purpose maps are:

- water bodies
- roads
- railway lines
- parks
- elevations
- towns and cities

superimposed: one item is placed over another so that they combine to create a new pattern

When all these features are superimposed, a general-purpose map is created. These maps give a broad understanding of the location and features of an area. The reader can gain an understanding about the type of landscape, the location of urban places, and the location of major transportation routes all at once.

THEMATIC MAPS

If you require very specific information about a place, **thematic maps** are useful. These maps are designed to show information about one particular topic. Because only one type of information

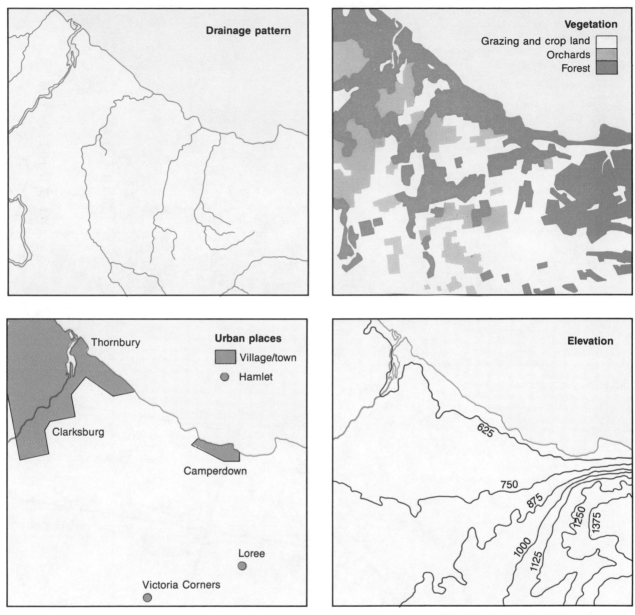

Fig. 30-3 Each of these thematic maps illustrates a different characteristic of the area shown in Fig. 30-4.

is presented, all the information can be clearly displayed. There is nothing extra on the map to hide this information. Study the examples in Fig. 30-3.

TOPOGRAPHIC MAPS

If you want to examine the characteristics of a small area of the earth's surface in detail, **topographic maps** are useful (Fig. 30-4).

Fig. 30–4 A topographic map of the Thornbury area on Georgian Bay in Ontario (scale 1:50 000). This is the same area as Fig. 30–3. NOTE: schools are shown as 🏫.

Topographic maps show:

a) physical features such as marshes, rivers, lakes, and wooded areas

b) human features such as political boundaries, highways, railways, bridges, and schools

c) direction and location: There are two ways in which topographic maps convey direction and location.
   i. latitude and longitude: Parallels of latitude and meridians of longitude are included on topographic maps to pinpoint location and to convey direction.
   ii. map grid: A series of blue vertical and horizontal lines is drawn on topographic maps to form a grid. This grid can be used to locate any feature on the map.

d) elevation: Elevation is the height of land above sea-level. It is shown in four ways on a topographic map (Fig. 30–5). Of these, contour lines are the most important.

Elevations on topographic maps are being converted from feet to metres. This conversion will take many years because there is a large number of maps to be changed.

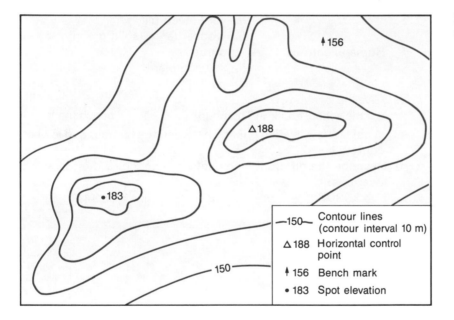

Fig. 30–5 Four ways of showing elevation on a map

Legend:
- —150— Contour lines (contour interval 10 m)
- △ 188 Horizontal control point
- ↟ 156 Bench mark
- • 183 Spot elevation

QUESTIONS

1. **a)** What are general-purpose maps used for?
   b) What features are found on general-purpose maps?
   c) Examine a road map. Which of the features from part b) are shown on the road map?
   d) Describe how five of the features are shown on the road map.

2. a) What is the purpose of thematic maps?
   b) Why are thematic maps useful?
   c) Find five examples of thematic maps in this book. Give the page reference and the theme of each map.
3. a) What are topographic maps used for?
   b) Describe the methods used for showing elevation on topographic maps.
   c) Describe the methods used for showing direction and location on topographic maps.

Information in Chapters 31 and 32 will help you to answer this question.

4. Refer to Fig. 30–4.
   a) i. What is the scale of the map?
      ii. What is the straight-line distance, in km, between the school in Loree and the main intersection in Clarksburg?
     iii. What is the shortest distance, in km, by road between the school in Loree and the main intersection in Clarksburg?
   b) In which direction does Indian Brook flow? How did you determine this?

Map grids are examined in detail in Chapter 31.

   c) Using grid co-ordinates locate an example of the following features:

   Physical Features   i. swamp
                       ii. very steep hill
                      iii. wooded area (solid green)
   Human Features   i. dump
                       ii. sewage plant
                      iii. park

   d) Give the location of:
      i. the school house in Thornbury   ii. a bench mark
   e) What is the elevation change between the highest and lowest contour lines?
   f) Describe the different land use(s) near each of the following locations:
      i. 493308   ii. 437282   iii. 433342

Locating Places on a Map

Imagine that you and your family have just driven into Calgary on the TransCanada Highway. Your parents have forgotten the route to your Uncle Fred's house so they have asked you to direct them using a street map of the city. You know where you are now (point A on Fig. 31-1) and where you want to go to (Uncle Fred's house is at point B on the map). Describe your present location and where you are trying to go. How will you get to your destination?

Finding a place on a street map of Calgary is easy because the roads are laid out in a grid, and because of the logical way that the streets and avenues are named. Locating places on most maps is equally simple. All you need to do is understand the system used on a particular map.

Key Terms

latitude
military grid

longitude
ranges

bearings

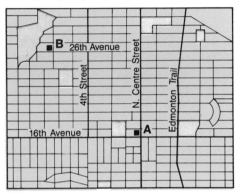

Fig. 31-1 Much of Calgary's road pattern follows a grid. The streets and avenues are measured from a central intersection in four directions (NW, NE, SW, SE).

■ GRID SYSTEMS

The most common way used to locate places on a map is with some form of grid system. Grids can be used on a global scale or on a more local scale. In this chapter we will look at three different grid systems.

LATITUDE AND LONGITUDE

If you use **latitude** and **longitude**, the geographic "centre of the world" is in the Gulf of Guinea off the coast of West Africa. Check in your atlas and you will see that this is 0° latitude and 0° longitude. From here a gridwork of lines extends north/south and east/west. Using this grid, you can determine the location of any place in the world as the intersection of a line of latitude and a line of longitude. Latitude and longitude are measured as angles, with the centre of each angle at the centre of the globe (Fig. 31-2). Latitude is measured north and south from the equator; longitude is measured east and west from the prime meridian.

Because of the curvature of the earth, latitude and longitude lines do not form a rectangular grid. Lines of longitude come together as you move toward the poles.

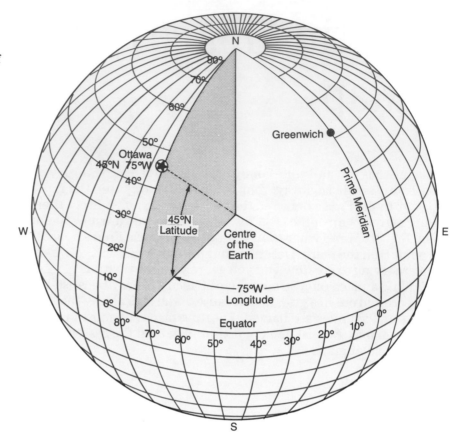

Fig. 31–2 Latitude and longitude are much easier to understand if we can picture each as an angle measured from the centre of the earth.

Q U E S T I O N S

1. From your atlas, determine the following:
   a) the name of the place at
      i. 49°N 123°W   ii. 35°S 139°E
      iii. 62°N 130°E   iv. 25°S 130°W
   b) the location of
      i. Cairo, Egypt   ii. Yellowknife, N.W.T.
      iii. Rangoon, Burma   iv. Nairobi, Kenya

GRIDS ON ROAD MAPS

Grids are used to locate places on many road maps. On most maps, grid squares are identified by a number along one side of the map and a letter along another side of the map. Fig. 31–3 demonstrates this for a portion of southwestern Ontario. The city of Windsor is in square N17 while Port Alma is in O18.

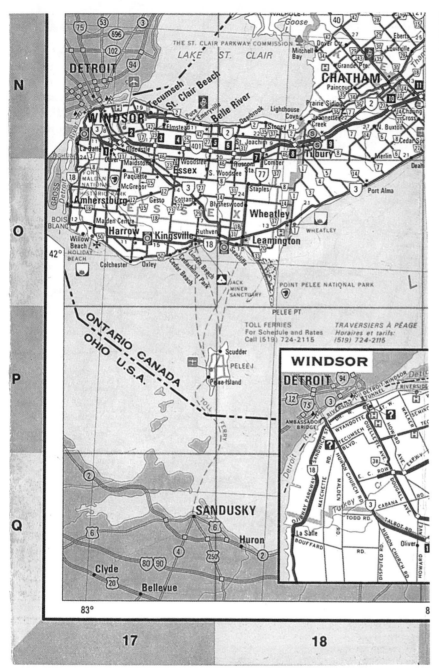

Fig. 31–3 Most Canadians are familiar with the use of grids to locate places on a road map.

1. **a)** Name the only village in Canada that is in P17.
   b) In which square is Chatham?

MILITARY GRID

You may have noticed a grid of blue lines on topographic maps. Each of these lines is identified by a two-digit number also printed in blue. Fig. 31–4 shows a typical example. Any point on the map can be located using a six-digit number. For example, point A on the map is at 825205. The first three digits indicate that A is located approximately 5/10 of the way from line 82 to line 83 – that is at 82.5. The last three digits indicate that A is about 5/10 of the way from line 20 to line 21 – that is at 20.5. Combine the two without the decimal points and you have the **military grid** reference for the place.

You can figure out which numbers go first if you remember the expression "Read **Right Up**". This means that you first read to the **right** of a vertical line and then **up** from a horizontal line.

Fig. 31–4 Military grid

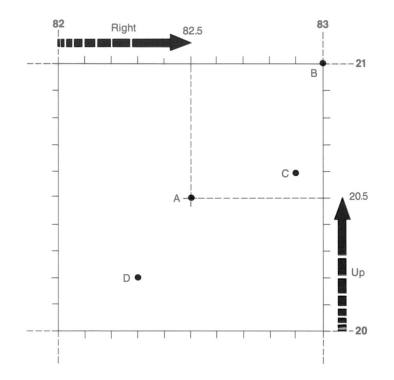

Q U E S T I O N S

1. What are the military grid references of points B, C, and D?

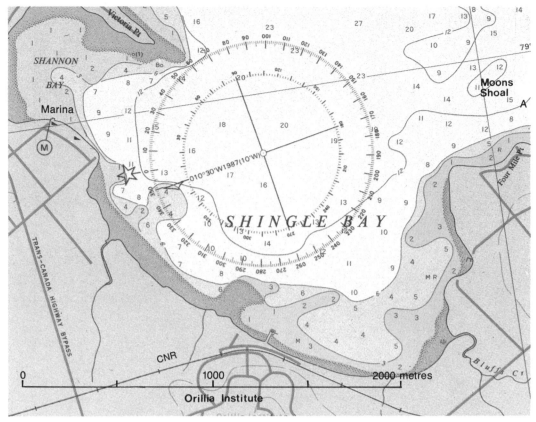

Fig. 31–5 A sample of a navigational chart

BEARINGS AND RANGES SYSTEM

Not all systems for locating places use grids. The system of **bearings** and **ranges** identifies a location by the use of an angle and a distance from a known location. Usually the angle is a compass bearing. For example, in Fig. 31–5 the location of the tip of Victoria Point from the dock at the Orillia Institute is 1975 m on a bearing of 082° True. The location of the marina in Shannon Bay is 3050 m on a bearing of 012° True from Four Mile Point.

Bearings and ranges are used for navigation by sailors, pilots and surveyors.

All of these bearings are compared to the North Pole (True North) rather than to the north shown by a compass (Magnetic North). On the compass rose in Fig. 31–5 True North is shown on the outer ring and Magnetic North on the inner ring. What is the difference in this part of Canada? Why does it exist?

QUESTIONS

1. **a)** What is the location of Moons Shoal (point A on map) from the mouth of Bluffs Creek?
   b) What is the location of the mouth of Bluff's Creek from Moons Shoal?
   c) What relationship do you see between the two?
2. What place is 2300 m on a bearing of 290° True from the tip of Victoria Point?

32 Scale Representation

In Chapter 30, you saw that a map must have a scale. The **scale** shows the relationship between distance on a map and the actual distance on the earth. Scale can be represented in three different ways: verbal, linear, and representative fraction.

Key Terms

scale   verbal scale   representative fraction
linear scale

■ VERBAL SCALE

A **verbal scale** gives the relationship between a distance on the map and a specific distance on the earth's surface. For example, 1 cm to 10 km. If you measure the distance between two places on a map and the distance is 1 cm, you would know that the actual distance between them is 10 km.

On the map in Fig. 32–1, the distance between "Here" and "There" is measured and found to be 3 cm. If the scale is 1 cm to 10 km then the distance on the earth's surface is found as follows:

$$\frac{1}{10} = \frac{3}{d}$$

$$d = \frac{3 \times 10}{1}$$

$$d = 30 \text{ km}$$

Therefore, the 3 cm distance on the map represents 30 km on the earth's surface.

An alternative method of solving this problem is as follows:

$$1 \text{ cm} = 10 \text{ km}$$
$$(3 \times 1) \text{ cm} = (3 \times 10) \text{ km}$$
$$3 \text{ cm} = 30 \text{ km}$$

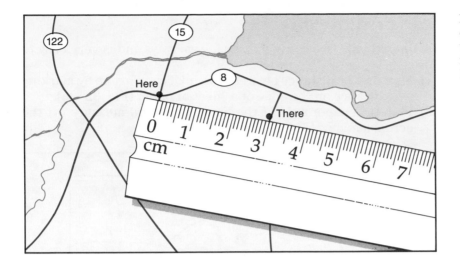

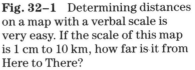

Fig. 32–1 Determining distances on a map with a verbal scale is very easy. If the scale of this map is 1 cm to 10 km, how far is it from Here to There?

QUESTIONS

1. What does 1 cm to 0.5 km mean?
2. Examine three different maps. You might choose from an atlas map, wall map, provincial road map, city street map, or topographic map. Write down the verbal scales of each.
3. Calculate the actual distance (on the earth's surface) between "Fee" and "Fie" and between "Fo" and "Fum" in Fig. 32–2.

Not every map provides a verbal scale

Fig. 32–2 If the scale of this map is 1 cm to 12 km, how far is it from Fee to Fie and from Fo to Fum?

4. Here is a list of distances between Canadian cities:
   a) Calgary to Edmonton   299 km
   b) Fredericton to Montréal   834 km
   c) Regina to Winnipeg   571 km
   Draw straight lines to show how each distance would appear on a map. Use a scale of 1 cm to 100 km.

■LINEAR SCALE

A **linear scale** is shown on maps in two ways and is very easy to use:

a) Measure the distance between two places on a map by marking this distance on the edge of a sheet of paper (Fig. 32–3a).

b) Place the paper against the linear scale and measure off the actual distance (Fig. 32–3b).

Fig. 32–3 Using a linear scale requires only a little practice. Follow the steps outlined here.

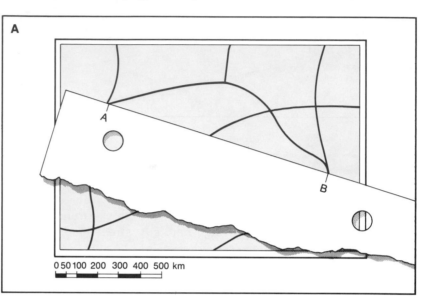

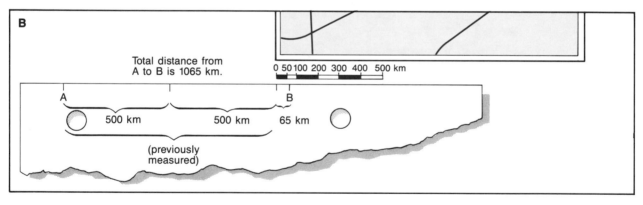

QUESTIONS

1. In an atlas, find a map of the provinces or part of the province where you live. Make sure the map has a linear scale.

   a) Measure the distance between two places.

   b) Using the linear scale, calculate the actual distance between these places.

   c) Do the same for two other pairs of cities or towns.

REPRESENTATIVE FRACTION (R.F.) SCALE

Another method for showing scale is the **representative fraction.** This fraction is a ratio and is shown in the following manner: 1:50 000. This means that 1 unit on the map represents 50 000 of the *same* units on the earth's surface. The units may be in any measure, such as millimetres, centimetres, and metres.

If the R.F. is 1:50 000, then 1 *cm* on the map represents 50 000 *cm* on the earth's surface. But usually we want to know the distance in kilometres. Therefore, we have to change the centimetres into kilometres. This is how it is done.

1. First remember that there are 100 000 cm in 1 km (100 cm = 1m; 1000 m = 1km).

2. Divide the second number in the R.F. by 100 000. This will give you the value in kilometres. In our example: 50 000/100 000 = 0.5. Therefore 1 cm on the map represents 0.5 km on the earth's surface.

   Let's take another example. The scale is given as 1:250 000. Divide 250 000 by 100 000. Therefore 1 cm on the map represents 2.5 km on the earth's surface.

RFs are easy once you remember the "magic number" of 100 000

QUESTIONS

1. In your own words, what is an R.F. scale?
2. In a scale of 1:8 000 000, how many km on the earth's surface are represented by 1 cm on the map?
3. Convert the following representative fractions to verbal scales.
   a) 1:125 000
   b) 1:25 000
   c) 1:500 000

When constructing a map, use whichever scale is best suited to the purpose of the map. Make sure that there is a scale on all your maps, regardless of which one you select.

33 Using Bar, Line, and Circle Graphs

Information is often best shown with visual aids like graphs. Bar, line, circle, and other kinds of graphs are frequently seen in textbooks, magazines and newspapers. Graphs like these present complicated numerical data in a simple, easily understood way. They also allow for the quick comparison of data. In this chapter you will learn how to construct some common types of graphs.

Key Terms

bar graph	line graph	proportional circle graph
circle graph		multiple line graph

■ BAR GRAPHS

Bar graphs are the simplest graphs to make. Bar graphs can be either vertical or horizontal. In the example that follows we will construct a bar graph with vertical bars. In a graph like this, the vertical axis of the graph usually represents the values to be shown. The horizontal axis usually represents the categories to be shown (e.g. different cities, kinds of cars, or years).

Now that you know the basic parts of a bar graph, let's go through the steps necessary to make one to show the information in Fig. 33–1.

Fig. 33–1 Infant mortality in Canada 1935–85

Year	Infant deaths per 1000 births
1935	72.5
1945	52.5
1955	31.3
1965	23.6
1975	14.3
1985	7.9

1. Choose the vertical scale first. What is the largest value to be shown? This helps us to determine the length of the vertical scale. If we were to use a scale of 1 cm to each 10 deaths/1000 births then the length of the vertical axis would be just over 7 cm long. On the other hand, if we were to use a scale of 1 cm to each 5 deaths/1000 births, the vertical axis would be just over 14 cm long. Choose a scale which makes the graph large enough to show the information well.

2. Now draw the vertical axis and label the scale on it. Be sure to indicate the units that you are using and give the axis a title.

3. Since information for six years is provided, we must draw six bars of equal width along the horizontal axis. You might choose to shade in each bar. Be sure to label the horizontal axis fully.

4. Be sure to give your graph an appropriate title and then you are finished (Fig. 33–2).

Infant mortality is a measure of the number of babies who die before reaching their first birthday.

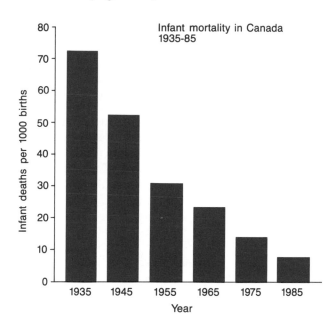

Fig. 33–2 This bar graph shows the information in Fig. 33–1

Assignment

Draw a bar graph to show the information given in Fig. 33–3.

Fig. 33–3

Bank Name	Number of Branches (1986)
Bank of Montreal	1192
Bank of Nova Scotia	1016
Canadian Imperial Bank of Commerce	1514
National Bank of Canada	564
Royal Bank of Canada	1450
Toronto-Dominion Bank	958

■ LINE GRAPHS

Line graphs are used most often to show how some value changes over time. The horizontal axis of a line graph usually represents time while the vertical axis represents the value to be shown. Suppose you want to show the number of national parks in Canada since 1876 (Fig. 33–4).

Fig. 33–4

Year	Number of parks
1876	0
1886	3
1896	4
1906	4
1916	8
1926	11
1936	15
1946	16
1956	17
1966	18
1976	28
1986	32

1. Choose the vertical scale in the same way that you did for a bar graph. Remember that the scale should produce a vertical axis that is of reasonable length. If you choose a scale of 1 cm for each park, how long would this make the vertical axis? Would this be a good size for a graph? When you have settled on a vertical scale, draw and label the vertical scale as before (Fig. 33–5).

Fig. 33–5 A line graph is an effective way to show the growth in the number of national parks in Canada.

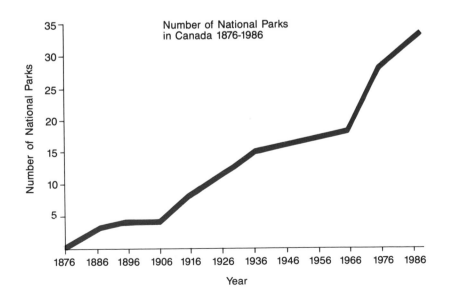

2. In the same way, choose a suitable scale for the horizontal axis. Your goal is to make the axis an appropriate length for the graph you are going to draw. In this case, which would be better: 1 cm for each year or 1 cm for each five years? Draw and label your horizontal axis.

3. Locate "data points" on your graph. For each year given, mark a dot at the appropriate value. Join the data points with a continuous line. Remember to give your graph a title and you are finished.

Assignment

If you want to compare several pieces of related information over time, a **multiple-line graph** can be useful. This means that more than one line is shown on the same set of axes. Draw a multiple-line graph to illustrate the information shown in Fig. 33–6.

Fig. 33–6 The populations in three Canadian cities in different years.

	1961	1971	1976	1981	1986
Montréal	2 216 000	2 743 000	2 802 000	2 862 000	2 921 000
Toronto	1 919 000	2 628 000	2 803 000	3 130 000	3 427 000
Vancouver	827 000	1 082 000	1 166 000	1 268 000	1 381 000

◼ CIRCLE GRAPHS

Circle graphs are used to show parts of a whole. They are frequently used to show information that is in percentage form, like that in Fig. 33–7. It is not difficult to construct circle graphs if you remember a few facts about angles and degrees.

Fig. 33–7

Province	Value of Coal Production (% of Canada's Total)
Nova Scotia	10
New Brunswick	2
Saskatchewan	26
Alberta	6
British Columbia	56

1. Convert each percentage into the equivalent number of degrees. The total should add up to 360°. For example,

$$10\% = \frac{10}{100} \times 360°$$
$$= 36°$$

2. Use a compass to draw a circle of the size that you desire. Use a protractor to draw the number of degrees that represent each percentage (Fig. 33–8).

Fig. 33–8 You will need a protractor to measure the percentages for your graph.

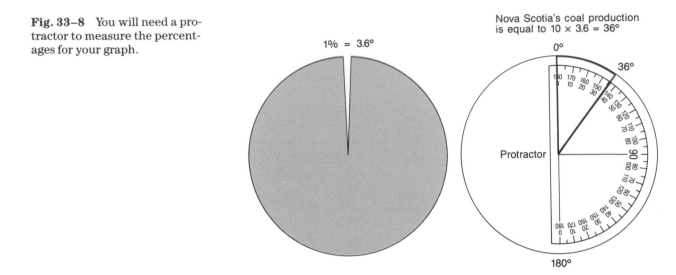

1% = 3.6°

Nova Scotia's coal production is equal to 10 × 3.6 = 36°

Protractor

3. Label your graph fully and give it a title (Fig. 33–9).

Fig. 33–9

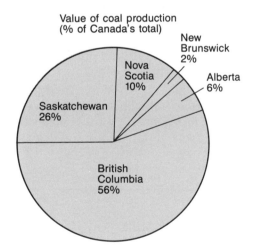

Value of coal production (% of Canada's total)

New Brunswick 2%

Nova Scotia 10%

Alberta 6%

Saskatchewan 26%

British Columbia 56%

Assignment

Draw a circle graph to show the information given in Fig. 33–10. Start by converting the numbers to percentages.

Fig. 33–10

Region	Full-time university enrollment (1985–6)
Atlantic Provinces	50 623
Québec	113 284
Ontario	185 016
Prairie Provinces	82 565
British Columbia	35 799

■ PROPORTIONAL CIRCLE GRAPH

Sometimes, graphs can be combined effectively with maps to show both the amount of something and its location. For example, if you want to compare the number of daily newspapers in each province, **proportional circle graphs** on a map of Canada could be used (Fig. 33–11). On a graph like this, a larger number of newspapers is shown by a larger circle. But how do you know what size each circle should be?

Fig. 33–11 Proportional circles can be used very effectively with a map of the areas being graphed.

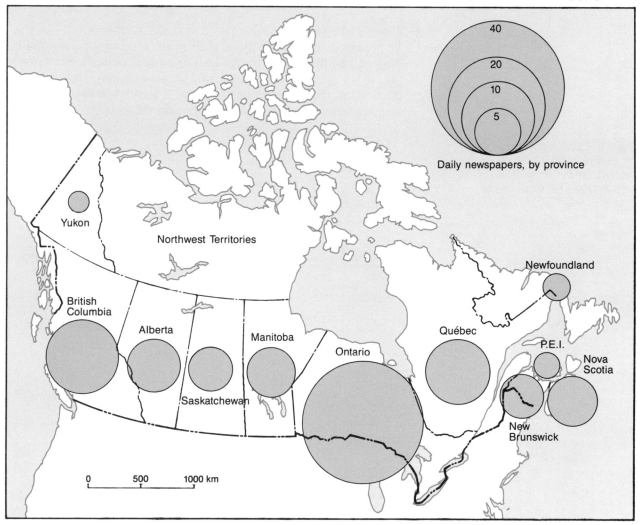

Proportional circles are drawn with their *areas* in proportion to the amount they represent. Let's work through an example to see how this is done. Suppose we want to draw proportional circles to represent the number of farms in Manitoba, Ontario, and Prince Edward Island.

1. Number of Farms:

Manitoba	Ontario	P.E.I.
29 400	81 700	3030

2. Since the area of a circle is equal to πr^2, the number of farms is in direct proportion to this:

for Manitoba   for Ontario   for P.E.I.
$\pi r^2 = 29\ 400$ $\pi r^2 = 81\ 700$ $\pi r^2 = 3030$

3. Since π is a factor of each of these equations, we can remove it and say that the number of farms is in proportion to the radius of the circle:

for Manitoba   for Ontario   for P.E.I.
$r^2 \propto 29\ 400$ $r^2 \propto 81\ 700$ $r^2 \propto 3030$
$r \propto 171$ $r \propto 286$ $r \propto 55$

$\propto$ stands for "varies directly with"

4. These radii values can be used to draw proportional circles. They may be used directly or, if they are too large or too small, they can be divided or multiplied by some factor. In our example, if we were to use these radii values in mm, the Ontario circle would be larger than this page. If we divide them each by ten, we would get circles of a more practical size (Fig. 33–12).

Fig. 33–12 Proportional circles are especially good for showing values that are very different, such as those for Ontario and Prince Edward Island. Why is this?

Number of farms

Manitoba
29 400

Ontario
81 700

P.E.I.
3030

5. Correctly title and label your graph. Be sure to indicate the scale used for your circles.

Assignment

Combine an outline map of Canada and proportional circles to show the information given in Fig. 33–13.

Fig. 33–13

Region	Number of Museums
Atlantic Provinces	86
Québec	70
Ontario	224
Prairie Provinces	192
British Columbia and Territories	114
TOTAL:	686

CHECKBACK

1. Look through *Canada: Land of Diversity* and find one example of each type of graph described in this chapter. Give the title of the graph and the page reference for each.

ANALYZE

2. What type of graph would be best for each of the following? Why did you pick this type of graph for this particular use? Make a sketch of what each graph would look like.

   a) The number of spectators at Toronto Blue Jays and Montréal Expos games in each year since each team was created.

   b) The amounts of money that the federal government spends for different purposes.

   c) The number of murders last year in each of Canada's ten largest cities.

   d) The number of doctors in each province.

34 Understanding Climate Graphs

If you had to describe the characteristics of the climate where you live, you would face two challenges. One would be to give an accurate description. The other would be to keep the description short and to the point. Fortunately, there is a simple way to describe the basic climate characteristics of temperature and precipitation. It is by the use of **climate graphs.**

Key Terms

total yearly precipitation   average yearly temperature
yearly temperature range   seasonal distribution of precipitation

Consider the case of Vancouver (Fig. 34–1). To make a climate graph from these statistics requires two steps:

1. Draw a line graph showing average monthly temperatures (Fig. 34–2). Note that the scale is written on the left vertical axis of the graph.

2. Draw a series of bar graphs representing average monthly precipitation. Put the precipitation scale on the right vertical axis (Fig. 34–3). A climate graph puts the bar graphs and the line graph together (Fig. 34–4).

    Now that you know how climate graphs are made, you can learn how to interpret them by studying Fig. 34–5 and answering the questions that follow.

Fig. 34–1 Climate statistics for Vancouver

	Jan	Feb	Mar	Apr	May	June	July	Aug	Sept	Oct	Nov	Dec	Year
Average Monthly Temperature (°C)	2	4	6	9	12	15	17	17	14	10	6	4	**9.8**
Average Monthly Precipitation (mm)	147	117	94	61	48	45	30	37	61	122	141	165	**1068**

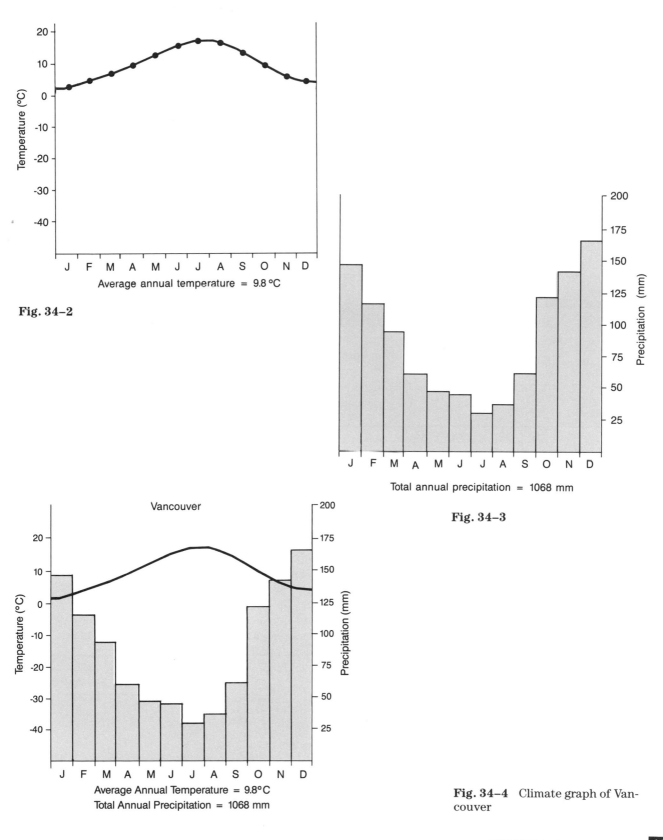

Fig. 34–2

Average annual temperature = 9.8 °C

Total annual precipitation = 1068 mm

Fig. 34–3

Vancouver

Average Annual Temperature = 9.8°C
Total Annual Precipitation = 1068 mm

Fig. 34–4 Climate graph of Vancouver

Climate Factor	How Determined	Importance
Average Annual Temperature	usually given below graph or the temperatures are added together and the total is divided by 12	indicates whether the place has a warm or cool climate
Annual Temperature Range	calculated by subtracting average temperature of coolest month from average temperature of warmest month	indicates whether the place has a continental climate (large temperature range) or a maritime climate (small range)
Total Annual Precipitation	usually given below graph or can be calculated by adding monthly precipitation amounts	indicates whether the place has a dry or a wet climate
Seasonal Distribution of Precipitation	determined by inspecting the graph. There are three major possibilities: a) even distribution of precipitation b) summer maximum of precipitation c) winter maximum of precipitation	indicates the climate influences at work and therefore different climate types

Fig. 34–5 A climate graph can tell you a lot about the climate of a place.

QUESTIONS

1. **a)** In your notebook, construct a climate graph for Calgary. Use the statistics given in Fig. 34–6.
   b) Calculate the average annual temperature and total annual precipitation. Write these figures below your climate graph.

	Jan	Feb	Mar	Apr	May	June	July	Aug	Sept	Oct	Nov	Dec
Average Monthly Temperature (°C)	-11	-7	-4	3	9	13	17	15	11	6	-3	-7
Average Monthly Precipitation (mm)	17	20	20	30	50	92	68	56	35	19	16	15

Fig. 34–6 Climate statistics for Calgary

2. Construct a chart similar to Fig. 34–7 to compare the climate characteristics of Calgary and Vancouver.
   a) Which city has the warmest annual temperature? Why?
   b) Which city has the largest annual temperature range? Why?
   c) Which city has the largest total annual precipitation? Why?
   d) In which season does each city receive most of its precipitation? Explain the conditions that account for this.

Fig. 34–7

	Calgary	Vancouver
Average Annual Temperature		
Annual Temperature Range		
Total Annual Precipitation		
Seasonal Distribution of Precipitation		

Use of Aerial Photographs

The first aerial photographs were taken in the 1850s from cameras attached to kites. Later that century, photographs were taken from hot air balloons. Although these early photographs were very crude, they did point out the potential usefulness of photographs taken from a great height. New techniques developed over the years improved the quality of aerial photographs tremendously. The result is that today, aerial photographs are an essential tool in the study of many aspects of geography.

Key Term

stereo pair

■ WHAT IS A STEREO PAIR?

Although a single aerial photo can be useful in the study of an area, the use of a **stereo pair** of photographs is even more helpful. These pictures are taken in rapid succession by a high-speed camera looking directly down at the ground. The camera is set so that the images overlap from photo to photo. Fig. 35–1 shows how this is done. As you can see, each photograph sees the same area from a slightly different position in the sky.

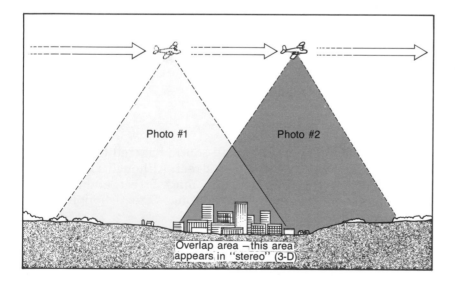

Photo #1

Photo #2

Overlap area —this area appears in "stereo" (3-D)

Fig. 35–1 A stereo pair works in a similar fashion to your eyes. In each case the same scene is seen from two slightly different angles.

When you position the photographs properly and view them through an instrument called a stereoscope, your brain sees an image in three dimensions. While the height of cliffs, trees, and buildings is exaggerated, this extra dimension allows you to see much more than is possible with a single photograph. Almost all of the exercises in this chapter can be done without a stereoscope, but many of them will be much easier if you use one.

■COMMERCIAL LAND USE

Fig. 35–2 shows part of downtown Toronto. What can we learn about Toronto from these photographs? The letters A to I on these photographs will allow you to locate items referred to in the following analysis.

The southern part of Toronto's central business district (CBD) is shown here. The CBD includes many of the most important commercial land uses found in the city; that is, the major office buildings and shopping areas.

OFFICE BUILDINGS

1. On a piece of tracing paper, trace the part of the CBD bordered by the tallest buildings.

2. Are these buildings concentrated in one area or spread out? Is this pattern surprising? Why or why not?

3. Canada's three tallest buildings are all found near the corner of King and Bay Streets (A). They are the First Canadian Place (Bank of Montreal) on the northwest corner, the Toronto Dominion Centre (TD Bank) on the southwest corner and Commerce Court (Canadian Imperial Bank of Commerce) on the southeast corner. Rank these buildings in terms of height. What colour might each be in real life? How do you know this?

4. The Toronto Stock Exchange is located in First Canadian Place. Because of this, what kinds of tenants might there be in the large office buildings nearby? How might the height of buildings be related to the type of business carried on and the wealth of these companies?

A fourth building, the Bank of Nova Scotia tower, was built after these photographs were taken.

SHOPPING

Yonge Street (B), which runs north-south, has traditionally been Toronto's most important shopping street. Although a lot of retail activity has moved further north on Yonge Street, and to suburban shopping malls, the downtown Yonge Street shopping area remains very important.

5. What height are most of the buildings along Yonge Street? Is this a surprise? Why or why not?

Fig. 35–2

6. Another form of shopping area can be found at C. This is the Eaton Centre, which consists of several hundred stores on several levels in an indoor mall. Give one advantage and one disadvantage of this type of development.

■ TRANSPORTATION LAND USE

Much of the transportation land use in this area is directly related to the commercial activities. Every weekday, hundreds of thousands of people must travel to the CBD to go to work. Most of them do so either by public transit or by car.

PUBLIC TRANSIT

1. a) The most important part of the downtown public transit system is the subway. The subway runs south on Yonge Street (B) and then loops westward to University Avenue (D) along Front Street (E). The Yonge and University subway lines join the rest of the Metropolitan Toronto subway system further north. Why was this particular route chosen? What effect has the existence of these subway lines had on the growth of Toronto?
   b) Show the subway route on your tracing.

2. The other part of the public transit system consists of a fleet of buses and streetcars. Can you suggest where three north-south and three east-west routes might be? Why do these streets not have subway lines on them? (Give two reasons.)

STREETS AND ROADS

Two types of roads are shown: expressways and city streets.

3. What is the purpose of expressways? In what directions do the expressways go from the downtown area?

4. What pattern is formed by the city streets? Is this pattern found where you live? How else can a city's streets be arranged?

PARKING LOTS

Since many thousands of cars enter the CBD each day, parking facilities are very important.

5. a) On your tracing, carefully locate and label all the parking lots you can see.

b) Describe the location of the parking lots in relation to the high density developments in the CBD. Why are the parking lots found in these locations?

c) How else can parking be provided other than by parking lots? Can you see this on the aerial photograph?

RAILWAYS

Both freight and passenger facilities are shown on the photograph.

6. Show the location of the passenger station (Union Station) on Front Street on your tracing. Why is this a convenient location?

7. The GO train, a commuter train, runs along the lakeshore tracks to Union Station. Show the GO train route on your tracing.

8. Where are the freight yards in relation to Union Station and the major buildings of the CBD? Why are they located away from the main part of the CBD? What is the purpose of these yards? What are the two "C-shaped" buildings at F? These freight yards are the location chosen for the Skydome domed stadium and much other redevelopment. Why is this a good location for a domed stadium to serve Metropolitan Toronto? What problems are there with this location?

HARBOUR TRANSPORTATION

9. a) How many freighters can you see in the harbour?

b) Look at the docks. What cargoes would be carried by these ships?

c) Add to your tracing a map of the area south of Front Street. Show the harbour facilities and the islands.

10. Ferry boats are used to move people and goods from the city to the recreational and residential areas on Toronto Island. Where are the ferry docks on the city side of the harbour? There are three different ferry docks on the islands. Where are they? Show these docks on your map.

AIRPORT

11. a) Show the location of the Toronto Island Airport on your map. How do people get to the airport?

b) This is not Toronto's main airport. Its runways are too short for large jets. What kinds of plane would use the island airport? State one advantage and one disadvantage of having an airport very near the downtown area.

■RECREATIONAL LAND USE

1. On your map, show the recreational land use in the downtown area. Include the following:
   a) island parkland
   b) city parks
   c) Canadian National Exhibition (G)
   d) Exhibition Stadium (H)
   e) Ontario Place (I)
   f) beaches (on Toronto Island)
   g) yacht clubs and marinas.

2. Be sure your map has a suitable title and legend.

■IN CLOSING...

In this exercise we have only begun to describe the uses of aerial photographs. As you continue your study of geography you will learn more and more uses for this valuable tool.

- Bonus Question
  This question will be a true test of your ability to interpret aerial photographs.

In what season, part of the week (weekday or weekend) and time of day were the photographs in Fig. 35–2 taken? Give evidence to support your answer.

Remote Sensing

36

When your grandparents were your age they could have seen the image in Fig. 36–1 only in their imaginations. It was taken by a satellite orbiting high above the border between Alberta and Montana. The 49th parallel, the border between Canada and the U.S., can be seen quite clearly because the land-use patterns are different in each country. In Canada, the land is used for grazing cattle, but south of the border grain crops are grown in rectangular fields. This exciting new geographic tool for studying the earth is called "remote sensing".

In this chapter we will examine the techniques used in remote sensing from satellites, the types of information gathered, and how this information is used.

Remote sensing using aerial photographs is discussed in Chapter 35.

Key Terms

Landsat	false colours	Radarsat

Fig. 36–1   In some places, the political boundary between Canada and the U.S. can be seen from space.

■ SATELLITE IMAGERY

Most aerial photographs are taken from airplanes at altitudes of 1000 m to 10 000 m. Photographs taken from these heights are useful for making detailed studies of relatively small areas. But they are not very useful for studying large areas. It is only since the 1960s that satellite technology has been available to study enormous areas of the earth. Each scene viewed by satellite measures 185 km by 185 km – an area of over 34 000 km².

Since the 1960s the U.S. has launched many weather and **Landsat** satellites. The Soviet Union and other countries, including Canada, have similar satellites. Even private companies are now building them.

Landsat: Land satellite

The Spot Image Corporation launched its first satellite, Spot 1, in 1986. This company is owned by governments and private companies in France, Sweden, and Belgium. The satellite is named Spot for: Systeme Probatoire d'Observation de la Terre.

■ COLLECTING AND SENDING INFORMATION

A Landsat satellite circles the earth in a near-polar orbit approximately every 103 minutes – 14 orbits per day (Fig. 36–2). Images are recorded from 81° N latitude to 81° S latitude. The orbits are set up so that the satellite appears over the same spot every 18 days.

The satellite moves across the earth at the same speed as the sun's apparent westward movement. This means that the satellite passes over each point at the same time on each pass and the information is collected under the same light conditions from season to season.

Landsat satellites orbit the earth at altitudes ranging from 700 to 920 km. They carry an electronic scanning system that collects more than a million items of information each second from the earth below. Since these scanners pick up reflected brightness and heat, the information is gathered only in daylight on noncloudy days.

Features as small as tennis courts are visible in the images. It is rumoured that top secret military satellites are able to pick out the print in a newspaper.

In the satellite, the information picked up by the scanners is converted into numbers. More than 30 million numbers are needed for each image. These numbers are transmitted to receiving stations located around the earth. They are fed into a computer and converted into black and white images (Fig. 36–2).

Colours are artificially added to the images to make the patterns more obvious. They are called **false colours** because they are not the colours a person would actually see from space. Although it takes years of experience to interpret such images fully, it is possible to gain some understanding by following this basic guide:

- shades of red indicate growing things (crops and other vegetation)
- shades of blue-green to grey indicate areas where there are few growing things, such as urban areas
- shades of blue to black indicate shallow and deep water

Be careful—both urban areas and areas with little vegetation appear a blue-green colour.

Fig. 36–2 A near polar orbit like this allows Landsat satellites to fly over the same location every 18 days. The transfer and processing of satellite data is a complex task involving many steps.

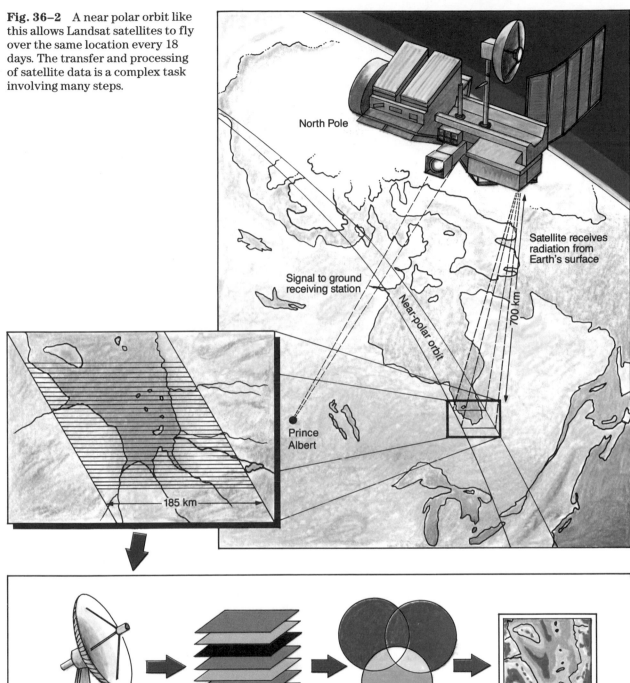

North Pole

Satellite receives radiation from Earth's surface

Signal to ground receiving station

Near-polar orbit

700 km

Prince Albert

185 km

1. Numerical data is sent from the satellite to a receiving station on Earth.

2. A computer converts the data into separate black and white images.

3. Filters or a computer add colour to make the image easier to interpret.

4. The final result is a false-colour image.

■ RECEIVING AND USING INFORMATION

Canada purchases the images from the Landsat and Spot satellites. The images that are received by the ground stations are sent to the Canadian Centre for Remote Sensing, in Ottawa, and the Ontario Centre for Remote Sensing, in Toronto.

The data from these satellites are received by ground stations around the world. Canada has three such stations: Shoe Cove, Nfld., Gatineau, Qué., and Prince Albert, Sask. Canada has been using satellite images since the early 1970s and has become a world leader in the field. Over the years, this experience has helped Canadian companies to design and build receiving stations and satellites for several countries around the world.

This early involvement by Canada with remote sensing is not surprising. Canada's vast size makes remote sensing less expensive than other methods of studying our resources. Remote sensing also provides a continuous record of changes on any parcel of land from which data are collected.

What can be done with this vast amount of remote sensing data? From a geographical point of view there is much that can be done. The information may be used:

- to study weather and climate
- for agricultural study and management
- for land-cover classification and forest management
- for map making and updating
- to study landforms, drainage patterns, and urban growth
- for mineral exploration
- to monitor surface mining and land reclamation
- to analyze water resources
- to study the impact of activities such as earthquakes and volcanic eruptions
- to study many types of pollution

■ THE FUTURE

Radarsat: Radar satellite

Canada's next major focus in remote sensing is the development of **Radarsat**. This satellite is being built at a cost of $635 000 000 for launch in 1994. Radarsat images will have several advantages over current Landsat images.

Radarsat images of the earth's surface can be made 24 hours a day under any weather conditions. They will provide information about such things as crop conditions, soil moisture, ice and snow depths, and ship movements through Canadian waters. This increase in knowledge about the earth's surface should help us use our resources more effectively.

QUESTIONS

CHECKBACK

1. Define the term "remote sensing".
2. **a)** Describe the characteristics of the orbit of Landsat satellites.
   b) Why are they set up in this manner?
3. Construct a chart or diagram to demonstrate the sequence of events necessary to produce an image from a satellite.
4. **a)** What are false colours?
   b) Explain what the false colours represent on a satellite image.
5. **a)** Why is Canada considered a world leader in remote sensing?
   b) Why is remote sensing technology important to a country like Canada?
6. How is remote sensing information used in the study of the earth?
7. Why will the images from Radarsat be an improvement over those from Landsat?

WHAT DO YOU THINK?

8. Satellite images provide information that may be used for many purposes. For example, industrial and political intelligence may be gathered from satellite images.
   a) Suppose a Canadian grain-marketing company purchases Landsat images that show the wheat-growing areas in other grain-producing countries. How might the company use this type of information?
   b) Food production in different countries can be predicted by studying the size of the agricultural regions; the impact of drought, disease, or pests; and the expected crop yield. How might an organization like the United Nations Food and Agricultural Organization use this information?

USING SATELLITE IMAGES

Now that we have seen how satellite images are made, let us examine some to see how they may be used:

- in the study of weather and climate
- for agricultural and forest management
- to study environmental pollution
- for map making

WEATHER AND CLIMATE

Most of us probably listen to or watch a weather report several times a week. These reports provide information on temperature, cloud cover, precipitation, winds, and storms. Forecasting weather accurately is a very difficult task because there are so many things to consider. The task, however, is becoming easier because satellites now provide images of the earth several times each day. Meteorologists interpret these images and can make accurate predictions about the weather. For example, they can determine the direction of a storm and warn people in its path a day or two in advance of its arrival (Fig. 36–3).

Information about weather conditions is useful to airplane pilots, farmers, forest firefighters, and ordinary people who want to know how they should dress before going outside.

QUESTIONS

1. A satellite spots a hurricane approaching the eastern seaboard of the U.S. and the Maritime provinces.
   a) How would the local weather stations receive this information?
   b) What damage could be avoided by early satellite warning?
   c) Why are satellite images more useful than local radar for observing such a storm?

Fig. 36–3 Satellite weather maps are the most familiar form of remote sensing for most people. Where is this hurricane located?

AGRICULTURE AND FOREST MANAGEMENT

The following information may be obtained from satellite images of farmland and forests:

Farmland

a) the types of farming in an area
b) the amount of land being farmed
c) the effect of drought or disease on crops
d) amount of production in a certain area

Forests

a) the types of trees
b) the effect of disease or insects on the forest
c) the area covered by each type of tree
d) amount and type of wood available for cutting
d) the location and size of areas being cut by forestry companies
e) the size and effect of forest fires

ENVIRONMENTAL POLLUTION

Damage to trees and crops from air and water pollution can be detected from satellite images. The false colours in Fig. 36–4 tell us the following about the forest:

- light red indicates hardwood trees and new growth
- dark red indicates coniferous trees
- blue-green indicates dying vegetation or very little vegetation

Fig. 36–4 What are the blue patches in this forested (red) area?

Q U E S T I O N S

1. What type of trees cover most of this area?
2. What evidence is there of dying trees?
3. Draw a diagram of the shape of the affected area.
4. Does there appear to be one or more than one source of the pollution that is affecting the trees?
5. What might be the source of this pollution?
6. If north is at the top of the photo, determine the prevailing wind direction in this area. Explain how you determined this.
7. How could you tell from satellite images taken over a period of time whether or not the industry causing the air pollution has taken measures to stop it?

MAP MAKING

Satellite images, like aerial photographs, may be used to draw maps. Here are two exercises that will show you how.

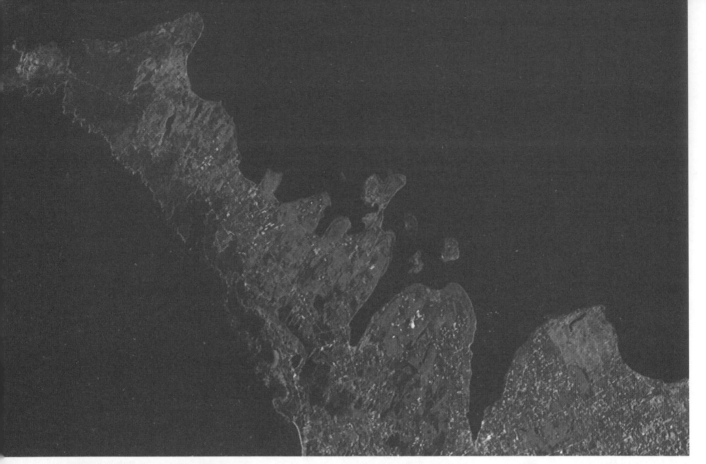

Fig.36–5 Bruce Peninsula of
Ontario

I From the satellite image of the Bruce Peninsula (Fig. 36–5)
draw a map as follows:

1. Place tracing paper over the satellite image and draw the
   shoreline.

2. The false colours in this image tell us the following:
   • bright red indicates farmland
   • light grey indicates broad-leaved trees
   • dark red indicates coniferous trees
   • dark blue indicates water
   Trace and shade in the areas that are mainly:
   • farmland
   • coniferous trees
   • water bodies

3. Label your map and provide a legend.

You have now drawn a map from a satellite image.

II Using the satellite image of Southern Ontario (Fig. 36–6) and
an atlas map of the same region, complete the following exercise.

1. Compare this satellite image to the map.
   a) What things can you see on both?
   b) What can only be seen on the atlas map?
   c) What can only be seen on the satellite image?

Fig.36–6 Southern Ontario: satellite images have both advantages and disadvantages compared to maps.

2. a) On a piece of tracing paper, trace the shoreline of all the lakes and rivers that you can see on the satellite image.
   b) Label the major lakes and rivers on your map.

3. a) Trace the boundary between the Canadian Shield and the Great Lakes lowland.
   b) How can you tell where this boundary is located?

4. Locate and label the following on your map:
   a) the boundary of the urban area centred around Toronto
   b) at least two other cities or towns
   c) the Holland Marsh

◼ IN CLOSING . . .

As you can see from these exercises, geographers have many uses for remote sensing using satellite images. Satellite images have a small scale showing a very large area. These images show the large patterns found on the land. Aerial photographs taken from an aircraft have a larger scale. Therefore they show more detail of a smaller area. By combining these two types of remote sensing, a great deal may be learned about an area without actually visiting it.

37

Evaluating an Issue: Being a Critical Reader

Fig. 37–1 Harp seal pup (white-coat)

Examine the animal in Fig. 37–1. Why would most people find it attractive? A number of studies have been done to determine what makes an animal attractive to people. These studies concluded that an attractive animal would have the following features: a rounded shape, a large head with big, dark eyes, short limbs, and light-coloured fur. These qualities are combined almost perfectly in harp seal pups. The hunting of these attractive animals led to an international controversy. As well, this dispute caused a fundamental change in the way of life of a small and unique group of Canadians.

One study was done by the Walt Disney Studios to help them redesign Mickey Mouse.

At first glance, the scene shown in Fig. 37–2 is shocking. A man with a large wooden club is about to kill a defenceless harp seal pup (called a whitecoat). Within seconds, the ice will be stained with blood as the whitecoat is skinned. Starting in the mid-1960s, photos and videotape of scenes like this appeared on television, in newspaper reports, and in advertisements by animal rights groups. Horrified viewers were told that this barbaric form of

barbaric: very cruel

Fig. 37–2 Photos like this were common during the battle over the seal hunt in the 1960s and 1970s.

hunting was being carried on in Canada. They were urged to support an end to this hunt. The whitecoat seal hunt has now ended and we are going to investigate what happened.

You might ask, "Why are we looking at a 'dead' issue; the seal hunt is over?" There are several reasons. Because this issue has been settled, it is easier to be objective about it than about a current issue that is still in dispute. In addition, the publication in 1986 of the report of the Malouf **Royal Commission** on Seals and Sealing provides us with a wealth of factual data. Finally, the sealing issue is typical of the kind of issue that Canadians face now and in the future. From it, you can learn how to be more critical of what you see and read and be better able to make your own judgements about important issues.

objective: fair, unbiased

Royal Commission: a body established by the government to make a detailed study of a problem or issue

Key Terms

endangered species   Royal Commission

■ BACKGROUND

Seal hunting occurs on all three of our coasts. In this chapter, however, we will examine only the hunt that occurred off the northeastern coast of Newfoundland and in the Gulf of St. Lawrence. Sealing has been practiced in these areas for as long as people have lived there. The hunt in Atlantic Canada occurred on the ice floes in the early spring. At this time of year, huge herds of harp seals migrate south to mate and have their young.

Since the seal hunt lasted for only a few weeks each year, it was not a full-time job. Fishermen traditionally took part in the hunt to provide income and food during a part of the year when fishing was not possible. Seals provided three main products. Most valuable of these was the fur, and in particular, the white fur of the harp seal pups. Most of the fur was shipped to Europe and used to make costly, high-fashion coats and boots. Seals also provided meat and oil.

Seal meat is considerably more nutritious than beef. Seal flippers are considered a delicacy.

■ THE DISPUTE

Controversy over the seal hunt erupted first in 1965 when an animal rights activist started a campaign to stop the hunt. The campaign used emotionally-laden photographs, like Fig. 37–2, along with statements such as the following:

1. "He goes to meet, in a curious, friendly, playful way, the first human being he has ever seen and is – by the same human – clubbed on the head and skinned on the spot, sometimes while he is still alive.

   "This sad, cruel episode is repeated over and over during the 'hunt' by hundreds of Canadian sealers who first kick away the mother and then drive home the message by bludgeoning the baby using a club, or the brutal, spike-tipped hakapik."

2. "I see the seal issue as representing a showdown for wildlife. These animals are symbolic, and if they can't be saved, it is probably not going to be possible to save any substantial population of wild creatures. The world will gradually fill with filth, and, one day empty of all but humans, this planet will become the loneliest place in the universe. Perhaps in saving the seals, humans may save themselves."

3. "It wasn't primarily a question of wildlife management or economics or . . . any of the other things that they tried to argue their way around. It fundamentally came down to a question of morality."

4. "The seal hunters are being exploited. If offered viable alternatives in the fast-expanding fishing or oil industry, they would certainly be the first to change their ways."

From these quotes it would seem to be a clear-cut situation. The seal hunt was a barbaric throwback to an earlier time. It primarily benefitted only those who owned companies in the industry and the wealthy people who used the products of this bloody business.

Opponents of the hunt were skilful in getting their message out. They went onto the ice and attempted to disrupt the hunt by scaring the seals away from the hunters or by spraypainting the whitecoats (Fig. 37–3). These campaigns were intensively covered by the world's press. People were encouraged not to buy seal products. Foreign governments were pressured to pass laws outlawing the import of Canadian seal products. The European Parliament received 3 000 000 letters from school children opposing the seal hunt.

Supporters of the seal hunt, including the Canadian government, fought back — but in vain. They presented studies that indicated that clubbing was a humane way to kill seals. They also showed how important the hunt was to the communities where the hunters came from. They showed that without the hunt, seal populations would grow and fish stocks would be reduced. But they could never overcome the mental picture that millions had of the whitecoats being clubbed and skinned.

hakapik: a club like a baseball bat with spikes in the end. If the hunter were to fall through the ice into the sea, the hakapik can also be used to help climb back onto the ice.

Spraypainting did not seriously affect the fur or harm the seals.

Fig. 37–3 Seal hunt protestors spray-painted seals so that their fur would be less attractive to hunters.

Demand for seal products dropped. Then the final blow came. The European Parliament banned the importing of Canadian seal skins. Canada's biggest market was lost. Even though the controversy had centred almost exclusively on the hunting of whitecoats, the demand for almost all seal products was gone. By 1982, the whitecoat sealing industry of Atlantic Canada was finished.

■ THE SEAL HUNT — A SECOND LOOK

As a result of the controversy, the federal government established a Royal Commission (chaired by Albert Malouf) to investigate seals and sealing in Canada. The Malouf Report concentrated on whether the killing of seals could be justified in three main respects.

1. Is the harp seal an **endangered species**?
   Some seal hunt opponents had stated that the hunt had made harp seals an endangered species. Malouf concluded that even with a kill of 130 000 whitecoats per year, the population of harp seals, numbered at about 2 000 000, was slowly on the rise.

2. Is there undue pain and suffering involved?
   This was perhaps the central issue. It was said that seal pups suffered greatly because of the methods used, and that mother seals suffered psychological damage watching their young die. Malouf concluded that the clubbing of seals was a very humane way to kill them. Scientists reporting to the Commission indicated that neither the pup nor mother felt any pain, and that the amount of cruelty involved was less than that found in sport hunting or in the killing of domestic animals such as cows and pigs. The Commission did suggest that the catching of seals by netting or by intentional wounding in the open ocean were in fact cruel, as the seals die slowly and in great pain.

*

*

*

*

These methods were not the subject of strong protests and continue on a limited basis today.

3. How important is the use of seal products?

*

*
*

If one is trying to decide whether the killing of an animal is justified, the importance of the end use must be considered. If a human life could only be saved by killing a seal pup, most people would support it. If the only purpose of killing is to provide furs to satisfy someone's vanity, most people would oppose it.

The Commission did not consider the question of whether the killing of any animal to meet human needs is justified. It considered this to be a question that each person must answer for themselves.

The Royal Commission concluded that much more was at stake than fashion. While the contribution of sealing to Canada's economy was very tiny, its importance in isolated parts of Newfoundland and Québec was great (Fig. 37–4). It typically provided 20 - 30 % of the annual income for those who hunted seals. In addition, the money came when it was most needed – at the end of the long winter when the sealers needed money to prepare their boats and gear for the coming fishing season. For the people of the sealing communities, there are no obvious alternative sources of income. At best, the former sealers would have to rely even more heavily on Unemployment Insurance. At worst, whole communities could be destroyed.

Seal hunting contributed more than money to the economy of this region. For many, sealing provided a source of high quality food. Furthermore, much of the community's social and cultural life centred on sealing.

Fishermen have always been concerned about the effects of growing seal populations on stocks of commercially important fish. Seals interfere with fishing in four ways. Obviously, they compete directly with fishermen for fish. Less obviously, they take fish from nets, at times taking one bite from each fish in the net. When they do this they may also damage the nets. Finally, seals harbor a parasite called the cod or seal worm. At one stage of its life, this parasite lives in the seal. It can be later transferred to cod, causing the fish to grow slowly and to be of poor quality.

Fig. 37–4 The seal hunt was an important part of the economy of small outport villages like this.

In total, the Malouf Commission concluded that sealing should continue in Canada and that there should be government efforts to help recapture lost markets. The Commission suggested that it may be necessary to encourage the hunting of seals so that seal populations do not get so large that fish populations are at risk. Malouf concluded, however, that the hunting of whitecoats should not be allowed. This decision was made not because this hunt was immoral or cruel, but because of the huge public outcry against it.

■ IN CLOSING . . .

Perhaps what the sealing issue teaches us is that we must be careful to balance emotional arguments with factual ones. When you consider the national and international issues that are important today, how can you be sure that you are making intelligent decisions? Here are some ideas.

When you read an article, see a film or video, or hear someone speak, consider the following:

- Who is giving the presentation? Are they on one side of the issue or are they neutral? Where did they get their information?
- What is the purpose of what they are doing? Are they trying to win your support or are they trying to provide information without "taking sides"?
- What is their approach? Is it logical and well-reasoned or is it based on emotion? Are arguments supported by facts?
- Is the presentation balanced? Are arguments on both sides of the issue examined equally critically?

When you are considering an issue, you are like the judge in a courtroom. You must examine the case that each side makes and then decide who wins; that is, which side gets your support. If you cannot tell which side has the better case, then you must search out enough facts to allow you to make your decision. In a free society like Canada's, everybody can get involved in the discussion of important issues. Your involvement and your decisions matter!

QUESTIONS

ANALYZE

1. On p.476, four quotes from sealing opponents are given. On p.477, some of the findings of the Malouf Commission are summarized. Relate each quote (or parts of them) to the Commission findings. What contradictions do you find? If these contradictions had been known earlier, might the results of the sealing debate have been different?

Hint: consider the three criteria for killing that were used by the Malouf Commission.

synonym: a word having the same meaning as another word

2. Why was the campaign by seal hunt supporters likely to fail right from the beginning?

3. a) The English language has many words that mean almost the same thing, but carry different emotional weight. In this chapter, the word "kill" has been used on several pages (look for a "*" in the margin). In each case, try substituting the words "harvest" and "slaughter", in turn, for "kill". How do these changes affect the impact of the text?

   b) In the sealing dispute, which side might have used each term?

   c) Try to think of other synonyms for "kill" and indicate how each could be used.

INVESTIGATE

4. With your teacher's help, choose a current controversial issue. Collect articles in support of all sides in the issue. Analyze these articles using the guidelines given on p. 479. What signs of bias did you find and how did you discover them?

WHAT DO YOU THINK?

5. a) If seal pups looked like rats, would the hunt have become a major international issue?

   b) Should the appearance of the animal involved affect the decision of how to treat it? Does it?

6. a) Do any of the activities of your life require the killing of animals? If yes, which ones?

   b) If your answer to a) was "yes", does this bother you? Explain your answer.

   c) On balance, remembering your answer to a), was the case against sealing sufficiently strong to cause the hunting to be ended? Why or why not?

Researching and Writing a Geographic Essay

38

The fateful day has arrived. At the beginning of the course your geography teacher announced that you would be expected to write an essay, and today it was assigned (Fig. 38–1). How do you make this experience a positive one in which you can take great pride? You must learn the skills of research and writing. In this respect, writing an essay is like doing algebra questions or shooting foul shots on the basketball court – a bit of background knowledge and a lot of practice will do the trick. This chapter will help with the background knowledge. The practice is up to you.

Genius was once defined as 5% inspiration and 95% perspiration!

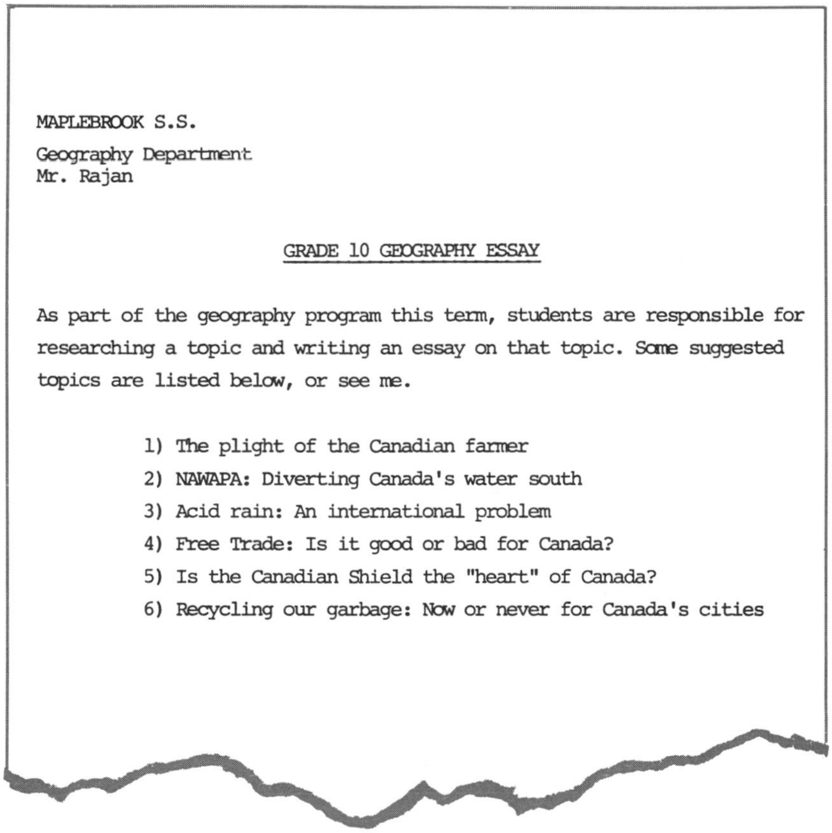

```
MAPLEBROOK S.S.
Geography Department
Mr. Rajan


                    GRADE 10 GEOGRAPHY ESSAY


As part of the geography program this term, students are responsible for
researching a topic and writing an essay on that topic. Some suggested
topics are listed below, or see me.


        1) The plight of the Canadian farmer
        2) NAWAPA: Diverting Canada's water south
        3) Acid rain: An international problem
        4) Free Trade: Is it good or bad for Canada?
        5) Is the Canadian Shield the "heart" of Canada?
        6) Recycling our garbage: Now or never for Canada's cities
```

Fig. 38–1 Writing essays is an important and useful learning skill. Like most other skills, it improves with practice.

Key Terms

thesis   bibliography

■IN THE BEGINNING

Before we start there are two important things to remember:

1. Your teacher is there to help you. At a number of points you should have your teacher check on your progress to date. These points are identified in marginal notes below.

2. Writing an excellent essay takes organization and *time*. Use your time wisely and start early. If your essay is due tomorrow, don't read this chapter tonight and expect that it will help you very much.

■RESEARCHING YOUR ESSAY

SELECT YOUR TOPIC

Confirm with your teacher that your topic is suitable.

A different term may be used in your school but the meaning will be the same.

Your teacher may supply a list of topics or you may wish to choose your own. It is important to pick something that interests you. Your topic may be something like "The Oil Industry in Atlantic Canada". This topic is so broad and general that you could never hope to do an excellent job on it. Instead, you should focus on only one important issue or idea within your essay. This is called your **thesis**. The purpose of your preliminary research is to give you the information necessary to choose a strong thesis.

A thesis is a clearly defined statement that the essay proves or supports. Having a clearly-stated and supported thesis is probably the single most important factor in writing a good essay. The thesis you choose should lend itself to analysis and not merely to description. For example, "How important will the oil industry become in Atlantic Canada?" From this question, you can state your thesis. Two possibilities would be: "The oil industry may bring great wealth to Atlantic Canada," and "The potential of the oil industry in Atlantic Canada has been greatly overestimated." You may find it helpful to get the reactions of a classmate to your thesis.

Your essay should concentrate on proving your thesis. Facts or ideas which are not related to the topic should be avoided. For example, you would not include information on how oil is formed or how an offshore oil rig works unless you could relate these to your thesis.

PRELIMINARY RESEARCH

The experience of doing research in even a small library can be both exciting and a little frightening. There is a lot of information available, but it may be difficult to find exactly what you want. Fortunately, there are easy-to-use methods for finding what you want from all that is available.

Card Catalogue

The card catalogue allows you to find books and other materials that have been indexed by subject, author, or title. Many libraries are converting from the use of cards to the use of either microfiche or computer terminals. These newer systems work in a way very similar to the traditional card catalogue system. No matter what system is used in your library, you might start your research by looking under "Atlantic Provinces" and "petroleum".

Vertical Files

Many libraries have a vertical file of clippings and brochures which are arranged by topic. The vertical files may be very helpful to you because they usually contain up-to-date materials.

FURTHER RESEARCH

Once you have decided on your thesis, you are in a position to research the specific information you need to prove it. In addition to the card catalogue and the vertical files, you may also consult the more advanced research tools described below.

Magazine and Newspaper Indexes

Much of the information useful for a geographic essay appears in magazines and newspapers. You can find the locations of helpful articles by using an index. An index is a listing of all of the articles that have been printed in one, or as many as 300, magazines and newspapers. Indexes are arranged by subject, and are published monthly or yearly. Some of the more helpful ones for geographic research are:

Canadian Periodical Index – lists about 300 Canadian popular and academic magazines

Canadian Magazine Index – lists about 200 Canadian and 15 American popular magazines

Canadian News Index – lists seven major newspapers from Halifax to Vancouver

Readers Guide to Periodical Literature – lists many magazines, mainly American.

Be sure to keep full references for all the materials that you use. You will need this information to do footnotes and a bibliography.

In addition to these general indexes, there are those published by individual magazines and specialized ones in areas such as business, economics, and social science.

To use an index, look up headings that are of interest. For example, if you look in the *Canadian Periodical Index* under "Oil and gas", it will tell you to see "Petroleum". Here you will see many entries arranged under numerous subheadings – including potentially useful ones like "Offshore Development" and "Atlantic Canada". With a little practice you can become very efficient at using indexes.

The next step is finding the magazines and newspapers that contain the articles you want. Most libraries have lists of the periodicals to which they subscribe. Articles in widely distributed periodicals such as *Maclean's* or *National Geographic* will be easier to obtain than those in more regional publications such as the *Hamilton Spectator*. If an article in a less easily available publication seems important enough, you may be able to get it on an inter-library loan or by visiting a larger library.

Curiously, if you look in the *Canadian Magazine Index* under "Petroleum", you will be directed to "Oil and Gas".

Computerized Data Bases

Some libraries now have access to computer data bases which have immense amounts of information in them. A good example is InfoGlobe. With it you can find and obtain any article printed in the *Globe and Mail* since the late 1970s. You find an article by searching, using either key terms (like those in an index) or a certain word (or words). The computer will find all articles containing the key term or word(s). Inefficient searches can be both expensive and time-consuming. Check with your librarian to be sure you know the most efficient method of using the computer to find information.

In 1987, the special educational price for InfoGlobe was $1/min.

■ WRITING YOUR ESSAY

By now you should have completed most of your research. Your research notes should be in some sort of logical organization. If your research was productive, you should feel very confident about your ability to write an outstanding essay.

PLANNING YOUR ESSAY

Your essay should consist of three parts:
The Introduction
The Body
The Conclusion

Before you start writing, you should outline what you intend to do in each section. This outline should be in point form and fairly detailed. Creating a well-reasoned outline will make the actual writing of the essay much easier and, in the long run, save you a lot of time. Take enough time at this stage to do a good job.

When your outline is complete, show it to your teacher for comments.

The Introduction

The importance of this section far outweighs its brief length. Here you must set the tone of your essay and state its purpose. Give necessary background information on your topic and then focus on the important question that your thesis seeks to answer. Finally, state clearly what your thesis is and how you will examine it. By doing this, you prepare your reader for what is to follow.

The Body

This is by far the largest and most important part of your essay. Here you must present the arguments that support your thesis. They should be organized in a logical way to support your case. Several paragraphs are normal, each dealing clearly with a segment of your research. Be very careful not to wander away from your thesis.

The Conclusion

The conclusion is the last opportunity you will have to impress your reader. It is therefore important to think it out carefully. You do not want to merely restate the facts from the body of the text. Rather, you want to remind the reader of what it was that you set out to prove and to sum up the evidence that supports you thesis.

FIRST DRAFT

Now you are ready to start writing. Your previous work should make this step much easier. When you write your first draft you should follow your outline carefully. If you decide to deviate from it, be sure that the change is an improvement and does not damage the logical plan that you made.

deviate: stray from your original plan

If possible, do your first draft on a word processor (Fig. 39-2). It will make revisions much easier. It will also make your final copy more attractive and easier to read.

It is beyond the scope of this chapter to teach you how to write English prose. But here are a few do's and don't's:

DO
- use proper grammar and spelling
- keep your text direct and simple
- avoid personal bias. What you write must be supported by facts.
- refer to any illustrations used (maps, diagrams, graphs) in the written text. If they are not directly related to the text, they should not be there.

DON'T
- use complex vocabulary if simple alternatives exist
- write in first or second person (I, we, you)
- use expressions like "etc.", or clichés like "at this point in time".

Fig. 38–2 A word processor makes essay writing much easier.

Some word processors check spelling and even grammar and style for you.

When you complete your first draft you are ready for the editing and revision stage. Re-read your first draft several times to help find errors of all sorts. A useful procedure is to read it aloud either to yourself or to someone else. Have a parent or classmate read it over as well. If you used a word processor to produce your draft it will pay dividends now. You can make as many drafts as you feel necessary, making improvements at each stage.

FINAL DRAFT

To produce your final draft you must do two things. Be sure that you have incorporated all the corrections and improvements from your revisions, and add necessary essay elements such as a title page, footnotes/end notes, and **bibliography**. Your teacher will probably specify how these things should be done. If guidelines are not provided, ask your teacher or check an essay style guide in the library.

If you work through all of these suggestions carefully, you will have an essay that you can take great pride in. Congratulations, and remember that each essay you write will make the next one that much easier.

■ QUESTIONS? — NOT REALLY!

If you have read this far in the chapter, it undoubtedly means that you have an essay to write and do not need any extra questions to answer. Use the suggestions included here to help you write that essay. Good luck!

Glossary

Aboriginal Rights rights claimed by Native people because they are the original inhabitants of the country.

Acid Rain created when sulphur dioxide and nitric oxides mix with water vapour in the atmosphere. Acid rain kills vegetation and turns lakes acidic, causing fish to die and wildlife to disappear.

Acid Shock when acid snow melts in spring, it rapidly increases the acidity of rivers. This prevents many fish eggs from hatching. If the eggs do hatch, the fish are often deformed.

Acidity on a pH scale, values less than 7 are acidic. The lower the value, the higher the acidity. See page 291 for a diagram of the pH scale.

Advance of Glacier if more snow accumulates than melts, a glacier will advance.

Aerospace Industry companies that supply parts or build vehicles such as airplanes, helicopters and spacecraft for use in the earth's atmosphere and in space.

Agribusiness agriculture + business. Operations include growing, storing, processing, and distributing food, and may be owned by a large corporation or a family.

Air Mass large body of air that has the same moisture and temperature conditions throughout.

Air Pressure the weight of air is called air pressure.

Alkaline having a pH level greater than 7.

Alpine Glacier glacier that occupies one or more valleys in a mountainous (alpine) region. Also called a valley glacier.

Anticlinal Trap a dome-shaped structure of rock layers created by folding. Oil and gas are often found in these traps.

Assimilation process by which immigrants lose their culture and adopt the culture of the society into which they moved.

Average Annual Temperature found by adding the monthly average temperatures together and dividing by 12. The average annual temperature is used to compare the climates of different places and to see whether they have warm or cool climates.

Balance of Payments similar to Balance of Trade, but also includes such things as interest, profits, and money spent by tourists.

Balance of Trade the difference between the value of exports and the value of imports. If exports are greater than imports, there is a trade surplus. If exports are less than imports, there is a trade deficit.

Band group of Indians that is recognized by the Canadian government. The government sets aside money and land (reserves) for use by the band. There are almost 600 bands in Canada.

Banks shallow areas of the continental shelf where there are many fish.

Bar Graph graph in which quantities are shown by proportional bars. Each bar has a length that represents its value. The bars do not touch each other.

Base Line line in a survey from which all other points are measured.

Bearings the direction between one place and another as measured by a compass.

Bedrock solid rock beneath the soil.

Bibliography list of resources used to write an essay. The bibliography is placed at the end of the essay.

Bilingual the federal government's policy of bilingualism ensures that people in all parts of Canada are served in either French or English. The concept of a bilingual Canada does not mean that every Canadian should speak both official languages.

Biomass the use of energy produced by living things (for example, firewood or gasohol).

Bitumen in oil sands deposits, each grain of sand is covered with a layer of water and a heavy oil or black tar called bitumen. This bitumen is processed into synthetic crude oil.

Block Parent community organization in which parents agree to help any child who comes to them for assistance.

Boreal Forest forest of needle-leaved trees that stretches from east to west across Canada. It is south of the Tundra but north of the Grasslands and Mixed Forest.

Branch Plant factory set up in Canada that is owned by a foreign company. A branch plant allows the company to sell its products in Canada without paying the tariffs on imports.

Breeding Stock the number of adult fish that must be protected if the total population of fish is to be maintained.

Broad-leaved Forest deciduous forest in southwestern Ontario that requires hot summers, mild winters, and plentiful precipitation.

Broad-leaved Trees species such as oak and maple that have thin, flat leaves. They grow in deciduous and mixed forests.

Bulk Cargoes things such as wheat, coal, gravel, and iron ore that are shipped in loose form rather than in packages. They are usually of low value and must be shipped as cheaply as possible.

Calcification in dry climates, water carrying dissolved minerals moves upward through the soil. At the surface, the water evaporates, leaving the minerals behind. The soil is called calcified.

Canada Land Inventory a federal government agency within the Department of the Environment. It produces land capability maps and summary reports on agriculture, forestry, recreation, wildlife, and sport fishing in the settled areas of Canada.

Canadian Shield see Shield.

Capital assets such as money, equipment or buildings, used to make a profit.

Capitalism system of government in which businesses such as farms, mines and factories are owned by private companies or individual people rather than by the government. A capitalist is a person who believes in this system of government.

Cash Crops crops that are sold by a farmer.

Cenozoic Era the most recent era. See Geologic Time.

Census Metropolitan Area (CMA) city of 100 000 people or more.

Central Business District (CBD) downtown area of a city or town where most of the important commercial and governmental activities are found.

Circle Graph a circle represents the total value and segments are drawn to represent different proportions or percentages of the total.

City urban place that is larger than a town. The population of a city is more than 10 000 people.

Civil Disorder activities that disrupt the normal functioning of society. Civil disorder includes assassinations, government crises, general strikes, acts of terrorism and revolutions.

Clear Cutting all trees in an area (except for very small ones) are cut at one time.

Climate the weather conditions of a place averaged over a long period of time.

Climate Graph graph that shows temperature and precipitation characteristics for a place.

Coal fossil fuel formed from undecayed vegetable matter laid down in ancient swamps. The vegetable matter was covered by clay and sand and was not exposed to the air. It was slowly changed into coal by heat and pressure.

Coat of Arms shield containing symbolic emblems.

Cold Front boundary between a warm air mass and an advancing cold air mass.

Colony a group of settlers in a distant land that is still governed by the settlers' homeland. A colony provides raw materials for the mother country and is a market for manufactured goods.

Commercial Forest part of a forest that has large enough trees and is close enough to a market to allow it to be used by the forest industry.

Commonwealth organization set up by countries that were once part of the British Empire. The Commonwealth allows these countries to cooperate through economic, cultural, and athletic exchanges.

Communications movement of information from place to place.

Communism system of government in which the government owns all the farms, mines, factories, stores, and so on. A communist is a person who believes in this system of government.

Commuter Train train used to move people daily between the suburbs and outlying areas of a city and the centre of the city.

Community Relations Police police who work within the community to prevent crime.

Concentrate an ore from which much of the waste rock has been removed.

Concentrated population is grouped in one area.

Concession System type of survey system used in most of Ontario whereby land is divided by concession roads and sideroads into squares and rectangles of varying sizes.

Condensation when water vapour is cooled, it changes from an invisible gas to liquid water.

Condensed water vapour is what forms clouds.

Conservation wise use of natural resources.

Conservation Tillage method of plowing that disturbs the soil as little as possible.

Conserver Society approach to living in which resources are used as efficiently as possible. This includes serious attempts to conserve energy and to recycle materials.

Consumption Growth index that measures the rate at which the economy of a country is growing.

Container metal box of standard size (2.4 m x 2.4 m x 4.9 m or 9.8 m) used for moving freight. The container is loaded at the point of shipment and remains sealed until it reaches its destination. Along the way, it may be moved by truck, train, plane or ship.

Contaminant substance that pollutes air, water, soil or food.

Continental Climate climate type that develops away from the influence of the ocean. The annual temperature range tends to be large and precipitation is low.

Continental Glacier glacier that spreads out to cover a large portion of a continent. During the last ice age, huge glaciers formed in northern Canada and moved southward.

Continentalism the belief that Canada and the United States should be joined so that the two countries can solve their common problems.

Continentalist a person who believes in continentalism.

Continental Shelf gently sloping outer edge of the continent that extends below the surface of the ocean to a maximum depth of about 200 m.

Contour lines lines on topographic maps that join places of the same elevation above sea-level.

Convectional Precipitation on hot summer days heated land causes the air above it to rise by convection. As the air rises it cools and condensation occurs. Rain or hail may fall from the thunderclouds that build up.

Cordilleran Vegetation there is a wide variety of vegetation in cordilleras because of differences in climate from one side of a mountain to the other. It ranges from forests of tall trees to desert shrubs and grasses.

Cost of Living   amount of money needed to buy food, shelter, and clothing.

County   the largest political unit within some provinces.

Cross-section   side view of an object showing the internal structure.

Cultural Diversity   the different customs, arts, and languages that exist in a country or region.

Cultural Exchanges   cultural organizations, such as those composed of writers, dancers, or singers, may exchange visits in order to show part of their country's culture to people in another country.

Cultural Fabric   the combination of cultural features that makes one country different from other countries.

Cultural Group   people of a region who have a distinct way of life.

Culture   beliefs, customs, skills, religion, arts and languages of a group of people.

Cycles of Boom and Bust   in many resource-based industries the price of the resource (such as wood, gold, agricultural products) may rise and fall on a regular basis. When the price is high, many jobs are created and there are good economic times (boom). When the price is low, many jobs are lost and there are poor economic times (bust).

Cyclonic Precipitation   when a warm moist air mass is forced to rise by a cool dry air mass precipitation occurs. This is called cyclonic or frontal precipitation.

Day Care   care provided for pre-school children of parents who work outside the home.

Decentralization   to distribute more evenly throughout the country or region. For example, the Federal Government decentralizes by moving some departments to cities outside the Ottawa area.

Deficit   occurs when the amount of exports is smaller than the amount of imports.

Demand   amount of a product that people are willing and able to buy at a certain price.

Deposition   the laying down of eroded materials (sediments).

Depression   bad economic times such as during the 1930s in Canada and other countries, when incomes fell and unemployment soared. Many people were forced to go on welfare (the "Dole") to survive during this time.

Deregulation   removal of regulations controlling certain parts of an industry. For example, deregulation of the airline industry removes rules controlling the price of seats and routes travelled.

Developed Country   country with a highly developed economy; its citizens have high incomes, abundant food, good housing, and can afford many luxuries.

Developing Country   country with a poorly developed economy; its citizens have low incomes, shortages of food, poor housing, and cannot afford luxuries.

Dispersed   spread out.

Diversified Urban Centre   town or city that has a variety of urban functions.

Diversity   having a lot of variety.

Domestic Response Teams   police units specially trained to respond to problems among the members of a family.

Drainage   removal of water from an area by means of lakes and rivers.

Drainage Basin   area drained by a river and its tributaries.

Dust Bowl   drought conditions of the 1930s on the Prairies, when crops and vegetation died and the exposed surface soil was blown away in severe dust storms.

Economic Base   economic activities that allow a community to exist. For example, a Native community may depend on trapping fur-bearing animals, and a town might exist because a mineral resource in the area is being developed.

Economic Diversity   the different types of jobs and industries that exist in a country or region.

Ecosystem   community of organisms interacting with one another and with the environment.

Emigrants   people who leave their country to live in another country.

Endangered Species   animals or plants that are in danger of extinction.

Energy Crisis   a world shortage of energy sources, particularly oil.

Entrepreneur   person who takes a risk by setting up a business in order to make a profit.

Environmental Impact   effects on the environment caused by the actions of people.

Equalization Grants   money that is collected by the federal government from the richer provinces and distributed to the poorer provinces.

Era   major division of geologic time (for example, the Paleozoic Era). See Geologic Time.

Erosion   erosion includes two processes:
a) the wearing away of the earth's surface;
b) the movement to other locations of materials that have been worn away.

Escarpment   steep cliff formed by erosion or faulting.

Ethnic   adjective used to describe groups of people distinguishable by their customs, language, common history, and way of life.

Exports   products and services produced in one country for sale in another country.

Extensive Agriculture   small amounts of labour, machinery, and fertilizers are used in proportion to the amount of land farmed. Most agricultural activities in Canada are of this kind.

Extractive Industry   industry that obtains raw materials for manufacturing from the natural environment. For example, miners take mineral ores from the ground and farmers use soil, vegetation, and climate to produce crops and raise animals.

Factory Freezer Trawler (FFT)   ocean fishing trawler that processes and freezes fish on board. An FFT may stay at sea for months at a time.

False Colours   when satellites take infrared images from space, the colours differ from those we see with our eyes. For example, living things show up as shades of red and non-living things show up as shades of blue-green.

Farm Consolidation   smaller farms are combined to make larger ones.

Farm Specialization   farm that specializes in one major activity. For example, a farmer may specialize in raising cattle, or raising dairy cows, or growing corn or wheat.

Faulting   movement along a crack (fault) or cracks in the earth's crust.

Federalism   belief that a union of states or provinces should agree to give certain specified powers to a central federal authority, and keep other powers for themselves. In Canada, the provinces control such things as education and the building of highways. The federal government manages such things as defence, international affairs and trade.

Financial Services   providing or managing people's money (for example, banking services).

Fiord   long, narrow inlet of the sea with steep sides. Fiords were created by glaciers that scraped out valleys. When the glaciers melted, the sea flooded the valleys.

First World   wealthy countries whose governments are non-communist. These include Canada, the United States, Japan, Australia, New Zealand, Argentina, Israel, and the countries of western Europe.

Folding   bending of rock layers.

Food Web   complex pattern of interlocking food chains.

Foreign Aid   people, money, and products sent by rich countries such as Canada to aid poorer countries.

Foreign Investment   investment of money in one country by citizens of other countries. For example, the United States and Japan invest in Canada.

Formal Relationships   relationships based on contacts between governments, such as trade agreements and military alliances.

Fossil   imprint in rock of the remains of a plant or animal that lived millions of years ago.

Fossil Fuel   any mineral that can be burned

to produce energy (for example, coal, natural gas, oil).

Francophonie organization of countries that are of French origin, similar in purpose to the Commonwealth.

Free Market economic system in which the forces of supply and demand are allowed to operate without government interference.

Front leading edge of an air mass. If the air mass is warm, the leading edge of this air is called a warm front. If the air is cold, the leading edge is a cold front.

Frost-free Period total number of days between the last expected frost in the spring and the first expected frost in the fall.

General-purpose Map map that contains many different types of information.

Generator in an electrical generating station, the generator (a magnet and coils of wire) rotates to generate electricity.

Geologic Time history of the earth from its formation to the present. The earth's history may be divided into several major time periods, called eras:
Cenozoic Era (most recent)
Mesozoic Era
Paleozoic Era
Pre-Cambrian Era (oldest)

Geothermal Energy the heat of the earth's interior. In the form of hot springs or geysers, this is sometimes used for heating buildings or producing electricity.

Glacier slow-moving mass of ice.

Global Village describes the idea that the world is becoming like one large village because of improvements in communications.

Grassland vegetation region where there are only grasses, cactus, and sagebrush because it is too dry for the growth of forests.

Greying of the Population population trend of the last quarter of this century, in which Canada's population is becoming, on average, older.

Gross National Product (GNP) total value of a country's yearly output of goods and services.

Gross National Product Per Capita GNP divided by the number of people in the country.

Groundfish fish, such as cod and sole, that live and feed near the bottom of the sea.

Ground Water water that is found below the earth's surface in the spaces of soil and bedrock.

Growing Season the period during which crops can grow. It is measured in two ways:
a) the length of time between the last expected frost in spring and the first frost in autumn;
b) the number of days between spring and autumn when the average daily temperature is above 5.5°C (the temperature at which most crops begin to grow).

Hamlet smallest kind of urban place. Hamlets generally have populations of less than one hundred people.

Hardwood wood produced from broad-leaved trees such as maple, oak, and elm. Hardwood is used to make furniture, sports equipment, tool handles, floors, and boats. Not all hardwoods are "hard"; for example, poplar and basswood are actually quite soft.

Heavy Metals metals such as lead, mercury, and cadmium, that are produced as waste by industries. They are highly poisonous to people and animals.

Hemisphere half of the world, either:
a) the Northern and Southern Hemispheres, divided by the equator
b) the Eastern and Western Hemispheres, divided by 0° and 180° lines of longitude.

Heraldry study of symbols for use on coats of arms or flags.

Herbicide chemical designed to kill unwanted plants (weeds). If used improperly, can become a pollutant.

Heritage cultural background of a person or country.

Highlands areas of high elevation containing mountains and plateaus.

High Lead Logging a system of forest harvesting in which large trees are cut into smaller lengths before being transported to mills. This system is used mainly in British Columbia.

Historical Head Start   a region that develops first tends to keep its lead in development over regions that develop later.

Hub and Spoke   method of organizing airline routes so that people travelling between smaller cities (spokes) travel to and change planes in a larger city (the hub). For example, a person wanting to travel from London, Ont. to Timmins, Ont. would change planes in Toronto.

Humus   dark portion of soil made up of partially decayed plant materials.

Hydro-electric Power   electricity produced by the movement of falling water.

Hydrogen-based Economy   in the future, hydrogen might replace fossil fuels as the energy source on which our society is based.

Hydrologic Cycle   the pathway followed by water from oceans and lakes through the atmosphere then back to the land and waterways.

Ice Age   time when glaciers covered most of Canada and the northern parts of the U.S. and Europe.

Igneous Rock   rock formed from the cooling of molten rock (magma or lava).

Immigrant   person who moves to a new country with the intention of settling there.

Imports   products that are brought into a country from another country.

Incentive Grant   money given to an industry to encourage it to operate in a certain area or in a certain way. For example, the government may pay a company to build a factory in a certain place or to hire workers in a time of high unemployment.

Index Value   way of measuring the change in the amount of something by comparing it to what it was at some earlier time. For example, if ten years ago the cost of a product was $223 (index value = 100) and today it is $446, then its index value today would be: 446/223 x 100 = 200.

Informal Relationships   non-government contacts between countries, including family relationships, sports, travel, and business contacts.

Inland Fisheries   commercial fishing in lakes.

Insecticides   chemicals that are sprayed on trees or crops to kill harmful insects.

Inshore Fishery   commercial fishing that takes place within a few kilometres of the ocean shoreline. Small fishing boats (less than 25 m long) go out to sea and return to shore each day.

Intensive Farming   large amount of labour, machinery, and fertilizers are used in proportion to the amount of land farmed. High yields per hectare are obtained. The growing of fruits is an example of intensive farming.

Intercity   movement *between* cities (for example, an intercity bus might travel between Toronto and Montréal).

Intracity   movement *within* a city (for example, an intracity bus moves people from their home to school).

Inuit   Native people who live in the Arctic region of North America and Greenland.

Irrigation   water is supplied to farmland using ditches, canals, or sprinklers. In times of dry weather, irrigated land can still grow crops.

Isolated Settlement   town that is located a great distance from the main populated parts of a country. Isolated settlements are often connected to the rest of the country only by airplane and/or ship.

Labour Force   total number of people working and looking for work in an area, province, or country.

Land Bridge   part of the ocean floor between Alaska and the U.S.S.R. that was exposed several times during the last ice age. This bridge allowed people and animals to travel from Asia to North America.

Land Capability   ability of land to be used for a certain purpose. For example, land capability for agriculture is based on soil quality, drainage, slope, and climate.

Land Claims   case put forward by Native peoples for the ownership and control of the lands on which they live or have lived. Land claims can be settled through talks with the government or by the courts.

Landforms natural features of the earth's surface such as mountains, valleys, or plains.

Landsat name given to a type of remote sensing satellite (*land sat*ellite) launched by NASA that collects information about the atmosphere, water, vegetation, rocks, and urban places using a variety of scanners.

Land Use type of activity carried out on the land. For example, land may be used for agriculture, residential, industrial, transportation, commercial or business activities.

Large-scale Map map that shows a large amount of detail of a small area, such as a map with a scale of 1:50 000.

Latitude distance north or south of the equator, measured in degrees. The equator is 0° Latitude and the north pole is 90° North Latitude.

Leaching in wet climates, the removal of minerals from soil by water as it moves down through the soil.

Leeward side of a mountain or mountain range facing away from the prevailing winds.

Legend portion of a map that explains the meaning of the symbols and colours used on the map.

Line Graph graph in which a line shows changes in value over time.

Linear Scale line divided into units (e.g. kilometres) that represents the actual units on the ground.

Linear Village village built along a road so that it is long and narrow. Linear villages occur in the long lot system.

Liveable Winter City city that has climate-controlled shopping malls and underground walkways that allow people to live in more comfort by avoiding winter weather.

Location Factors factors such as historical head start, market, location of raw materials, power and fresh water, labour, transportation, and political factors that help to explain the location of cities and industries.

Logging cutting of trees by forest industries.

Longitude distance east or west of the prime meridian, measured in degrees. The prime meridian is 0° Longitude.

Long Lot System type of survey system used in southern Québec and some other areas of Canada. Individual lots tend to be long and narrow and extend back from major rivers or roads.

Lowlands areas of low elevation containing plains and hills.

Mammals warm-blooded vertebrate animals such as humans and whales.

Manufacturing Industries industries that process raw materials into a more finished state. For example, making lumber from logs is primary manufacturing, and making furniture from lumber is secondary manufacturing.

Map representation of the earth's features drawn on a flat surface.

Marginal Farming area where farming conditions (such as rainfall, soil fertility, and growing season) are close to the minimum required for success.

Maritime Climate climate type that is strongly influenced by the closeness of a large water body, such as a large lake or an ocean. The annual temperature range tends to be small and precipitation is high.

Marketing Board government agency that sets quotas for production and price for the product.

Mechanization replacement of human and animal labour with machines.

Melting Pot society in which cultural groups are encouraged to adopt the main culture of the society and to stop practicing their own customs.

Meridians imaginary lines (meridians of Longitude) on the earth's surface that join the North and South Poles.

Mesozoic Era major geologic time period in which reptiles such as dinosaurs were the dominant forms of life. See Geologic Time.

Metallic Minerals minerals that yield a metal when processed. For example, iron, gold, uranium, and silver.

Metamorphic Rock type of rock formed when sedimentary or igneous rocks are subjected to great heat and pressure.

Métis person of mixed European and Indian descent.

Meteorologist   person who studies and forecasts the weather.

Metropolis   can be either the dominant city of a country, or a major city with great political, economic and cultural power.

Metropolitan Dominance   one or more metropolises dominate the economic, cultural, and political life of a country.

Microwave Transmission   movement of information by radio signals (electromagnetic radiation).

Migration   movement of large numbers of people from one place to another.

Military Alliances   agreements between two or more countries to help each other in times of war or threat of war.

Military Grid   a grid, composed of blue lines and numbers, used to locate places on a topographic map.

Mill   factory where raw materials from mining or forestry are processed. For example, sawmill, pulp and paper mill, steel mill.

Mineral   valuable substance that is taken from rocks by mining.

Mineral Reserves   known quantity of minerals in a country or area.

Mixed Farming   includes both the growing of crops and the raising of animals.

Mixed Forest   vegetation region that contains both broad-leaved and needle-leaved trees. It is a transition zone between the Broadleaved Forest and the Boreal Forest.

Mobility   freedom of movement.

Model   a simplification of the real world that helps make a complex situation more easily understood.

Moderating Effect   effect that large water bodies have on the climate over nearby land areas. Winter temperatures are warmer and summer temperatures are cooler than areas located away from large water bodies. The result is a small annual temperature range.

Moraine   material deposited by a glacier, often in the form of hills. For example, a terminal moraine is formed at the furthest position reached by a glacier.

Multicultural Society   society composed of many cultural groups that are encouraged to maintain their heritage. In 1971 the federal government established a policy of multiculturalism that recognizes the value of the contributions of the many cultural groups living in Canada. The policy encourages people to share their culture with other Canadians so that all may benefit from Canada's diversity.

Multi-factor Region   region that is determined on the basis of more than one thing. For example, an urban or natural region.

Multinational Corporation (MNC)   large company that operates in more than one country. Some "multinationals" have great economic and political power.

Multiplier Effect   the total effect on the economy caused by an expansion or contraction in one part of it. For example, a new mine employing 300 people may cause 900 other jobs to develop in manufacturing and services.

Muskeg   spongy, water-logged ground.

Nationalism   belief and loyalty in one's country. This may produce a policy of national independence. In Canada, this often means greater independence from the United States.

Native Peoples   all persons who have descended from Canada's original inhabitants. The term includes Indians, Métis, and Inuit.

Natural Gas   fossil fuel formed under conditions similar to those which produce oil. Natural gas occupies spaces in porous sedimentary rock.

Natural Region   region that is determined using only environmental factors such as climate, landforms, vegetation, and soil.

Natural Resources   valuable items found on the land and in the waters of a country. For example, fish, trees, oil, gas, minerals, furs, and fresh water.

Natural Vegetation   plants that would grow in an area in the absence of human influence.

Needle-leaved Trees   trees that have needles rather than broad leaves. Found commonly in the boreal forest, they include pine, spruce and fir.

Neighbourhood Watch   neighbours in a community agree to watch each others' property and to call the police if there is unusual activity, such as strangers entering the property when the owners are away.

Neutralize   a substance is made chemically neutral by mixing it with another substance. For example, an acidified lake can be made non-acidic with the addition of lime, which is alkaline.

Non-Commercial Forest   part of a forest that has trees too small or too far from the market to use.

Non-Metallic Minerals   minerals that yield non-metals when processed. For example, salt, potash, and asbestos.

Non-Porous Rock   rock such as shale or granite that does not contain tiny pore spaces. Liquids or gases cannot pass through non-porous rock.

Non-Renewable Resource   resource that can only be used once. For example, oil.

Nuclear Energy   energy produced by using the heat from nuclear fission (the splitting of atoms), usually to generate electricity.

Nuclear Fission   the splitting of atoms to produce heat to make electricity.

Nuclear Fusion   the joining together of hydrogen nuclei to produce heat to make electricity. Fusion is the process that powers the sun.

Nutrients   mineral substances that are absorbed by plant roots.

Offshore Fishery   ocean fishing done from boats longer than 25 m. The boats stay at sea several days before returning to shore with their catch.

Oil   a fossil fuel, also called petroleum. Millions of years ago the microscopic remains of marine plants and animals were covered with silt under warm seas. These remains were chemically changed into oil.

Oil Sands   mixture of heavy crude oil, sand, and water.

Open-Pit Mining   the mining of ore found near the earth's surface by digging a large hole.

Ore   rock that contains enough valuable minerals to make mining profitable.

Orographic Precipitation   see Relief Precipitation.

Overburden   soil and rock above a mineral deposit that must be removed before open-pit or strip mining can begin.

Overexpansion   growth of a company or farm's activities to a size beyond what the market will support.

Paleozoic Era   major geologic time period in which fish and other sea life were the dominant life forms. See Geologic Time.

Parent Company   company that sets up another company in a different country. For example, a Canadian company may be owned and controlled by an American-based parent company.

Parkland   vegetation region that is a transition zone between Grassland and Boreal Forest.

Peat   partially decomposed plant matter that can be burned when dried.

Pellets   after poor quality iron ore has some of the waste rock removed, the remaining ore is made into balls the size of marbles. These are called pellets. They are made to reduce the cost of shipping the ore to steel mills.

Per Capita Income   income per person, calculated by dividing the total income for a country or province by the population.

Permafrost   ground that does not completely thaw in the summer.

Personal Services   businesses that provide services needed by people. For example, barbers, hairdressers, dry cleaners, restaurants, movie theatres.

Pesticides   chemicals designed to kill harmful plants (these are called herbicides) and harmful insects (insecticides).

Petrochemicals   chemicals made from petroleum.

pH Scale   scale used to determine which substances are acids and which are bases. The scale measures values from 0 to 14. The midpoint, 7, is neutral. Values below 7 indicate acids and values above 7 indicate bases. Normal rainwater has a pH of 5.6.

Physical Diversity   different landforms, climates, soils, plants, and animals that exist in a country or region.

Phytoplankton microscopic plants that live in the sea.

Piggyback movement of transport trailers by rail. Usually this involves shipment over a long distance by rail followed by local delivery of the trailer by road.

Plateau elevated flat area (see Highland).

Polar (Polar Climate Region) the areas north of the Arctic Circle (66.5°N) and south of the Antarctic Circle (66.5°S). These areas have cool or cold temperatures all year.

Population Density calculated by dividing the population of a region by the region's area.

Population Distribution pattern showing where people live in an area. For example, a scattered distribution, or a linear distribution along a coastline or road.

Porous Rock rock with tiny spaces or openings that may contain air, water, oil, or gas. Liquids or gases may move through these spaces. Sandstone is a porous rock.

Potash name given to potassium compounds such as potassium chloride, which is mined mainly in Saskatchewan.

Power Grid system of electric power lines that connects large generating stations to those who use electricity.

Prairies grasslands that occupy the southern parts of Alberta, Saskatchewan, and Manitoba. The natural grasses of this region have been largely replaced by wheat.

Precambrian Era first era in the earth's geologic history. There were vitually no life forms at this time. See Geologic Time.

Prevailing Winds winds that are most commonly found in an area. For example, over most of Canada the prevailing winds are Westerlies, which blow from west to east.

Prime Meridian the line of Longitude on maps or globes that joins the north and south poles and runs through Greenwich, England. Longitude is measured 180° east and 180° west from this line (0°).

Privatization process whereby government-owned crown corporations are sold to private industry.

Profile side view. Differs from cross-section by not showing internal structure.

Proportional Circle Graph the size of the circle is proportional to the size of the value it is representing.

Protective Tariff tax on imports, designed to give goods made in a country a price advantage over imported goods. Also known simply as a tariff.

Public Transit government-controlled transportation system, using vehicles such as buses and subways to carry people within a city.

Pull Factor factor such as freedom of speech or employment opportunities that attracts a person to a country.

Purchasing Power amount of money that people have to spend on their needs.

Purse Seine fishing net that encircles fish. It is then closed at one end (like a purse) to lift the trapped fish onboard the fishing boat.

Push Factor factor, such as the lack of freedom of speech or unemployment, that makes people want to leave their country and move to another one.

Quality of Life measure of how comfortable life is in a country.

Radarsat Canadian satellite to be launched in 1994 that uses radar to take images of the earth's surface.

Rainshadow area on the leeward side of mountains with little precipitation.

Ranges distances from one point to other points on the earth. With a bearing (compass direction), a range can be used to determine a location.

Raw Material something used by an industry to be processed into a more finished state. For example, iron ore (raw material) is made into steel (product), and steel (raw material) is made into an automobile (product).

Region area possessing characteristics that make it different from neighbouring areas.

Regional Disparity differences in wealth between various regions of a country.

Regionalism   division of a country into small administrative units.

Relief   the elevation of an area, and the difference between the lowest and the highest elevation.

Relief Precipitation   precipitation created when an air mass rises to cross a mountain barrier. Also called orographic precipitation.

Remote Sensing   study of the characteristics of the earth using photographs taken from aircraft, and electronic images taken from satellites.

Renewable Resource   resource that replaces itself unless badly mismanaged. For example, trees grow to replace those cut down or lost to fire or disease; polluted water is cleaned by the environment.

Representative Fraction   method for showing the scale of a map by using a ratio, such as 1:50 000.

Research and Development (R and D)   process of conducting research to develop a new product and then developing this product for sale. Companies spend great sums of money to:
a) decide what products will be needed in the future, and
b) determine how these products can be built as cheaply as possible.

Reserves   areas of land set aside for the use of Native people.

Reservoir   artificial lake built to store water for use in a hydro-electric generating station, for irrigation, or for flood control.

Residential Density   measure of the number of housing units per hectare (or km²).

Resource Base   the extent and quality of natural resources that are found in an area.

Resource-based Community   settlement that owes its existence to the use of a mineral, forest, or fishing resource.

Resource Development   the building of facilities, such as mines, mills, and pipelines, that are needed to obtain resources.

Resource Management   wise use of resources so that they will last as long as possible.

Retail Trade   sale of goods to the public.

Retailing   selling goods to the public in stores.

Retreat of Glacier   a glacier melts back (retreats) when the rate of melting is greater than the rate of snow build-up.

Rift Valley   valley that is created when the portion of land between two faults (cracks in the earth) drops down. The St. Lawrence River Valley is a rift valley.

Royal Commission   panel of experts assembled by the government to investigate a problem and to recommend ways of solving it.

Rural   areas outside towns and cities.

Satellite   manufactured object that is launched by a rocket and circles the earth. Satellites are used to communicate, to study the earth's resources, and to aid the military.

Scale   measurement on a map that represents an actual distance on the earth's surface. For example, a scale of 1:50 000 means that one centimetre on the map represents 50 000 centimetres on the earth's surface.

Seasonal Distribution of Precipitation the time of year when a place receives its precipitation. For example, if a place receives most of its precipitation in the winter, it is said to have a winter maximum of precipitation.

Second World   wealthy countries that have communist governments. These include the U.S.S.R., Poland, Czechoslovakia, and other countries of eastern Europe.

Section   unit of land, 1.6 km by 1.6 km (1 square mile), that is part of the survey system used in most of the Prairie provinces. When settlers first arrived, they were given a quarter-section of land to farm.

Section System   type of survey system used in most of the Prairie provinces. It is based on the division of land into sections.

Sedimentary Rock   rock usually formed in layers from the compression of sediments over millions of years.

Sediments   eroded materials that are deposited by water, wind, or glacial ice.

Selective Cutting   only trees of a certain type, size, and quality are cut.

Self-sufficient being able to supply all of one's own needs.

Separatism belief held by some people of a province or region that they would be better off if they were independent of the rest of the country. In Canada, there are groups in Québec and in Western Canada who would like to separate.

Service Centre community whose main function is to provide goods and services (such as food, clothing, education, and health care) for the surrounding area.

Service Industries industries that provide services needed by other industries and society in general. They include such things as retailing, education, health care, communications, and government services. Services industries are the largest part of Canada's economy.

Services all types of jobs in the economy except those that actually produce a product.

Settlement process that occurs when an area becomes inhabited, or a term for a small urban place such as a hamlet or village.

Settlement Pattern distribution of homes, farms, villages, towns, and cities in an area.

Shaft Mine ore deposits deep in the earth are mined using vertical and horizontal tunnels. Some tunnels are drilled to a depth of more than 2 km. They are large enough to allow the use of large equipment. See also Underground Mining.

Shield large area of Precambrian rock that forms the core of a continent.

Single-factor Region region that is determined on the basis of only one thing. For example, on the basis of its geology or farming type.

Single-industry Town community that depends on one industry for its economic survival.

Small-scale Map map that shows a small amount of detail of a large area, such as a map with a scale of 1:250 000.

Social Progress measure of the quality of life, determined by combining a wide variety of factors.

Soft Fruits fruits like peaches, plums, and apricots which are easily damaged by frost.

Softwood wood produced by needle-leaved trees.

Soil surface layer of the earth, composed of mineral and organic materials, air, and water.

Soil Profile the different horizons (layers) in the soil and the rock layer (bedrock) below the soil. Each horizon has different physical, biological, and chemical characteristics.

Solar Heating heating of a building using heat from the sun.

Solution Mining recovery of a mineral by injecting hot water into the mineral deposit. Solution mining only works if the mineral (such as salt or potash) dissolves easily in water.

Speculators people who buy something, such as land, hoping the price will rise in the future. When the price has risen they sell the land for a profit.

Spillway deep valley created by large amounts of water flowing from a melting continental glacier. Today, such a valley may be occupied by a small stream or river called a misfit stream.

Sport Fishing fishing done by people who do it for sport rather than to make money.

Stereo Pair pair of aerial photographs that, when looked at through a stereoscope, show a 3–dimensional image.

STOL Aircraft *S*hort *T*ake-*O*ff and *L*anding airplanes. They can operate from very short runways.

Structural Material material that is used in the construction industry. For example, sand, gravel, and limestone.

Subsidiary company controlled by a larger company, often in another country. For example, Imperial Oil of Canada is controlled by Exxon in the U.S.

Subsidy money provided by a government to help a company to continue to operate even though it is losing money.

Supply amount of a product suppliers are willing and able to sell at a given price.

Supply Management arrangement among farmers, usually through a marketing board, to control the supply (and therefore the price) of a farm product.

Surface Strip Mining   mining of minerals located on the earth's surface by stripping off the layer(s) of the deposit. For example, coal deposits in Alberta are strip mined.

Surplus   occurs when the amount of exports is greater than the amount of imports.

Survey System   pattern of land division used in an area.

Sustained Yield Management   use of a renewable resource at a rate that allows the resource to renew itself. For example, the number of fish caught should not be greater than the number of fish reaching maturity.

Synthetic Crude Oil   processed oil obtained from the heavy crude oil of oil sands.

Tar Sands   see Oil Sands.

Tariffs   taxes charged on goods which are imported into Canada.

Technology   level of technical development in an industry or country.

Telecommunications   information sent electrically through wire or through the air.

Temperate   climate that has warm summers and cool winters.

Thematic Map   map containing information on only one topic or theme.

Thermal-electricity   electricity that is produced by the burning of fuels like coal, oil, and natural gas.

Thesis   statement that forms the central theme of an essay. The essay should attempt to prove the truth of the thesis.

Third World   less developed countries of the world, found mainly in South America, Asia, and Africa.

Tidal Power   use of tidal flows to generate electricity. Can only be attempted where a dam with generating equipment can be installed across an inlet of the sea with very high tides.

Till   eroded material deposited directly by the ice of a glacier. Usually a mixture of materials of all sizes.

Till Plain   flat to gently hilly area created by deposition under a glacier.

Topographic Map   large-scale map showing both natural and human-made features.

Topography   natural features of the landscape.

Tossed Salad   a reference to Canada's multicultural society in which cultural groups are encouraged to maintain their heritage. It is the opposite of Melting Pot. See Multicultural Society.

Total Annual Precipitation   amount of precipitation received each year in a certain location.

Town   urban place that is larger than a village and smaller than a city. The population ranges from approximately 1000 to 10 000 people.

Township   subdivision of land used (with different meanings) in the survey systems of Ontario, the Prairies, and southern Québec.

Toxic Chemicals   chemicals that are harmful to humans or to the environment.

Transformer   device that converts electrical voltages either to a higher voltage for transmission or to a lower voltage for use.

Transition Zone   area where the characteristics of one region gradually change into those of another.

Transportation   movement of people and things from one place to another.

Tree Line   boundary between the tundra and boreal forest zone. North of this line it is too cold for trees to grow.

Tropical (Tropical Climate Zone)
1. area between 23.5°N and 23.5°S. In this region no distinctive winter season occurs.
2. any area with climate conditions typical of the tropics.

Tundra   northern-most vegetation region, found in areas too cold for trees to grow. Bushes, grasses, mosses, and similar plants dominate.

Turbine   machine that causes an electrical generator to turn; it is driven by either moving water or steam.

Two Hundred Nautical Mile Limit   Canada claims control of the oceans within 200 nautical miles (370 km) of the shoreline. The purpose of this limit is to allow proper management of the resources in this area.

U-shaped valley valley that has been widened to a U-shape by the movement of a glacier.

Underground Mining mining carried out below the ground, often at great depth, using shafts and tunnels.

Unemployment condition of not having a job.

Unit Train train that carries large amounts of only one cargo along a route. For example, coal is carried from the interior of British Columbia to Vancouver for shipment to Japan.

United Nations organization to which most of the world's countries belong. It is designed to foster international co-operation and prevent conflicts.

Urban referring to towns and cities.

Urban Functions activities that occur in an urban place and allow it to exist. For example, manufacturing, retail trade, and government.

Urban Renewal process of rebuilding older parts of a city.

Urbanization process of changing from rural to urban.

Urban Sprawl low density development around the fringes of a city.

Verbal Scale map scale given in words. For example, 1 cm to 20 km.

Village urban place that is bigger than a hamlet and smaller than a town. The population ranges from approximately 100 to 1000.

Warm Front boundary between a cold air mass and an advancing warm air mass.

Water Consumption water usage in which water is not returned to streams and lakes after being used. For example, irrigation.

Water Deficit exists in an area when the demand for water is greater than the supply.

Water Diversion movement of large amounts of water from one drainage basin to another.

Water Pollution contamination of water by substances that make it unclean or unhealthy for animals, plants, and people.

Water Surplus exists in an area when the demand for water is less than the supply.

Water Table top of the zone in the soil in which all pore spaces are filled with water. Above the water table, the pore spaces are filled with air.

Water Use water usage in which water is returned to streams and lakes after being used for purposes like hydro-electric power and industrial cooling.

Weather condition of the atmosphere at any given time. Weather includes temperature, precipitation, air pressure, humidity, cloudiness, and winds.

Weathering breakdown of rock into small particles.

Wheat-Fallow System technique of farming on the Prairies which involves alternating years of wheat growing and fallowing (not planting a crop).

Wholesale Trade buying and selling of goods *other* than to the public. For example, sale of goods by manufacturer to distributor.

Wind horizontal movement of air over the earth's surface, caused by differences in air pressure.

Wind Power action of the wind on a windmill is used to generate electricity or to pump water.

Wind-chill Factor measures the combined effect of both temperature and wind to indicate how cold it feels.

Windward side of a mountain or mountain range that faces the prevailing wind.

Yearly Temperature Range difference between the average temperature of the warmest month and the average temperature of the coldest month.

Zone of Accumulation part of a glacier where snow builds up and turns to ice. The glacial ice moves outward from here.

Zoning laws, usually passed by city governments, that control the kind and amount of development in an area.

Zooplankton tiny animals that live in the sea and eat phytoplankton.

Index

Credits and Sources

Unit Opening photos: Unit One: John Wallace/Bruce Clark. Unit Two: A.J. Casson, *White Pine* (see Fig. 5–17). Unit Three: Department of Regional Industrial Expansion. Units Four, Five, and Six: Eduvision. Unit Seven: James Loates/Julian Cleva. Unit Eight: courtesy of the Canada Centre for Remote Sensing, Energy, Mines and Resources Canada.

Text Photos:
Fig. 1–1: Greg Abel. Fig. 1–2: courtesy of Alberta Travel. Fig. 2–1 (pg. 13-left): courtesy of Canadian National Railway. (pg. 13-right): Paul Pope, Department of Development and Tourism, Newfoundland. (pg. 14-top left): John Wallace/Bruce Clark. (pg. 14-top right, lower right): Parks Canada. (pg. 14-lower left): Eduvision. Fig. 2–3 (top left): courtesy of Canadian National Railway. (lower left; top, centre and lower right): Eduvision. Fig. 2–5: Dept. of the Secretary of State. Fig. 3–2: courtesy of Alberta Travel. Fig. 5–4, 5–9: Parks Canada. Fig. 5–5: Government of Alberta. Fig. 5–6: John Wallace/Bruce Clark. Fig. 5–8: Eduvision. Fig. 5–11: Government of British Columbia. Fig. 5–17: A.J. Casson, 1898–, *White Pine*, c.1957, oil on canvas, 76.0 x 101.3cm; McMichael Canadian Art Collection, anonymous donor, 1966.16.119. Fig. 5–18: Wm. G. Roberts, 1904–1974, *Hillside, Lake Alphonse*, 1942, oil on canvas, 48.5 x 74.0cm; McMichael Canadian Art Collection, purchased 1984; 1984.20. Fig. 5–19: Wm. Kurelek, *No Grass Grows on the Beaten Pathway*, from *Fields*, Wm. Kurelek, © 1976, Tundra Books. Fig. 5–20: James Spencer, *Mount Jacobsen #2* Fig. 6–8:, Fig. 6–9: Atmospheric Environment Service. Figs. 7–4, 7–5, 7–8, 7–12: Eduvision. Figs. 7–6, 7–7: John Wallace/Bruce Clark. Fig. 7–9: Government of Alberta. Fig. 7–10–5: Alberta Travel. Fig. 7–11: Parks Canada. Fig. 9–3, 9–6: Dept. of Regional Industrial Expansion. Fig. 9–7: Parks Canada. Figs. 9–8, 9–12: Imperial Oil Ltd. Fig. 9–19: Eric Grace. Fig. 9–11: Eduvision. Fig. 9–16: Transport Canada. Fig. 10–15: John Wallace/Bruce Clark. Fig. 10–6: C75992, Public Archives of Canada. Figs. 10–8, 10–11: Eduvision. Fig. 10–9: PA 29090, Public Archives of Canada. Fig. 10–10: PA 37769, Public Archives of Canada. Figs. 11–4, 11–5, 11–9: Eduvision. Fig. 11–7: Energy, Mines and Resources Canada, National Air Photo Library. Fig. 12–9: Keith Minchin/City of Fredericton. Fig. 12–10: Economic Development Commission, Regional District of Alberni-Clayoquot. Fig. 12–11: John Wallace/Bruce Clark. Fig. 12–14: Eduvision. Fig. 13–1: John Wallace/Bruce Clark. Fig. 13–14: John Wallace/Bruce Clark. Fig. 13–7: Ontario Ministry of Natural Resources. Figs. 14–1, 14–2: John Wallace/Bruce Clark. Fig. 14–3: Strathcona Mineral Services Ltd. Fig. 14–4: Brian Hicks, courtesy Metropolitan Toronto Police Force. Fig. 15–3: John Wallace/Bruce Clark. Fig. 15–7, 15–10: Boeing Canada, deHavilland Division. Fig. 15–9: Imperial Oil Ltd. Fig. 16–2: (top): PA 48413, Public Archives of Canada. (centre): Air Canada. (lower): John Wallace/Bruce Clark. Fig. 16–3: courtesy Canadian National Railway. Fig. 16–4: Canadian Airlines International. Fig. 16–10: Eduvision. Fig. 16–12: Transport Canada. Fig. 16–13: Syncrude Canada. Fig. 17–3 (left): PA 4992, Public Archives of Canada. (top right): PA 29468, Public Archives of Canada. (lower right): Teleglobe Canada. Fig. 17–4: NASA. Fig. 17–6: CNCP Telecommunications. Fig. 17–9: Infomart. Fig. 17–10: Department of Communication. Fig. 18–4: Kellogg's. Fig. 18–5: Eduvision. Fig. 18.6: John Wallace/Bruce Clark. Fig. 18–7: courtesy of Ontario Hydro. Fig. 18–8: Eduvision. Fig. 18–9: courtesy of Toronto Stock Exchange. Fig. 18–10: Department of Communication. Fig. 19–4: Volvo Canada. Fig. 20–4: Tourism P.E.I. Fig. 20–10: Transport Canada. Fig. 20–11: Ontario Ministry of the Environment. Fig. 21–1: John Wallace/Bruce Clark. Fig. 22–1, 22–20: Eduvision. Fig. 22–9: Ontario Ministry of Agriculture and Food. Fig. 22–10 (left): Metropolitan Toronto and Region Conservation Authority. (right): John Wallace/Bruce Clark. Fig. 22–13: Landsat imagery courtesy of the Canada Centre for Remote Sensing, Energy, Mines and Resources Canada. Fig. 22–17: Bill Hapgood. Figs. 23–3, 23–13: courtesy of Abitibi-Price Inc. Figs. 23–7, 23–9, 23–15: Eduvision. Fig. 23–16: Ontario Ministry of Natural Resources, Maple District. Figs. 24–3, 24–5: Eduvision. Fig. 24–11: John Wallace/Bruce Clark. Fig. 24–13: Denison Mines Ltd. Fig. 25–5: Imperial Oil Ltd. Figs. 25–6, 25–7: Eduvision. Fig. 25–13: Hydro-Québec. Fig. 26–9: Department of National Defence. Fig. 26–12, 26–15: John Wallace/Bruce Clark. Fig. 27–4: Petro Canada. Fig. 27–8 (top): reproduction by permission of IBM Corporation. The logo is a Registered Trademark of IBM Corporation. (centre): INCO Ltd. (bottom): BATA Industries Ltd. Fig. 31–3: Ontario Ministry of Transportation and Communications. Fig. 31–5: Department of the Environment — Not for Navigation. Fig. 35–1: U.S. Department of Commerce, National Oceanic and Atmospheric Administration, Environmental Data Service. Fig. 35–2: Energy, Mines and Resources Canada, National Air Photo Library. Figs. 36–1, 36–4, 36–6: Landsat imagery courtesy of the Canada Centre for Remote Sensing, Energy, Mines and Resources Canada. Fig. 37–1, 37–2, 37–3: Greenpeace. Fig. 37–4: Eduvision. Fig. 38–2: John Wallace/Bruce Clark.

Text Sources
Fig. 29–1: reprinted by permission of the Toronto Star Syndicate.